Courtier to the Crowd

Ivy Lee and the Development of Public Relations in America

RAY ELDON HIEBERT

"Public sentiment is everything. With public sentiment nothing can fail; without it, nothing can succeed. Consequently, he who molds public sentiment goes deeper than he who enacts statutes or pronounces decisions. He makes statutes or decisions possible or impossible to be executed."
ABRAHAM LINCOLN
In debate with Stephen Douglass
August 21, 1858

"The people now rule. We have substituted for the divine right of kings, the divine right of the multitude. The crowd is enthroned. This new sovereign has his courtiers, who flatter and caress precisely as did those who surrounded medieval emperors."
IVY LEDBETTER LEE
In a speech to the American Railroad Guild
May 19, 1914

Ivy Ledbetter Lee, 1877–1934

RAY ELDON HIEBERT

ABOUT THE AUTHOR, First edition, 1966

RAY ELDON HIEBERT is chairman and professor of journalism, public relations, and broadcasting at The American University, Washington, D.C., and director of the Washington Journalism Center. A graduate of Stanford University, the Columbia University Graduate School of Journalism, and the University of Maryland, from which he received M.A. and Ph.D. degrees in American Studies, Dr. Hiebert taught at the University of Minnesota before joining the staff at The American University in 1958.

He has worked for newspapers in Los Angeles, New York City, and Washington, for the news department of NBC, and for the government in Washington as a speechwriter and consultant. He has edited two books, *The Press in Washington* (Dodd Mead & Co., 1966) and Books in Human Development (Agency for International Development, 1965); he also has written two monographs, and many articles in *Journalism Quarterly, Public Relations Quarterly, Public Relations Journal* (for which he also serves as Contributing Editor), and other periodicals.

Dr. Hiebert has served as a special regional observer for the Pulitzer Prize Committee, is vice-president of the Public Relations Division of the Association for Education in Journalism, and is a member of the Educational Advisory Council of the Public Relations Society of America.

ABOUT THE AUTHOR,
Second edition, 2017

RAY ELDON HIEBERT is founding dean and professor emeritus, College of Journalism, University of Maryland.

During his long academic career, he also served as director of the Washington Journalism Center (1965–68), academic advisor to the Voice of America and director of the VOA's Summer Fellowship Program for journalists from developing countries (1980–90), director of the University's Journalism Center is Budapest (1990–95), and Fulbright Fellow in Liberia (1982). He has also been visiting professor or lecturer in thirteen different countries in Africa, and in six countries of Eastern Europe, in Korea, Japan, the Philippines, and most recently in China. He has lectured at universities in the Netherlands, Germany, the United Kingdom, and Spain.

In 1999, he was given the University of Maryland's "Landmark Award" for his achievements in international service.

He has served as a consultant to a number of U.S. government agencies, including the State Department, Agency for International Development, Justice, Labor, Housing and Urban Development, Health and Human Services, and Defense. He has also been a consultant to a number of nonprofit organizations, including the Boy Scouts of America and the American Red Cross.

He is author, co-author, editor, or co-editor of twenty academic books, including *Mass Media*, a widely-used textbook. He is also author or co-author of three other biographies and three histories.

For forty-two years, he was editor of an academic journal he founded, *Public Relations Review*, which now has a worldwide circulation.

He resides in Carmel, California.

Courtier to the Crowd: Ivy Lee and the Development of Public Relations in America

By RAY ELDON HIEBERT

© 2017 Ray Eldon Hiebert
All rights reserved. Printed in the U.S.A.
First edition, 1966
Second edition, 2017
Library of Congress Control Number: 2017942370
ISBN 978-0-9990245-0-8

This book or any portion thereof may not be reproduced or used in any manner whatsoever without the express written permission of the publisher except for the use of brief quotations in a book review.

Published by PRMuseum Press, LLC, New York, New York

PREFACE

THIS BOOK IS THE RESULT of deep interest in the written word and its influence on American culture. The printed page has had an extraordinary impact on our civilization because of the importance of public opinion in a democracy and because of the development of particularly effective means of public communication in the United States. Effective communication not only brought democracy into existence but allows it to continue by providing for the expression of a variety of opinions which alone can preserve a balance of powers.

In the late nineteenth century, however, the industrial revolution created an increasingly complex and technical society in America which hampered individual expression. The change from a rural to an urban society altered the role of public opinion and ultimately threatened the very foundation of democracy. The mass culture of an industrial civilization with its mass production and mass communication seemed to be better suited to a monolithic rather than pluralistic social structure. For a time, especially from the beginning of the twentieth century to the late 1930s, many thoughtful Americans felt that democracy could not exist in a mass society, and they looked instead to more authoritarian political and economic concepts, especially to communism at one extreme or to fascism at the other.

During Ivy Lee's lifetime, 1877–1934, the crisis of democracy in a mass society reached its climax. His work was central to the entire problem of public communication in a complex and industrial environment. He devoted most of his life to the written word, in a way that was peculiarly American. A pragmatist, he was concerned with the word as a tool of power rather than an object of beauty. In one sense he was in the American tradition of Sam Adams, Tom Paine, Alexander Hamilton, Thomas Jefferson, and Abraham Lincoln. Like them, he understood the necessity for using words to get people to understand his point of view. Unlike them, however, he lived in an age when words could be used increasingly to maintain rather than prevent an excess of power—an age when America was confronted by the questions: Can a variety of views be expressed meaningfully in a mass society? And, if so, how?

Lee not only answered yes to the first question but also provided the means to answer the second. He recognized the breakdown in individual communication caused by the industrial revolution. He was concerned with the weakened fabric of democracy that resulted. He seriously studied the alternatives of communism and fascism but argued that they were not satisfactory solutions, that a pluralistic society could be maintained and democracy preserved in the face of twentieth century difficulties. He spent a good part of his life helping develop techniques which would allow a variety of groups to achieve public expression and gain public understanding for their points of view.

The use of these techniques eventually became known as the practice of public relations, that activity which provides the means for relating the ideas of one group to another, of one public to another. Lee helped bring professional status to those who devoted their time to this kind of activity, and those who have followed in his footsteps regard him as a founder of "modern public relations."

More important, the techniques which Lee helped develop did aid in the preservation of democracy in a mass society. Instead of any one group dominating the channels of communication, many are now able to place their views before the public. Despite the complexities of today's technological age, any group can apply Lee's techniques to its own problems and achieve public understanding of its point of view. Thus we have in public relations the mechanism for maintaining a pluralistic society.

For a time during the second half of the nineteenth century, industrial leaders turned to monopoly as a solution to their economic problems. By the turn of the century, however, a reversal was taking place, largely as the result of a new kind of communication that appealed to mass man: "yellow journalism" with its practice of "muckraking." This gave to such anti-industrial groups as the agrarians and grangers, populists, labor unions, and progressives a new power over public opinion that allowed them to counterbalance the might of the industrial captains, for a while even threatening the continued existence of their power by bringing into question the basic idea of free enterprise.

Ivy Lee arrived on the scene at a moment when capitalistic forces no longer seemed to have the upper hand in the struggle for public opinion. During the first decade of the twentieth century he directed his attentions to the problems of the industrialist and businessman, who more than others needed new techniques of public relations since they rarely understood the dynamics of public opinion and cared little for communicating their ideas to the crowd. The resulting problems were solved by Lee and others who joined him. The techniques they devised were not only useful to those businessmen but are still being practiced by all kinds of groups in business, labor, politics, and government.

Lee criticized the "muckrakers" whom he considered to be taking advantage of the confusion in industrial life to suit their own ends, distorting communication for their own purposes. He regarded them as demagogues and called them "courtiers to the crowd." But the phrase can be applied to Lee as well. He believed implicitly in the power of public opinion and sought to serve the people, whom he considered the kings of democracy. In seeking the understanding of people, he paid them the supreme flattery of attributing to them intelligence. He was a courtier to the crowd, as are all practitioners of public relations who flatter the people with information in the hope that they will understand and accept and provide the necessary power to make any idea succeed.

Pioneering in establishing acceptable public relations, Lee made an impact on American life far out of proportion to his fame. Newspaper and magazine articles were devoted to him and his work during his lifetime, most of them critical and many failing to view objectively his role in American society. Since his death in 1934 nothing of any substance has been published about him, although most books on journalism, publicity, public relations, propaganda, and public opinion today pay tribute to him as a prime mover in his field. Analysis of his life and contribution has remained fragmentary, primarily because source material was made available only recently. This, then, is the first full-length biography of the public relations pioneer.

RAY ELDON HIEBERT
Washington, D.C.
January 1966

PREFACE TO THE SECOND EDITION

THIS IS A BOOK I PROBABLY would not have chosen to write today. In fact, I've resisted all entreaties to republish this for more than fifty years. And yet, in some ways this book may now have new relevance for our age, a new time of moguls and robber barons, a new age of growing economic disparities, a new era of unfettered social media conjuring up the lawless wild west of nineteenth century America.

In the first third of the twentieth century, Ivy Lee helped dampen down the "public be damned" capitalism of the nineteenth century robber barons, and in doing so, I believe, he did much to save capitalism from the far-left revolutions that rocked much of Europe and brought about the communist revolution in Russia. Because of that, Lee had many critics on the left. At least one called this book a whitewash of avaricious capitalism, of the kind once represented by the Rockefellers. I once came across a far-left website of the "fifty most dangerous books ever published," and *Courtier to the Crowd* was 37th on the list. I doubt it would really be considered that way by most readers, then or now.

One important point about Ivy Lee's "crowd." He worked before the age of scientific public opinion research, which got started shortly after his death. George Gallup, then a professor of journalism at Northwestern University (and later Columbia Graduate School of Journalism), in the mid-1930s began using statistical analysis of polling data to get a scientific reading of public attitudes and opinions. Today that is the common way to understand public opinion and develop ways to influence it.

Lee started his professional career as a journalist, working as a reporter for newspapers in New York City, including covering Wall Street for the *New York Times*. From his myriad contacts and his sharply honed journalistic instincts, he developed a strong feeling for what the crowd was thinking and feeling. This was the basis for the advice he gave—without scientific research—about the opinions of the crowd.

On a summer vacation in Sacramento many years ago, as I was searching through the state library to find a topic to develop for my PhD dissertation, I came across a book that said Ivy Lee was the father of the modern press release. My PhD advisor, Carl Bode, an authority on American popular culture, approved my proposal for a study of the impact of Ivy Lee and the press release on American history. This was in the early 1960s.

In addition to a lot of reading, I interviewed anybody and everybody I could find who might have something to say about Ivy Lee. I talked with Lee's widow at her home in Wilton, Connecticut. I spent much time with his sons, James, who had worked in Lee's firm but had retired to a run an inn in Dorset, Vermont, and Ivy Jr., who had his own public relations firm in San Francisco. I spoke at length with T. J. Ross, who had worked his way up in the firm to be Lee's chief partner, then got his name on the door (Ivy Lee and T. J. Ross), and ended with just his name, long after Lee's untimely death at the age of 57.

Ross made sure I understood he couldn't give me all the material I might have wanted to investigate. The firm's relationship with its clients was, by mutual understanding, confidential. The Lee firm might prepare material for a client, but clients issued the material in their own names, and the nature of Lee's work on the client's problems remained confidential. Ross pointed out that this was no different from the relationship between doctor and patient or lawyer and client.

In the Lee situation, that policy might have led to much of the misunderstanding that has plagued Ivy Lee's reputation, especially his interest in Soviet Russia and his brief work for the I. G. Farben company in Germany.

However, the complete record of his relationship with his clients was carefully maintained by Lee's firm, in large three-ring binders. They were called M.S.O.s (messages sent out) and were labeled with the client's name and dates. These were not available to me. They were not included in the original gift of the Lee papers given to Princeton University Library. I received a grant to catalog the Lee papers in the mid-1960s, a marvelous opportunity for any scholar. But the M.S.O.s were not in the Princeton collection that I catalogued, nor in the book I wrote.

Many years later, as the firm was winding down its work and T. J. Ross closed its doors, the M.S.O.s were finally given to Princeton. Today, any scholar can examine the work of the Lee firm more closely than I had been able to. Scott Cutlip, the principal historian of public relations, was able to read the M.S.O.s for his 1994 book, *The Unseen Power: Public Relations, a History*. Cutlip concluded that those three-ring binders held no material that could raise any doubts about my interpretation of Lee's significance or prove Lee had been a secret agent of the Nazis or the Soviet Union or imperial Japan. Cutlip wrote in his history that *Courtier* was the "authoritative" biography of Ivy Lee.

#

On rereading this book fifty years after I wrote it, I've concluded that Ivy Lee really was of two minds about his field. His firm could and did distribute promotional material and publicity on behalf of its clients. But he did much more than that, although he often felt he couldn't adequately describe his work. Fifty years after I wrote this book, I have a better idea of what Ivy Lee did, and would frame it somewhat differently today.

This new edition, however, is not a revised edition. It is a replica of the original, even though my thoughts about it now are different. In the last fifty years, at least three important concepts have been developed which weren't in the literature that Ivy Lee had available when I wrote this book. Those concepts are now known as "social responsibility," "public diplomacy," and "conflict resolution." Those terms would better describe much of Lee's work.

Lee's public relations counseling, as in the case of the Rockefellers and the railroads, was in reality "conflict resolution." He felt that, in almost any situation, if both sides of a conflict could lay out their positions honestly, clearly, convincingly, and publicly, understanding and acceptance would be the result.

He often said he didn't know how to describe his work, perhaps because there was as yet no glossary for what he did. Looking back, it's evident Ivy Lee was practicing social responsibility, conflict resolution, and with his international interests, public diplomacy long before those terms were conceived.

I hope this book will help today's generation of public relations practitioners gain a better understanding, not only of Lee, but also about the history he helped to shape.

RAY ELDON HIEBERT
Carmel, California
July 2017

INTRODUCTION

RAY ELDON HIEBERT HAS PERFORMED A SERVICE by gleaning from records and memories the story of a man who will go down in history as the "father of public relations." His biography of Ivy Lee is a significant historic document. We lack similar knowledge of many other public relations pioneers because few records have been available, and those that were have not been woven together with the meticulous care and comprehension that Professor Hiebert has used in this volume. Appreciation should be given to the corporations involved and to Ivy Lee's family for making material available for this study.

This book traces the story of Lee through his early training in the family of a Methodist minister and in schools, in the newspaper office, as a fledgling publicist, and then as a pioneer public relations counsel for some of the greatest corporations in the world. He was one of the first exponents of the philosophy of "full disclosure" in news. He tore away the insulation of the "corporate veil" from the acts of his clients and allowed the piercing eye of press and public to become acquainted with the facts.

Ivy Lee was born at a crucial moment in history. In the last half of the nineteenth century, the industrial revolution brought exploitative capitalism to a crisis. Unbridled competition was suffocating business from the inside, while public clamor for more control was stifling it from the outside. Lee understood that organization and cooperation were indispensable for success in the new order. And he realized that public acceptance was necessary in a democratic society. To win acceptance, the public had to be fully informed, but it also had to be fully understood. Lee's own success in persuading corporate adoption of these new methods of dealing with the business public made him one of the most influential and controversial men of his time.

Of course he made mistakes of head and heart, and Professor Hiebert has portrayed these candidly. But in summation, Lee's errors were minor compared with the good work he performed. He persuaded many leaders of business and industry to clean house and become socially conscious. Thus he helped to pave the way for the cooperative and beneficent capitalism that has helped keep the West free during the rapid developments of the twentieth century.

These pages are a stimulating combination of history, biography, economics, theology, and journalism. The book should have a place on the shelf of every person who practices in the fields of public relations or journalism, and readily available as a source of information and guidance for corporate executives, businessmen, clergymen, politicians, lawyers, newsmen, and editors.

RAYMOND W. MILLER
Lecturer Emeritus, Harvard University
Graduate School of Business Administration

Boston, Massachusetts
January 1966

CONTENTS

About the Author, First Edition, 1966 4

About the Author, Second Edition, 2017 5

Preface 7

Preface to the Second Edition 11

Introduction 15

Contents 17

I. THE MAN
"He who molds public sentiment"

1: The Crowd is Enthroned 20

2: Heritage of a Courtier 36

3: The Power of the Word 48

4: Press Agents or Muckrakers 59

5: The Anthracite Coal Strike 70

II. PUBLIC UTILITIES
"The Divine Right of the Multitude"

6: Wreck on the Main Line 85

7: Campaign for Freight Rates 97

8: Humanizing the Subways 108

9: One Big Happy Family 118

10: Public Relations for Public Utilities 129

III. THE ROCKEFELLERS
"End of the Rear Door Philosophy"

11: The "Ludlow Massacre" 140

12: Dimes for Human Interest 156

13: Playing No Favorites 168

14: Biographers for Billionaires 178

15: Policies for the People 192

IV. THE CAPITALISTS
"Before the Court of Public Opinion"

16: Counsel for Corporations 208

17: Steel: Armaments for Bethlehem 222

18: Adjustments in Oil, Copper, and Coal 246

19: Cooperation in Foods, Cotton, Sugar, and Tobacco 257

20: Analyzing Attitudes Toward Travel and Aviation 268

21: Mass Entertainment: Uniting the artists 279

22: Banks: Rising from the Fall 290

23: Autos: Faith Instead of Inflation 304

24: Politics: The Failure of Moderation 314

25: Religion: Divided Protestants 325

26: Big Men: A Network of Interests 332

V. FOREIGN INTERESTS
"At the Council Table of the World"

27: Red Cross: Humanizing America 347

28: Problems of International Propaganda 363

29: Loans for France, Poland, and Romania 376

30: Russia: A colossal Axe to Grind 386

31: Germany: An Experiment that Exploded 402

VI. FINAL TRIAL
"The Judgments of the People"

32: Prosecution by the Critics 416

33: Verdict From the Crowd 432

Appendices 447

A note on Sources and Acknowledgements 447

Acknowledgements, Second Edition 451

Notes 452

Selected Bibliography 453

Index 463

RAY ELDON HIEBERT

I

THE MAN

"He who molds public sentiment"

1: THE CROWD IS ENTHRONED

ON AN EVENING IN JUNE 1958 the Republicans in New York held a one-hundred-dollar-a-plate dinner to select a candidate for governor. Back and forth across the hall of white ties and dinner jackets one name kept rising and falling among party faithful: Nelson Aldrich Rockefeller. To old-time, back-room politicians the name of Rockefeller was a political liability no party could afford, a name that would never get the popular vote. But even as cigar smoke thickened in the room, a new generation was getting ready to take over. For these men, with their understanding of public opinion backed by computer statistics, the Rockefeller name had new charm.

As the tinkle and clatter of dinnerware died, a party officer arose to address the gathering. He lined up a series of ten charts, each showing results of opinion polls on the gubernatorial candidacy of Nelson Rockefeller, grandson of a man once called "the greatest robber baron." The official spoke passionately. "I believe in this man! You can look at these charts and see that he will probably be a more popular candidate than anyone else we can put up. I say that the organization has to go for Rockefeller—and if it doesn't, I will step out as state chairman."

The party agreed to go along with the polls. Rockefeller was given the nomination and the charts proved to be correct as voters turned out en masse to confirm his popularity. His election as governor of the most populous state of the Union climaxed one of America's most significant public relations dramas. Only fifty years earlier, the John D. Rockefellers, Sr. and Jr., were among the least liked men in the United States. If either had been put on a ticket for county dogcatcher, he would have been booed out of town. And, unlike the later generation, neither would have cared a drop of oil about public opinion charts and popular attitudes.

The change began fifty years earlier on a dark day in 1914. The elder Rockefeller was out on his private golf course at Far Hills for a leisurely game, unperturbed by the world around him. More cautious, the younger Rockefeller—"Mr. Junior" as he was known—waited in the stone mansion at Pocantico Hills. A labor dispute in a Colorado coal mining company owned by the Rockefellers had caused an incident that was being called the "Ludlow massacre." Agitators were quick to make this another heinous crime to lay at the feet of the oil kings.

For years newspapers and magazines had carried muckraking headlines and articles about the capitalistic excesses of the Rockefellers: their stinginess, their ruthlessness, their lack of concern for public welfare. Their very name had become associated with imperialism, greed, insensitivity, "dog eat dog, root hog or die" capitalism. For many Americans, the Rockefellers meant monopolies, inhuman working conditions, slums, and filth. Through the years the tycoons had felt secure in the knowledge that they were not guilty, and so they ignored the charges. The headlines screamed and slapped, but with good Baptist humility the Rockefellers lifted their faces and turned the other cheek.

The Ludlow affair, however, proved to be too much. Crowds picketed the Standard Oil building in Manhattan; rabble rousers went up into Westchester County to throw stones at the Pocantico Hills mansion. And Mr. Junior, always more sensitive than his father, decided that something had to be done—they could no longer ignore the public. He turned for advice to a man who might know something about the masses, his friend Arthur Brisbane, then a socialist-leaning Hearst editor. "If you are concerned about public opinion," Brisbane said, "I know someone who could help you." And he suggested a thirty-six-year-old former newspaper reporter with the unlikely name of Ivy Ledbetter Lee.

Lee was a preacher's son from Georgia who had worked his way through Princeton and had gone on to newspaper work in New York around the turn of the century. A perceptive man with a sharp mind and a keen understanding of economic and social currents of his time, he had left journalism to become a new kind of press agent. Between 1904 and 1914 he had worked for various clients, chiefly for the Pennsylvania Railroad, and had also spent two and a half years in Europe for a stockbroker. The railroads had been prime targets of hostile public sentiment, but Lee had been amazingly successful in his work and was assistant to the president and key advisor to the Pennsylvania when John D. Rockefeller Jr. called upon him for help.

"Tell the truth," Lee told Rockefeller, "because sooner or later the public will find it out anyway. And if the public doesn't like what you are doing, change your policies and bring them into line with what the people want."[1] That was the essence of his advice. It was disarmingly simple and proved to be effective. It was so artless yet so efficacious that a generation of cynical critics suspected Ivy Lee of sinister machination and callous manipulation. John D.

Rockefeller Jr., however, liked Lee's point of view and took his word.

The result was that the Rockefellers opened their books, told their side of the story, and changed many of their policies, the most important being in management-employee relations. Until the Colorado strike they had believed in the theory that owner and worker should not mix. The proprietor should be silent and stoney-faced in his puritanical dignity; the laborer should be industrious, honest, and aware of his station. But on Lee's advice, the sheltered, august, white-gloved John D. Rockefeller Jr. went out to Colorado, talked with the miners, danced with their wives, learned their problems, communicated his, and achieved new appreciation and understanding on both sides. From that moment on, he urged closer relations and greater communication between manager and employee in the companies in which the Rockefellers held investments. He helped spread these ideas through a booklet, "The Personal Relation in Industry," an influential appeal for benevolent enterprise.

Over the years popular feeling toward the Rockefellers changed as they brought their policies into line with public thinking. Nelson Rockefeller, following his father's footsteps, enjoyed nationwide admiration from 1958 to 1962 and became a leading contender for the 1964 Republican presidential nomination. But the dramatic loss of public approval he suffered in 1963 following his divorce and remarriage showed that no stunts nor press-agentry nor manipulation of public opinion could stop the downward trend of the popularity charts once he had taken a course that went against the grain of the people. This was proof of Ivy Lee's basic philosophy that publicity was not enough to counteract the opinions of the public toward policies or actions with which the public did not agree. The policies and actions themselves had to be sound.

Because of the Rockefellers' wealth and influence, their acceptance of Ivy Lee's principles opened a new era for business and public relations. Even before his association with the Rockefellers and certainly thereafter, Lee attracted the big businessmen of America and showed them what they must do and how to secure public understanding. At one time or another he served as an advisor in public relations to such men as George Westinghouse, Thomas Fortune Ryan, Charles Schwab, Walter Chrysler, Harry F. Guggenheim, Alton B. Parker, John W. Davis, Henry P. Davison, Dwight Morrow, Otto Kahn, Winthrop Aldrich, Benjamin Javits, Charles Lindbergh, and George Washington Hill. He aided some of the largest and most powerful corporations, including the Pennsylvania Railroad, Standard Oil, Bethlehem Steel, Interborough Rapid Transit, Chrysler Corporation, American Tobacco, Armour and Company, General Mills, and United States Rubber. He gave counsel to the coal trust, public utilities, sugar cartels, banks, shipping interests, investment houses, and foreign countries. He donated his services to universities, foundations, charities, and churches.

Ivy Lee was never quite sure of the title of his profession, confessing toward the end of his life that even his children did not know what to call him. He was not a press agent, not a promoter, not an advertising man. He did many of the things they did, but he did much more. As his work grew and his ideas took shape, he spent less time with publicity and press releases and more time thinking, analyzing public opinion, and giving counsel on public problems.

Above all, he became a catalyst for the men with whom he dealt. He sparked new ideas, touched off the formation of new practices, generated the formulation of new policies. He helped spawn influential organizations such as the Daniel Guggenheim Foundation and the Copper and Brass Research Institute. He spurred the programs of the Rockefeller Foundation and the American Red Cross. He not only dealt with the popular mind but concerned himself with the leaders of the world. He conferred with Churchill, Mussolini, and Hitler, and with every president of the United States from Grover Cleveland to Franklin Roosevelt.

Just a few months after Lee's death in 1934, a British writer, Terence O'Brien, asked his readers: "How far will the governments of democratic countries be compelled to adopt the kind of methods which Ivy Lee and his followers have already evolved?" Now, thirty years later, an assessment can be made. The answer, of course, is that these methods are today an indispensable part of nearly every organized activity in democratic life. Without public relations, democracy could not succeed in a mass society. Today in every democratic government a significant part of the budget is allocated for public relations services. In the United States, an entire Federal bureau, the U.S. Information Agency, is devoted to improving public relations between the United States and foreign countries.

At the end of Lee's life, only a handful of men were practicing his arts. By 1960, the U.S. Census listed more than 30,000 in the profession, and other estimates ran as high as 100,000. The total amount of money annually spent for public relations activities is estimated to be more than two billion dollars. Today, America is a civilization of organization men influenced largely by policies derived from an awareness of public relations.

Lee was certainly not the world's first public relations practitioner. Most men of history who succeeded in public life must have had some understanding of the principles Lee employed. But he was probably the first to devote his time to these activities as an independent professional agent on behalf of individual clients, and he gave expression to basic principles now widely accepted by those who have followed him in his practice. Historian Merle Curti calls him "the first great figure in his field...the prototype of subsequent public relations counsels"[2]

Perhaps no better way to understand the historical development of modern public relations could be provided than through the story of Ivy Lee. He played such an intimate role and was the archetype of so many who shared the stage with him that his story is larger than himself. It is a story of a changing America from Reconstruction to the Great Depression. His short lifetime—1877 to 1934—spanned that momentous period in our history. But he did more than bridge the gap between the Victorian nineteenth and the revolutionary twentieth centuries—he played an important role in the metamorphosis.

Lee's concern with public opinion was directly in the American tradition. Abraham Lincoln voiced the *raison d'être* of public relations when he said that without public sentiment, nothing in America could succeed. The earliest American settlers, freed from the shackles of older societies and established on new frontiers, could act as individuals. As individuals, they had new importance; their opinions counted. When these individuals formed groups and their opinions were unified, they had power. The public is "the fountain of all power," Lee once wrote. In a democracy, he said, "we have substituted for the divine right of kings, the divine right of the multitude. The crowd is enthroned."[3]

So Samuel Adams found when, through newspapers and pamphlets, he and his Sons of Liberty and Committees of Correspondence courted the opinions of colonial Americans and stirred them to insurrection. So Thomas Jefferson found when he stimulated the colonies to settle the matter of independence with his ringing "Declaration." So Tom Paine found as he rallied the population with his pamphlet, "Common Sense," and revived a weary army with his "Crisis Papers," a series of press releases sent to colonial newspapers. The authors of the *Federalist Papers* also engaged in unifying the crowd by writing for the public media. With careful timing, stirring rhetoric, and considered logic, Hamilton, Madison, and Jay explained the compromises of the new Constitution to a disparate crowd of Tories, Federalists, Republicans, merchants, farmers, and backwoodsmen, persuading them to agree to a democratic government on a scale never before tried or achieved. The *Federalist Papers*, in the judgment of historian Allan Nevins, was "the greatest work ever done in America in the field of public relations."[4]

In the nineteenth century the press agent became a familiar figure in American life. It was his job to woo and win the crowd through the printed word in the penny press, that medium for reaching the greatest number of people in the shortest amount of time. But his work was limited largely to politics and entertainment. Amos Kendall and Francis Blair, two newspapermen in Andrew Jackson's "Kitchen Cabinet," brought the press secretary, publicist, and ghost writer into the White House as the masses assumed new importance in government and politics. In entertainment, press-agentry was frequently based on fraud and hoax. Washington Irving, for instance, stirred public interest in his books by creating a fake character, Diedrich Knickerbocker, to obtain newspaper publicity. P. T. Barnum became the prototype of the nineteenth century press agent through his skill at creating headlines with contrived and often underhanded stunts.

On the other hand, business in the nineteenth century had little use for press or public. Its leaders held aloof from the crowds and avoided involvement with the masses. "The public be damned" was the prevalent attitude. If press agents were employed, their job was to prevent true facts from reaching the public or to let people know that they ought to mind their own affairs. Ivy Lee grew up in a period when free enterprise reached a peak in American history, and yet at that very climax the tide of public opinion was swelling up against business freedom, primarily because of the breakdown in communication between the businessman and the public.

Ironically, increasing literacy in the nineteenth century and technological developments in communication led to more power for public opinion and less choice for the individual. The great movements late in the century, the Grange, Populism, Progressivism, and others, proved the masses could be swayed and that aroused public opinion could effectively influence legislation, direct governmental action, and create the climate in which society operated. But the power came from mass communication and mass movements, not from the individual. These circumstances weakened the liberty of the individual and threatened to shape a more authoritarian structure such as that of communism or fascism. By the end of the nineteenth century, a free and open society was in peril.

Out of this milieu grew public relations. It did not spring full blown from Ivy Lee's head. Its starting point was the nineteenth century press agent, its maturation the contemporary public relations counsel. Lee played a key role in its evolution, changing the direction from fraud, hoax, distortion, and stunts to factual information, understanding, and sound policies. His own thinking, which was so important in public relations development, can be expressed in five points:

1. Lee believed in individual liberty and felt that economic freedom as expressed in some form of capitalism was most conducive to growth and progress.

2. He believed in democracy where the people were the government and public opinion the final law.

3. He accurately assessed the growing conflict between the individual freedom necessary for industrial success and the power of public opinion in a mass society.

4. He realized that the individual whose activities had public consequences, especially the businessman, must make his actions circumspect in order to preserve his freedom in a mass society.

5. He saw that where individuals, groups, and masses come into conflict, channels of communication must be opened to provide information necessary for them to understand each other and find solutions.

None of these ideas is in itself original. The final argument is only another way of stating Thomas Jefferson's rationale for freedom of the press to represent all points of view. Only with all sides presented can society avoid an excess of power in the hands of a few, whether that power be political, governmental, private, or industrial. In the complex, specialized, and technological age of mass communication and mass production, a specialist was needed to provide advice on public actions and to communicate those actions to the public in understandable terms. This was the role that Ivy Lee and his colleagues grew into.

In providing advice on public activity, Lee was acutely aware of what he called "revolutionary" changes in society. The "protestant ethic" of the nineteenth century had given way to the "social ethic" of the twentieth. The "inner-directed" man was becoming "other-directed." The fierce struggle and individualism of earlier generations had to be replaced with cooperation and organization. In terms that perfectly described our mid-twentieth century organization man, Lee analyzed the changed industrialist. "The power of a dominant personality which was of the utmost importance in the early years of pioneering industrial life, is far less effective in today's large-scale organization." Rather, he contended, "sympathy, unselfishness, a tendency to play for the whole team, those things which enable a man to work effectively with others, are now, I believe, of greater importance." In short, Lee maintained, business had to change its policies of closed, individualistic, competitive capitalism to new programs of open, cooperative, and benevolent enterprise![5]

But as business must understand the public, so the public must understand business. In the case of the railroads, where "demagogues" and "muckrakers" had stirred up public insistence on reforms that could place unfair limitations on the companies, the people must understand that a railroad "can do no more than it can offer the prospect of rendering a fair return for. All other considerations are bound up in those stern economic laws."[6]

When public opinion and the freedom to follow those stern economic laws came into conflict, as they did in the 1914 Colorado strike, the only solution lay "in a proper understanding of those laws, and in a proper adjustment of the intimate and far-reaching relations arising out of that understanding." It was necessary for understanding and compromise on both sides, or as Lee put it, a "proper adjustment of the interrelations" of public and business, for only in such adjustment "must rest the orderly and healthy development of American business in the future."[7] He gradually assumed the role of providing the adjustment of relations between public and business. He often thought of himself as a new kind of lawyer, one representing his client in the court of public opinion, which in a democratic society made judgments with as much certainty and finality as any court of law.

Lee was interested in the whole range of human relationships: trade relations, employee relations, industrial relations, government relations, community relations, even international relations. He first called his work "publicity," a term now used primarily to describe the techniques of communication which he helped to perfect rather than the interrelationships with which he was concerned. The broader role of adjusting relationships is more aptly described by "public relations," a phrase Lee did not use extensively until later in his career in the twenties.

By publicity, Lee meant "the entire gamut of expression of an idea or of an institution," not only in newspapers but through "the radio, the moving picture, magazine articles, speeches, books, mass meetings, brass bands." Yet he always argued that one's publicity should not be separate from one's relations with the public. Publicity was "everything involved in the expression of an idea or an institution—including the policy or the idea expressed." In its ultimate sense, he said, publicity means "the actual relationship of a company to the people, and that relationship involves far more than saying—it involves doing."[8]

He counseled that publicity as he conceived it must be neither censored nor distorted but an open airing of the truth. "A man who goes into a policy of publicity must believe absolutely that he is right and that he can justify his policy upon the theory that 'truth loves open dealing,' and that he can rely absolutely upon the refining and sterling value of the truth." A company that devotes itself to telling the truth must have a worthwhile truth to tell if it wants to retain the goodwill of the public. "An elementary requisite of any sound publicity," he said, was "the giving of the best possible service."[9]

Lee was often attacked, especially by those on the political left, champions of the workers and spokesmen for labor unions, whose most legitimate criticism was that his policies of truth and good service were followed only because they were more effective means of destroying individual differences, of unifying individuals into a crowd, and thus maintaining power for his clients. Indeed, the contemporary Madison Avenue opinion molder is often guilty of promoting conformity in order to sway the masses.

Lee recognized that crowds were inherent in twentieth century society. As the frontier had passed away and life had become more complex, group action had had to replace individual initiative. The way in which crowds organized in a free and democratic society depended upon the voices that were heard. By their nature, he said, crowds need to be led, but the important thing was to have courtiers for all points of view in attendance before the throne of this new king—otherwise the public could not make accurate and sound judgments. People were intelligent, he said, and if given all the facts, they would not submit to deception or duplicity.

Those on the political right criticized Lee for being too naïve, for giving the masses too much credit, and for complying with impossible demands of a blind and bumbling crowd. They felt a certain betrayal in Lee's idea that publicity was a weapon that cuts both ways, and "unless a man is willing to be absolutely honest, he had better not monkey with publicity." He told his business clients that "a company cannot sing of its prosperity to security holders and at the same time cry over its poverty to tax appraisers and its workingmen."[10]

He felt that most criticism of his ideas—from both labor and management, left and right—was based largely on a lack of faith in people and in the democratic process. One side thought that the public *could* be misled and the other that it should be misled. When a group of electric railway executives berated him for his faith in the people, he answered sharply: "If we cannot trust the people, I'm afraid we must reconsider the very question of democratic government. Unless we can trust the people, democratic government is in danger, and I, for one, am not prepared to admit that that is true."[11]

Perhaps Lee's chief attribute was his ability to stand up under attacks from both left and right and hold to a democratic, middle-of-the-road policy. He argued against government ownership, unfair union demands, and commission-set rates that would not allow sufficient profit for business growth. But he could also boldly rebuke the isolationism of the United States Chamber of Commerce, bluntly criticize the lack of action by Herbert Hoover, and soundly debunk ill-conceived policies of John D. Rockefeller. Lee worked for the interests of his corporation and millionaire employers, but to the extent that he honestly advised them on public matters, frequently against their personal interests and business profits, he was a man of pluck and backbone, at times bordering on nerve and gall.

He did not conceive of himself as anybody's tool or mouthpiece. To the contrary, he considered it imperative to remain an independent agent in order to maintain his integrity and provide forthright advice to his clients. In 1916, after little more than a year's association with the Rockefellers, he left their full-time employ of his own accord and worked for them thereafter only on retainer, primarily so he could maintain his independence and thereby be most useful to them as a public relations counsel. Today few in the profession who are not independent counsels can claim to be practicing public relations with the objectivity that Ivy Lee felt was essential to his work.

There still are insufficient regulations for the practice of public relations, but during Lee's lifetime there were none at all. Since he operated on a new frontier he created his own guidelines as he went along. He was not always right, but in retrospect it is remarkable how often he was. He made mistakes, but considering the context of the disorderly period in which he lived, it seems surprising how few transgressions he committed. His sins were primarily sins of faith, optimism, and enthusiasm. His tragic flaw, perhaps, was his wholehearted acceptance of the traditional democratic belief in the innate goodness of man and the American virtues of working hard, thinking shrewdly, and rising to the top.

"I have found," he once told an interviewer, "that the biggest men are the simplest, the humblest, and the most trusting."[12] His own trust on a few occasions led him to accept half-truths as whole or to put too much faith in individuals or crowds. It was one thing to believe Rockefeller, a man of good intentions to begin with. But on at least one occasion a Rockefeller subordinate abused Lee's trust and led him to publicize half-truths which, when uncovered, led to nationwide criticism at the hands of his enemies and earned him the lifetime nickname of "Poison Ivy." Lee made a tragic mistake, perhaps even contributing to his untimely death, when he put too much faith in the German people, thinking that they would accept his policy of open dealing and that the resulting publicity about Hitler would expose the Führer for the maniac that he was and allow people to restore sound policies in Germany. That failure did not disprove the efficacy of Lee's principles, but it emphasized the complexities of the problems of communicating truth to man in a mass society.

In spite of his sincere faith, Lee was not a simple man. There were many parts to him and many motives. He had a desire to serve society, but he was ego-serving as well. He pursued his ideals assiduously, yet at the peak of his career, as the golden age of American business careened toward its climactic Black Friday of 1929, Lee was so torn by serious doubts about American business and his own contribution that he considered giving up his work altogether. In spite of his human doubts and ego, he had unusually perceptive insights into the problems of the revolutionary twentieth century, and the solutions that he devised proved to be unusually effective. This made him more than the ordinary press agent; it made him a new kind of "courtier to the crowd."

---

[1] U.S. Congress, Senate, Commission on Industrial Relations, *Final Report and Testimony*, 1915, Vol. VIII, pp. 7899 ff.

[2] Merle Curti, *The Growth of American Thought* (New York: Harper & Bros., 1951), p. 652.

[3] Ivy Lee, *Human Nature and the Railroads* (Philadelphia: E. S. Nash & Co., 1915), p. 8.

[4] Allan Nevins, *The Constitution Makers and the Public* (New York: Foundation for Public Relations Research and Education, 1963), p. 31.

[5] Quoted by M. K. Wisehart, "How Big Men Think and Act," *The American Magazine*, July 1929, p. 30.

[6] Ivy Lee, *Railway Progress in the United States* (London: B. F. Stevens & Brown, Publishers, 1912), p. 31.

[7] Ibid., pp. 9, 32.

[8] Ivy Lee, *Publicity: Some of the Things It Is and Is Not* (New York: Industries Publishing Co., 1925), pp. 7–8, 48.

[9] Ibid., p. 48.

[10] Ibid., p. 45.

[11] Ivy Lee, *Publicity for Public Service Corporations* (New York: privately printed, 1916), "Questions and Answers" section, p. 4.

[12] Quoted by Wisehart, loc. cit.

RAY ELDON HIEBERT

2: HERITAGE OF A COURTIER

AS THE NINETEENTH CENTURY ENTREPRENEUR gained wealth and stature, he withdrew from association with the common folk. The typical newspaper reporter, on the other hand, was often conspicuously a part of the crowd, frequently appearing with unkempt hair, dirty fingernails, bohemian dress, and the stench of liquor on his breath. The higher a man rose in life, the more he avoided contact with this creature of the press. The story is told of how John Pierpont Morgan was once surprised into a rare interview when he fell into conversation with a well-dressed man with white gloves and polished speech. After their talk had progressed for some minutes, Morgan was surprised to learn that he was speaking with a newspaper reporter, but he was so pleased to have found a gentleman in the crowd that he allowed the interview to continue. And the reporter had a scoop.

When, just out of Princeton, Ivy Lee went to work as a newspaperman in New York City, he was the gentlemanly type, impressing the Wall Street barons of finance with his courtly manner, his Southern dignity, his careful questions, and his guarded speech. He brought an uncommon polish to the New York newsrooms. Handsome and engaging, he stood six feet tall and had the lean physique and erect carriage of an ambitious man. His face was open and honest, with a large mouth, straight nose, and intent blue eyes. His chin was sharp and forceful, his forehead high and crowned with soft chestnut hair. One leg, broken in his youth, was slightly shorter than the other, but he limped a bit only when tired.

His dignity and decorum went with him as he moved from the newspaper world to become a press agent. Deane Malott, later president of Cornell who worked for Ivy Lee in the twenties, described him as starchy, encrusted with dignity, courtly and formal, with immaculate dress and a steel-blue gaze. This was in sharp contrast to the "circus-hawker" press agents of that period with their brown derbies and checkered suits.

Yet Lee could be homespun and folksy. Even when he rose to fame and sat in a plush skyscraper office overlooking New York, he retained close identification with his impecunious Georgia relatives and his sense of belonging to the common man. When he was interviewed at the peak of his career by a reporter from a southern magazine, he smiled and bowed as they were introduced. "The assignment wasn't going to be difficult," the reporter wrote. "I knew at once he was 'folks'." Lee had the rare ability to understand and be part of the common man, even while he could speak man to man with the Rockefellers, the Chryslers, and the Schwabs. He was always able to communicate in the other's language, on the other's terms, bridging the gulf between men, no matter who or what they were.

Ivy Lee was endowed with rich qualifications to be an intermediary between people. His father's side of the family could trace its line back to Richard Lee I of Virginia and his mother's to the father of George Washington, and from the Washingtons to Margaret Butler and her illustrious ancestry that took in almost all the kings of Europe, including Arthur and Charlemagne.[1] Lee's grandfather, Zachary Lee, had been a Georgia planter and grist mill owner; his grandmother, Emma H. Wideman, was the descendent of a German soldier who fought in the American Revolution.

Ivy Lee's father, James Wideman Lee, was born in the small village of Rockbridge in 1849. The grist mill gave the Lees sufficient wealth to send James off to Bawsville Academy before the Civil War. But the family fortune was lost when General Sherman burned the mill on his march to the sea. And two months after the war,

Zachary lost his life while trying to save the house during another fire. With the family in ruin, James had to quit Bawsville and finish his education at the public high school at Grantville. A bright young man and a hard worker, he attracted the interest and confidence of a well-to-do family friend, Ivy Sewall, who gave him the money to complete his college education at Emory (then a Methodist institution primarily preparing young men for the ministry).

After graduation in 1874 James W. Lee joined the Georgia Conference of the Methodist Episcopal Church South and was ordained for the ministry in 1876. He started serving a circuit of small churches around Atlanta, including Spring Creek, Rockmart, Long Cane, Carrollton, Dalton, Rome, and within ten years had worked his way to the big city of Atlanta. Early in this tour he met Rev. Dr. L. L. Ledbetter, a prominent Methodist minister also serving the community as a physician, whose property, like the Lees', had been desolated by Sherman's men.

When Rev. Lee came to the Ledbetter home in Cedartown as a circuit preacher, he was much taken with one of the twelve children, Emma Eufaula. But she was not quite thirteen years of age, so he was not allowed to visit her in the parlor of the house. He came around to the kitchen and courted her over the pages of the Bible as he taught her the scriptures, and they were married a short time later, in 1876. Emma was one month shy of being fourteen when her first child was born on July 16, 1877. They named him Ivy, after the friend who had helped his father through college, and Ledbetter, after his mother's family. Two brothers, James Wideman Jr. and Lewis, and three sisters, Kate, Alice, and Laura, later arrived to complete the family.

Ivy Lee's mother was a remarkable woman. Born in the middle of the Civil War and growing up in the poverty that followed, there was little hope that she could acquire an education and lead a cultured life. But she taught herself to read and often would sit in the kitchen behind the open door listening intently to the conversation of the men in the parlor. Her intellect encompassed such broad interests that later as a preacher's wife she could easily make her household the center of public affairs in whatever community she was living. After her husband's death she traveled widely as a popular lecturer at women's clubs and church functions. She died in 1951 at the age of 89, having outlived her first-born and famous son by seventeen years.

Ivy's father was every bit as remarkable. He became one of the most popular ministers at the Trinity Church in Atlanta and later at the Park Street Church. In 1893 he was transferred to St. John's in St. Louis, returned to Trinity and Park Street in 1906; then back to St. Louis in 1909, serving there until his death in 1919. He was the Presiding Elder of the St. Louis district and narrowly missed becoming a bishop of the Methodist Church.

For young Ivy, listening to sermons in church was a lesson in conciliation. Most of his father's sermons were about thrift, love, diligence, and moral duties. But for the more sophisticated congregations in Atlanta and St. Louis, he delved into more complex problems of theology, being especially concerned with the widening gulf between science and religion.

Earlier in the century the work of Charles Darwin had shattered Protestantism in much the same way that the Civil War ravaged the South. Reverend Lee preached many sermons and wrote several books in an effort to heal the wound and prevent the gulf from widening. He took a conciliatory position between the fundamentalists and the evolutionists. An evolving human being, he maintained, was not out of line with Biblical teaching; evolution was merely the way in which God revealed his handiwork. Such a position was radical in the Deep South.

But Rev. Lee was a master at winning friends and influencing people. According to his biographer in the *Dictionary of American Biography*, he had "unmistakable friendliness and persistent optimism...hundreds of people of all classes and in all regions voluntarily testified to his influence on them personally."[2] He was expert at fundraising. "He never had a charge," wrote his son later, "without leaving some visible witness of having been its pastor." He built a parsonage at Dalton. He raised the money and oversaw the building of one of the most imposing churches in the state when he was at Rome. He rebuilt Trinity, built a new edifice at Park Street, and raised $200,000 for one of the most expensive churches in St. Louis. As Presiding Elder his chief role was raising money for educational and charitable purposes.

The minister was a persistent visitor to the homes of his parishioners. He knew and remembered the names of all the members of his congregation and their children. During his vacations he sent postcards to all the Sunday School scholars and their parents. When he visited Palestine in the 1890s he sent flowers from the Garden of Gethsemane to every family in his church. His greatest fondness was for clipping the papers and magazines for articles of interest which he would send to his friends. In all, wrote his son, he "kept in touch with the members of the different charges he served, from his first circuit down through all the other charges for forty-four years."[3]

Just as he tried to bridge the gap between fundamentalists and evolutionists, so he held to the middle of the road between radicals and conservatives. When Emma Goldman and her women anarchists came to St. Louis, he struck out at them from his pulpit—and thus made the headlines. A few weeks later when a race incident came to light, he criticized reactionary attitudes. METHODIST PASTOR LAUDS JEWISH RACE—the headlines read. He worked for Negro education and demanded that Catholics and Jews be admitted to the Y.M.C.A. Later he proposed a "Cathedral of Cooperation" in Atlanta for all faiths, Protestant, Catholic, and Jewish. Ivy Lee's father had a warm respect for people and the ability to bridge the gulfs between them. His many techniques for maintaining personal relations with people were later adopted by his son Ivy in a new profession.

The South, during the Reconstruction period that followed the Civil War, had greater need for conciliation and persuasion and human relations than any other place in America. Not only was it devastated, but Reconstruction made it possible to keep the South defeated, its old ways changed politically, socially, and economically. Most Southerners resisted Reconstruction, and it finally failed. New leaders emerged who knew how to restore old ways of life by more devious means. These men, the Bourbons, recognized that through cooperation with Northern industrialists, they could slip out from under the heavy hand of Reconstruction, so they agreed to raise a commercial South from the ashes of the old plantations. The result, they expected, would be an industrial rather than agricultural aristocracy.

Unlike the old planters, however, the Bourbons understood the new order. They knew that the only way to restore power to a political and economic aristocracy was by swaying the new and powerful crowd with a spread-eagle oratory that would rally the farmers and poor whites. In this new Bourbon South of the late 1870s and 1880s, merchandizing, money lending, building factories, promoting railroads, and developing resources became more important than planting tobacco or cotton. Thus the planter gave way to the demagogue, eventually to the Ben Tillmans, Tom Watsons, and Huey Longs, reversing the welfare policies of the Reconstruction, emphasizing states' rights and *laissez faire*.

Increasingly they turned to the Northern capitalist to stand as godfather to Southern commerce and industry.

Ivy Lee grew up in the midst of talk about the "New South." Constant visitors in the Lee home were businessmen, politicians, bishops, and journalists. Most important to Ivy were the Howells family that ran the *Atlanta Constitution*, their famous writer, Joel Chandler Harris, and equally famous editor, Henry W. Grady. Unlike the Bourbons, this circle in Atlanta grew steadily more liberal, influenced by such men as Woodrow Wilson, Walter Hines Page, and George Washington Cable. They sought more education for Negroes, stronger policies of civil rights, and more positive governmental programs.

Henry Grady was the most respected apologist for the industrial New South, using his newspaper to publish factual stories pointing up the need for greater industrialization and editorials to nail down the arguments. "He did not tamely promote enterprise and encourage industry," wrote a contemporary. "He vehemently fomented enterprise and provoked industry until they stalked through the land like armed conquerors." Grady's famous New York speech in 1886 on the New South was a masterpiece of conciliation. He praised Lincoln as the first genuine American, a fusion of Puritan and Cavalier. He drew a rosy picture of Southern race relations: "We found that in the summing up, the free Negro counts for more than he did as a slave." But he reminded his Northern audience that "your fathers sold their slaves to our fathers."

Grady was neither a boorish Bourbon nor a Southern Quisling—he was essentially an adjustor of relations, one who sought reforms in Southern industry and agriculture while promoting their growth. His position stirred an amazingly sympathetic response in newspapers across the country, and he returned home from his New York speech a hero in the land. He was not only hero but idol for young Ivy Lee, who visited his editorial offices, worked for his paper while in college, and thought of no other career than Henry Grady's newspaper business. Lee absorbed all of Grady's interests: Wall Street, the stock market, banking and investments, the relationship of big business to the little man. Most important, perhaps, Lee was impressed with Grady's honesty and sincerity and his ability to turn a phrase. He later gave Grady much credit for what he had learned from him about influencing people.[4]

But while Grady was the prophet of the New South, Joel Chandler Harris was chronicler of the old. And young Ivy often sat at his feet and learned a different side of life, a more human, common, mellow, and sympathetic side. Harris would often gather the Lee children around him and tell them Brer Rabbit stories of the plantation, of slaves and white folks, of the old order that was gone. Lee later wrote and published a memorial volume about Harris, just as Lee's father had written a biography in eulogy of Grady![5]

These heroes of young Ivy Lee spent a great part of their lives trying to heal the break between North and South. It was a South of many opposites: reconstructed and unreconstructed; Bourbons and liberals; decaying aristocrats and the rising common man; capitalists and reformers; agrarians and industrialists; old and new. It was a land where oratory and demagoguery, publicity and promotion were the most effective means of healing wounds. The heroes of Ivy Lee were essentially interpreters of the South to the North and the North to the South. A few years later, their young protégé would fill the same office for big business and the common man.

When Ivy Lee went North for his education at Princeton the ideas he had learned at church, home, and community were given a more sophisticated rationale but one that was congenial to his background. At Princeton the intellectual atmosphere was dominated by President James McCosh, a leading exponent of the Scottish common-sense philosophy. Individualism, freedom from government interference, the right of property, and acquisition of wealth were basic doctrines. Shortly before Lee arrived on the New Jersey campus, President McCosh wrote that "God has bestowed upon us certain powers and gifts which no one is at liberty to take from us or to interfere with. All attempts to deprive us of them is theft. Under the same head may be placed all purposes to deprive us of the right to earn property or to use it as we see fit."

It was a doctrine which dovetailed with the ideals of industry and thrift that had been taught Lee as a boy. The Methodist circuit riders throughout the United States had followed Francis Asbury's example and spread the Calvinist doctrine that one's moral duty was to be diligent to his earthly calling. "If you want to win the game of life and honor the God who made you, work hard and save." This doctrine taught to James Wideman Lee as he prepared for the ministry at Emory College was passed on to his son in countless sermons.

At Princeton the doctrine of evolution, with which Ivy's father had flirted, was easily made to fit a philosophy of industriousness. The world was a place where the fittest survived. The competitive struggle of the marketplace weeded out the weak and incompetent and selected for positions of power those individuals who were set apart, predestined by their initiative, vision, judgment, and powers of organization. Since leaders rise in society through natural competition, McCosh taught at Princeton, the function of the state is to maintain order and protect property. To do so, the state naturally seeks to increase its power by interfering with business. But the individual must constantly protect himself against such interference, and it is this balance of power, this struggle between state and individual, which provides equilibrium in a democracy.

However, the last decades of the nineteenth century were years of extremes in American life, years when a few men became fabulously wealthy, but also years of vast slums, destitution, and social ills. Poverty, according to McCosh, sprang from laziness; civilization, on the other hand, sprang from industriousness. The questions remained: How can the pursuit of wealth prevent social ills? How could it result in the common good?

The answers were best summed up in the phrase, "the gospel of wealth." Seven years before Lee arrived at Princeton, this creed had been given its name and most complete statement by one of the country's greatest capitalists, Andrew Carnegie, in an article entitled "Wealth," printed in the *North American Review* in 1889.[6] Carnegie had been a friend of Joel Chandler Harris so Lee knew of the Scottish millionaire's ideas firsthand.

For Carnegie, the answer to the world's social ills lay in the duties of the man of wealth, and the first of these was "to set an example of modest, unostentatious living, shunning display or extravagance; to provide moderately for the legitimate wants of those dependent upon him; and after doing so to consider all surplus revenues which came to him simply as trust funds, which he is called upon to administer, and strictly bound as a matter of duty to administer in the manner...best calculated to produce the most beneficial results for the community."[7]

Lee shared Carnegie's strong feelings that this code provided the true antidote for social ills, for the temporary unequal distribution of wealth, the conciliation of rich and poor. Lee, too, felt that the use of great fortunes for the public good would ultimately bring, in Carnegie's words, "a reign of harmony, another ideal, differing, indeed, from that of the communist in requiring only the further evolution of existing conditions, not the total overthrow of our civilization."[8]

Here were the seeds of public relations, the key to most of Ivy Lee's thoughts. The essence of Lee's contribution was that he helped to give Carnegie's ideas a new technique, a voice which enabled them to survive during the first half of a twentieth century infinitely more complex politically, economically, and socially than the last half of the nineteenth had been. Lee helped to *further the evolution of existing conditions* while much of the rest of the world was seeking an antidote for social ills through a communist or fascist revolution, the total overthrow of civilization.

Woodrow Wilson, a Princeton professor of jurisprudence and political economy and one of Lee's chief mentors, also was becoming increasingly concerned about social ills and the public welfare. While at Princeton, Wilson began to move away from his earlier distrust of the state; ultimately he accepted the popular Germanic idea that the state was a beneficent organ of society capable of harmonizing individual rights with public duties and social development.

Although Ivy Lee never went as far as Woodrow Wilson, the effect of Wilson's influence can be seen in Lee's ideas. For instance, he told railroad owners in 1910 that government regulation of rail lines would "serve a sound public purpose" if the owners themselves would not adopt effective measures "to stop the old practices of discrimination and favoritism, of special rates and secret rebates, and of unequal treatment of shippers."[9]

However, the loss of freedom which government regulation posed was alien to Lee's ideals. Only one solution remained: Carnegie's. Business itself must bring its policies into line with the aspirations of the public and thus preserve its franchise. Lee played an intermediary role between business and public to gain conciliation for their differences. His heritage had equipped him well for that task.

---

[1] Genealogy of the Lee-Ledbetter family, Mrs. Kate Lee Trueblood, St. Louis, Mo.

[2] C. C. Pearson, "James Wideman Lee," Vol. XI of *Dictionary of American Biography*, ed. Robert Livingston Schuyler (22 vols.; New York: Charles Scribner's Sons, 1958), p. 111.

[3] Ivy Lee, "Introduction," James Wideman Lee, *The Geography of Genius* (New York: Fleming Revell Co., 1920), p. xvii.

[4] Raymond B. Nixon, *Henry W. Grady; Spokesman of the New South* (New York: Alfred A. Knopf, 1943), p. 23.

[5] Ivy Lee, *Memories of Uncle Remus* (New York: privately printed, 1908).

[6] Andrew Carnegie, "Wealth," *North American Review*, June 1889, pp. 653–664. Also reprinted in *Democracy and the Gospel of Wealth*, ed. Gail Kennedy (Boston: Heath and Co., 1949), pp. 1–8.

[7] Ibid.

[8] Ibid.

[9] Ivy Lee, *The American Railway Problem* (London: B. F. Stevens & Brown, Publishers, 1910), p. 5.

3: THE POWER OF THE WORD

AS A COURTIER, LEE'S CHIEF CONCERN was the effect he had on his prince, "the crowd." A sincere believer in the ideas that were part of his heritage, he had almost a religious devotion to his work. He was concerned only in a peripheral way with money or social position, preferring to spread his gospel.

Lee once persuaded John D. Rockefeller Jr. to write and publish a book; Rockefeller did so only when he could find a publisher to undertake the job and sell the book over the counter for a fair price. The important thrust in Rockefeller's life was to make a profit, and he counted the royalties carefully.[1] But when Ivy Lee published a book he often did so at his own expense, not because publishers turned him down but because he wanted to say his own piece, to put it in his own typographical style, and to distribute it to his own list of thousands of people that he felt were important readers. He was not interested in royalty dollars but in influence, in the spread of the ideas in which he believed.

Indeed, his disregard for money bordered on improvidence. His wife has said that when they were first married, if he had enough money in his pocket for lunch and dinner, he would forego his meals to take her for a buggy ride through Central Park. She often had to put her foot down on his prodigal spending. Even after he was earning a small fortune he spent little money on himself, choosing instead to be generous with everyone else, especially his family.

He had a warm relationship with his father, and after he left home the two carried on an almost daily correspondence. His father's handwriting, however, was all but illegible, and the story is told by the family that part of the first money Ivy earned in New

York was used to buy his father a typewriter so they could correspond more easily. Later, on trips overseas, he often bought trunkloads of clothes and gifts for his family. One Christmas he paid to bring twenty-one members of his and his wife's families together from all over the country to their home in New York where he not only entertained them but provided Christmas gifts for all.

As a high school student he once gave much of his own clothing away to one of his Sunday School pupils, George Gibson. "George is a poor boy who appreciates his condition and wants to do well," Lee wrote in his diary. "He has a world of pride, and is intensely humiliated by his condition, and I am very interested in him and trust I can do something to help him." When Ivy was only 32 years old, with a young wife and three young children to support on a limited income, he gave a thousand dollars to Emory College for its Alumni fund. This was in 1909 when that amount of money would have purchased a comfortable home. The next year he set up for Emory an annual debating and writing award of twenty-five dollars.

Lee spent money lavishly to maintain his relationships with his business associates and paid generous salaries to his employees. He kept a luxurious suite of offices at a prestige location, complete with objects of art on the wall, rugs on the floor, and a doorman. His club dues and restaurant bills, to say nothing of his travel expenses, would have staggered the normal professional man. But influence was his profession. Because he used his money and position to spread his ideas, he was not a wealthy man in the normal sense, even though his office took in large sums of money for the work Lee and his associates did. When he died, the *New York Times* carried a story saying that he owed more than $100,000 in taxes and debts, and his net estate was valued at less than $24,000.[2]

But for Lee the chief tool of influence was the word—not money. John D. Rockefeller Jr. once asked him about the public relations potential of such proposed projects as the Williamsburg restoration in Virginia and The Cloisters in New York. Lee responded that they could have "the greatest possible educational value," but only if the knowledge of such projects could get out to the people. "And as museums and exhibits cannot be transported," he said, "the only substitute is the printed word."[3]

Lee's fascination with words was nourished by his early association with the *Atlanta Constitution*, where the newsroom buzzed with activity, papers littered desk tops, phones jangled, typewriters clacked, and the smell of printer's ink filled the air. The men in these offices dealt with facts and ideas; they molded the opinions of their readers; they stirred legislatures; they influenced business; they got things done. Lee loved the clutter, the excitement, the sense of importance that pervaded the air. For the remainder of his life he functioned best in this atmosphere. His father was author of a dozen books on theology, history, biography, and travel, and while traveling in Mexico was a correspondent for the *Constitution*, and later served as the editor of a popular Methodist magazine. Perhaps more important was his father's influence on Lee's ability with the spoken word.

His father enjoyed the Southern gift of rhetoric and oratory. Shortly after he took over the Trinity Church in 1886; Rev. Lee was asked to New Jersey to speak on "The Correlation of Spiritual force" at the American Institute of Christian Philosophy, a meeting of some of the most important religious thinkers of the day. It was a rare honor for a clergyman from the South. An article in the *Western Christian Advocate* by Rev. Howard Henderson, entitled "Lee-Preacher, Poet, Philosopher," described the speech as "an ambitious topic for a tyro among academicians," and the young preacher as "smooth-faced, almost boyish looking, evidently timid, and, at first, hesitating; while handsome, faultless in dress, graceful in carriage and action—he did not seem a sage, and inspired more curiosity than confidence." Henderson added that "besides, he was from the South, and what could a Southerner know of metaphysics."

But, once he got into his subject, Rev. Lee swept all doubt from the skeptical Northern minds in the audience. "The structure of his thesis was as solid and stately as a cathedral and as brilliant as its diaphanous windows and colored effigies," wrote Henderson. The speech made philosophy "radiant with rhetoric.... The silver trumpet of a Levite could not have breathed more mellow yet martial tones with which those words were transported from lip to ear." From that triumphant hour, wrote Henderson, "Dr. Lee's position as philosopher and poet was secure."[4]

Reverend Lee went on to give some memorable sermons and speeches. One at the World Parliament of Religion in Chicago in 1893, "Christ, the Reason of the Universe," was widely reprinted because it had stirred much response. His talk on "What Is Science" at the Lewis and Clark Fair in Portland in 1905 won much praise. His speech, "Abraham Lincoln: A Tribute," delivered in Atlanta in 1909, gained wide attention as an eloquent statement of the new, liberal Southerner. Another address, "The South of Tomorrow," became an important statement on enlightened Southern hopes and plans.

Ivy's early dexterity with words, inherited from his father, naturally caught the attention of his teachers. Nina Mitchell of the Ira Street Grammar School in Atlanta had a great respect for him and they corresponded with each other as long as she lived. William M. Slaten of the Boys High School in Atlanta wrote that Lee's work was marked by "diligent application, the highest integrity, and excellent scholarship." He had a "certain dignified reserve," and was "easily regarded by his classmates as a young man of extraordinary mentality."[5]

In the Atlanta high school Lee was secretary of the Ciceronian Literary Society and president of the Alciphronian Literary and Debating Society. At Central High in St. Louis, where he finished his senior year after the family moved from Atlanta, he was the first ever to be named president of the Boys' Literary Society before becoming an advanced senior.

His dream of going on to Princeton, the prestige Northern college for the proper Southerner, had to be postponed for lack of money, so he returned to Georgia and his father's alma mater, Emory College. Here he succeeded with ease; his greatest difficulty was keeping from talking too much in class. He was a constant organizer and was the originator of what became a popular group, the Current Topics Club, a natural outlet for his broad interests in literature, art, politics, and baseball. But he was never much of an athlete. He did play football once and that evening expressed surprise in his diary at "not getting hurt at all!" But at Emory his lack of athletic prowess did not matter. "In the Southern college of that day," a writer later said, "it was in the debating societies, rather than on the gridiron, that fame was won." Lee became a champion debater and also served as the college editor of the *Atlanta Constitution*. At the end of his sophomore year, he was voted "best debater" (both on preparation and impromptu), "best informed," "best read," and "best writer," in the entire college.

Lee did so well in his first two years at Emory that he began to think of bigger worlds to conquer and turned his thoughts again to the possibility of entering Princeton. He rounded up letters of reference, gained admission, was given a loan, and entered in 1896. At Princeton his life exemplified nineteenth century American ethics: he studied diligently, worked part time to help pay his way, saved his money thriftily. He intended, above all, to rise and make his mark on civilization.

In his first year he joined the staff of the *Daily Princetonian*, and the following year was elected managing editor of the *Alumni Princetonian*. More important, he found he could already begin to pay his way with his pen. He became the eastern football correspondent for other college newspapers. The *Tulane College Spirit*, which subscribed to his service, said that "Mr. Lee's superior in facts and news about football in the East cannot be found." This was undoubtedly a plug from the correspondent's own best press agent: Ivy Lee. *The Vanderbilt Hustle* said, "We predict that Mr. Lee's light will not long be under a bushel at Old Nassau."[6]

A great many events other than football games went on at Princeton, such as lectures and concerts, in which the newspapers were interested. Since reporters were paid by the column inch, Lee began to send his stories to the local papers and soon became their regular campus correspondent. He published material in all the New York papers, including the *Journal*, the *American*, the *World*, the *Press*, the *Herald*, the *Sun*, the *Tribune*, and the *Times*. He also sold reports to the *Trenton State Gazette, Trenton True American, Philadelphia Press, Philadelphia Ledger, Philadelphia Inquirer, New Haven News*, and *New Haven Post*. It was not long before Ivy Lee received a letter from Frank N. Mack, manager of the Associated Press in New York. "Mr. Halstead...advises us that in his judgment, based upon inquiry and personal observation, you are best qualified to take up the work of serving the Associated Press with such news as it should have from Princeton."[7]

Lee's first big scoop of his career came from Grover Cleveland. The President had recently retired from the White House to his home in Princeton. In typical nineteenth century fashion he refused to make any public statements; in fact, he valued his privacy so much that reporters were afraid to interview him and the newspapers had to go wanting. One evening young Lee organized a group of his fellow students to go to the Cleveland home and serenade the ex-President with college songs and cheers. Cleveland was moved by the gesture and at length came out onto the front porch where he made a little speech to the students. Lee was in the front row, pencil and pad in hand, and took down every word. It was Cleveland's first public utterance since leaving office. Lee wired his story to New York and awoke the next morning to find his exclusive in front-page headlines.[8]

Lee developed a close relationship with Cleveland and was given several exclusive stories by the ex-President. When the battleship Maine was blown up in the Havana Harbor in 1898 Lee raced to the Cleveland home to break the news. "This is terrible!" Cleveland said.

"Would you permit me to wire that?" Lee asked, taking out his pencil.

Cleveland agreed but asked for the pencil and wrote out carefully for Lee: "I am deeply distressed to learn of the lamentable disaster to the Battleship Maine and sincerely hope that subsequent information will tend to mitigate the apparently horrible circumstance." Lee frequently used this story as an illustration of how important men were often clumsy in their attempt to use words to communicate with the people."[9]

The most important attribute of any man who worked for Lee was the ability to write with simplicity and clarity. He had shelves full of dictionaries and encyclopedias as well as books on writing techniques and texts on semantics. Whenever a new man would join the firm, he was given two books: Sir Arthur Quiller-Couch's *On the Art of Writing*, specifically for the chapter "On jargon," and Havelock Ellis's *Dance of Life*, for its chapter on expression.

Although his staff writers were excellent, Lee could usually improve any copy which he went over with his editor's pencil, and he was appreciative when associates edited his own copy. In the end, the printed material that went out of his office had a clarity, simplicity, and polish that seemed to have been achieved effortlessly because of its smoothness, but actually had involved much intense labor in preparation.

Another of Lee's interests was economics, and he was at the head of his Princeton class in that subject. "What he doesn't know about trusts," said the yearbook about him, "is not worth knowing."

He also began to seek out and attract important people. Added to his close relationship with Cleveland was a friendship with Woodrow Wilson. "I remember so well," he later said, "those long walks which Wilson and I used to take in the beautiful country surrounding Princeton."

Although he had the respect of his fellow students, they ribbed him for his worship of important people. The "Class Prophecy" in the 1898 *Nassau Herald* said of him: "Our Lee! Our Great Lee! Hail! Hail! Hail! The great Lee bestowed a benignant smile upon [his classmates]. Under his arm he carried a book which had made him famous, entitled 'Great Men Who Have Met Me.' As he proceeded with great condescension to join his classmates, he hummed to himself a little song of his own composition, entitled, 'Only Me, Ivy Lee.'"[10]

His interest in important people was not entirely egotistical. He may not have been humble, but he was sincere. He was able to be a conciliator, a bridger of worlds, because he was frankly and deeply interested in other people. One key to his success was his ability to write and speak with a simple and genuine forthrightness. He was the original "really sincere guy."

If anything, Lee took life too seriously. He had difficulty passing off problems with a casual joke and was not disposed to idle humor. As a boy he took school and church with great earnestness, was a faithful member of the Epworth League, and taught Sunday School. Fraternity brothers from Emory said he pledged "with all the solemn, grim-faced determination of a man donning the garb of the priesthood."

He was, indeed, a puritan. While at Emory he wrote in his diary that he was "horrified" that Smith College girls took newspapers out of the library. He once wrote in his diary about a girlfriend who "seems to be quite fond of cigarette pictures, but I gave her such a talk on the subject that I don't think she will care for them much more."[11]

He himself never smoked until he was 49 years old and under great pressure from involvements with dozens of high-level, nerve-wracking negotiations and enterprises. Then at a banquet with one of his sons, he shocked everybody by asking for a cigarette, which he puffed amateurishly. Thereafter, on occasion, he would smoke a light Philippine cigar, but he never inhaled.

His sexual life was dominated by the same straight-laced puritanism. As an adolescent, he was highly attractive to girls but never was able to bring himself to take advantage of their affection. "I sometimes think," he wrote in his diary when he was seventeen, "that perhaps girls occupy too much of my attention and that it would be best for me to leave them alone altogether."[12] After his marriage, he was a devoted husband and father. Raymond Fosdick later remarked to Mrs. Lee that he would never forget the "warm and graceful way—it was almost a ceremony—in which Ivy always held your chair at the table and kissed you as you sat down."[13]

Usually soft spoken and urbane in business relationships, perfectionist Lee could erupt in monumental wrath when a job was not perfect or things did not go as planned. One reporter, Henry F. Pringle, wrote that "he flies into rages when a statement is prepared without the proper finesse, when terms and phrases are used carelessly." He could lose his temper with his superiors as well as his subordinates, could be as blunt about the truth with Rockefeller as well as his office boy and frequently expressed his anger to his clients over inept policies and stupid mistakes. "These rages are terrifying but short lived," Pringle noted. "During them Mr. Lee proclaims loudly that stupidity is the prevalent characteristic of mankind. He pounds upon his desk until the inkwells rattle. But after a short while the storm is over, and then not infrequently, he begs forgiveness with tears of contrition and Christian brotherhood in his eyes."[14]

In spite of his temper, Lee rarely swore. He considered it a luxury he could not afford, a sign of ignorance used by stupid people who could not find more effective ways of expressing themselves. Lee's mastery of language enabled him to find more meaningful words.

Throughout his mature career and after his death, Lee was accused of spreading lies and deceit on behalf of his clients. Nothing could have been further from his own idea about himself. There were times, such as in the Ludlow Affair or the German campaign, when haste or gullibility led him into a trap of exaggeration, distortion, or untruth. But this was alien to his personality, to his ideals and ideas. A central theme of his entire heritage—religious, political, intellectual—was that the truth would make one free. As a courtier to the crowd, he felt that the truth was the most effective way to flatter the people in a democratic society, that sooner or later, if the system could be trusted, the truth would be known, and thus a policy of honesty was the most direct means to public approval.

1. Letters from Ivy Lee to John D. Rockefeller Jr., Aug. 23, 1923 and Dec. 21, 1927, Rockefeller Archives, New York.

2. *New York Times*, Nov. 30, 1935, p. 16.

3. Letter from Ivy Lee to John D. Rockefeller Jr., June 22, 1928, Rockefeller Archives, New York.

4. Quoted by Ivy Lee, "Introduction," James Wideman Lee, *The Geography of Genius*, loc. cit.

5. Letter from William M. Slaten to Dr. James Wideman Lee, Jan. 5, 1915, Ivy Lee Papers, Princeton.

6. *Princeton Scrapbook*, Ivy Lee Papers, Princeton.

7. Letter from Frank N. Mack to Ivy Lee, Dec. 14, 1897, Ivy Lee Papers, Princeton.

8. Arnold Berlin, *"Ivy Lee"* (unpublished thesis, Princeton University, 1947), p. 10.

9. Ibid.

10. *Nassau Herald* (Princeton University, 1898), p. 57.

11. Ivy Lee Diaries, June 23, 1894, Ivy Lee Papers, Princeton.

12. Ibid.

13. Letter from Raymond B. Fosdick to Mrs. Ivy Lee, Jan. 1, 1957, Mrs. Ivy Lee's personal papers.

14. Henry Pringle, "His Master's Voice," *The American Mercury*, Oct. 1926, p. 151.

4: PRESS AGENTS OR MUCKRAKERS

IVY LEE HAD OFTEN THOUGHT OF becoming a lawyer, but realized he did not have enough money for the years of law school. But during his final semester at Princeton he entered the important Lynde Prize Debate as a member of the Whig Hall delegation to the American Cliosophic Society. This was the most important debate of his life and, always a champion in this arena, he won first prize and a $500 award.

After graduating cum laude in the Princeton class of 1898 he spent two months at his parents' home in St. Louis mulling over career possibilities and, realizing that even the $500 was not enough for law school, decided to return to Princeton for a post-graduate course in journalism. He returned to the East Coast in August, visited some of the New York newspaper editors for whom he had been writing while in college, and decided he could earn his way through law school by freelance writing. The editor of the *New York Sun* gave him encouragement and the editor of the magazine *Success* suggested he start with a series on "How to Make One's Way Through College."

In September Lee enrolled in the Harvard Law School, certain that with the remains of his $500 award and with freelance success, he would soon be a member of the bar. By the end of the first semester, however, all of the money was gone and nothing was coming in. Early in 1899 twenty-one-year-old Ivy Lee went back to New York City to look for a job as a journalist. The story goes that he had $5.25 for a room, a sandwich, piece of pie, and cup of coffee, and then used his last nickel for a subway ride downtown to the offices of the *New York Journal*, the Hearst paper.[1]

Charles Edward Russell, then editor of the *Journal* (who went on to become a noted socialist writer and was twice the socialist candidate for the New York governorship) had read Lee's stories from Princeton and he put the young man on as a reporter at $12 a week. This association developed into a friendship that lasted the rest of their lives, even though they did not agree politically. Lee started out as a police reporter but got a full range of assignments covering everything in the city from the East Side and Tenderloin areas to drama, from sports to finance and Wall Street. His first assignment was a story typical of the front pages of Hearst papers: "Bean Jilts Many to Wed a Laundry Girl." This wasn't completely Ivy's province and the story had to be rewritten.

He quickly mastered the techniques, and his exclusive interview with Major General Wesley Merritt, commander of the American Army at Manila, explained the Philippine situation so thoroughly that the editors recognized Ivy had a knack for getting a good story out of important people. When a girl under the care of a Christian Science practitioner died, the *Journal* made a crusade out of it. On the day of the girl's funeral Lee got a scoop by going to the house of the minister before the service and getting his notes on his sermon. The story won him a sixty-six percent increase in his salary.[2]

Unlike many newspapermen of that era, Lee was not the happy-go-lucky, bohemian type. He concentrated on his work, his eye on that distant goal, success. "He did what most newspaper men don't," said a fellow reporter, John K. Mumford. He "made a business of his business." Lee kept a newspaper morgue of his own; he regularly clipped interesting and important items and filed them away for his own reference. When assigned to do drama reviews, he made a diligent study of criticisms and put together several scrapbooks with careful notations on Shakespeare and the legitimate stage. He gave himself wholeheartedly to digging into a story. When he got an assignment in Brooklyn, Mumford related, instead of taking the nearest streetcar across the East River, as most reporters would do, Lee set out for the public library or a friendly law office to do background research on his assignment before covering it. It was a familiar picture, John Mumford said, to see Lee on an assignment with half a dozen big books under his arm.[3]

One of his assignments was to cover the training of boxer Tom Sharkey, who was preparing for his famous World championship bout with Jim Jeffries. Lee made arrangements to live with the fighter, worked out with him in the ring, and even rode a bicycle with him while he did his roadwork. The experience made him a fight fan for the rest of his life.

Perhaps his most famous newspaper story was about a raid on a gambling house run by one Dick Canfield. Lee was covering an uptown dinner event, and when he got back to the office, the night editor, having learned of the raid, assigned Lee to cover it. None of the reporters from other newspapers could get much information about Canfield or the raid, and they had little to write about. But Lee, with uncanny foresight and news instinct, had been collecting clippings and information about Canfield for more than a year, and was able to turn out a column and a half about Canfield's past and present activities that made the banner story of the day and scooped the other papers.

Unlike most of his fellow reporters, who maintained an attitude of cynicism toward the prominent men whose virtues and vices made front-page news, Lee was impressed by important and newsworthy people. He made the most of every opportunity to cultivate his contacts with prominent men and often succeeded in making an impression with his own talents and personality.

Lee later moved over to the *New York Times* where he worked under Adolph Ochs's famous news-gathering editor, Carr Van Anda. And, like all old-time journalists who did not consider themselves true professionals until they had worked for three papers, Lee finally went over to his third, Joseph Pulitzer's *New York World*. Along the way he acquired a good education in economics, a natural interest in the stock market, and became a specialist in Wall Street and financial coverage.

This environment was eminently congenial to his taste and interest. Wall Street was where big men congregated and great activities with world-shaking implications took place. Some years later, Pendleton Dudley, a pioneer public relations colleague of Lee's described the atmosphere. "Both Lee and I had a great zest for people of all sorts," he said, "particularly for persons who did things in a big way. As the Wall Street of that day was the central arena for business action and the clash of big business personalities, Lee and I gravitated to it as naturally as small boys to a circus."[4]

The big men of finance pulled the strings of government as well as business. Especially during the administration of William McKinley, an extraconstitutional government, to use the phrase of William Allen White, was dominant in the land. Wall Street was, for all practical purposes, the capital of the country. The constitutional government punished crimes of violence directed against individuals, but the extraconstitutional government of big business protected the crimes of cunning directed against public rights.

The age of big business had increased the wealth of the country, stretching railroads across the land, erecting urban centers, building manufacturing facilities, providing electricity for better power and lighting, oil for better heating and energy. From 1800 to 1900, even with the surging increase in population, the per capita wealth had increased from $200 to $1200. In 1900, however, one-half of the people owned practically nothing, and one-eighth of the people owned seven-eighths of the wealth. In fact, one percent of the population owned fifty-four percent of the wealth; one family in every hundred was able to buy out the other ninety-nine and still have plenty left over.

New and transplanted Americans worked in factories where assembly-line techniques of mass production were taking the craftsmanship and creativity away from the individual worker, giving him a monotonous routine. The hours were long, days off few, and pay poor. In order to meet household expenses, children were sent off to the factories often before they became teen-agers. The vote which democracy promised them was frequently sold away or manipulated into the hands of political bosses who were themselves tools of the men who owned the factories.[5]

The main concern, after all, was making a profit, the one goal worth striving for. Human life and natural resources were expendable in that endeavor. One journalist estimated that 500,000 workers were either killed or maimed each year. An inventor declared that a timesaving device could be sold in twenty factories, but a lifesaving device in none. Railroads killed thousands each year at grade crossings, but little money was spent changing the crossings or putting up necessary warning devices. In one factory, a man's legs were caught in the machinery; quick calculation by the manager indicated that removing the man intact would require dismantling the machine and would cost thousands of dollars in lost production. On the other hand, by amputating the man's legs, production time would be saved, and the man could be discharged and sent to the hospital with no recourse against the company.[6]

Much of the business world in America, of course, was not guilty of such extreme excesses, but all eventually suffered because of those businesses which were. At first the press was banned from most industrial endeavors, because public knowledge of the facts would have been fatal to many operations. At times press agents were hired to serve as buffers between business and the public to prevent the truth from getting out. Yet, despite the fact that the public often did not know what was going on, there were constant demands for reform. Laws were proposed to curb the powers of the trusts; meetings were held to organize the workers into unions to strike for higher wages and better working conditions; crusades were started against slums, drinking, and disease. Finally, efforts were increased to make the facts public.

This last and most important endeavor amounted to a revolution in journalism. Newspaper owners and editors during the nineties had begun to assume a new role. The editorial function which had been so important in the eighteenth century had given way in the middle of the nineteenth to the reportorial function, inaugurated by men such as James Gordon Bennett in the era of the penny press. Toward the end of the nineteenth century, journalists realized that they could do more than report the news; they could, by their very reporting, *make* news.

Pulitzer, more than most other publishers, realized that the new urban American—immigrant or transplanted farmer—wanted more than dull, gray editorial columns; he had to be stirred and entertained. Pulitzer reached thousands of new readers with a newspaper full of pictures, comic strips, and human interest stories. If there was insufficient material for human interest, the newspaper could create events. Pulitzer sent Nellie Bly around the world so that a series of stories could be written about her escapades.

Hearst took the techniques of Pulitzer and carried them to logical ends. He manufactured events and sensationalized news to create headlines. Some historians claim that his enthusiastic coverage of the volatile Cuban situation helped fan into flames the Spanish-American War, while selling millions of newspapers.

S. S. McClure, meanwhile, was gaining success by creating news through the exposé and crusade. He sent reporters out to dig up news of graft and corruption in the clandestine operations of big business and government. McClure and his fellow journalists between 1895 and 1905 were learning that they could influence the public mind and sell their products more through hard-hitting, factual-type stories than through the rational arguments of editorial columns.

In 1899, when Lee arrived at the offices of Hearst's *Journal* in the midst of these changes in American journalism, he observed firsthand the work of the "muckrakers," as Teddy Roosevelt later called them. Among them were such writers as Lincoln Steffens, Ray Stannard Baker, Ida Tarbell, Upton Sinclair, and Samuel Hopkins Adams, whose factual writing crystallized public opinion to bring pressure for reforms.

Steffens' exposés of municipal and political corruption brought about city reform movements and weakened the power of political bosses and machines. Baker's and Tarbell's disclosures of big business excesses—especially in railroad, coal, and oil trusts—stirred new legislation that put teeth into antimonopoly measures. Sinclair's revelation of meat packing industry frauds and Adams' attack on patent medicine brought into being the Pure Food and Drug Act. Lee was never a muckraker, but he could see that the policies which the capitalists followed, mainly that of ignoring public interest, opened them to attack.

These were exciting days for journalism, but the life of a newspaper reporter was limited and Lee had bigger dreams. While he worked a night beat, he enrolled for postgraduate courses in political science and literature at Columbia University, where he became particularly fond of one of his professors, Dr. George E. Woodbury, a popular author and poet. Under Woodbury's spell, Lee seriously considered quitting the newspaper business to try his hand at writing novels.

He had left his boarding house on an invitation to live at John Mumford's home where he met another journalist, Lewis Bigelow, a young man from St. Paul. Lewis and his sister, Mrs. Ethan Allen, had invited a younger sister, Cornelia, to come from St. Paul for Thanksgiving, 1900. They invited Ivy Lee to join them for dinner, and an immediate attraction developed between Ivy and Cornelia Bartlett Bigelow.

Cornelia was a lovely, intelligent, and proper girl. She was a direct descendent of Josiah Bartlett, first governor of New Hampshire and a signer of the Declaration of Independence. Her father, born in 1820, had been one of the original settlers of St. Paul, having left his New Hampshire village because its expanding population of 5,000 no longer had enough room for him. He became a prominent Minnesota lawyer as the attorney for James J. Hill, president of the Great Northern Railway. As a child, Cornelia had found a great friend in the railroad tycoon.

When Ivy and Cornelia met, Lee was the epitome of Southern courtliness. Tall, thin, and handsome, with a quick mind and a passion for success, he had much to offer. They fell in love and were married in St. Paul the next year. He brought Cornelia back to an apartment on 94th Street, near the elevated, the best his $22 a week would allow. Still working the night shift, he would often come home at three in the morning and Cornelia, hearing him arrive, would get up and put supper on for him.

Lee was still driven by his aspirations. Like many another young man with a literary bent, he wanted to write the great American novel, but he didn't want to starve in a garret while doing it. For a time he thought of buying a small country newspaper so he could be a man of influence in his community, get things done, make $10,000 a year, and still have time to write his novel. It was, however, a pipe dream. He saw a more immediate and realistic opportunity in freelance, nonfiction writing and had some success in 1902 selling articles about Wall Street and big business to the magazines. In November of 1902 their first child, Alice, was born to Ivy and Cornelia Lee. Making more money became imperative.

Sale of his magazine articles encouraged him, and the next summer when Cornelia decided to go with their child to St. Paul for a vacation, Lee quit his job as a reporter at the *World* and stayed at home to do some serious writing. Not one to burn his bridges behind him, he had first gone to see his editor at the *World*, Bill Thayer, who assured him that he could have his job back if he did not succeed. "You can always write a pot-boiler if all else fails," a friend assured him.[7]

The very day he quit the *World*, at least according to legend, he got his first important publicity opportunity. He ran into Capt. Arthur Cosby, a New York political boss, who asked him if he knew someone who could handle the publicity for a coming campaign against the Tammany organization. "How about me?" Lee asked, and he was given the job.[8] His work was to help reelect Seth Low as mayor of New York. Low ran on the Fusion ticket, backed by the New York Citizens Union, essentially a reform organization bucking the entrenched Tammany machine and its candidate, George B. McClellan. The Fusion ticket had managed to defeat Tammany in the previous election and had already legislated some needed reforms.

As Press Representative of the Citizens Union, Lee sat in with the campaign committee and prepared its literature. Later, he wrote the campaign book for the election, his first big production as a press agent. The result was a 160-page book entitled *The City for the People: The Best Administration New York Ever Had*. It contained many of the features that were to be common to Ivy Lee's publicity efforts in the years to come. In plain language, dramatized typographically by numerous headlines, bold type, and underscored sentences, Lee told the Fusion story. The Citizens Union, he wrote, stood for the idea that "the business affairs of municipal corporations shall be conducted upon their own merits, uncontrolled by State and National politics," meaning political machines such as Tammany.

Lee pointed out how the last Tammany administration of Mayor Van Wyck had been guilty of graft in every department of the city. He described the Fusion record under Seth Low by contrast as one of watchfulness, care for the city's public works, interest in the outlying boroughs, provision for future needs, resistance against harmful legislation, correction of abuses and fortification against the obstructionism of the Tammany machine, as well as construction of subways, tunnels, and bridges.[9] Despite Lee's efforts, the Fusion ticket lost the election to Tammany's McClellan.

This experience, however, and his successes with his freelance magazine articles, opened up the possibilities of a new career for Lee. He knew he could never be either a loud-mouthed press agent or a crusading journalist. His successful articles about banking, law, investments, and Wall Street led him to feel that he had some talent for explaining complicated and misunderstood facts to a popular audience. With the increasing complexity of life, there was a greater need for such skill, especially in the business and industrial world, and it ought to be worth money, Lee felt, to have the causes of increased misunderstanding clearly and effectively explained. Lee saw that here was an opportunity to combine his literary and legal interests; he could use his pen to account for and defend ideas and actions before the court of public opinion, that great new audience of American readers.

---

[1] Eric F. Goldman, *Two-Way Street* (Boston: Bellman Publ. Co., 1948), p. 5.

[2] *1899 Scrapbook*, Ivy Lee Papers, Princeton.

[3] John Mumford, "Who's Who in New York, No. 55," *New York Herald Tribune*, Apr. 5, 1925.

[4] Pendleton Dudley, "Current Beginnings of Public Relations," *Public Relations Journal*, Apr. 1952, p. 9.

[5] C. C. Regier, *The Era of the Muckrakers* (Gloucester, Mass.: Peter Smith, 1957), pp. 4 ff.

[6] Ibid.

[7] Mumford, loc. cit.

[8] Ibid.

[9] Ivy Lee, *The City for the People* (New York: Citizen's Union, 1903), pp. 5 ff.

RAY ELDON HIEBERT

5: THE ANTHRACITE COAL STRIKE

AT THE TURN OF THE CENTURY the coal mine operators suddenly found themselves faced with a challenge from their employees greater than any they had ever met. As business had consolidated during the nineties so had the labor unions, and by 1902 the recently organized United Mine Workers union was strong enough to lead 150,000 miners out on strike in the anthracite coal regions of Pennsylvania. The miners demanded a reduction in their working day from 10 hours to 9, a 20 percent increase in wages, payment according to the weight of the coal mined, and owner recognition of their union.

The strike was one of the most spectacular of a period marked by labor unrest. The owners would not give in and the strikers held their ranks firm from May until October. As winter approached, a country dependent on coal was gripped with fear, and President Theodore Roosevelt was determined to bring an end to the strike. The coal mine operators were controlled by the eight railroads that tapped the anthracite region, which were in turn dominated by J. P. Morgan and the other powerful capitalists of the day. The leader of the operators was George F. Baer of the Philadelphia and Reading Railway.

Throughout the strike the operators not only refused to give in to the demands of the miners, but refused to be concerned. They cared little about public sentiment and nothing at all about the press. When reporters came to the offices of the coal operators, honestly seeking their story so that both sides could be presented, they were told by a clerk: "Mr. Baer is not here today. I'm sorry, but I really can't tell you where he is or whether he will be back. A meeting of the operators? I haven't heard of any; certainly no meeting has been held in this office."¹

On the other hand, John Mitchell, leader of the United Mine Workers, gave reporters every consideration, treating them with sincerity, frankness, and directness. The results of this contrasting treatment of the press caused pro-operator observers to accuse the newspapers of showing pro-union bias in their stories. But, when a joint conference of operators and miners was held, it was Mitchell's point of view that was published because he made a complete statement to the press, while the operators told the reporters they had "nothing to say." One observer said about Mitchell, "it has never been charged that he misrepresented things, but facts, like figures, are open to varying interpretations, and may be made to indicate conditions that do not exist. Therefore the public was influenced to sympathize with the miners rather than with the operators."²

Throughout the strike, George F. Baer made only one important public statement to the press. When that statement appeared in the newspapers as the entire presentation of the operators' position, the reaction of the public was obviously damaging. "The rights and interests of the laboring man," Baer had told the press, "will be protected and cared for not by the labor agitators, but by the Christian men to whom God in his infinite wisdom has given the control of the property interests of the country."³

The operators not only turned their backs on the press and the public, they also refused to cooperate with Roosevelt. Finally, the President's threat to operate the mines under the supervision of federal troops forced the operators to a compromise. But by that time public opinion had swerved to support the miners, and they won a considerable victory that included a shorter work day, a 10 percent wage increase, and the right to a union check-weigh-man at the scales.

Roosevelt was sensitive to public opinion, and as the crowd turned against business because of the coal strike, business began to feel the heavy side of Teddy's big stick. In his first message to Congress, Roosevelt noted that there was now "a widespread conviction . . . that the great corporations were in certain of their tendencies harmful to the public welfare" and he urged that they should be "not prohibited, but supervised and within reasonable limits controlled." Roosevelt was still a Republican, and like the Old Guard, supported the high tariff, the gold standard, and imperialism. But he differed from McKinley in his belief that the government had to protect its own people, even if this meant government interference. He was not an unqualified subscriber to the theory of *laissez faire*.

Business was in a state of transition from the last decade of the nineteenth century when the investment bankers of Wall Street had undertaken to remedy some of the evils that had developed under the system of economic liberalism, especially extreme competition. Factory owners had driven out the small craftsmen and then had turned to drive one another out of existence until large numbers went into bankruptcy during severe depressions. As Harvard business historian N. S. B. Gras put it: "Steamship lines competed until they drove 'their nearest rivals onto the rocks. Railroads carried passengers and freight for less than cost till their rivals were bankrupt. Oil operators outsold their competitors till they got all the business."[4]

During the nineties, investment bankers had undertaken to do what the government, motivated by strict adherence to *laissez faire* democracy, refused to do. Bankers were the first to suffer from the unrestrained competition that caused bankruptcy and depressions, and consolidation of unsound businesses seemed to them the logical solution—to snuff out the hopelessly weak companies and strengthen the strong, to build up the working capital of the companies they championed, to insist on multiple functions carefully integrated. In the process, however, the Wall Street investment broker ignored the interests of the common man—the workers and farmers. When the press began exposing Wall Street practices, the common man saw only that Wall Street was seizing powers which only a government could safely wield.

As a Wall Street reporter, Ivy Lee had seen many of the mistakes which the investment bankers were making, especially in their dealings with reporters who fed information to the public. Most newspapermen had good reason to despise the big capitalists; the capitalists, in turn, hated newspaper reporters, who had the "scent of bloodhounds and the disposition of public executioners." It was increasingly evident that big businesses needed their interests represented by intelligent reporters. Lee felt that there was great public interest in the stock market dealings, but stock market operations were so complicated that few reporters were capable of making this material meaningful to the average man.

Lee felt he could make a contribution to businessmen by accurately translating their information for the people, as one of his first freelance magazine articles demonstrated. The article entitled "Savings Banks," written in 1902, attempted to show that such institutions had sociological as well as financial implications in a democratic society. "Teaching the working classes to save is of vital importance, especially in a country with a free ballot," he wrote. "It is essential to the development of good citizenship that the savings of the poor should be invested for them, and that this work should be done with such ability and honesty as will prove both an object lesson and a practical benefit."[5]

Lee argued in the article that "sound finance demands that the savings of the people should be made available for the productive needs of the community." He praised the principle of teaching savings in the public schools and of such companies as the Baltimore and Ohio Railroad which established a savings bank for its employees. "These public-spirited men who are struggling to instill ideas of saving in the minds of the poor, giving time and thought to the problem, have made themselves creditors of civilization," Lee wrote. "The money market and industrial organizations owe it to savings banks...to make their securities really secure, so that they may be of value to the working classes and those classes of benefit to them."[6]

The article led to one of Lee's first independent accounts. A group of New York bankers, trying to establish the New York, Port Chester, and Boston railroad line, were buying franchises on property for the right-of-way. But they had great difficulty convincing property owners to sell and, at length, they asked Lee to help them. He went to each of the towns along the proposed right-of-way to talk to its influential citizens; he convinced them of the integrity and goodwill of the bankers behind the railroad, and that the railroad would be good for the community. As the climate of opinion changed, the investors were gradually able to buy up the franchises.[7]

A few stories about Lee's activities in this period pictured him as the typical press agent of the day, complete with gimmicks and stunts. One attributed to him the responsibility for an accident to a circus which he supposedly served as press agent shortly after leaving newspaper work. Apparently as the circus came into New York, the monkey wagon was wrecked on the Brooklyn Bridge. Monkeys proceeded to scamper all over the many cables of the structure. The riotous confusion necessitated calling in half the

New York police force. The event, so the story goes, made front-page headlines in all the New York papers, and headlines were the best kind of publicity for his circus client.[8] Lee denied this story all his life. From the first he thought of himself not as a maker of headlines, but as a new kind of lawyer.

In an article he wrote about lawyers in 1904 he stated that in this age of commercialism, every business needed within its establishment a lawyer to tell it what it could do within the law, to set up trusts which did not violate the antitrust act, to make legal financial deals. "'Show me how I may do this thing'—that is often the command of the capitalist to the counselor. The lawyer does not inquire into the motives—be they sinister or benevolent—of his clients. It is frequently his work merely to devise means by which the proposed object may be realized without transgressing the letter of the law."[9]

Increasingly, as journalists stirred public opinion and public opinion caused the government to set up laws to curb business, Lee saw an equation between the court of law and the court of public opinion. Did not business need someone to advise it on means by which a proposed object could be realized without arousing the indignation of the public? Was not a new kind of lawyer, or a new profession, needed? Lee felt that there was, and after he quit his job at the *World*, he devoted the rest of his life to it.

Lee's job as press representative for the Fusion Party's 1903 campaign was successful in one sense—it brought him into contact with George Parker, then press agent for the Democratic National Committee and a man with many contacts. Parker asked Lee to join him in directing the publicity for the Democratic Party in its bid to defeat Roosevelt in the 1904 campaign. The 1904 convention proved to be typical of the many ironies of American politics. The Democrats had finally turned away from William Jennings Bryan after three unsuccessful attempts to get him into the White House. Instead, they turned to a conservative, gold-standard Democrat of the Grover Cleveland school, a New York judge, Alton B. Parker. Running on a conservative platform, Parker faced an incumbent who espoused progressive ideas but was backed by old-guard Republicans and financed by big business.

Together, George Parker (no relation to the Judge) and Ivy Lee began to prepare material for Judge Parker's campaign. One of the techniques that Parker and Lee used was to distribute throughout the country this card: "The President's Dream of War," it would say on one side, quoting from Roosevelt's writing to document his sanction of American imperialism; "Judge Parker's Plea for Peace," it would say on the other. Another card had on one side Roosevelt's statement about greater freedom for the press and on the other it quoted his "gag order" forbidding bureau chiefs in the government to give out information to the newspapers. Such tactics may not have been completely original, but they got headlines from time to time.

Parker and Lee's press releases had some distinction. They were printed exactly like regular newspaper columns and distributed on galley sheets, making it easy for editors to use the story intact. Furthermore, unlike so much political publicity of the day, the stories were written in good newspaper style.[10]

In spite of these tactics, Roosevelt was far too dynamic a public figure for the colorless though genteel Judge Parker, and Teddy swept the election easily. Again, however, it was not a complete loss for Lee because he gained a partner. When, late in 1904 they joined together in a firm which they called simply "Parker & Lee," they took a small office at 20 Broad Street in the Postal Telegraph Building adjacent to the New York Stock Exchange. Parker, being older and more widely experienced, was made the senior partner, and Lee was to handle "such selling as would be needed." To the apparent surprise of both partners, selling was needed. Neither big business nor little business came running in droves for the services Parker & Lee offered.[11]

From the first, the two men had differing ideas about the role of their firm in business life. Parker was the old type of press agent. A native of Indiana and educated in Iowa, he had been a newspaperman in that state before Lee's father had even finished college; he was, in fact, older than his partner's father by two years. In 1873 he had started the *Tribune* in Indianola, Iowa, and in 1876 he had bought half interest in the *State Leader*, a newspaper in Des Moines. He returned to Indiana as an editorial writer on the Indianapolis *Sentinel* in 1880 and got into politics shortly thereafter as private secretary to William H. English, the losing Democratic candidate for the vice presidency in 1880, a campaign where press material and publicity were used for the first time on a mass scale.

From that campaign, Parker had drifted around in various journalistic jobs on the *Washington Post*, the *Manchester* (New Hampshire) *Union*, and the *Philadelphia Times*. He resigned from that paper to receive a political appointment as Assistant Postmaster of Philadelphia. He helped to set up a newspaper in New York, the *Press*, and in 1888 returned to full-time political publicity as editor of the campaign book and manager of the Literary Bureau for the Democratic National Committee during the election of President Grover Cleveland. The incumbent candidate lost, but when he regained the Presidency in 1892, he appointed Parker to the post of United States Consul at Birmingham, England, a post which the press agent kept until 1898, even through two years of William McKinley's Republican Administration.

In all, Parker worked with the Democratic National Committee on five presidential campaigns and had much to do with changing the party literary bureau into a press bureau. He served in England as commissioner for the Louisiana Purchase Exposition, and promoted European participation in the St. Louis World's Fair of 1903–04. After Grover Cleveland retired from public life and was appointed to the board of trustees of the Equitable Life Assurance Society, the ex-President brought along Parker as secretary of that board, a position which he continued to occupy even after the formation of the firm of Parker & Lee.

Parker was able to bring to the young firm many powerful contacts in the world of big business and politics; he introduced Lee to an important circle of associates that, like a chain reaction, provided him a lifelong entree to many of the world's leaders in government and industry. But Parker also brought to the new firm the old nineteenth century ideas of press agentry, and Ivy Lee wanted to be more than a press agent. The *New York Times* observed later that "Lee brought something new to the business of publicity. When he was young...there were numerous press agents in town who promoted the theaters and stage stars, but there was no specialist in publicity for corporations who conferred on terms of equality with the boards of directors of great corporations. His life spanned that change, and he had much to do with the change."[12]

Lee wanted to move in this newer direction and Parker's friendship with such men as George Westinghouse, inventor and manufacturer, and Thomas Fortune Ryan, financier who had amassed a $200 million fortune through his streetcar-subway lines built with Tammany contracts, enabled the Parker & Lee firm to contract publicity work for both Westinghouse and Ryan. Ryan came to believe in Parker & Lee so thoroughly that once he wrote out a check for $10,000 in anticipation of their publicity efforts in his behalf.

This account encouraged the two men so much that they looked for staff members, and Daniel T. Pierce was invited to join them. A lawyer and editor of a publication called *Public Opinion*, Pierce understood the ideas Lee was trying to promote, but he was not sure of the potential of the firm until Lee showed him the $10,000 check from Ryan.[13]

But all was not that easy. In the voids between clients the partners often took offbeat jobs—Lee, for instance, chased promoters of fraudulent stock notes around the Panama Canal Zone for a time to keep the business going. Some jobs, even though small, led to bigger things. Lee did a brief publicity job for the International Harvester Company, and another for the Pennsylvania Railroad that led to a major job for Lee and brought to Parker an important account with the Union Pacific Railroad. Perhaps the most important client at that time was the Anthracite Coal Roads and Mines Company. In fact, it was the work Lee did for this account that established his new and important philosophy.

In 1906 another strike was impending against the coal operators, but by this time the business interests represented by George Baer were learning their lesson. Somebody recommended to Baer the work of Ivy Lee, and the young publicist was hired to help with the imminent strike. One of the first things Lee did in virtually revolutionizing the policies of the operators was to send out this announcement to all newspapers: "The anthracite coal operators, realizing the general public interest in conditions in the mining regions, have arranged to supply the press with all possible information. Statements from the operators will be given to the newspapers through Ivy L. Lee. He will also answer inquiries on this subject and supply the press with all matter that it is possible to give out."[14]

The policy represented a complete about-face for the coal operators. Lee not only sent out this and many succeeding statements, but he sent them as the signed statements of the men he represented, a Coal Operators' Committee of Seven, and he named them specifically: George F. Baer, W. H. Truesdale, J. B. Kerr, David Willcox, Morris Williams, E. B. Thomas, and J. L. Cake. Weary of anonymous interviews, of underhanded methods, of getting only one side of the story, the press now welcomed these signed statements almost daily.

Furthermore, this simplified the work of the reporters on the coal strike story—they were given advance information on the place, time, and topic, and within a few minutes after the meeting had ended, a complete report of the proceedings. Most important for the operators, Lee knew what was newsworthy, and he was able to get published many columns of news items concerning the coal trust which had never been released before. As a result, the public got both sides of the issue so that the solution could be worked out equitably and rationally.

Perhaps the most important result of the entire affair was Lee's drafting of what he called his "Declaration of Principles," which he sent to city editors of newspapers along with his first statement to the press. This set the tone for the practice of publicity for many years, and is still quoted as a standard of ethics by publicists. Lee wrote:

> This is not a secret press bureau. All our work is done in the open. We aim to supply news. "This is not an advertising agency; if you think any of our matter ought properly to go to your business office, do not use it. Our matter is accurate. Further details on any subject treated will be supplied

promptly, and any editor will be assisted most cheerfully in verifying directly any statement of fact.

Upon inquiry, full information will be given to any editor concerning those on whose behalf an article is sent out. In brief, our plan is, frankly and openly, on behalf of the business concerns and public institutions, to supply to the press and public of the United States prompt and accurate information concerning subjects which it is of value and interest to the public to know about. Corporations and public institutions give out much information in which the news point is lost to view. Nevertheless, it is quite as important to the public to have this news as it is to the establishments themselves to give it currency. I send out only matter every detail of which I am willing to assist any editor in verifying for himself. I am always at your service for the purpose of enabling you to obtain more complete information concerning any of the subjects brought forward in my copy.[15]

The statement brought about a revolution in relations between business and the public. Where formerly business pursued a policy of "the public be damned," from now on business increasingly followed a policy of "the public be informed."

A few other companies saw the efficacy of Lee's advice. A Senate resolution to investigate the monopolistic practices of the International Harvester Company also brought Lee an opportunity to put his policies into practice. The company allowed him to proclaim in writing that the officers "were not only willing that their company should be investigated, but that they would welcome and facilitate such an investigation by every means in their power." Through Lee's work, the company not only indicated to the people and the government its own confidence in its integrity, but it won the confidence of people and government. If such a company is to be attacked, Lee said, "it can only be attacked on the grounds that it is large, not that it is dishonest, illegal, or unfairly managed."[16]

Lee defended a large company because it could have better relations not only with the government and the public but with its own employees. Hours are generally shorter, he said, and workers' rights acknowledged. He praised the International Harvester Company for building a clubhouse for its workers and for creating harmonious working conditions. "The time has passed," he wrote, "when the employer and the working man can afford to be at 'outs'; and the employees are beginning to realize that the employers are willing to meet them more than half way in the endeavor to bring about more amicable relations and more unified effort."[17]

Ivy Lee quickly acquired many imitators. These men, said Pen Dudley who himself joined their ranks, were "first and last newspaper reporters who had worked on first-order metropolitan dailies, where mental keenness is prerequisite. Thus equipped, they had perfected the techniques of searching out newsworthy facts and incidents, however difficult of access. Once they had the news they knew how to report it clearly and 'unslanted' in words that would catch and hold the fleeting interest of the average newspaper reader."[18] This helped establish the new profession—the practice of public relations.

The firm of Parker & Lee adopted for itself the motto: "Accuracy, Authenticity, Interest." The most important fact was that the firm attracted the faith and aroused the interest of the entire newspaper world, according to *Editor & Publisher*, the magazine of newspaper people. By 1908 that magazine, which later became one of Ivy Lee's most vigorous critics, said of his firm that after "little more than three years...this publicity bureau has established itself firmly in the estimation of editors and publishers of the United States."

Editor & Publisher asserted that the Parker-Lee firm "has never made any attempt at deception; matter is sent to the press with the frank statement that it is in behalf of the client, and that no money will be paid for its insertion in the columns of any newspaper." It said of Parker-Lee material that it was "never sensational, never libelous, always accurate, always trustworthy, always readable," and significantly, added: "In newspaper offices no question of the merit of its matter is raised nowadays, but only the question of its availability for the paper which has it under consideration."[19]

The masters of finance ultimately realized that they had a new force to reckon with—the force of an informed public opinion. The corporations at first had taken measures to stop the growth of public indignation over their policies by attempting to distort the facts, withholding them from the press, or even bribing the press to win its favor. As the new century wore on, business increasingly realized the need for new policies of openness and truth. Ivy Lee helped to win acceptance for those principles.

---

[1] Sherman Morse, "An Awakening in Wall Street," *American Magazine*, Sept. 1906, p. 458.

[2] Ibid.

[3] Quoted in Merle Curti, op. cit., p. 634.

[4] N. S. B. Gras, "Shifts in Public Relations," *Business Historical Society Bulletin*, Oct. 1945, p. 119.

[5] Ivy Lee, "Savings Banks," *World's Work*, Sept. 1902, p. 2489.

[6] Ibid., p. 2490.

[7] Berlin, op. cit. pp. 45–46.

[8] Ibid., p. 45. See also *Detroit Free Press*, Nov. 10, 1934.

[9] Ivy Lee, "Modern Lawyer," *World's Work*, June 1904, p. 4879.

[10] Ivy Lee, *Political Scrapbooks*, 1903–4, Ivy Lee Papers, Princeton.

[11] Dudley, op. cit., p. 10.

[12] *New York Times*, Nov. 10, 1934, p. 15.

[13] Berlin, op. cit., p. 48.

[14] Morse, op. cit., p. 459.

[15] Ibid., p. 460.

[16] Lee, "An Open and Above Board Trust," *Moody's Magazine*, July 1907, pp. 158, 164.

[17] Ibid., p. 163.

[18] Dudley, loc. cit.

[19] *Editor & Publisher*, Jan. 18, 1908, p. 2.

II

PUBLIC UTILITIES
"The Divine Right of the Multitude"

6: WRECK ON THE MAIN LINE

PUBLIC UTILITIES—FAVORED WITH GOVERNMENT PRIVILEGES in their infant years—rapidly grew into a complicated national problem. Favoritism was essential in developing public power and transportation for industrial expansion, and the government indulgently provided lavish incentives and permitted complete freedom of operation so the United States could be webbed by a vast network of rails and lines to carry the power and the products upon which business operation and profits depended. But in the twentieth century a government concerned with protecting the people began to reconsider the proposition of private ownership of public utilities.

The railroads found themselves at the center of the problem: unions were organizing their employees; Congress and state legislatures were creating new restrictions and regulations; the press and the public were complaining of poor service, faulty rates, and multiplying accidents.

Public hostility towards the railroads had been growing since the Civil War. Railroad owners had become vehement proponents of imperialistic, *laissez faire* capitalism, their business ethics justified by such creeds as Herbert Spencer's competitive individualism: in the struggle of the free marketplace, the strong and able win, the weak and foolish lose, and thus does civilization make progress.

As early as the 1880s public protest of railroad practices caused a Senate investigation and the January 1886 report of the Senate group, the Cullom Committee, listed many of the railroad abuses and corrupt practices of that day: unreasonably high local rates; discriminations between persons, places, and types of freight; special secret rebates and kickbacks; passes; watered stock, causing excessive capitalization; and managements that were extravagant and wasteful.

Many of America's great nineteenth century capitalists and financiers—the "Robber Barons" Jay Gould, Jim Fisk, Daniel Drew, Cornelius Vanderbilt and his son William, Edward H. Harriman, James J. Hill, and many others—were contributors to the profligation and corruption of the industry. Through such politicians as Senator William M. (Boss) Tweed of New York, these entrepreneurs and their associates often were able to legalize their manipulations and maneuverings. Through the banking offices of John Pierpont Morgan and other financiers, they executed all manner of chicanery.[1]

The railroad owners themselves were frequently caught in the pincers of the monopolistic capitalism of their fellow industrial and financial barons. Rockefeller, for instance, was able to force the railroads to give his Standard Oil Company millions of dollars worth of freight rebates. In Ohio, while Standard paid a freight rate of 10 cents a barrel, its competitors paid 35 cents a barrel, and the 25-cent difference was refunded to Standard. In one year-and-a-half period alone, four railroads paid more than $10 million in kickbacks to Standard Oil.[2]

Thousands of such incidents increased public agitation for government regulation. Farmers and merchants were among the first to raise their voices because they suffered most from rate discriminations. Farmers, organizing the Grange movement, found that their concerted opinions were able to influence various legislative reforms early in the 1870s.[3] In the 1880s and 1890s railroad labor slowly organized and exerted pressure on management and legislation. The Progressive movement of the 1890s, bringing together farmer, small merchant, and laborer, did much to swell the public voice. Finally, the growing popular press spread the word, and when muckraking became the loudest cry, public indignation over railroad practices became a national attitude.

Of all the large industries, the railroads were used most by the public, and yet the owners cared least about public opinion, believing that "charge all the traffic will bear" was an unassailable economic law to determine rates. This disdain for regulation was given wide publicity by the press. "Law?" the newspapers quoted Commodore Vanderbilt, "What do I care about Law? Hain't I got the power?" The Commodore's son William used a phrase that accurately reflected the attitudes of the railroads and became an epitaph for all business of that period. Questioned about the public's interest in the removal of a fast New York Central train from the Chicago line, young Vanderbilt reportedly said: "The public be damned.... I don't take any stock in this silly nonsense about working for anybody's good but our own because we are not. When we make a move we do it because it is in our interest to do so."[4]

Railroad owners, increasingly aware of their bad publicity, tried to win the goodwill of reporters by bribing them with free passes, but continued to refuse to give out complete and accurate information. Joseph Dorney, railroad editor of the *Cincinnati Enquirer*, wrote in 1917: "It wasn't so many years ago that a newspaperman was as welcome in the office of a railway official as a secret service agent is in the cabin of a moonshiner. The reporter sent to cover a wreck or run down a railroad story had to be an improved edition of Sherlock Holmes to get the facts of the case." Dorney pointed out that when a train jumped the track or a trespasser was killed, no one in the entire railroad organization would say anything about it. Naturally the press only got the other side of the story, and this in turn was all the public received.[5]

Rising public resentment over railroad abuses inspired state after state to set up regulatory commissions. These actions and the Cullom Committee's investigation resulted in the creation of the Interstate Commerce Commission to set rates and make regulations on a national basis. The Sherman Antitrust Act of 1890 was, among other things, an attempt to curb railroad consolidation. This did not prove effective until the Expedition Act was passed in 1903, speeding the court procedure under the Sherman Act. Also in 1903 the Elkins Act strengthened the prohibition of railroad rebates.

The strictest legislation of all came in 1906 when Congress passed the Hepburn Act which increased the size and extended the powers of the Interstate Commerce Commission. The Act abolished the granting of passes, strengthened the law against rebates, required the railroads to separate themselves from such enterprises as company-owned coal mines, and, most important, empowered the I.C.C. to establish "just and reasonable" maximum rates. Later laws increased regulation of railroads, such as the Mann-Elkins Act of 1910, further extending powers of the I.C.C., and Robert M. LaFollette's Railroad Valuation Act of 1913, requiring the I.C.C. to assess the value of all railroad property. But the Hepburn Act of 1906 made railroads cry out most loudly against what they felt was their strangulation at the hands of the government.

Alexander J. Cassatt, president of the Pennsylvania Railroad, recoiling from these legislative blows, remembered the firm of Parker & Lee that had earlier worked for the Pennsylvania in an effort to counteract a series of articles in the *Philadelphia North American*. The articles had attempted to expose railroad officials who had supposedly been given stock in certain coal mines in exchange for passes, rebates, and other favors, and Parker & Lee had tried to neutralize this with favorable publicity. But the Pennsylvania was not ready at that time to adopt the policies which Lee proposed.

In May and June of 1906 Ivy Lee was in Panama combining work on a stock fraud case with a vacation and giving attention as well to the building of the Panama Canal and its railroad line because he saw potential public relations problems inherent in the project. Unexpectedly, he received a cable from Cassatt, asking if he would return immediately for an interview. Sensing the importance of the telegram to his career, Lee quickly set sail for the United States. There was no information on railroads available from which he could study the problems and have a program ready, so he was somewhat worried when he met Cassatt immediately upon arrival in Philadelphia because he had not one suggestion to make for a publicity policy for the Pennsylvania Railroad.

Instead of asking Lee about such a policy, however, Cassatt asked him about Panama, the Canal that was being built, and the railroad situation on the Isthmus. Lee gave detailed answers from his own close observations. "As it happened," he said later, "I had made quite a study of the Panama railroad situation, going over the line and talking with a number of engineers." Cassatt was impressed with the young man's keen observations, even in matters that had been of only indirect concern at the time, and gave him the job of advising the Pennsylvania on its publicity problems without ever inquiring about Lee's suggestion for a program for the railroad.[6]

This experience taught Lee a life-long lesson that helped him acquire many other accounts—by being shrewdly observant of everything with which he came into contact, he gained background knowledge from which to build publicity for the organization with which he was dealing. Lee's careful study of railroads eventually made him one of the country's authorities on public transportation problems. He gave speeches across the country and in Europe, lectured at American and European universities and at scholarly meetings of the Academy of Political Science and the American Academy of Political and Social Science, and wrote bulletins and articles on railroad topics.

When he took on the Pennsylvania account, he brought in his brother, James Wideman Lee Jr., as a full-time publicity writer for the railroad while Ivy made policy decisions and supervised the account through his firm of Parker & Lee. Wideman, as he was called, had followed in Ivy's footsteps. He had been born in Dalton in 1882, had been graduated from Emory College, and had gone directly into the newspaper business. He had been city editor of the *Columbus* (Georgia) *Ledger* from 1904 to 1905, and was state political editor for the Atlanta Georgian when he joined Ivy to promote the railroad business.

Ivy Lee's years as an advisor to and spokesman for the Pennsylvania Railroad and, through it, for the entire railroad industry encompassed the most hectic period in American railroad history, during which railroads were reaching their peak growth and starting their long decline.

Many an old-timer with the railroad was dismayed when, almost immediately, Lee began revolutionizing things, putting into effect his theories about absolute frankness with the press. An accident occurred to a Pennsylvania train on the main line near Gap, Pennsylvania. The company, following ancient tradition, automatically suppressed all news of the accident. Learning of the situation, Lee promptly reversed the company directive and personally invited reporters to travel to the scene of the accident at the railroad's expense and set up facilities for gathering facts and taking photographs. He offered reporters material for which they had not even thought of asking. This reversal of hallowed practice sent the Pennsylvania executives into an uproar of angry protests.

At almost the same time, however, an accident had occurred on the New York Central line, the Pennsylvania's long-time rival. The Central, adhering to conventional policy, put restrictions on information about the accident. When newsmen learned of this censorship they responded with fury, particularly since the Pennsylvania had already changed its policies. Editorials and columns criticized the Central's actions and praised the Pennsylvania's. When the commotion settled, the Pennsylvania found that it had a good press for the first time in many years.[7]

To Lee a good press, fundamental to good public relations, was obtained not by bribing reporters with passes but by providing them with the information they needed to write their stories and perform their jobs. Also fundamental was that the organization should tell its side of the story. Then, with a good press, both sides might be told and the public might have a fairer picture from which to form a better judgment.

Lee increasingly devoted himself to the railroad, not limiting himself to publicity puffs and press releases about railroad activities, but delivering speeches and writing articles that were penetrating analyses of the railroad situation, presented as logical arguments and explanations for railroad actions. His attempt always was to counteract the critics by giving public voice to the side that had been so long silent. One of his first magazine articles for the railroad industry illustrates his ideas and methods of expression. Entitled "Railroad Valuation," it argued the railroad's side of the debate raised by Senator LaFollette. If the I.C.C. were to set rates according to the Hepburn Act, then some means must be provided to set just rates. LaFollette maintained that the Commission should undertake a physical valuation of each railroad, exposing watered stock and arriving at a true value of the property upon which just rates could be set.

To Lee such an action would be not only extremely costly but completely unrealistic. First of all, he wrote, the real value of a railroad is the outcome of its earnings, and it is impossible to derive rates from such value when the value is the consequence of rates. Second, rates are properly made by economic law, by commercial conditions, by the exigencies of business, by competition of one product with another, and by the competition of one market with another.

As an example, he pointed out that a rate is made on Oregon lumber coming to the Middle West enabling the Pacific Coast producer to compete with Michigan. Without a rate substantially the same as that paid by nearer producers, Oregon lumber would have no eastern market. "Rates cannot be made independent of economic laws," he wrote. "Those economic and commercial forces...are as absolutely beyond the control of its managers as are the orbits of the planets." Finally, he argued, the only logical way to evaluate the railroads is through the stock market. "The average market price, over a period long enough to remove the element of manipulation, is unquestionably a nearer approach to ascertaining actual value than anything else that has been devised."[8]

Lee's job, as he often said, was "interpreting the Pennsylvania Railroad to the public and interpreting the public to the

Pennsylvania Railroad." The *public* was his prime concern. He saw that to serve the public was simply acting in "enlightened self-interest." That term, used by Lee in another 1907 magazine article, has become the axiom for twentieth century American capitalism. "The directors of the Pennsylvania," wrote Lee, "believe that with a railroad, as with an individual, the more it does for the public and the more it makes of its opportunities to serve, the more the public will reward it. The better treatment it gives to its employees, the more loyal and the more efficient they will be." Such a policy of "cooperation and encouragement," he wrote, was simply the "policy of broad common sense."9

Lee listed many of the things that railroads were already doing for public service: agricultural education to develop new and better farming techniques; training courses for young men interested in railroad work; aid to and establishment of Y.M.C.A. clubs and buildings; scholarships for young men in college; clubhouses for railroad workers; pension plans for retired employees; savings funds; and voluntary relief plans. He told with special fondness how the Pennsylvania had sold fourteen acres of its land at a vastly reduced price to the city of Harrisburg, for extension of its park system. He later predicted that this kind of action would spread. "Before a great while," he told the London School of Economics in 1910, "you will find that our more progressive companies will have a profit-sharing scheme, a system of old-age pensions, and a plan of employers' liability. This will make for stability and safety of employment and will add to the permanent efficiency of the companies."10

The Pennsylvania was an ideal place for Lee to put his ideas into effect. "The job gets bigger every day," he wrote to his father soon after he joined the company. "It is one of the most beautiful jobs I ever saw, because all the work is pitched on such a high key. The activities of the Pennsylvania are of an exceptionally high order, everything they do being carried out in the best way possible, regardless of expense. The consequence is that we have beautiful raw material with which to work." Lee also characterized the nature of the individual needed for his kind of work. It requires, he wrote his father, "a peculiar combination of knowledge on economics, politics, journalism, and business generally."[11]

Throughout 1907 Lee remained a member of Parker & Lee with the Pennsylvania as his chief account. On the recommendation of Samuel Rea, vice-president of the Pennsylvania, he took on other railroad accounts, including the Delaware and Hudson, and the Harriman lines—the Union Pacific, the Southern Pacific, the Oregon Railroad, and the Oregon Shortline. One duty was to travel across the country inspecting their lines. He was especially concerned with general conditions and industrial development of territories which the railroads served. The panic of 1907 had made business aware that it needed to grow to survive. Lee prepared publicity material emphasizing the scenic, industrial, and agricultural features of California and the West for Harriman promotion. Later, in the twenties, when business was flourishing in these areas, Lee recommended publicity emphasis on California's educational and scientific resources rather than scenery and agriculture.

In 1908 Ivy Lee withdrew from his partnership in Parker & Lee to devote himself exclusively to the challenge of ideas that he found at the Pennsylvania Railroad. The next year a partner in the Wall Street brokerage firm of Harris, Winthrop, and Company offered Lee a new challenge, the job of setting up their offices in Europe. It was a tempting opportunity, even though he was absorbed with the railroad business, because it would give him the chance to gain a more detailed knowledge of investment and finance. It would also give him and his family—now made up of a daughter Alice, and two sons, James II and Ivy Jr., in addition to his wife—a chance to travel and learn about Europe.

Instead of quitting the Pennsylvania, he asked for and received a leave of absence and turned his work over to his brother. He retained an active interest in railroads and studied the European systems, where the lines were largely government owned and operated. He spoke to European railroad officials, gave speeches on American railroads, and frequently lectured at the London School of Economics on railroad topics.

Meanwhile, other lines throughout the United States were adopting Lee's policies of absolute frankness, especially in matters of accidents where the public was directly concerned, and within a few years, the railroads were actually competing to make known what they earlier had struggled to keep hidden.

In his article on railroad press agents, Dorney provides a good example of the far-reaching effects of Lee's influence. After a train accident near Cincinnati in 1917, Dorney called the general manager of the railroad and "although he was up to his ears in work, he gave me a detailed statement of the disaster—seemed pleased to do so—and told me if there was anything else I desired to know later he could be found at his office until six o'clock and at his home afterwards." Dorney told of another incident when a wreck occurred in Kentucky, and even before the "bulletin" had been received in his office, the railroad vice-president called and offered to take the reporter on the relief train to the scene.[12] Such treatment would have been rare, if not unheard of, only eleven years earlier.

Earl Newsom, prominent public relations counsel, told a convention of the Public Relations Society of America in 1963: "This whole activity of which you and I are a part can probably be said to have had its beginning when Ivy Lee persuaded the directors of the Pennsylvania Railroad that the press should be given all the facts on all railway accidents—even though the facts might place the blame on the railroad itself."[13]

Lee deserves credit for an even more important contribution to fellow citizens: in helping railroad management grow up, putting away its corrupt "public be damned" youth for a more responsible "public be served" maturity, he opened the door for all businesses to follow—and this led to improvements in the living scale for all workmen as well as giving immeasurable impetus to industrial expansion that put the United States far ahead of competing nations.

---

[1] John F. Stover, *American Railroads* (Chicago: University of Chicago Press, 1961), pp. 104 ff.

[2] Ibid., p. 118.

[3] Harold Underwood Faulkner, *American Political and Social History* (New York: Appleton, 1948), p. 475.

[4] Stover, op. cit., p. 111. See also, *New York Times*, Oct. 9, 1882, p. 1.

[5] Joseph Dorney, "The Railroad Press Agent," *Railway Age Gazette*, May 4, 1917, p. 960.

[6] Quoted in M. K. Wisehart, op. cit.

[7] Goldman, op. cit., p. 8.

[8] Ivy Lee, "Railroad Valuation," *Bankers' Monthly*, July 1907, p. 94.

[9] Ivy Lee, "Indirect Service of Railroads," *Moody's Magazine*, Nov. 1907, p. 580.

[10] Ivy Lee, *The American Railway Problem*, p. 14.

[11] Ivy Lee to his father, Nov. 21, 1906, Ivy Lee Papers, Princeton.

[12] Dorney, op. cit.

[13] Earl Newsom, "Business Does Not Function by Divine Right," *Public Relations Journal*, Jan. 1963, p. 4.

7: CAMPAIGN FOR FREIGHT RATES

IVY LEE RETURNED FROM EUROPE in December of 1912 to accept the position of "executive assistant" to the president of the Pennsylvania Railroad. To be in constant contact with the company's executives, Ivy moved his family to Ardmore, closer to headquarters in Philadelphia.

With his brother successfully directing publicity for the railroad, Lee broadened his responsibilities of policy direction to include a study of the activities of the company, to criticize at any point where criticism was deserved, and to bring a detached viewpoint to the service of the railroad. He advised officers on matters which would interest the public and on how to present them. His advice, he said, was that "publicity would pretty much generally take care of itself providing the things to be made public were in themselves interesting and praiseworthy," and therefore railroad policies "should commend themselves to an enlightened public opinion."[1]

Lee's position as an officer of the company allowed him freedom to express himself and put into practice the concepts that he had been developing. During this period, according to one of his associates, Daniel Pierce, Lee was able to use the gigantic corporation of the Pennsylvania Railroad as an industrial guinea pig to test his theories and ideas.

Although American railroads continued to grow until they reached their peak in 1916, their rate of growth began to decline in 1906, the year of the Hepburn Act. The Panic of 1907 brought bankruptcy to many lines, and railroad receipts in 1908 declined by about $300 million. Railroads had less money to spend on extending and improving lines, and by 1912 production of new railroad cars and new track had been curtailed to such an extent that much of the bumper farm crops of that year was lost because it could not be taken to market.

In retrospect, the causes for this decline were probably more varied than Lee would have admitted. It was impossible, even without government interference, for the railroads to keep up the growth of the nineteenth century. New competition from electric streetcars and automobiles undoubtedly played a part in the decline. But Lee attributed most of the blame to the public's clamor for regulations that prohibited rates which could bring a profit. He was not against government regulation *per se*. He agreed with Professor Woodrow Wilson, as he told the London School of Economics in 1910, that it was "absolutely necessary that effective measures should be taken to stop the old practices of discrimination and favoritism, of special rates and secret rebates, and of unequal treatment of shippers."[2] But such regulation should not go so far that it curtailed growth.

The causes for public clamor, according to Lee, were in part the results of the old demagogues and muckrakers who suppressed information about worthwhile accomplishments of the railroads while they magnified and distorted the unworthy out of all proportion. The railroad decline from 1906 to 1912 was brought about first, because of a "natural anxiety on the part of railroad managers as to the public's attitude toward railroad property," and second, because of "a reasonable apprehension lest the public through legislation and commission interference might prevent that return upon further investments in railroad improvement to which holders of railroad securities should feel themselves entitled."[3]

However, the fault also lay with the railroads themselves because railroad men neglected "the human nature of the situation," and while "loud-tongued politicians dilated upon the evils, railroad men sat still, attended to their jobs, and said nothing of the good." Ivy Lee urged railroad men to insist, in and out of season, and to put forth the facts to prove it, "that no matter what fly-specks might be produced on the wall, the structure itself was safe and solid and something to be proud of."[4]

The railroad debate centered on the freight rates, the roads insisting that rates be raised to make enough profit to keep the companies growing, the shippers insisting that rates be lowered. The shippers' fight was carried on principally by Louis D. Brandeis, later Supreme Court Justice but then a lawyer for shippers' interests. Brandeis caught the public fancy with the slogan that "the railroads wasted a million dollars a day."

The fight lasted from the middle of 1913 to the end of 1914. In that period Lee made numerous contributions to public relations theory and practice, and gave eloquent, though never systematized, expression to the main tenets of his central policy: first, that public opinion is powerful and righteous; second, that there are certain economic laws within which business must operate in order to grow; and third, that in the case of a conflict between public opinion and economic law, publicity would bring understanding to the problem. "Publicity," he said, "is an effective cure for most railroad financial evils. Focus the bright light of day upon any transaction and men will be extremely careful to see to it that the transaction is legitimate."[5]

More important, Lee developed the techniques of a full-blown publicity campaign to fight for a rate increase. He was named publicity representative of a "President's Committee" of three major eastern railroad lines, the Baltimore and Ohio, New York Central, and the Pennsylvania, with the job of publicizing the railroad's side of the freight rate debate. It was his first opportunity to develop a complete publicity campaign.

Having concluded that the methods used in his earlier work for the railroads were "unfortunate in that we had not taken our case to the people," he now told the I.C.C. in advance about his plans. Realizing the final decision of the Commission would be jeopardized if someone raised the point of unfair influence, Lee told the Commission, "we don't intend to rely upon the casual newspaper reports for the people of this country to learn the reasons which we shall present to you and upon which we ask for this increase in rates."[6]

He proposed instead that after each I.C.C. hearing of the rate debate, he would extract every important fact that the railroads presented and give it distribution not only in breadth but in depth, using every medium at his disposal to reach those people who could influence the outcome of the I.C.C. decision. He devised, organized, and waged the campaign with all the thoroughness of a general in full battle. It was an all-out struggle with public opinion.

A campaign to change public opinion swiftly was, first of all, a logistical problem in the distribution of facts and ideas. In 1913 the chief medium for the distribution of this material was still the newspaper, so the first phase of the distribution plan was to give information verbally and in printed form to the press in Philadelphia, and then to send, when he had time, copies of that information to papers throughout the Pennsylvania system.

Quickly, however, Lee realized there was a much broader field to cover. He began to seek ways to get the attention of people he could not reach through newspapers. In studying the constituencies of the Pennsylvania Railroad he found the company had many publics: about 112,000 shareholders, about 200,000 bondholders, about 250,000 employees, and about 500,000 daily passengers. These people, who had a direct relationship with the company, had to be given more information than could be put into the newspaper, either as news, features, or advertising material.

He started by publishing leaflets, then advanced to the idea of bulletins posted in railway stations. Shortly he began placing in passenger cars small folders containing information of interest to all. He also realized that there was an additional public far more important than passengers and employees—the people who influenced other people: congressmen, state legislators, mayors, city councilmen, college presidents, economists, bankers, writers, lecturers, clergymen, and many more "leaders of opinion" as he called them. To these he sent quantities of bulletins and leaflets containing literate and logical arguments with frequent quotations from influential and respected men.

The campaign also included a speaker's bureau. Railroad executives were sent around the country to make speeches before important community and business groups such as the local chambers of commerce and boards of trade. These meetings were covered by the local press and reported to the public in news stories. Lee himself made speech after speech telling the railroads' side of the story, always emphasizing that his speeches had not been edited by management. "I am alone responsible for the opinions expressed," he said. He clearly intended his statements to be for railroads in general, and in the course of delivering them developed ideas that contributed significantly to the growth of the new profession of public relations.

The story Lee told was, first of all, that railroads were suffering from many burdens—floods, increasing wages and taxes, and expensive legislation. Furthermore, these burdens were hard to carry for several reasons: there were different tribunals for wages and rates; the railroads were compelled to compete by the anti-trust laws and kept from competing by rate laws; there were conflicts between law and business customs; there was a demand for more passenger service along with a demand for lower fares; there were contradictory local demands; and there was inadequate pay for carrying the mails.

Always ready with a persuasive analogy, Lee likened the railroad situation to that of a hotel which rented two-dollar rooms. Along comes the government and demands that the hotel install baths in every room, marble floors, rugs, and picture windows, and then forbids the hotel to raise its two-dollar rent. He then would ask, "Who would be foolish enough to invest money in required hotel improvements when the hotel is not allowed to raise its rates accordingly to recoup the investment?"

What was needed, he argued, was constructive, not destructive, treatment. For this there were three fundamental propositions. (1) The public must agree to pay for what it gets; he contended that the roads were vastly underpaid for parcel post and did not have the money to meet the public demands for safety equipment and other improvements. (2) A definite policy must be established; commissions and regulations were inevitable, he felt, but what was wrong were policies and commissions and regulations which contradicted each other. (3) Lee maintained that "we must restore the faith of the public in the good intentions of earnest men who happen to be successful. Let us pin our faith to the enterprise of the individual. Let us see to it that as regulators we have men striving to serve the public and not to promote private political ambitions; let all railroad commissions work with the railroad and not against them. Let us abandon the thought that material success should be an object of suspicion."[7]

Included in the campaign were all the major issues in the railroad situation, issues which are still basic to the problems of capitalism in modern society. On increased safety precautions by the railroads, for instance, Lee asked for greater understanding of what the public demanded. Railroads were more than willing, he said, to have automatic signals, straight track, steel cars, electric locomotives, even beautiful stations in every city, and all the ideal conditions which every railroad officer dreams of.

But he said all could not be done at once. To replace every wooden passenger car in the country with a steel one would cost $600 million. It would cost another $600 million for the Pennsylvania system alone to remove all its grade crossings. A cheaper, more effective way to achieve greater safety was by inspiring greater care and caution in the railroad workers themselves. He told a convention of master boilermakers in Philadelphia, "Let us concentrate on the MAN. Not in rules or mechanics will we find half the safety we will in the fidelity and the enthusiastic service of conscientious MEN."

For the rising problem of labor and labor unions, he had a similar solution. "It seems to me it is not merely a matter of pay for our men," he said, "for we must see to it as far as we can that each class of labor is paid fairly, and that certain classes are not permitted to force an unwarranted share for themselves." But, more important, the railroads must get their men "to see something of the value of doing good work for the sake of good work."

Finally, the invasion by government of railroad management was, for Lee, one of the disquieting elements of the future. He felt that government regulation, although sound in theory, only developed a situation where increased and improved service did not pay its way?[8]

The campaign stirred much criticism. Albert B. Cummins, Senator from Iowa, told Congress it was "the most comprehensive, energetic, and persistent campaign he had ever witnessed to make the people of the country believe that the effort of the government to regulate railroads, railway rates, and railway practices has resulted in dismal, disastrous failure." Cummins called the railroad program an effort to "mislead and pervert" the people, trying to "awaken sympathy by false pretenses," and trying to deceive the country with "exaggerated cries of suffering and distress." The campaign, he said, had "filled the newspapers with headlines and dispatches." It had provided dinners and public banquets where the "eloquence of orators paints lurid pictures of empty treasuries, of worn-out tracks, of falling bridges and dilapidated equipment."[9]

To this Ivy Lee replied, "We have been chided in the past for not having taken people into our confidence. When we take the people into our confidence...some of our friends in Washington think the devil has surely been at work somewhere."[10]

Senator LaFollette called the campaign a "monument of shame" and denounced it on the floor of Congress. "The Baltimore & Ohio, New York Central, and Pennsylvania railroads conducted a publicity campaign through the publicity agent of the Pennsylvania Railroad," he said. "Thirty-two anonymous ex parte bulletins...have been issued and scattered broadcast over the country. They have formed the basis of thousands of news items, editorials, and addresses. They found their way into the weekly newspapers. They played no small part in influencing a large proportion of the upward of 2,200 newspapers in the United States."[11]

LaFollette submitted to Congress a detailed diagram showing the influences bearing on the Interstate Commerce Commission, and showing how the railroad presidents, officials, directors, and agents, through the Pennsylvania publicity bureau, influenced the I.C.C. directly, and swayed it indirectly by persuading newspapers, magazines, trade journals, financial journals, stock- and bondholders, meetings of commercial clubs, traffic clubs, and boards of trade, the business public, members of 'the Cabinet, members of Congress, the President, and labor organizations.

The Senator inserted into the *Congressional Record* a complete file of the publicity material for the campaign.[12] It included the bulletins issued by the railroads, a series of pamphlets containing speeches delivered by railroad officials, copies and lists of newspaper and magazine articles and editorials that were for the most part based on the statement contained in the bulletins and pamphlets. LaFollette also included a large number of letters that had been sent to the President and forwarded to the I.C.C., letters sent to Congressmen and to the I.C.C. Commissioners themselves. These were often letters by bankers, businessmen, boards of trade, and even labor unions, which had been instigated in the first place by the original publicity bulletins, pamphlets, speeches, and newspaper articles.

This mute testimony to the effectiveness of Ivy Lee's first large-scale publicity campaign demonstrated clearly how influential people had indeed been reached, and how they in turn brought pressure to bear upon the proper body. This was Lee's theory translated into practice. He later said that it had cost the railroads about $12,000 for the publicity of the campaign, and he added, ironically, that it had cost the people of the United States about $12,000 to have it all reprinted in the *Congressional Record*.[13]

The campaign gained so much attention from Congress that Lee's activities for the railroads were investigated by the Senate Commission on Industrial Relations. Lee's brother explained to this committee that the object of the Pennsylvania publicity bureau was to "keep the public advised of the company's activities" and to "take the public into its confidence." On controversial matters, the publicity bureau was to make sure that the public understood the company's position. "The company started its publicity work some nine years ago by first inaugurating a plan of full publicity regarding all accidents," he told the committee, and added that "in the same way, if we go a year, or two years as we just have, and do not have a single one of all the 181,000,000 passengers carried killed in a train accident, we make that fact public."[14]

The success of the campaign was evident when on December 16, 1914, the Commission granted the advance in rates by a vote of five to two, representing an about-face by the Commissioners and a clear victory for the railroads. The president of the Pennsylvania said that the decision marked "the beginning of a broad, constructive policy in railroad regulation."[15]

By the end of 1914 there were other signs that public opinion might be turning to a small degree in favor of the railroads. In addition to the victory in the rate advance, President Wilson wrote to a committee of railroad executives pointing out that the railroad situation should have sympathetic treatment because railroads represented "the one common interest of our whole industrial life." Other indications of a turning tide came when a committee of Congress reported that railroads were underpaid for carrying the mails, and when the people of Missouri overwhelmingly voted down extra-crew laws.

Oswald Garrison Villard, noted journalist and head of the *New York Evening Post*, viewed the work of Ivy Lee in the freight rate campaign as a monumental advance. "I have never been able to understand," he said, "why railroads that are playing the game squarely have not each taken a man like Mr. Lee, made him vice-president, and told him to do nothing else than to be a link between the press, the public, and the railroads."[16]

Even the opposition agreed. When Brandeis was asked to publicly criticize Lee's railroad publicity campaign, he answered: "If

I were in the railroads' place, I would do exactly what they are doing."[17]

---

[1] U.S. Congress, Senate, Commission on Industrial Relations, *Final Report and Testimony*, 1916, Vol. VIII, p. 7897.

[2] Ivy Lee, *The American Railway Problem*, p. 5.

[3] Ivy Lee, *Railway Progress in the United States*, p. 6.

[4] Ivy Lee, *Human Nature and the Railroads*, p. 14.

[5] Ibid., p. 79.

[6] Ibid., pp. 57-58.

[7] Ibid., pp. 105-113.

[8] Ibid.

[9] Ibid., p. 56.

[10] Ibid.

[11] U.S., *Congressional Record*, 63rd Congress, 2nd Session, 1914, LI, Part 8, pp. 7736 ff.

[12] Ibid., pp. 7735-8093.

[13] Ivy Lee, "The Enemies of Publicity," *Electric Railway Journal*, Mar. 31, 1917, p. 600.

[14] U.S. Congress, Senate, Commission on Industrial Relations, op. cit., Vol. XI, p. 10,243.

[15] Ivy Lee, *Human Nature and the Railroads*, p. 126.

[16] *Railroad Age Gazette*, June 25, 1915, p. 1480.

[17] Quoted in "Publicity and Corporations," *Ivy Lee's Publicity Book*, p. 14, Ivy Lee Papers, Princeton.

RAY ELDON HIEBERT

8: HUMANIZING THE SUBWAYS

IN THE EARLY PART OF 1916 the subways and street railways of New York City found themselves faced with employee unrest that led to a major strike. Public opinion was distinctly hostile to the companies. Even more than the railroads, the subways and streetcars were used by the crowds, and their managements had a special responsibility to maintain a circumspect relationship with the public in order to maintain private ownership.

A natural solution was to improve public relations, and one of the major companies, the Interborough Rapid Transit, called upon Ivy Lee. Lee had worked exclusively for the Rockefellers from the end of the freight rate campaign until April 1, 1916, at which time he opened his own independent firm. He wrote to his father on that day: "My feeling is that I have devoted the whole of my life to the present time, to preparing for the work which I am just now undertaking. Of course, the whole of my life is an education, and my life will continue to be one, but I feel that now I ought to begin to realize on the preparation which I have had."[1]

His ideas had been tested on some of the most difficult issues of the first decades of the twentieth century—the anthracite coal strikes, the railroad situation, the freight rate debate, and the Rockefellers' problems—and they had not been found wanting. Much of the business world was now aware of its new dilemmas, and Lee's success gave him confidence he held the key to the solutions. "It is very evident that I am going to have all the business that I can possibly take care of," he wrote his father. Even before he opened the doors of his new agency, the Rockefellers and the Pennsylvania Railroad retained him to continue to serve as their special consultant, and their names attracted new clients such as the I.R.T. and Bethlehem Steel Corporation.

He took two partners into his new firm, once again recruiting his brother Wideman, who severed his full-time relationship with the Pennsylvania to join the agency. The other partner was W. W. Harris, a former newspaper reporter and editor. The firm—Lee, Harris, and Lee—opened for business on April 1 at 61 Broadway.

The chief advantage in having a firm independent of his clients was the ability it gave him to express his ideas freely, without being tied to the purse strings of any one corporation. "It is certainly delightful to be free," he wrote to his father, "to be able to do what you please, and with nobody to tell you what to do. It is what I have dreamed of being able to do for a great many years."[2]

He studied the I.R.T. problems carefully. The company had just taken a big loss as the result of the employee strike. Now uneasiness was setting in again, and another strike seemed imminent. But to Lee, the employee representation plan that had worked in Rockefeller's Colorado coal mines could work just as well in the New York subways. After some convincing of both sides, the plan was accepted and it averted a second violent strike.

As a means of communication from company to public, he advised the use of streetcar cards and posters that would be interesting, pertinent, and newsy, and that could be changed as often as possible. He felt that a great publicity potential existed in the company's monthly and annual reports, and he advised that the I.R.T. prepare its own publications in magazine format for employees, patrons, and public. These would "arouse the interest of employees; form the basis for information or editorial comment for newspapers; provide a medium of communication with city officials, taxpayers' organizations, and the like." He felt that they should not be issued on a regular periodical basis but "only when one has something important to say."³

Eventually, the company was able to gain the confidence of its men by interpreting its needs and problems so effectively that, several years later, it could explain why a reduction in wages was needed and gain the employees' agreement to it—an almost unprecedented achievement in the twentieth century. While the subways had improved their relations with their own workers, they continued to be plagued with public problems instigated by passengers and citizens in general who could use weight at the polls to influence the operations of public utilities. Politicians, offering the kind of *quid pro quo* peculiar to their calling, gladly promised to maintain subway fares at five cents if the people would elect them. But without an increase in fares, the companies had limited budgets for expansion and improvement. This meant that equipment was not always new and safe, service was not always the best, and the company had to look for ways to cut jobs and save money.

Lee felt the public needed to understand the human factors in the situation, to see that the subway companies, as any other business, were not corporate machines but a group of human beings just like the members of the crowd, operating under certain fixed conditions, and trying their best to serve the public and make a profit. In portraying the subway companies in this way, Lee was of course drawing upon his previous successes.

There were only a few basic elements to Lee' "psychology of the multitude," and these he had learned from the lessons of history, not from the science laboratory. All the great "statesmen, preachers and soldiers have from time immemorial recognized these principles when they sought to lead people," he said. They were:

1. Success in dealing with crowds rests upon the art of getting believed in.

2. Getting believed in requires leaders who can fertilize the imagination and organize the will of the crowds.

3. Since crowds do not reason, they can only be organized and stimulated through symbols and phrases.

While people are intelligent and fair, he maintained, "the crowd craves leadership. If it does not get intelligent leadership, it is going to take fallacious leadership." Referring to muckrakers, he said, "men utilize skill to produce emotion and opinion in favor of reform and against the wrong." Therefore, "why should not the same process be utilized on behalf of constructive undertakings, on behalf of ideas and principles which do not tear down but really build up."[4]

Lee called his crowd psychology seeing the "human nature" of the situation. One of the first things to understand about "human nature" is that one cannot reason with multitudes. In developing a policy of publicity, one should not expect "merely to reason the case out, merely to present statistical data and arithmetical equations," because "people are interested in their own affairs, they are not very much interested in your affairs and they will not analyze statistics."[5]

By the same token there is no gain in pointing out "the logical inconsistencies of other people's statements or arguments, however erroneous they may be." For this reason Lee was not interested in a policy of defense but a policy of dynamic and constructive action. "If we cannot answer what they say with something that will appeal constructively to the imagination or emotion of the public, with something which will *supplant* the erroneous statements, it is hardly worthwhile to go into the case at all."

Far better than any abstraction is concrete detail. "A public to be influenced must feel.... To make the public feel, we must be concrete," Lee urged. For instance, he felt that the best way to counter the claim that the railroads were run by a small group on Wall Street would be to put forth the concrete details in terms of human beings: the names of shareholders; how they are increasing; the women among them; the life insurance companies owning stock; the names of the trustees. "That is a statement of fact that produces an effect upon the people's imaginations and emotions," he said. "It tells its own story, it supplies its own inference."[6]

As an example of constructive action, Lee suggested that the subway guards be given freshly laundered white linen suits each day. During the long, hot summer, the thousands of tired and sweaty passengers pouring through the stations would be greeted by fresh, clean, white-suited employees. This would impress the public mind with the idea that the Interborough was looking out for its men, a subtle inference that the company was looking out for its passengers, also.

Perhaps nothing was more important to Lee than to be natural, to use the language of the people. "The greatest thing that could be done for the street railways and the steam railroads, in fact for all the utilities of the United States," he said, "would be to do for them what Billy Sunday has done for religion." He admired Billy Sunday because "he speaks the language of the man who rides the trolley car and goes to ball games, who chews gum and spits tobacco juice." Lee felt that the abstract, obscure, and cold legal phraseology of the lawyer was often to blame for the misunderstanding of the public. "Whenever a lawyer starts to talk," Lee said, "he shuts out the light."[7]

Lee felt that the crowd understood symbolic words and phrases better than it understood logic. When muckrakers created symbols that moved the public for their causes, often giving a false impression, business had to create new symbols and phrases to replace those of the opposition in the public mind. "The labor people," he said, "were very happy in their selection of that term 'full crew.' Now, if we had referred to that from the beginning as the 'extra crew,' it seems to me we would have made considerably more headway than we did."

The phrase "what the traffic will bear" was another that hurt the cause of the railroad because it was a phrase people remembered with suspicion. "It is scientifically correct, no doubt," Lee admitted, "but it conveys a most unfortunate suggestion to the popular mind—the thought that the rate is 'all the traffic will bear,' a suggestion absolutely contrary to the fact."[8]

Lee's work for the subways resulted in two of his most famous publications: the *Subway Sun* (underground edition) and its sister publication, the *Elevated Express*, written in language the people could understand, made up in newspaper format on posters to be pasted in subway stations and trains. For many years thereafter they were produced in Lee's offices and became a permanent and popular part of New York City life.

These publications did not contain any direct advocacy of the subway management's position, but were well illustrated with feature pictures and touched upon the little things, the human interest aspects of life, glimpses of old New York, schedules of programs being provided by the city's recreational facilities, suggestions to improve the service, and so on. To be read they had to be interesting, and this interest was bound to be reflected in goodwill for the company.

The *Subway Sun* and *Elevated Express* also contained messages of advice and personal attention, usually from the president of the I.R.T. himself. "DANGER WARNINGS," the headline might read, followed by: "Every day our guards warn you more than 150,000 times to 'watch your step.' They speak for your safety.

Won't you listen? (signed by) Theodore Shonts, President." The message served not only to lessen the accident rate but to make the subway rider feel that the president of the I.R.T. was personally concerned about his safety."[9]

Sometimes the *Subway Sun* backfired, and Lee's office had to use great care and delicate handling in dealing with the subway public. The *Sun* once printed a request that riders make an effort to break the growing habit of holding the pneumatic doors open, which delayed the trains. The result, however, was that more people learned that they could make the trains wait for late-comers by holding the doors, and the *Sun*, by telling people, only increased the problem. For the most part, however, the two publications became useful and permanent institutions for communicating with the subway riders of New York.

A large part of the human interest appeal came from putting human beings into the picture. Lee told the Electric Railway Association that it was important to "put the personality of the management forward in such a way that the people will realize that the men who run their streetcars have red blood in their veins." He added that the public statements of most companies were cold and mechanical. For instance, a notice of change on a streetcar line posted on the window would read:

> Effective Oct. 1, 1917. Notice—Green streetcars will run south through to Thirty-Fifth Street and return northbound by First Avenue, instead of Broadway.

No wonder people thought that streetcar managers sat up nights thinking of ways to irritate them, Lee said. How much more human it would be if the president of the line would put a folder on all the cars explaining the change and showing the personal concern of the manager for the convenience of the riders.

He advised executives to sign their own names to their public statements. He had learned earlier from poster bulletins prepared for the Pennsylvania Railroad which were too impersonal and too cold when signed at the bottom of the poster: The Pennsylvania Railroad Company. The same poster reissued over the signature of the company president, Samuel Rea, was much more effective.[10]

But while these techniques helped to "humanize" the I.R.T., and, through a central publicity bureau, all subways and streetcars, they did not succeed in winning for the companies an increase in fares. When Lee returned to his office after World War I he tackled the dominating problem—low fares. The subways were overcrowded and could not properly take care of the great number of customers who demanded service. In a normal free-enterprise situation, the company would raise its rates to buy more cars, provide better service, and meet the demand. But in the I.R.T. situation, the rates were frozen by the New York State Transit Commission at five cents. The only way to solve the problem would be to let the people know precisely what the problem was.

In the early twenties Lee organized a campaign for a fare increase along much the same lines as the 1914 campaign for the freight rate increase. The subway fare became an important political issue in New York City. Lee was the target of editorial cartoons, particularly in the socialist papers, where he was pictured as the editor of the *Subway Sun*, with a greedy grin on his face, grinding out little newspapers screaming for a rate increase while in the background the capitalists grew fat on the money they were thus squeezing from the poor, oppressed subway riders of New York.

Ultimately, in 1926, the argument reached its climax in a New York State Transit Commission hearing on the proposed rate increase. In the hearings, Samuel Untermyer, chief counsel for the commission, seized upon Ivy Lee as the crucial witness in his attempt to deflate the argument in favor of the increased fare. Untermyer put Lee on the stand and grilled him about his role in the publicity campaign for a fare increase.

Lee testified that he had not done much but give advice to the company and make suggestions which others carried out when the company desired. The chief counsel then subpoenaed the books of the I.R.T. and with Lee on the stand pointed out that between 1916 and 1926, he had been paid a salary of $128,129 and an expense account of $125,269. Under the transit contract between I.R.T. and the city of New York, these were charged as operating expenses and were paid by the city. These figures, Untermyer charged, represented "illegitimate expenditures" which simply placed "additional burdens upon the car-riders of the City.... It thus appears that while the announced policy of the City officials on the strength of which they were elected to office was and is for the maintenance of the five-cent fare, the company has been spending the City's money toward the defeat of that policy."[11]

Lee protested, saying that it was in the interest of the city and the subway riders to increase the fare because ultimately it would mean better subways and safer service. "Do you think," Untermyer returned, "that it was proper for you to assume that you knew what was in the interest of the City, when the duly elected City authorities were opposed to it?"

"Yes, sir," Lee responded, "it is conceivable that their favoritism for a five-cent fare was to get votes."[12]

Untermyer subpoenaed examples of Lee's work for the I.R.T. and Lee produced eight large, bound volumes of newspaper clippings, magazine articles, pamphlets, folders, posters, and other materials that his office had prepared. It was impressive evidence of the thoroughness of the Lee campaign. But unlike the earlier railroad freight rate debate, this time the companies lost to the commissions. The five-cent rate remained.

Lee's interpretation of the subways to the public and the public to the subways was not without effect, however. Safety and service steadily improved, labor problems eased, and passenger satisfaction increased. In time, the rates were increased, and somehow there was even a growing feeling among the crowd that those who operated the great chain of cars that clanked overhead and the grinding machines that ran in the bowels of the earth below needed some human sympathy like everyone else.

---

[1] Ivy Lee to his father, Apr. 1, 1916, Ivy Lee Papers, Princeton.

[2] Ibid.

[3] Ivy Lee, "The Technique of Publicity," *Electric Railway Journal*, Jan. 6, 1917, p. 18.

[4] Ivy Lee, "The Human Nature of Publicity," *Electric Railway Journal*, Aug. 4, 1917, p. 182.

[5] Ivy Lee, *Publicity for Public Service Corporations*, p. 9.

[6] Ivy Lee, *Human Nature and the Railroads*, pp. 17–18.

[7] Ivy Lee, *Publicity for Public Service Corporations*, pp. 21–22.

[8] Ivy Lee, *Human Nature and the Railroads*, pp. 16–20.

[9] Ivy Lee, "Interborough Solicits Complaints," *Electric Railway Journal*, Apr. 7, 1917, p. 638.

[10] Ivy Lee, "Personality in Publicity," *Electric Railway Journal*, Aug. 11, 1917, p. 223.

[11] New York State Transit Commission, *Report and Recommendations of Special Counsel* (by Samuel Untermyer), 1927, pp. 63–64.

[12] Ibid.

Ray Eldon Hiebert

9: ONE BIG HAPPY FAMILY

IVY LEE'S WORST FEARS FOR THE RAILROADS—Government ownership—came true in a sense on December 1, 1917, when President Wilson took over the entire rail system of the United States and put it under Army control to meet the emergency transportation requirements of the war effort. Wilson named his Secretary of the Treasury, William G. McAdoo, as Director General of the railroads. One of McAdoo's first acts was to fire Ivy Lee from his job as independent consultant to the Pennsylvania. He appointed his friend Alfred H. Smith, president of the New York Central, the Pennsylvania's chief competition, as Eastern Regional Director of the railroads.

No impressive records were made during the period the Government operated the railroads—from December 1917 to March 1920. The Government did raise the wages of the worker, but the roads already had a decent score in this category. In 1917, the average railroad worker's compensation was 27 percent higher than the average for workers engaged in manufacturing. By 1920, through Government raises, the railroad average was 33 percent higher. To offset the raises in wages, the Government found that it had to do what it would not let the private companies do—raise rates and fares. Without even explaining to the people the reasons for such increases, the Government announced a 28 percent rise in freight rates and an 18 percent increase in passenger rates.

In spite of the higher rates, the efficiency of the operation dropped off drastically under Government control. In 1916, under private ownership, the railroad operating ratio (actual operating costs, exclusive of new equipment and improvements) was an excellent 65.5 percent. By 1918 it had fallen to 81.5 percent; by 1920 it was all the way down to 94.3 percent. The total railroad operation cost the United States Government over $900 million, not including another $200 million which the Government had to pay the railroads to settle court claims for equipment that had been damaged during Government operation.[1] The $1.1 billion came out of the taxpayers' pockets, and no one made any real attempt to explain this expense to the man on the street.

When the Pennsylvania regained control of its lines on March 1, 1920, the company was faced with the huge job of rebuilding. Not only were equipment and facilities in bad shape, but morale of the personnel was low, partly because workers feared that the wage increases granted under McAdoo would not be continued. Soon thereafter General W. W. Atterbury, designated to become the new president of the line, asked Lee if he would consider becoming a vice-president in charge of public relations to solve all the company's problems.

Lee answered that "it would certainly be most unwise to suggest that by a change in organization involving the appointment of the Vice-President in Charge of Public Relations other officers of the railroad would, to some extent, be relieved of their public relations responsibility." Lee said that any announcement of the appointment of a public relations officer should serve as public recognition that the railroad was accepting "its obligation to keep the public informed of all railway matters," and "as has been the practice of the Pennsylvania Railroad for a number of years, every officer should consider himself a public relations man."

A vice-presidency should be created, Lee told Atterbury, not because the title carries weight, but "because the importance of the work to be handled warrants it. A railroad should keep close to the public and have the machinery to do it. Furthermore, everyone in authority should be charged specifically with this responsibility." He suggested that he serve instead as a consultant and "not attempt to be the one spokesman for the company."² Atterbury took this sound advice, and Lee became an independent consultant, attached to the staff of the vice-president in charge of operations. He attended regular staff meetings, and advised on publicity, public relations, and personnel relations for the entire company.

A subsequent Pennsylvania president, Martin W. Clement, explained that it was not Lee's duty to plan or carry out policies or procedures. "But, through his position with the officers, he had a good deal to do with the planning of policies in the discussion stage.... And, it was his job to see that once they had been determined upon, they were kept, so that they would not be in conflict with public opinion." Clement characterized Lee's work as "keeping the officers from getting mad at each other and from getting into fights with the public." When the public accused the Pennsylvania "of not doing the things we should have done, Lee's advice was always to show them how we were doing it."³

The Pennsylvania wanted to rebuild the lines to make up for ground lost under Government control, particularly since it felt that Regional Director Smith had given favorable treatment to the New York Central. The Pennsylvania had to make itself competitive in order to win back its customers. But the railroads could not compete by lowering rates, for I.C.C. rates were set for all. The only area in which they could compete was service, and this was the responsibility of each individual employee.

Employees not eager to make the operation a success could make it a complete failure by a kind of passive sabotage. Suppose, Lee said, an employee walking through the station at Harrisburg taps a journal box on a limited train, finds it hot, does not stop to oil it but lets the train go on. A few miles out of the station, the entire train would be wrecked. "The employee must want to do his job for all it is worth or that may happen." The management agreed and decided that the way to get men to *want* to do their job well and *want* to provide the best service was to *pay* them more than they would get on any other railroad. But the national unions set pay scales and, ironically, in order to pay the men higher wages, the Pennsylvania had to fight to keep the national unions from organizing the men.

Following the war, agitation for national representation had been increased by the unions. The engineers, firemen, conductors, and trainmen were organized, but the rest of the company's 250,000 men were not. To offset the agitation, Atterbury put forward a Plan of Employee Representation, or a company union, where the workers would have a system of collective bargaining without getting involved with the unions and workers of other companies. But the plan only created more trouble for the Pennsylvania, including lawsuits and the opposition of the United States Railroad Labor Board. The independent unions were vigorously opposed to it and seized every opportunity to flay the Pennsylvania for its position. Atterbury wanted Lee to win public sympathy for the "company union" idea.[4]

Lee, however, warned against it. "I deprecate very much the idea of a controversy on the subject of the labor union as contrasted with the company union," he wrote Atterbury. "I hate the phrase 'company union' as I do not think it properly expressive of the idea.... This is a problem calling for exploration of new ideas...rather than for propagandizing with reference to any particular theory. Everybody knows that the problem of employee representation has not yet been worked out. The labor union of the United Mine Workers type...which limits production and has no secret ballot is certainly not the ideal organization. I am frank to say that I don't think the so-called company union, exclusively controlled by company finances, is ideal either."

Instead, Lee felt that the problem needed some "middle ground which will give the employees actual representation, a feeling that they are represented by men of their own choice without duress from any direction, and the opportunity to give all they have in the way of effort, advice and experience to the management through promotion of the common interests of the company for which they work, as well as of themselves."[5]

Lee believed that competitive salaries were fine, but he suggested a better way to get employees to work for the common interests of the Pennsylvania and give the best possible service: that the company promote the idea that its workers belonged to the "Pennsylvania Family," as he called it. This would help restore the sense of identity which the employees had lost during Government operation. More important, it would give employees something to work for and be proud of. Typically, Lee proposed a program of communication to promote the family feeling. On his advice the company set up newspapers in each of the four regions where it operated. Each paper had an editor and assistant who doubled as publicity men for that region to coordinate the entire communication setup.

These regional newspapers devoted 90 percent to news about the employees and their families—such as births, deaths, marriages, and outstanding job performances. Lee felt that the men would take pride in the fact that a great corporation wants to publicize them to their fellows. No advertisements for the company, pictures of the officers, or propaganda were allowed in the publications, although space was given occasionally to activities of the railroad of personal concern to the rank and file.

Lee also started the *Pennsylvania Standard*, a paper to communicate between management and employees. Here were expressed frank statements of the management's point of view and explanations of various situations on the railroad in which the employees would be interested.

There also was need for better communication between official personnel. Lee set up monthly letters to keep officers advised of outstanding developments affecting the Pennsylvania operations, as well as the industry as a whole, and business generally. Lee also suggested that letter communications would create a more intimate contact with employees.

In addition to these channels of communication, the company was also urged to adopt policies that would fill out the picture of the Pennsylvania as one big happy family. Lee advised that Atterbury and other officers of the railroad go over the lines, meet the men, shake hands with them and talk to them. "Let the men look into the faces of the officers of their company," Lee said. "Let them see the character that is expressed in those faces. Then the men will be able to interpret the acts of the management in the terms of the personality of its officers."

Lee suggested the development of a *Who's Who on the Pennsylvania Railroad*, to show the workers and the world who and what the Pennsylvania is. By calling attention to the many years of education, training, and experience that were behind each man on the railroad, the public would gain confidence in the ability of the men and, so Lee hoped, decrease agitation for outside control.

Another activity which Lee publicized was the Women's Aid of the Pennsylvania Railroad, a unique organization with the company president's wife as head of the league and vice-presidents' wives as her chief assistants. There was a risk in this way of organizing, Lee said, because the men's wives were not always on the same levels as their husbands, but it was the only way to get the society started. The ladies of the Women's Aid visited families of sick men; helped families in distress get back on their feet; attended marriages, baptisms, and funerals; sent congratulations and flowers to aliens who became citizens; and in general strove to keep up the morale of the men on the road. By the mid-twenties, Lee was happy to report that 122,000 mothers, wives, and daughters of Pennsylvania employees were dues-paying members of the league.

To emphasize the need for such an organization, Lee told this story: A crack Pennsylvania train had a bad accident causing injury to more than 300 people; later it was discovered that the engineer of the train had been up the entire night before fighting with his wife. It was this kind of "morale hazard" which the Women's Aid could help to eliminate. Their activities could "spread happiness among the homes of the men and thus create a morale which will back them up in their work."

Lee also recommended the company undertake psychological studies to help show what could be done to improve the environment and working conditions of railroad men so they would be happier and more contented. This would not only increase their efficiency but make them less likely victims of agitators and malcontents.

An idea that Lee always tried to push was a profit-sharing plan. He told the Pennsylvania executives that "all the company would have to do is give out the facts for publication and the newspaper reporters and editors will do the rest." He was sure the favorable publicity resulting would be worth far more than the cost to the company. It would dramatize the spirit of the Pennsylvania in the public imagination more effectively than any other action. But this was a greater sacrifice to the image of the Pennsylvania Happy

Family than even a paternal management was yet prepared to make. There was no profit-sharing plan.

But the happy family concept was not dropped, and Lee pursued it more vigorously than ever, even broadening it to include the general public. He insisted that it was important for the public to know about the Pennsylvania "family." His office continued to publish newspapers for the employees, to write speeches, to prepare pamphlets, and to send out press releases to tell the man on the street or in the office what the Pennsylvania was doing.

One human interest story that got wide coverage was this: on a particularly cold January day, the general manager of the Pennsylvania issued this simple command—whenever a train was approaching, the foreman not only should blow a whistle to warn the men to get out of the way but, since men probably would be wearing earmuffs and wouldn't hear the whistle, the track foreman ought to take special care to see that the men got off the track. It was a routine item, but it caught the public fancy and was carried as a feature news story all over the United States.

The railroad at this time did a limited amount of advertising, primarily for passenger traffic business, usually in the form of ads for railway excursions to Luray, Virginia, or Atlantic City. But Lee wanted the company to splash the Pennsylvania in newspapers all over the United States as the premier railroad of America. He never forgot that the railroads had to strive for the approval of the crowd. Beyond the ranks of those who worked on the railroad or bought from the railroad stretched the vast army of those who legislated at voting booths. "Unless an institution like the Pennsylvania can interpret itself to this element in such a way as to give the fundamental feeling of its being a great, enlightened, honest, and efficient institution, it cannot get the support which it must have in order to be a success," he said.

It was not enough for the company to ship freight, Lee said; the customer must be made to feel that his interests are the company's interests. He promoted a bureau to supply information to shippers on the progress of their freight—if a New York shipper sent a car to St. Louis, he could find out when that car would be in Pittsburgh, when in Indianapolis, and when it would reach its destination. No law compelled the railroads to do this; it was simply good customer relations.

One of the most important passenger relations measures which Lee promoted—equal to the *Subway Sun*—was the introduction of the Pennsylvania dining car menu. It is surprising how people will talk about a good dinner they had on the train, he said, and if the railroad can give its passengers a wonderfully good meal, they will tell everybody what a delightful trip they had. If the meal was good, then dinner time would be a felicitous moment for telling people about the Pennsylvania, and the menu offered the perfect medium. Lee's office produced different two-page inserts for the Pennsylvania menu each week, and 54,000 copies went into the railroad dining cars. A typical menu would have on page one a photograph of a trainman carefully oiling the wheel bearings of a railroad car and a few lines about the Pennsylvania and what it was doing. On the other page would be a story about the national railroad situation or articles about the Pennsylvania supplied by the mayors or Chambers of Commerce from towns through which the railroad ran.[6]

The Pennsylvania did not always carry out Lee's suggestions. By 1927 he was advising that to give more of a family feeling to the workers, the company should distribute an annual report to employees. He wrote to Clement, then a vice-president: "Of course, this is an entirely original idea, and I do not think that General Atterbury will approve of doing it." But he went on to list sixteen important types of information that such a report should contain, including a full statement on wages, earnings, grievances, and pensions.[7]

Clement disagreed. He did not feel that the employees were entitled to know how well they were being directed. "If a general in charge of a great army led his troops to disaster, he is in no way responsible to the men, only to his country," wrote Clement.[8] The implication was clear: the business executive was responsible only to his company. Lee shook his head. Even in an enlightened company like the Pennsylvania, it was not easy to overcome nineteenth century attitudes. The day arrived, however, even though Lee did not live to see it, when annual reports to employees had become a commonplace feature of American business life.

In 1937, Clement, then president of the Pennsylvania, testified before a Senate Subcommittee on Interstate Commerce investigating railroad holding companies. Did he believe that a company executive was in no way responsible to the men? Or did he believe in the advice of Ivy Lee? Without a doubt, he said, Ivy Lee had been right.

Though they rejected a few of his suggestions, generally the Pennsylvania officials had the common sense or good intentions to listen to Lee's advice on public relations, and this made their company a perfect laboratory in which he could test his ideas. He once told a gathering of his own staff that the Pennsylvania account was their most highly developed and technical job in all of its ramifications. "Our experience with the Pennsylvania has taught us more for application to other jobs," he told his associates, "than any other client that we have ever had."[9]

---

[1] Stover, op. cit., pp. 181 ff.

[2] Ivy Lee to W. W. Atterbury, June 10, 1920, Ivy Lee Papers, Princeton.

[3] M. W. Clement to R. E. Hiebert, Apr. 19, 1963.

[4] "Transcript of Staff Conference, Ivy Lee and Associates," Jan. 25, 1925, pp. 17–35, Ivy Lee Papers, Princeton.

[5] Ivy Lee to W. W. Atterbury, Dec. 15, 1927, Ivy Lee Papers, Princeton.

[6] "Transcript of Staff Conference," loc. cit.

[7] Ivy Lee to M. W. Clement, Jan. 18, 1927, Ivy Lee Papers, Princeton.

[8] M. W. Clement to Ivy Lee, Jan. 21, 1927, Ivy Lee Papers, Princeton.

[9] "Transcript of Staff Conference," op. cit., p. 35.

10: PUBLIC RELATIONS FOR PUBLIC UTILITIES

PERHAPS MORE THAN ANY OTHER ACTIVITY, Lee's work with public utilities provided the experience out of which he formulated his ideas of public relations, as opposed to press agentry, as a job to provide clients with advice on the policies that would keep them operating in the public interest.

The kind of advice he was best at giving is illustrated by the action taken at one of the regular Monday conferences of the Pennsylvania Railroad executives. Lee attended and listened to various reports on the company's plans and procedures. One report showed that a great variety of unavoidable accidents in the railroad yards and along the line caused an enormous amount of window glass to be shattered in passenger cars. The officer responsible for the report pointed out that by changing from plate glass to pressed glass, the company could save about $100,000 a year. After the officers discussed this proposal from various points of view, the operating vice-president turned to Ivy Lee.

"What would the public think about this question?" he asked.

"Before I answer," Lee said, "I'd like to know if pressed glass distorts vision?"

"Yes it does," said the author of the report, "but the distortion is slight. It doesn't amount to much."

"Nevertheless," said Lee, "in that case you have no choice. You cannot put window glass which distorts vision in the cars of the railroad that carries three hundred million passengers a year. You have no right to use glass that is going to strain the eyes, even though the strain is so slight that the people are not aware of it."

The officers agreed, and the pressed glass proposal was dropped altogether.[1] Not only did such a policy make good publicity when it was announced but it made the public aware that people had to squint when looking through the windows of other railroads to see what was clearly visible from the Pennsylvania cars. In effect, this was "public relations" in the best sense of that phrase.

Lee did not invent the term "public relations"; he did not even employ the phrase extensively until the twenties, relatively late in his career. "Public relations" was used in the nineteenth century, though not in its present meaning. In 1882 a lawyer addressed the Yale Law School on "The Public Relations and Duties of the Legal Profession," by which he meant relations for the general good. In 1908 Theodore Vail, president of the American Telephone and Telegraph Company, used "Public Relations" as the title for his annual report. If questions about investments, returns, and distribution are satisfactorily answered, he wrote, "there can be no basis for conflict between the company and the public."

From 1906 on, Lee made regular use of such phrases as "inter-relations" and "human relations." Soon such terms as "industrial relations" and "trade relations" became popular and were frequently used in the titles of government committees and commissions. The application of "public relations" to the activities in which Lee was engaged has been attributed to a colleague, Daniel Willard, president of the Baltimore and Ohio Railroad, which Lee represented in 1914 during the rate campaign. Willard set up his own "public relations" department during that period, directed by Hampton Baumgartner, another pioneer in the field.

By 1916 Lee frequently used "public relations" as a blanket phrase to cover all the various activities in which he was engaged. "The advisor in public relations," he wrote in 1917, "should be far more than a mere publicity agent."[2] But he continued to call the technical aspects of his work "publicity." Even in the early twenties he referred to himself as a "publicity advisor," "publicity expert," or "publicity director," and referred to his work as the profession of publicity, although he gave one of his office publications the title of *Public Relations* in 1921.

But apparently the term "public relations *counsel*" was first used by another pioneer, Edward Bernays, who had started his career as a press agent in 1913. Bernays used the word "counsel" to describe his activities in 1922, and Lee used the word frequently thereafter. By 1928 the Metropolitan Life Insurance Company issued a report entitled "Functions of a Public Relations Counsel," and while it indicated that such activity was rapidly gaining wide acceptance, it listed only two practitioners: Edward Bernays and Ivy Lee.[3]

Out of his work for the public utilities came some of the most important published statements of Lee's philosophy. The first was *Human Nature and Railroads* (1915), a collection of speeches he made during the freight rate campaign. Another was a series of articles for the *Electric Railway Journal* (1917) while he was working for the subways. His most important statement was *Publicity For Public Service Corporations* (1916) from a speech he delivered to the Electric Railway Association.

"Publicity must not be thought of as it is by a good many as a sort of umbrella to protect you against the rain of an unpleasant public opinion," he told the rail executives. "Publicity must not be regarded as a bandage to cover up a sore and enable you to get along pretty well with the real trouble there. Publicity must, if your trouble is to be cured, be considered rather as an antiseptic which shall cleanse the very source of the trouble and reveal it to the doctor, which is the public." Publicity meant letting the people know exactly what one was doing, and if what he was doing was right, he would succeed. "An elementary requisite of any sound publicity must be, therefore, the giving of the best possible service."

Traditionally, capitalists had used the argument of expense as an excuse for not providing better service. But Lee pointed out that "good service consists in many things which do not involve money." It includes the courtesy of one's employees to the public, and of one's self to his employees. All companies could, without cost, cultivate a pleasant tone of voice and a friendly attitude, a mind open to innovation and change; they could avoid complacency and satisfaction with the way things were while preserving an attitude of sympathy to the public. It did not cost money to give serious and thorough attention to complaints, Lee pointed out. If the company could not correct the situation, then "nothing will do more good than a frank and candid explanation...giving reasons why it cannot be helped."[4]

Lee's work for the Pennsylvania Railroad and the Interborough Rapid Transit Company led him into the problems of the public utilities as a whole, and he frequently gave advice to associations of utilities which had common problems. He helped to found and advise both the Association of Railroad Executives and the Bureau of Railroad Economics. He worked closely with the Electric Railway Association and streetcar owners and executives, as well as individual companies such as the American Transit of Detroit. He also worked for power firms, including the Long Island Lighting Company, New Orleans Railway and Light Company, the Montana Power Company, and the Georgia Railway and Power Company.

Unfortunately, Ivy Lee's was often a voice crying in the wilderness, especially during the late twenties in the arena of public utilities. One of the worst examples of publicity used to conceal the truth was brought to light in 1928 during an investigation by the Federal Trade Commission of publicity methods practiced by public utilities. The publicity of the National Electric Light Association, for whom Lee had never worked, came under particular scrutiny from the Commission hearings. Testimony revealed that, under threat of Government investigation, the organization had in a few weeks increased its publicity expenditure from $750 to $140,000. But instead of spending that money for a forthright public explanation of its position, the association had instead resorted to the old tactics of bribery and underhanded dealing to assure victory.

College professors who gave courses in the problems of public utilities and Government ownership were employed to present the association's views. Newspapermen were put on a regular salary to write association material. Writers identified with radical movements and former high government officials were given large sums of money while writing books containing the association's opinions. The association also sent out published material without identifying itself as the source of that material.

It increased advertising in newspapers which would in turn be friendly to the association's views. In Iowa, for instance, advertising expenditures were increased 1,000 percent, and the investigation revealed that additional editorial matter had appeared in the Iowa papers which should have cost another $80,000 if the space had been purchased at advertising rates.

Lee insisted that all of these surreptitious practices were ineffective in getting control of public opinion because in the long run the people would learn the truth. Lee's earlier plan for a publicity bureau for the Electric Railway Association recommended a platform far different from that of the National Electric Light Association. Such a central bureau, Lee said, should be guided by four general principles in any campaign:

1. The source of all printed matter circulated should be made known. In fact, "every act should be taken in the full light of day."

2. Expenditures should be restricted to payments for advertising, printing, postage, and necessary salaries and expenses in connection with work actually performed.

3. There should be no criticism of commissions, individual commissioners, or anybody in public life; similarly, there should be no attacks, direct or indirect, upon labor organizations or leaders.

4. It should be the policy to restrict whatever was published to data contained in official records. Every fact stated should be carefully verified before publication, although statements of fact should not be colorless, but put forward in a way that carried conviction.[5]

The manner in which Ivy Lee prepared his clients for a Congressional investigation can be best seen in a case he handled for the Pennsylvania. The Walsh Commission, a Senate committee to investigate industrial problems, was anxious to get at the heart of railroad labor problems and called on General Atterbury to testify. Before the railroad president was scheduled to appear, Lee advised that he request every official of the road to go back over the files and note every labor dispute which might in any way be subject to criticism. Lee and his staff digested the results that were disclosed and prepared for the problems that might come up before the Walsh Commission.

After sifting through all possibilities, they knew that the one thing Walsh would ask about was the private arsenal of 5,000 rifles which the company maintained at the Broad Street Station. It was easy to imagine the headlines that would result when Walsh wrung from Atterbury a confession that the Pennsylvania had such an arsenal with the implication that it was to be used to shoot down strikers.

Company officials didn't want to admit anything, but Lee persuaded them to announce all the facts. He then prepared a bulletin discussing every important labor dispute that the railroad ever had. He made no attempt to conceal the fact that the railroad had an arsenal but explained in simple terms that such a large company in which the money of thousands of Americans was invested must be prepared in any eventuality to safeguard the lives of its passengers.

Just before Atterbury took the stand as a Congressional witness, the bulletin was handed out to the press. It effectively cut the ground from under Chairman Walsh's feet. The points from which he was going to draw inferences were already clearly spelled out and explained, and the public was told a good deal that the railroad wanted it to hear, particularly that the Pennsylvania was earnestly endeavoring to settle labor disputes in a spirit of fairness to both workers and stockholders.[6]

Earlier Lee had given similar advice to John D. Rockefeller Jr., who was also examined on the witness stand by Walsh. Lee was familiar with the tactics of the experienced and clever investigator. Walsh knew when the reporters for the afternoon papers had to leave the hearing room to meet their deadlines, so he always made it a point to get in his charges while the reporters were present, then permitted the examinees to answer only after the deadline was past and the reporters gone. The result was that the afternoon papers would carry essentially Walsh's point of view. Lee knew what Walsh's questions would be and advised Rockefeller to write out his answers in advance and have them distributed to the press, enabling the reporters to meet their deadline with both sides of the story.

In essence Lee's work was to advise his clients on what they must do to bring their policies into line with public thinking and then insure a public hearing for their actions. Unlike the publicity agents for the National Electric Light Association, he was not simply a hireling putting out the statements of his superiors. He often heard a different voice, the voice of the crowd, and disagreed with the executives he served. Pennsylvania President Atterbury once characterized Lee as "the only publicity man I've ever found who would stand up and fight me when he thought I was wrong."[7]

But with the exception of a few public utilities that understood Lee's point of view, most were still engaged in undercover operations. Throughout the twenties, the utilities were consolidating at a rate faster than ever. More than 3,700 individual companies disappeared through mergers from 1919 to 1927. By 1930 it was estimated that half of the electric power in the country was generated by only three great holding companies. The increased consolidation enlarged the fears of the people, and the revelations of the FTC investigation of 1928 further alienated the public from the cause of the utilities. By the thirties, the "Power Trust" was a major political issue, and one of the most important actions of Franklin Roosevelt's New Deal was to provide laws establishing effective federal regulation over the utilities, abolishing unnecessary holding companies, and setting up Government-owned utilities such as the Tennessee Valley Authority.

To counteract the growing sentiment for federal regulation and control in the thirties, the companies organized the Public Utilities Executive Committee. This time, however, they hired Ivy Lee and his firm. During the Roosevelt administration, the chief concern of the public utilities was the proposed Wheeler-Rayburn bill to limit holding companies. The Lee firm provided advice to the Public Utilities Executive Committee and engaged in telling its side of the story forthrightly by assembling the facts and putting them out in releases to newspapers, magazines, and radio stations. In 1935 a Senate Committee headed by Hugo Black, Senator from Alabama who later became a Supreme Court justice, investigated the publicity of the utilities and the activities of Lee's firm. The committee revealed that the firm was paid $5,000 a month for its work, but the investigation verified that no bribery, subsidy, or subterfuge had been used to tell the facts to the public.[8]

The Wheeler-Rayburn bill as it was finally passed by Congress, under the title of Utilities Holding Company Act of 1935, did not bring about Government ownership of public utilities, the worst fear of most utility executives. No doubt the bill was not harsher because Ivy Lee's advice had engendered better public understanding of the problems of the utilities. By the same token, understanding of the public point of view made the utilities executives increasingly face their responsibilities. The Wheeler-Rayburn bill brought many needed reforms to the utilities, enabling them to be among the first companies to pull out of the depression, and any public problems since then have been minor. Today they are among the most public relations minded of any business groups in America. With the utilities operating efficiently and in the public interest, there is less reason for any clamor for public ownership.

Lee's advice was not always right, it was not always taken, and the problems were not always solved. But for the most part his diagnosis was sound. Edward Bernays once commented that the difference between his public relations work and Lee's was that his was a science and Lee's was an art. Lee did not engage in much public opinion research, but he understood the problems and sought solutions by intuition and insight. One Pennsylvania Railroad executive, when asked why his company deferred to Lee's opinions, answered: "Because we have learned that, in certain matters, his opinion, based on long experience, is as valid as a fact tested by experiment."[9]

The railroads are the best example of Lee's accurate intuition and insights. In the 1960s the problems of railroads were of the same kind, if greater in degree, than they had been in Lee's day. Railroad historian John Stover has written that in the sixties the main problems were in four areas: public opinion, government relations, employee relations, and railroad management. Lee was intimately concerned with all of these. His central attention on public opinion was most important. And even in the 1960s, according to Stover, "to the extent that the railroad problem is political rather than technical, a public opinion that is at least neutral toward the railroads is absolutely essential."

Ivy Lee started the railroads on their campaign to understand and respect public opinion and to put forth their side of the story in an effort to neutralize conflict. Later, largely through the Association of American Railroads but also through each individual company, a continued campaign of public information and education has been carried out for this purpose.

Lee was able to make a significant contribution to the evolving relationship between railroads and utilities and the public because he understood the change that had come over America. "There was a time when railroad managers thought they were running a private business," he once said, "but they have come to find they are . . . running a business over which the public itself has assumed complete supervision and control." He told railroad executives that "the crowd is in the saddle, the people are on the job, and we must take consideration of those facts, whether we like them or not."[10]

---

[1] Recounted by Wisehart, op. cit.

[2] Ivy Lee, "The Technique of Publicity," *Electric Railway Journal*, Jan. 6, 1917, p. 17.

[3] Edward L. Bernays, *Public Relations* (Norman: University of Oklahoma Press, 1952), pp. 91, 96–97.

[4] Ivy Lee, *Publicity for Public Service Corporations*, pp. 1 ff.

[5] Ivy Lee, "What a Publicity Bureau Could Do," *Electric Railway Journal*, Aug. 18, 1917, pp. 265–267.

[6] Ivy Lee, "Publicity and Corporations," *Ivy Lee's Publicity Book*, p. 12, Ivy Lee Papers, Princeton.

[7] Quoted in Bronson Batchelor, *Profitable Public Relations* (New York: Harper & Bros., 1938), p. 190.

[8] *Editor & Publisher*, June 20, 1935, p. 12.

[9] Quoted by Wisehart, op. cit.

[10] Ivy Lee, *Publicity for Public Service Corporations*, frontispiece.

III

THE ROCKEFELLERS

"End of the Rear Door Philosophy"

11: THE "LUDLOW MASSACRE"

ONE DAY IN MAY OF 1914, while he was heavily engaged in fighting for the freight rate advance on behalf of the railroad industry, Ivy Lee received a call from John D. Rockefeller Jr., son of the greatest capitalist of them all, asking the publicist to meet him for a conference. Realizing the importance to his career of such an invitation, Lee dropped his railroad work in Philadelphia for the moment and went to New York.

"I feel that my father and I are much misunderstood by the press and the people of this country," said Rockefeller when the two met. "I should like to know what your advice would be about how to make our position clear."[1] This was, typically, an understatement. The Rockefeller name was being denounced from one end of the country to the other with unprecedented fervor, and the younger Rockefeller, who had managed to remain relatively free from earlier attacks on his father, was now the center of abuse. The new wave of resentment against both Rockefellers had its origins in the Colorado strike in general and the so-called "Ludlow Massacre" in particular.

The Colorado strike had begun on September 23, 1913, when about 9,000 coal miners walked out in the southern Colorado coal fields. The largest company involved in the strike was the Colorado

Fuel and Iron Company, of which the senior Rockefeller was principal stockholder. However, he had turned responsibility for the stock over to his son, who was held by many people to be personally responsible for the developments.

It was an age of conflict between employer and employee, an age which already had witnessed the rise of labor unions, the growth of socialist and communist movements. The United States Congress had set up the Commission on Industrial Relations in 1912 to investigate the problems of industry in the first decade of the twentieth century. According to George P. West, who wrote a summary of the Colorado strike for the Commission, it was the "most serious and most portentous...of all the conflicts between employers and workmen that occurred during the life of the commission." Furthermore, he said, it offered unequalled opportunity to study some of the 'major problems of industrial unrest.[2]

The Colorado strike involved a central issue of capitalistic democracy: the right of owners to run their businesses in their own way, without interference from their employees; and the right of workers to enjoy their full political and social rights, especially in situations where owners control the entire lives of workers. In the case of the Colorado Fuel and Iron Company, for instance, workers lived in company houses in a company town, bought their provisions in a company store, and when they voted, cast their ballots for candidates put up by the company. There was a one-way flow of information from company down to worker. The officials established no channels for communication from worker to company nor provision for relationship between the two.

Agitation by employees of the Colorado Fuel and Iron Company culminated in a strike in September; miners packed up their families and belongings, left company camps and moved into neighboring tent colonies set up by the United Mine Workers of America. Both sides were armed, and company guards were backed by deputy sheriffs. Gunfire started on October 17 when deputies drove an armored car through the tent colony, firing a machine gun that riddled the tents and killed several men. This brought about a general state of war, and the Colorado State Militia was called in to restore the peace.

Shortly thereafter the Commission on Industrial Relations began to investigate the strike. Meanwhile Rockefeller, as chief stockholder, was getting news about the strike from the company's officers, especially L. M. Bowers, chairman of the board, and J. F. Welborn, president. Both men convinced Rockefeller that "the workers were thoroughly satisfied with conditions in the mines and that the strike represented a vicious attempt on the part of the union to foment dissatisfaction, or if this failed, to intimidate workers into going on strike."[3] When Rockefeller was called to testify before the Commission toward the end of March 1914, he simply repeated what he had learned from the company officers and said he could do little but stand by those in charge of the company's affairs.

Many people charged him with "absentee capitalism." Just a few weeks later an event occurred that brought the entire public into the critic's circle. On April 20 an accidental shot started another battle, ending when several strikers and, more important, two women and eleven children had been killed. This was the "Ludlow Massacre" that sparked full combat. Mine structures were attacked and burned. Buildings were looted. The entire state was gripped with the fear of anarchy. Finally, the Governor's plea to President Wilson brought federal troops to the scene to stop what was officially declared a state of insurrection.

The attack on Rockefeller grew more bitter than ever before. William Green, an officer of the International United Mine Workers Union, telegraphed him to "stop killing of men, women, and children." Newspapers raged. The *Cleveland Press* wrote that "the charred bodies of two dozen women and children show that *Rockefeller knows how to win.*" Upton Sinclair staged a demonstration outside the Rockefeller home in Tarrytown. Mobs in the streets of New York listened to soap-box orators urge listeners to "shoot [Rockefeller] down like a dog." "Never before," said one of his biographers, "had the younger Rockefeller been so keenly and painfully aware of his isolation from the American public."[4]

Many people had offered advice to Rockefeller; others offered to sell out to him. He was told to buy great quantities of newspaper advertising space to counteract the wave of criticism. He was even urged to start a newspaper of his own. More devious, perhaps, were offers of help that came from such people as Elbert Hubbard, a magazine publisher and philosopher-of-sorts, who offered to devote an issue of his magazine to a Rockefeller defense if the Colorado Fuel and Iron Company would guarantee the purchase of thousands of copies for distribution. C. F. Carter, a journalist, offered to write a book clearing the Rockefeller name, again if the sale of a specified number of copies could be guaranteed.[5]

John D. Rockefeller Jr., suspicious about this kind of guidance, sought counsel from men who were sympathetic to his critics. He had known Arthur Brisbane from other associations and turned to him for help. Brisbane, son of a well-known socialist, Albert Brisbane, was famous in his own right as an editor of Pulitzer and Hearst newspapers in New York where he had become acquainted with Ivy Lee. Brisbane suggested Lee as a man who knew about public opinion and was completely honest.

When Rockefeller asked him what do, Lee responded that "the first and most important feature of any plan of publicity should be its absolute frankness; that there should be no devious ways employed." Lee bluntly said that newspaper advertising would be "in the highest degree unwise" and told him that "no money should be used in any way directly or indirectly to influence the attitude of the press." Rather, Lee urged, if the coal mine operators had a story to tell, "they ought to tell it themselves, and tell it frankly, and tell it fully."[6]

The younger Rockefeller agreed. "This is the first advice I have had that does not involve deviousness of one kind or another," he said. Lee, however, was engaged in the biggest job he had yet undertaken for the Pennsylvania Railroad. And when Rockefeller asked Samuel Rea, then the Pennsylvania's president, if he could borrow Lee's services for the time being, Rea refused, but would allow Lee to advise the Rockefellers so long as it did not interfere with his regular duties for the Pennsylvania.

The next seven months must have been the most hectic period yet for a man who had already lived an unusually eventful life. As his regular job Lee directed the publicity campaign for the railroad rate increase until December 1914, when the case was won by the roads. In his "spare time" he began the major battle for the Colorado mine operators.

By the beginning of June, only days after his first talk with Rockefeller, Lee had his basic campaign planned. He had asked to be put in touch with Welborn to get the mine operators' side of the story. Welborn in turn supplied him with material which unfortunately expressed management views so blatantly that it brought about one of the gravest errors of Lee's career.

At this moment the excitement in Colorado had died down; federal troops were maintaining order, and few newspaper stories were being written. Lee later told the Industrial Relations Commission that "it was obvious, therefore, that the newspapers would not print any information that would be given to them." So Lee planned the same kind of campaign he had waged for the railroads—material sent out to the opinion leaders of the country.[7]

In a long letter to Rockefeller on June 5, 1914, he outlined his plans for his new employer's approval. He suggested a series of bulletins entitled "The Struggle in Colorado for Industrial Freedom." (Meanwhile, the United Mine Workers of America brought out a pamphlet of their own entitled "The Ludlow Massacre.") Lee sent Rockefeller the galley proofs of the first bulletin and suggested the topic for the second. He would follow these with others of the same kind, "the idea being to make them all dignified, free from rancor, and based as far as possible upon documentary or other evidence susceptible of proof, if need be. The distribution of these through an extended period will, I am quite certain," he told Rockefeller, "create a great deal of discussion."[8]

The bulletins consisted primarily of press notices and articles on aspects of the Colorado situation that put the operators in a favorable light. These were supplied by a committee of mine operators including, besides Welborn, John C. Osgood and D. W. Brown, presidents of two other mining companies. Lee's work was primarily that of an editor. He chose the material, in some cases wrote introductory or transitional paragraphs, set the style for the bulletins and saw them through their printing.

The bulletins were sometimes loaded on one side, leaving the door open for criticism. Bulletin Number 8, for instance, contained a quotation from Mrs. Helen Grenfell, vice-president of the Law and Order League, to the effect that the Ludlow disaster was precipitated by the strikers, that the fire had been started accidentally by "an overturned stove or an explosion" and that the two women and eleven children were suffocated, not shot.

While in retrospect this appears to have been the truth, Lee did not include in the bulletin the fact that Mrs. Grenfell was the wife of a railroad executive and that the Law and Order League had been organized after the strike to counteract the effects of the prolabor Women's Peace Association.

Bulletin Number 11, entitled "How Colorado Editors View the Strike," contained statements from a report which vindicated the operators. The report was based on a conference held by the editors, but out of the 331 editors in the state, only fourteen took part in the conference and only eleven signed the report. All eleven were from papers controlled by the coal companies. These omissions provided open ground for critics.[9]

Most of the bulletins contained matter which on the surface was true but which presented the facts in such a way as to give a total picture that was false. The only sin of commission was in regard to salaries. From an annual report of the United Mine Workers, sent to Lee by the coal operators committee, he took the figures for the salaries of some of the prominent strikers. Somehow, what was meant to be a year's salary was translated into nine weeks' salary. The result was that the incomes of prominent strikers were listed as: Frank J. Hayes, salary and expenses for nine weeks, $5,720.12, or $90 a day; John McLennan, $66 a day; John R. Lawson, a nine weeks' salary of $1,772.40; Mother Jones, $2,668.62, or $42 a day, indicating that the strike leaders and the unions were profiteers.[10]

These bulletins were printed from material sent by the operators before Lee himself was able to go to Colorado and conduct his own investigation. Meanwhile, Rockefeller was growing wary of the information he was receiving from the mine officers and was anxious to send Lee on a trip through the mines as soon as the publicity advisor could get away from his work at the Pennsylvania Railroad. Rockefeller had also recently hired the Canadian industrial relations expert, Mackenzie King, later Prime Minister of Canada.

Lee had scheduled a vacation for August and was planning to take his family to Europe, but he sent them separately while he went out to Colorado to try to get at the heart of the problem. He found quickly that the reports sent by Bowers and Welborn had been biased and exaggerated and that in reality the officers did not have a progressive attitude toward labor-management conditions. From that time on he advised Rockefeller that changes had to be made in the company management.

Lee made a personal visit to the mines at Primero, Sugundo, Frederick, Sopris, Morley, Tabasco, and Berwind. He visited tent colonies at Starkville and Ludlow. He lunched with mine superintendents and with miners in their boarding houses. He talked with miners' wives, military officers, mine operators, politicians, and citizens of Colorado. He reported back to Rockefeller that public opinion was not with the operators, but he felt that the unions had overplayed their hand. The present sentiment, he told Rockefeller, was one of indifference toward the operators and latent hostility toward the miners' union. "Partly to meet this situation," he said, "we have arranged to put the names of the lawyers and clergymen of the state on our bulletin mailing list."[11]

He found that the name of Rockefeller roused hostility in many Coloradans, and he urged that this be combatted vigorously. "One way of doing this will be to publish a bulletin, detailing the relationship of yourself and your father to the CF&I," he wrote. He suggested that the Rockefellers have prepared and sent to Colorado a statement showing their entire holdings in CF&I, how much they paid and how much they had received from each class of security. "I want to contrast the amount paid to you with the amount put into the property out of earnings, showing your policy has been to build up the Company (and thereby to build up Colorado) rather than to get quick profits or to exploit the people here," he wrote.

Most important, he met with Welborn and Bowers personally and persuaded them to adopt a broad publicity policy toward both the employees and the public. Lee felt that the chief source of trouble had not been lack of sufficient pay but rather lack of a two-way communication. "The men are afraid to complain or appeal," he wrote to Rockefeller. "There is distinctly a missing link here. There is no safety valve for the men to get petty grievances out of their system." A policy of publicity, he felt, should be the initial move toward establishing better lines of communication.

"The first step in this direction is to be the placarding of a series of posters at each mine telling of the work of the Company and its relations with the men," he said. The first poster he prepared was an open letter from Welborn to the men, thanking them for their loyalty during the strike. Subsequent posters told of the end of the strike, gave facts and figures on exactly how much coal was being mined, expressed the desire of the company to treat all the men fairly, and invited them to send in their complaints. Lee also advised that leaflets be placed in the homes of the men, where the women would see them. "Women are voters in the state, and their influence is important in every way."

"I believe this publicity policy will be of substantial value *as a start* in getting the complete confidence of the miners and the public of this state," Lee wrote Rockefeller. But, "it is of the greatest importance that as early as possible some comprehensive plan be devised to provide machinery to redress grievances. Such provision would not only take the wind out of the Union sails but would appeal, I am confident, to the soundest public opinion."[12]

Gradually, thereafter, the wind did fall out of the union sails, and by December 1914, after the strike had dragged out for eight months, the men voted to go back to work. Without a doubt Lee's bulletins and posters had accomplished one of their purposes: they had created a "great deal of discussion." The public was talking about two sides of the issue, and opinion was already to some extent neutralized.

At this point, the United States Commission on Industrial Relations again came into the picture and made the whole affair a matter of record. The Commission was composed of nine persons representing employers and employees. But the chief counsel, Frank P. Walsh, was an undisguised partisan of the employees and was accused by many of conducting an inquisition of top industrialists rather than an investigation of the problem. The Commission turned to the Colorado strike as a prime example for its examination of the disturbed industrial situation.

John D. Rockefeller Jr. met with Ivy Lee and other members of his staff before he appeared as a witness on January 25, 1915. Lee's brother, Wideman, later told how, during the meeting, someone called to find out which entrance at the New York City Hall, where the hearing was scheduled, would be used by Rockefeller. Jerome Green, a staff member, replied automatically, "Oh, the rear door, of course." At this, according to his brother, Lee sprang to his feet. "The days of the rear door philosophy are over," he said. "Mr. Rockefeller will have to enter through the same door as everyone else."[13]

Rockefeller not only used the main entrance, but he walked down the center aisle of the crowded courtroom—somewhat nervously, no doubt—shaking hands with such famed strikers as

Mother Jones, and pleasantly greeting others who had vigorously denounced him. Mrs. Bella Zilberman, who had been arrested a year earlier for picketing the Standard Oil building, came forward to shake hands with Rockefeller, and Mrs. Gertrude Wilde Klein, a unionist, started a discussion with him. During a recess, the capitalist even managed to joke with reporters about their weariness at having to listen to him again. When asked about his relationship to publicists and propagandists, Rockefeller told the courtroom that "if a publicity agent would not tell the whole truth, I would not want him near me."[14]

All in all, the overwhelmingly hostile courtroom was completely disarmed by Rockefeller's behavior. Instead of making Rockefeller the star witness, the investigators focused on Ivy Lee, the publicist behind the capitalist. Lee was on the witness stand on January 27 and 28, 1915, in New York, and on May 22 and 25, 1915, in Washington. Throughout the testimony, Walsh attempted to show that Lee was an important and mysterious force behind the scenes, nefariously manipulating the railroads, the Rockefellers, and the coal mine operators.

The Commission, Walsh contended, was making an effort to fix the responsibility for the industrial situation in Colorado and elsewhere. Since Rockefeller had vastly greater wealth and influence, he was the most significant factor as far as stockholders were concerned. Now Walsh wanted to determine who was responsible for Rockefeller, "whether the action taken by Mr. Rockefeller is really his action and the statements made by him are really his statements, or yours, for instance," Walsh told Lee on the stand.[15]

Lee replied that his view of his job was that he was simply an advisor and his advice was to tell the truth. He did not follow "the old theory of a publicity agent" which was to take what his employers gave him to the press and then to use his influence to get it published. This, he said, "was totally foreign to my idea. My idea is that the principal himself should be his own publicity agent. That the function of a person like myself, for example, when acting in that capacity, should be to advise with the man who is to take the responsibility for the act itself as to what he should do and what he should say."[16]

When asked just how much Rockefeller accepted this counsel, Lee answered: "I have never known a man to be more careful and more conscientious and more painstaking about scrutinizing every line that went out over his name, whether he wrote it or whether somebody else assisted in writing it or not."[17]

Lee's contention that he was an independent advisor with no axe to grind except his policy of truth to win public goodwill seemed to be borne out by the Lee-Rockefeller correspondence, subpoenaed by the Committee and made part of the record. In one letter, for instance, he had sent Rockefeller a copy of an important speech he had delivered to the American Railway Guild, "desiring as I do that you should understand some of the ideas by which I work."[18]

In another exchange of letters, Rockefeller had asked Lee's advice on the suggestion that Lee personally refute misstatements of fact every time such appeared in print. Lee answered that he felt "constructive, positive publicity was of more importance." The subpoenaed correspondence showed that Lee had vetoed the suggestion that Rockefeller buy Elbert Hubbard magazines in return for a sympathetic article. "You will realize," he had written to Rockefeller, "that up to the present time it has been the theory of the bulletins that they be confined to statements of fact from sources or people in Colorado itself." Lee had been blunt about his policy of buying favors from no one. He had told Rockefeller that

Hubbard might go out to Colorado and write an article after seeing the situation but that it should be made clear that Hubbard was on his own initiative and at his own expense.[19]

The results of the testimony showed for the most part that Lee had been pursuing his policy of advising Rockefeller to tell the truth and reshape his management to be acceptable to public opinion. The one instance which the Commission could pinpoint where that policy had not been followed was the error in the bulletins about the union workers' salaries, and that mistake damaged Lee's entire position. It was the only untruth which the Commission on Industrial Relations could attribute to Lee during the investigation and Walsh grilled him long and hard about the matter.

According to Lee's version of the story, the first fifteen bulletins had been put together into a booklet entitled *The Facts Concerning the Struggle in Colorado for Industrial Freedom*. This was printed in Philadelphia "in order that the typography might be as effective as possible." But the bulletins and addressed envelopes were sent in bulk to Denver, where they were mailed individually "if they met the approval of the operators...in order that the full responsibility for the bulletins should be placed upon the operators."

While the bulletins were en route to Denver, Lee said he received a telegram from Welborn saying there was an error in one of the bulletins and asking whether it could be corrected in the completed pamphlet. Lee said he wired back about October 1 that, since the pamphlet was already on its way, he suggested an errata slip be printed in Denver and enclosed with the pamphlets when sent out. I did not know what the error was," he testified. "It never occurred to me that it was an error of any consequence."

Even though the telegram had been sent about October 1, the error was not corrected until January 1, and by that time the damage had been done. As a result of the testimony it was difficult for members of the Commission to agree that Lee's policy had been wholly one of telling the truth. Commissioner Austin B. Garretson brought the hearing room to laughter after the testimony about the error when he asked of Lee: "Your mission was that of the average publicity agent, was it not, to give the truth as the man you were serving saw it?"

"That would be a characterization on your part, Mr. Garretson," Lee replied.[20] But the Commissioner had made his point. Lee had made the grave error of initially accepting and circulating as true all facts and figures given him by the mine operators. It got headlines across the nation and won him the nickname of "Poison Ivy." It stuck in people minds, and the lesson was unforgettable to Lee.

The month of December 1914 was climactic in the career of Ivy Lee. The freight rate advance was passed by the Interstate Commerce Commission. The Colorado strike came to an end. And within a month, the Congressional Commission had revealed to the whole world that Ivy Lee had been personally responsible for those momentous developments. Finally, the Commission hearings revealed that Ivy Lee was now the right-hand man to senior John D. Rockefeller himself. In the popular mind, Lee became the man behind the scenes manipulating the world's greatest industrialists and solving their problems.

Several months after the investigation of the Colorado strike, Ivy Lee suggested to John D. Rockefeller Jr. that he go to Colorado to see for himself at firsthand the conditions of the mine employees as Lee had done. The unprecedented trip proved to be a landmark in public relations. For two weeks Rockefeller visited mining camps, talked with the miners, went to their homes, met their wives and children, and even attended their social functions. At one social affair, after giving a short talk, he suggested that the floor be cleared for a dance, and he ended the evening only after dancing with almost every miner's wife present. It was an extraordinary performance for the shy and serious-minded Rockefeller.

"You ought to have seen the newspaper men run for the phones when the dance began," an aide to Mackenzie King later said. "But that incident, and the publicity that was given to it throughout the state, was more effective in fostering good-will than a dozen speeches or conferences."[21] When Rockefeller returned to New York, Lee helped him draft a plan of employee representation which provided for adjusting the grievances and improving the working conditions of the miners. It was overwhelmingly accepted by the workers in a formal vote.

In the years that followed, John D. Rockefeller Jr. acquired a wide reputation as a "new voice in industrial relations." Under Ivy Lee's counsel, he gave speeches, wrote magazine articles, and even authored a book, all on the theme central to Lee's ideas of public relations: the need to create a more personal relationship between capital and labor. "The Colorado strike was one of the most important things that ever happened to the Rockefeller family," John D. Jr. said years later, and he expressed gratitude to his public relations advisor for the important role he had played in that momentous crisis."[22]

---

[1] Quoted in Wisehart, op. cit., p. 126.

[2] George P. West, *Report on the Colorado Strike* (Washington, D.C.: Commission on Industrial Relations, 1915), p. 5.

[3] Quoted in Raymond B. Fosdick, *John D. Rockefeller Jr., A Portrait* (New York: Harper & Bros., 1956), p. 146.

[4] Ibid., pp. 151–53.

[5] Rockefeller-Lee correspondence, in U.S. Congress, Senate, Commission on Industrial Relations, *Final Report and Testimony*, Vol. IX, pp. 8871–8881.

6 Ibid., Vol. VIII, p. 7899.

7 Ibid.

8 Ibid., Vol. IX, p. 8867.

9 George Creel, "Poisoners of Public Opinion," *Harper's Weekly*, Nov. 7, 1914, p. 436.

10 U.S. Congress, Senate, Commission on Industrial Relations, op. cit., Vol. VIII, p. 7908.

11 Ivy Lee to John D. Rockefeller Jr., Aug. 16, 1914, p. 3., Rockefeller Archives, New York.

12 Ibid.

13 Quoted in Berlin, op. cit., p. 80–81.

14 *New York Times*, Jan. 28, 1915, p. 4.

15 U. S. Congress, Senate, Commission on Industrial Relations, op. cit., Vol. IX, p. 8718.

16 Ibid., Vol. VIII, p. 7911.

17 Ibid., Vol. IX, p. 8718.

18 Ibid., p. 8871.

19 Ibid., p. 8881.

20 Ibid., Vol. VIII, pp. 7899–7910.

21 Quoted in R. B. Fosdick, op. cit., p. 162.

22 Ibid., p. 167. See also John D. Rockefeller Jr. to Mrs. Ivy Lee, Aug. 26, 1936, Rockefeller Archives, New York.

Ray Eldon Hiebert

12: DIMES FOR HUMAN INTEREST

Ivy Lee's handling of the Colorado strike was so successful that he won the attention and interest of John D. Rockefeller Sr., at that time thought to be so insulated from the world that nobody could approach him. John D.'s son persuaded him to listen to Lee, because he felt Lee's ideas would be as valuable to the head of the family as they had been to him.

Until January 1, 1915, Lee was still technically employed by the Pennsylvania, although he had been working almost completely for John D. Jr. On the first of the year he officially resigned from the railroad, with public expressions of regret from both sides, and formally joined the personal staff of John D. Rockefeller Sr. His position in the empire was made clear in a letter the elder Rockefeller sent to Senate Committee Chairman Walsh: "In compliance with your request...the present members of my personal staff are my son John D. Rockefeller Jr., Starr J. Murphy, and Ivy L. Lee."[1] The boy from Georgia had reached rarified atmosphere.

He moved his office back to New York to be close to the Rockefellers and their interests. Ironically, his departure from the Pennsylvania caused the railroad some unfair publicity when newspapers accused it of being owned by the Rockefellers since one of its officers had stepped into the Rockefeller problem in Colorado. Other observers felt that the appointment was unfortunate because Lee's relationship with Rockefeller would only bring further opprobrium to the name.

For Lee, the elder Rockefeller was a classic example of an industrialist who needed counseling in public relations. From his earliest life the senior Rockefeller had a facility for organizing men; he used this talent to create an oil industry, and in the process—

because of the industrial revolution, the machine, the automobile, and the new need for oil and gasoline—he became one of the wealthiest men in history. But he had shunned publicity at all costs and had done nothing to take the public into his confidence.

At the same time, Rockefeller was generous as well as shrewd. Since his youth he had regularly contributed a significant portion of his income to his church and other charities. As he grew wealthier he gave larger shares of his money away. When he retired from active business in 1896 he brought the same talent for organization to his philanthropies that he had brought to the oil industry. As a result, the $550 million he gave away in his lifetime was not wasted on lost causes but was intelligently directed to improving the lives of people all over the world.

Prior to the second decade of the twentieth century, however, these facts were not commonly known, primarily because Rockefeller cared little for what the public thought and never took the trouble to correct inaccuracies and misconceptions. By nature, he was quiet and reserved, and business and family burdens made him further withdrawn and reticent. As a result few people really knew the man, and the popular press thrived on misconceptions.

Few people thought of Rockefeller as a human being, but only as a billion-dollar machine that crushed everything in its path. He was pictured as a stingy old man who would step on anyone to make another dollar. He was commonly described as morose and mean, fearful of being attacked by people he had ruined, and ringed by bodyguards. When he gave sizable sums to church or charity, it became "tainted money" with which he was seeking to salve his guilty conscience. Nevertheless, Rockefeller maintained a policy of silence. He didn't even announce his retirement, and years after he was no longer active in Standard Oil, he was still being blamed for actions with which he had little connection.

When the president of Rochester University, a political economist, offered to write a text in 1884 that would show that petroleum products were cheaper and better because of the organization that Rockefeller had brought to the industry, Rockefeller turned him down partly because he did not want the man to be attacked for his association with the industrialist. "You know that great prejudice exists against all successful business enterprises," Rockefeller wrote, "the more successful, the greater the prejudice."

In 1884 a woman wanted to write a short biography of Rockefeller for a magazine series devoted to eminent Americans. She requested an interview because "it is a good thing for the *world* to know that the *President* of the *great* Standard Oil Company is a *Christian*, a gentleman, an earnest *temperate* man, and generous in all good works." To this Rockefeller replied firmly: "In accordance with a decision reached some time since, I have declined to allow anything to be written in the manner as suggested, but I appreciate the kindness of my friends desiring to say something favorable for me and that might be helpful to others."[2]

Press abuse of Rockefeller hit its full stride with the muckrakers after the turn of the century. Chief among writers who exposed him was Ida M. Tarbell; her *History of Standard Oil*, published serially in *McClure's* between 1902 and 1904, provided factual proof that the capitalist was devoid of ethical considerations, that he would stop at nothing, not even the ruin of his friends, to create an oil monopoly. Another muckraker, Thomas W. Lawson, created a popular sensation with his attack on Rockefeller in *Frenzied Finance*, which appeared serially in 1904 in *Everybody's* magazine. Across the land, newspaper articles and editorials struck out at him as the "Robber Baron" and "The Great Octopus." It was not long before Standard Oil was in court, and Judge K. M. Landis handed down the famous decision fining the oil corporation $29 million for violations of the antitrust act.

The story is told that John D. was playing golf when news came of the court action. A messenger handed him a yellow envelope and received a dime from Rockefeller, who proceeded to read the message without a change of expression and returned to his golf. One of his partners, a Standard executive, blurted out, "How much is the fine?" Rockefeller, concentrating on his game, murmured, "twenty-nine million dollars," and proceeded to drive a long shot down the center of the fairway. He reportedly finished nine holes with a score of 53, lowest he had ever made.[3]

Rockefeller had often been advised to end his policies of silence and aloofness. His son did not believe in them, and some of his former associates at Standard Oil were against them. In 1905 Standard had given in and hired a press agent, J. I. C. Clarke, a former reporter on the *New York Herald*. Clarke opened the doors to reporters, but he remained little more than a press agent for the company, not for the Rockefeller family. Standard Oil's press agentry and publicity were of the nineteenth century variety, not Ivy Lee's type. The company resorted to bribery to battle the bad press it was receiving. John D. Archbold, vice-president of Standard, was accused of spending thousands of dollars buying off magazines. And that only led to further trouble. The Hearst papers did some bribing of their own and got hold of letters showing how Archbold was trying to bribe not only the press but, as the antitrust suit came to a head, legislators as well.

From 1905 to 1915 the elder Rockefeller had opened up a bit. He appeared in public, allowed an occasional interview, permitted his few speeches to be republished, even gave his "reminiscences" to the magazine *World's Work*, which published them serially and then in book form. But while he had organized great industries and great charities, Rockefeller brought no great organizational innovation to publicizing his endeavors; he was content to leave the full story to history. The history that was being written by the popular press was severe, and the Rockefellers refused to bribe or cajole their way out of it. Allan Nevins later wrote that "the wide acceptance of Miss Tarbell's 'character study' was largely the result of Rockefeller's refusal to countenance any reply.... Along a lengthening shadow, the policy of silence was responsible for misunderstanding, suspicion, and hatred."[4]

The shadow grew longer still in 1915 with the Colorado strike. But men like Lee and Mackenzie King were beginning to offer suggestions for dissipating the darkness, and the Rockefellers were wise enough to listen. Two other men, George Vincent, head of the Chautauqua Institute, and Raymond Fosdick, a New York attorney, served with Lee and King after 1915 as a sort of public relations council to guide the Rockefeller interests in an enlightened manner.

King, a labor relations expert, was influential in persuading the Rockefellers to take a more personal and human interest in the affairs of their businesses, an idea basic to Lee's entire philosophy. Lee became a close personal friend of King's and a close confidant even after King became Prime Minister of Canada in 1921.

Lee undertook the job of publicizing the human nature of the Rockefellers with perhaps even more enthusiasm than he had devoted to the same job on behalf of the railroads. Shortly after he joined the Rockefeller staff in 1915 the Walsh committee, grilling him about the Colorado strikes, asked about his new relationship:

Walsh: What are your duties as a member of the personal staff of John D. Rockefeller Sr.?

Lee: I represent Mr. Rockefeller on various boards of directors and have intrusted to me various confidential matters relating to a great many of his interests, as much as my time will allow me to take care of. I have very little to do with publicity, as a matter of fact.

Walsh: Well, have you given up the publicity idea altogether? That is, as to circulating alleged facts with reference to their industries, and all that?

Lee: I have not given up the idea of publicity, because I believe that publicity is the biggest idea that we can develop. I believe that the great fault committed by the Rockefeller interests in the past has been the absence of publicity.

Walsh: So you are an advocate of their giving everything the widest publicity?

Lee: Absolutely; every chance that develops. I believe that they ought to make known to the public their business and feelings and any facts about their affairs that they feel the public should be interested in.[5]

Lee found it easy to consult with the Rockefellers on bridging the communication gap between them and the public. He later told his friend Pen Dudley that the Rockefellers were a very human group of businessmen who in no way held themselves remote from others and were profoundly disturbed at finding their operations misunderstood and themselves distrusted by their fellows.

In spite of Rockefeller's long history of silence, he cooperated with Lee. He realized most men of extensive business had difficulty keeping in step with the people and he knew one of his greatest needs was to be closely associated with someone who was not only sensitive to public reactions and attitudes but able to reflect them accurately. He told Lee that he should not spare any Rockefeller feelings but at all times report the facts exactly as he found them.

Lee felt that the supreme power of the elder Rockefeller's mind was that it was an instrument of judgment rather than creativity. Almost never, Lee said, would Rockefeller put forward his own ideas. Rather, he would listen to his advisers and, with uncanny judgment, choose the way that was successful.

Lee told the story of how he would spend a great length of time explaining in minute detail a particular policy. Rockefeller would then ask him to give all the reasons on the other side why such a policy should not be adopted, and he would not act unless Lee was able to present both sides of the argument.

Lee embarked on a program of letting the world know about the Rockefeller philanthropic activities. "You doubtless saw the announcement we made Saturday relating to the Rockefeller Institute," Lee wrote the younger Rockefeller in July 1914. "I enclose a copy of it for your information, together with a number of newspaper clippings showing the way in which it was handled." He proposed to Rockefeller that this activity should continue. "We are planning to make an appropriate announcement next Monday regarding the transfer of the money to Johns Hopkins University," he wrote. "I am making a study of the work of the General Education Board, as well as that of the Rockefeller Institute, and will no doubt be able to formulate, a little later, more detailed plans for continued publicity for that organization."[6]

Lee knew that by making a feature story out of Rockefeller charities, he would have no trouble getting newspaper space. After releasing the Johns Hopkins gift story to the press, he was pleased with the resulting publicity, which he sent on to Rockefeller with this comment: "In view of the fact that this was not really news, and that the newspapers gave so much attention to it, it would seem that this was wholly due to the manner in which the material was 'dressed up' for newspaper consumption. It seems to suggest very considerable possibilities along this line."[7]

The younger Rockefeller was gratified with the results. He had seen the newspaper articles, he wrote, but he had not known where they had come from. Several times he wrote with a tone of surprise and pleasure: "The articles are generally excellent.... Let the good work go on."[8] But Lee soon discovered it was so easy to get publicity for a Rockefeller gift that there was a danger in creating an image in the public mind of Rockefellers as loud-mouthed breast-beaters. He thenceforth advised the Rockefellers to cease announcing their gifts, allowing the recipients to make a public announcement in their own way if they desired.

Lee continued to make sure that other worthwhile and interesting activities of the Rockefellers were brought to public attention. Features were prepared on Rockefeller playing golf, talking with neighbors, going to church. When World War I burst on the scene Rockefeller's contributions to the war effort were increased and statements were released from Rockefeller urging all to get behind the country. When twenty-five men from the Rockefeller estate enlisted in the army, it made news stories in the nation's papers.

Rockefeller birthdays were especially good for feature material, invariably producing stories and pictures in newspapers around the world. When the elder Rockefeller reached his ninetieth birthday in 1929 Lee wrote to the son, John D. Jr., that if he could only get his father to permit one more interview, "I know the country would read it with the greatest interest. The interview could be so written that it would bring forth the most charming reaction."[9]

As the number of birthdays increased, the sympathy of the reaction multiplied. Indeed, Rockefeller became a leading subject of newspaper human interest stories. The irony of the world's richest man living on a strict diet made the Sunday supplements. And of course when he passed out dimes, it made the feature pages of the world's newspapers.

The dime episode was perhaps the most curious publicity that came out of Lee's relationship with the Rockefellers. According to Rockefeller biographer Nevins, it first attracted press attention during World War I when Rockefeller purchased a home in Florida, "The Casements," near Ormond. Despite his age, his health and spirits were excellent and he began to enjoy getting out in a crowd. According to Nevins, he attended the Ormond Union Church on Sunday and after the services he stood on the lawn and distributed bright new dimes to the Sunday School children. However, the origin of the practice of giving away dimes is not certain. It has been said that Rockefeller started giving away dimes as tips to his golf caddies. And someone has suggested that he first started giving away nickels but changed to dimes because they were lighter.

In any case, many people scorned the practice as a publicity stunt and attributed it to Ivy Lee. The myth grew, especially at the hands of publicists who were anxious to use the dime episode as a simple object lesson in the effectiveness of publicity. The story was that Lee arranged for Rockefeller to hand out the dimes, and by this simple expedient, according to publicity experts, the fact that "Rockefeller was a human being was established with the American people. Ivy Lee humanized the Midas of his day, and he did it with dimes," wrote the author of a widely read publicity textbook.[10]

Actually Lee probably did not invent the dime idea. His son, Ivy Lee Jr., Thomas Ross, and many others close to him have denied that he was solely responsible. More likely, as Nevins suggests, Rockefeller spontaneously gave away some dimes and found that it was a "rite that put people in good humor, bridged awkward moments, and enabled him to point a lesson in thrift." He enjoyed the act for the rest of his life.[11]

Whether Lee was responsible or not, he was the catalytic agent that spurred the activity and stirred the press. From this action, popularized throughout the world, the Rockefellers emerged as real and understandable human beings. The important thing about these human interest stories was their inherent truth. There was no exaggeration, whitewashing, or distortion as practiced by some theatrical press agents or circus publicists to get newspaper space for their clients. The Rockefellers were thrifty above all else, and the giving away of dimes was simply a dramatic illustration of the fact that they recognized the value of even this small amount of money.

As for the Rockefeller thrift, Lee was fond of telling of a time when he drove out to Pocantico Hills one evening with John D. Jr. for a discussion with the father. As they were leaving late at night, the elder Rockefeller noticed that both men were lightly dressed for a long ride in the open roadster. He brought out several of his famous paper waistcoats, but both declined, saying they were already well equipped for the ride. The old gentleman put his hands on a shoulder of each and said: "Boys, let me give you a piece of advice. Don't ever be afraid of a surplus."

The Rockefellers were thrifty in their relationships with their employees, including Lee—not parsimonious but realistic. When Lee joined the Rockefeller staff on a full-time basis, he was paid $1,000 a month, a handsome salary for 1916, but not what one would expect for one of the three personal staff members of the world's richest man. Later, Lee was given a $1,000 monthly retainer, but that was a smaller amount than he got for less work from other clients.

When Lee performed a special job, John D. Jr. would give him a fee beyond the retainer. Lee never suggested a figure and would take whatever Rockefeller decided was proper. After his work on the Teapot Dome scandal (discussed later) J.D.R. Jr. sent him a check for $10,000, a good fee but not an overly generous one. On the other hand, Lee's relationship with the Rockefellers undoubtedly brought hundreds of thousands of dollars worth of other accounts to his firm.

As the Rockefeller public reputation visibly improved, the family came to depend more on Ivy Lee and gradually exchanged their previous policies of silence for those of constructive action, including the correction of misconceptions. In 1924 the elder Rockefeller wrote to his son: "In some of the papers we notice from time to time the statement that after I had accumulated the great fortune I began to give it away. I think that gradually, and carefully, through Mr. Lee...this should be corrected, and made to appear as it really was, that in the beginning of getting of money, away back in my childhood, I began giving it away, and continued increasing the gifts as the income increased and that it was a work of my whole business career and not of the last end."[12]

The Rockefellers had come to depend on Ivy Lee for their public image, even though he had not remained in their full-time employ. In 1915 Lee tendered his resignation so he could set up his own independent consulting office—the only way he could operate in a true public relations sense.

"What's the matter, aren't we paying you enough?" asked the elder Rockefeller.

"On the contrary," Lee replied, "I never expected to be surrounded by so much visible evidence of wealth. I'm afraid that I'll become so conditioned to it all that in five years I'll be too timid to give you my real opinions, for fear of losing my job." He explained that in his own company, "I'll never be entirely dependent on any one, and will be in a position to give advice no matter how unpalatable."[13]

After establishing his agency he continued to advise the Rockefeller family and their interests until his own death. He served on boards, committees, and staffs, always representing and protecting the public reputation of the Rockefellers. After Lee's death, his firm continued the relationship until the deaths of both Rockefellers, the elder in the thirties and John D. Jr. in 1960.

---

[1] U.S. Congress, Senate, Commission on Industrial Relations, op. cit., Vol. IX, p. 8462.

[2] Quoted in Allan Nevins, *Study in Power: John D. Rockefeller* (New York: Charles Scribner's Sons, 1953), Vol. I, pp. 332–333.

[3] Albert H. Carr, *John D. Rockefeller's Secret Weapon* (New York: McGraw-Hill, 1962), p. 150.

[4] Nevins, op. cit., Vol. II, p. 350.

[5] U.S. Congress, Senate, Commission on Industrial Relations, op.cit., Vol. IX, p. 8855.

[6] Ibid., p. 8890.

[7] Ibid., p. 8875.

[8] Ibid., p. 8876. See also letter, p. 8869.

[9] Ivy Lee to John D. Rockefeller Jr., July 1, 1929, Rockefeller Archives, New York.

[10] Herbert M. Baus, *Publicity in Action* (New York: Harper & Bros., 1954), p. 294.

[11] Nevins, op. cit., Vol. II, p. 414.

[12] John D. Rockefeller Sr. to John D. Rockefeller Jr., July 25, 1924, Rockefeller Archives, New York.

[13] Quoted by Merryle S. Rukeyser, International News Service correspondent, undated clipping, Ivy Lee Papers, Princeton.

13: PLAYING NO FAVORITES

AFTER ESTABLISHING HIS OWN AGENCY, Lee considered the Rockefeller family his number one client and was acutely aware of carrying the full responsibility for their public relationships. "I do want you to feel," he wrote to John D. Rockefeller Jr., "that you can go away with full assurance that all your interests, insofar as I am watching out for them, are in good shape and receiving adequate attention."[1]

Perhaps his most important contribution during his 20 years with the Rockefellers was his careful tending of the fertile Fourth Estate. He was an anxious gardener of the press, pruning and clipping, urging the growth of strong stories in one plot and stamping out poisonous news in another. A bad weed sprouted suddenly early in 1920 when the Hearst papers carried a story telling how the "stingy" Rockefeller paid slave wages to his servants at Pocantico Hills. Rockefeller suggested to Lee that he prepare a public statement refuting the Hearst story.

Lee immediately saw that such action would alienate the reporters and editors. He suggested instead that a memorandum be prepared and privately sent to Arthur Brisbane and the Hearst organization "as to exactly what the facts are so as to save them perhaps from referring to the matter again in this inaccurate way."[2] The press saved face, the story was not picked up by other papers, and it did not attract much attention.

In another episode of potentially bad publicity, the Teapot Dome affair in which the Rockefellers had become unwittingly entangled, the situation was so explosive that had only a part of the story been told, it would have damaged the Rockefeller reputation and perhaps public interests. Lee advised that the press would get some of the facts sooner or later anyway, so he notified all the papers that Rockefeller had an important statement and they should send their best reporters. At this conference Rockefeller Jr. told the entire story. However, because of conditions in Standard Oil which he could not control, he could not yet make any public statement but said, "I am going to leave this entirely to your own sense of responsibility as to what is wise and in the public interest in this situation to be published." All the reporters treated the facts with discretion.[3]

Lee explained in the beginning that he must be fully and quickly informed of all developments concerning the Rockefellers and their activities. Although the family took Lee into their confidence, he sometimes was caught between the Rockefellers and rumors. Early in 1924, for instance, a report suddenly went over the nation that John D. Sr., then 85, had died at his home in Ormond. The newspapers could not confirm this and editors around the country kept Ivy Lee's telephone ringing most of the night. Lee was at a loss because he could not contact the Rockefellers himself to get confirmation of the report, but he felt sure that the family would have informed him had something happened, so he told the newspapers it was probably a rumor and nothing was published.

Lee later told John D. Jr. that newspapers did not publish the rumors only because the editors "were sufficiently sure of the likelihood of my knowing about it if it were true to accept my statement and let the matter drop." Such situations, he said, came up constantly and could be handled effectively only if he had complete information so the press would come to trust his judgment. "I want," he said, "to be in a position to be very frank at all times with the newspapers," and he insisted therefore that he always be "one of the first to be advised" on all developments.[4]

Lee also insisted that Rockefeller meet with members of the press from time to time. He spent a great deal of his energy and ingenuity restraining the press, but he could keep the goodwill of reporters and editors only if on occasion Rockefeller acceded to their wishes. "I have kept a vast horde of people away from you for many months past," he wrote to J.D.R. Jr. "Hardly a day goes past but somebody wants to get an interview with you."[5]

On many occasions he urged Rockefeller to allocate some time to the press. "Both these people," he once wrote about two New York reporters, "are pressing me very hard to get this promptly, so if it is possible I would appreciate it if you could arrange to give a half hour, say, to each one.... If you cannot arrange a half hour, fifteen minutes would, I think, accomplish all that is necessary." Sometimes he soft-pedaled the demands of reporters and presented them to Rockefeller in a more palatable form. He told Rockefeller that one reporter wanted "to write a sort of character story and simply have contact with your personality...so you need have no anxiety about anything you say being quoted."[6]

Most of the reporters who were assigned to write about the Rockefellers came to depend upon Lee for accurate and complete statements of their subject's opinions. They frequently allowed Lee to review their work and check it for accuracy or taste, an indication of how far many of them had come to trust Lee's relationship with the press and the Rockefellers. In such cases Lee was most discreet in making suggestions about fact or taste, bending over backwards to avoid any implication of censorship or dictatorial methods.

For instance, a play was submitted to Lee in which the leading character was modeled after John D. Sr. It was a sympathetic treatment in which the protagonist was an oil millionaire who spent time trying to find out how his workers lived. The only feeling Lee had was that the play unnecessarily identified Rockefeller as the prototype and that it would be a better play if the principal was more a composite of prominent businessmen. "Could you not revise your play to accommodate this suggestion," Lee wrote to Brock Pemberton, the author, "without in any way impairing its dramatic value?"[7]

A large part of his work for the Rockefellers consisted of analyzing editorial sentiment and news coverage and sending the clippings to the Rockefellers. This was handled by Lee's office staff, but he would make the reports to the Rockefellers himself. Lee got them to adopt a policy of answering editorials with a letter of acknowledgment. If the editorial was good, John D. Jr. would thank the editors for their courtesy. If it was unfavorable, he would acknowledge the expression and make a courteous but firm statement of whatever he felt the true facts were. These letters were prepared in Lee's office but signed by John D. Jr. himself.

Perhaps the chief reason why Lee was able to keep the goodwill of the press was that he persuaded Rockefeller to play absolutely no favorites and give out no exclusives. If one newspaper got a story, all newspapers should get the story. This appealed to the newsman's sense of fair play and allayed his fear of being scooped by the opposition. And it was always a good rationalization for not allowing a lone reporter to interview the boss. Instead, when the demands were great enough, a press conference was held with representatives of all the papers.

At times, however, this policy backfired and Lee was criticized for spoiling exclusives. The most vehement criticism of this sort came during the Abby Rockefeller courtship in 1925. Miss Abby had been arrested on a traffic charge and the family hired a young attorney, David Milton, to handle her case. He won a suspended sentence for her and the story was in all the newspapers. A few months later Hearst's *New York American* received a tip that Miss Abby, after an apparently secret romance, was to be married to Milton. The Hearst paper sent its best reporter, Henry Doherty, to the Rockefeller home to check on the rumor. When Doherty arrived, Mrs. Rockefeller was giving a reception and could not see him; instead, she apparently sent a message scribbled on the back of a letter telling the reporter to go to 111 Broadway and see Ivy Lee.

Doherty caught a cab back downtown to the Lee office and, on his way, examined the letter on which Mrs. Rockefeller had written the note. To his surprise, so the story goes, he found that the letter was from a family friend congratulating Miss Abby on her pending marriage to Milton. That should have been proof enough, but Doherty continued to the Lee office where he demanded confirmation from the publicist. As soon as Lee saw that Doherty had the facts of the Abby-Milton courtship, he immediately called all other papers and gave them the news so it would not appear that the Rockefellers had played favorites. The cry of foul went up from Doherty and the Hearst papers for spoiling a scoop.

The story has several versions, but in any circumstance it is a bit suspect.[8] It seems unlikely that Mrs. John D. Rockefeller Jr. would have given a reporter a letter from a friend, and it is equally unlikely that a Hearst reporter would have sought further confirmation if he had had such a letter. Nevertheless, it was true that Lee frequently spoiled an exclusive about the Rockefellers by insisting on equal treatment of the press.

The entire matter of the Abby Rockefeller wedding was a difficult exercise in press and public relations. Every reporter and every photographer wanted a front row seat, as did thousands of those listed in the Social Register to whom an invitation was a symbol of social approval. Lee made elaborate arrangements with the press, handing out one invitation to each newspaper, assigning reporters a separate section in the church, and providing them with a logical and careful explanation of the family's reasons for imposing detailed restrictions on the activities of the press. Most newsmen accepted the explanations, understood the problems, and abided by the rules. Lee later told J.D.R. Jr. that he was "perfectly delighted with the way in which the newspapers have handled this matter."

Lee was of course greatly concerned with the reaction of the general public to the wedding and he devoted considerable attention to the effect the stories of the wedding could have on the reader in the street. He felt it was of the greatest importance to avoid any show of "gorgeousness" or give any impression which would suggest "regality." For this reason he refused to let the photographers take pictures of Abby in her wedding gown and he refused to give the press details about gifts. He was able to achieve his purposes, he explained afterwards to Rockefeller, because he had given the newspapers names of prominent people and other substantial material "in such quantities and of such quality that they could not be ignored—thus absorbing the space that would otherwise be occupied by embellishments that we did not want."

Both press relations and public relations of the wedding turned out to be harmonious, giving, as Lee said, "Abby and David a happy public atmosphere in which to start their married life." He insisted that the wedding also provided "a further revelation to the public of the attitude of John D. and Mrs. Rockefeller toward life itself."[9] The Rockefellers greatly appreciated Lee's work and sent him a warm note of thanks. "We do not see how a more accurate and favorable public impression could have been given," J.D.R. Jr. wrote. He said that many of their friends had the highest praise for Lee's careful planning and wise handling of the wedding.[10]

As J.D.R. Sr. grew older, the newspapers pressed him even more for interviews and exclusives. Photographers especially wanted his picture and gathered around him every time he appeared in public. "On arrival of our train in Ormond," he complained to his son, "we were greatly annoyed by having a large number of photographers and movie cameramen taking pictures as we alighted, with none of whom we had had acquaintance or special relations."[11] The same was true, he said, at the Pennsylvania Station in New York. But if photographers did not get a good picture, the press grumbled. Lee solved the problem by hiring a professional photographer, Brown Brothers in New York, to come in and take pictures, then making reproductions available simultaneously to all newspapers and other media.

The movies increased efforts to get shots of Rockefeller for newsreel features after the advent of the talkies in the late twenties. Lee's policy of playing no favorites was upset on the occasion of the sixtieth anniversary of Standard Oil of Ohio. The Hearst newsreel company, Movietone News, scored a clean scoop by getting Rockefeller (without Lee's knowledge) to say a few words about Standard Oil for the talkies. The possibility of using newsreels for publicity purposes was something Lee had been suggesting for a long time. He wrote to J.D.R. Jr. that the people "obtained a more intimate impression of your father [through the newsreel] than they have ever had before and it is all to the good."

Unfortunately, all the other movie companies descended on Lee and demanded the same favor accorded Movietone. Lee could only tell them that he had not arranged the Movietone interview, and now could not burden the old gentleman with an appointment to remake the movie. Movietone of course would not release the rights. Lee pleaded with J.D.R. Jr. that "at any time your father feels disposed in the future to allow motion pictures or talking pictures to be made of himself, that we pursue a policy that such pictures would be made available to all companies. We feel that it is important that we keep the friendship of the motion picture people just as we seek to keep that of the newspapers."[12]

The younger Rockefeller took up the issue directly with his father. He congratulated him on his entrance into the "Movietone star realm" and asked that might it not be best to have Lee apprised in advance of any further pictures you may be willing to have taken? J.D.R. Sr. answered that he was heartily in accord and would try earnestly and honestly to carry out his son's and Ivy Lee's suggestions. But, he argued, there were many times when this was impossible. For instance, when Harvey Firestone visited the elder Rockefeller at his son's suggestion and they had a game of golf together, the photographer came out and took pictures. "This of course was not my photograph," he wrote to his son. "It was Mr. Firestone's, with Mr. Rockefeller in it."

At times the elderly gentleman must have chafed under Ivy Lee's strict advice that he play no favorites. "I do not presume that I am expected under such conditions to embarrass my companions by either declining to be taken or attempting to communicate with Mr. Lee before giving assent as to their publication," he wrote to his son after his picture had been taken with Firestone.[13] Most of the time, however, he saw the wisdom of the counsel and agreed with Lee. A few days later, for instance, he played golf at his winter home in Ormond with an Associated Press correspondent. The A.P. man wanted to write something about the game, but Rockefeller told him that in order to guard his commitments to other newspapers, he could not allow anything to be written without Ivy Lee's approval.

In the end the policy of playing no favorites and giving the press all reasonable cooperation in getting stories paid handsome dividends to the Rockefellers. Sometimes, of course, Lee was exasperated with the press. Sending a clipping of a sarcastic article from the *New York Herald* to Rockefeller, he commented that "it was written by some rattle-brained reporter who thought to write along old lines would be effective."[4] But for the most part the press stopped writing along old lines. The reporters and editors came to respect the Lee-Rockefeller relationship and to respect Lee and the Rockefellers as individuals.

By 1925 the president of the United Press, Karl A. Bickel, could in good journalistic conscience turn directly to Ivy Lee for advice about the Rockefellers. Bickel was to give the commencement address at Marquette University on "Opportunity Today," and he wanted to get some apt Rockefeller quotations that he could pass along to the graduating students. Expressing the judgment of many of his fellow newsmen, Bickel wrote to Lee: "Mr. Rockefeller's success in life both materially and otherwise has been established."[5] Ten years earlier that attitude would have been widely mocked and derided, and no newsman would have made such a statement.

---

[1] Ivy Lee to John D. Rockefeller Jr., Sept. 29, 1925, Rockefeller Archives, New York.

[2] Ivy Lee to Starr J. Murphy, May 17, 1920, Rockefeller Archives, New York.

[3] Recounted by Ivy Lee in a speech given at the Columbia University School of Journalism, 1932, Ivy Lee Papers, Princeton.

[4] Ivy Lee to John D. Rockefeller Jr., Jan. 23, 1924, Rockefeller Archives, New York.

[5] Ivy Lee to John D. Rockefeller Jr., Nov. 17, 1926, Rockefeller Archives, New York.

[6] Ivy Lee to John D. Rockefeller Jr., Feb. 15, 1928, Rockefeller Archives, New York.

[7] Ivy Lee to Brock Pemberton, Mar. 5, 1926, Rockefeller Archives, New York (The play was entitled "The Forgiving.")

[8] For one version of the story, see Pringle, op. cit.

[9] Ivy Lee to John D. Rockefeller Jr., May 21, 1926, Rockefeller Archives, New York.

[10] John D. Rockefeller Jr. to Ivy Lee, May 20, 1925, Rockefeller Archives, New York.

[11] John D. Rockefeller Sr. to John D. Rockefeller Jr., Feb. 6, 1930, Rockefeller Archives, New York.

[12] Ivy Lee to John D. Rockefeller Jr., Jan. 24, 1930, Rockefeller Archives, New York.

[13] John D. Rockefeller Sr. to John D. Rockefeller Jr., Feb. 6, 1930, Rockefeller Archives, New York.

[14] Ivy Lee to John D. Rockefeller Jr., Aug. 13, 1923, Rockefeller Archives, New York.

[15] Karl A. Bickel to Ivy Lee, May 29, 1925, Rockefeller Archives, New York.

Ray Eldon Hiebert

14: BIOGRAPHERS FOR BILLIONAIRES

ONE OF THE MOST IMPORTANT PROJECTS in Ivy Lee's public relations plans for John D. Rockefeller was the preparation of an adequate biography that would correct distortions which remained in historical treatments as a residue of the muckraking period. When he first joined the Rockefeller staff, Lee tried to find someone who could write biographical material about Rockefeller. Curiously, one of Lee's last acts, two weeks before his death in 1934, concerned the same problem.

Prior to 1915 Rockefeller had turned down all biographers and had not released any material about his life. As a result, almost all the writing was based primarily on second-hand sources. Ida Tarbell had used Standard Oil material subpoenaed in court actions against the company. But personal detail about the Rockefellers was harder to come by than a million-dollar gift for a good cause.

Early in 1915, before the "no exclusives" edict had been issued, Lee got in touch with a newspaper acquaintance, William O. Inglis, then a top reporter for the *New York World*. Inglis was a clever writer; Raymond Fosdick later called him a man of rare intelligence. But more important, he was a debonair newspaperman who played a gentlemanly game of golf and had a finely tuned sense of tact. Lee did not tell Rockefeller that he had a newspaperman who wanted to interview him for biographical material. Instead, he suggested that he had a reporter who was good at golf and would like to have a round with Rockefeller, perhaps to write a story about the game afterwards. Rockefeller said he would be pleased to play golf with Inglis but would prefer not to have anything written for publication.

However, if Inglis wrote about their game and submitted it to Lee, he would not object if Lee approved the story. Rockefeller told Lee he would "leave it in your hands to see that nothing objectionable was published."[1]

Lee gave Inglis a letter of introduction and the reporter went out to Far Hills in New Jersey, the old gentleman's private golf course. The two men played their round and Inglis succeeded in winning his opponent's favor. They chatted pleasantly about trivial things, but Inglis filed the details carefully in his mind and then went home and wrote his story. It appeared on November 13, 1915, in the *World* under a banner headline, PLAYING A ROUND OF GOLF WITH JOHN D. ROCKEFELLER. It was a pleasant piece, full of human interest and personal touches, accompanied by pictures of John D. swinging his clubs. This was the beginning of a long series of feature stories about the billionaire on the golf course, an opening wedge in the humanizing of the Rockefellers.

Lee saw Mr. Rockefeller's liking for Inglis as an opportunity for a competent writer to gather personal material. Rockefeller began cooperating and granted interviews in which he told Inglis about his past life and experiences. The two men played golf together frequently; Inglis even accompanied Rockefeller south when he went to Ormond for the winter. They enjoyed each other's company so much that the old gentleman once complained that they were having too good a time and Inglis wasn't spending enough hours each day (at least five) getting down to business.

The younger Rockefeller was delighted; there was nothing he wanted more than to have the world learn the true story of his father's life and know the truth about his personality. And the old man held the key to the facts. For the next few years, Inglis became Rockefeller's Boswell, soaking up all the atmosphere and information he could get. The elder Rockefeller cooperated on the venture partly because he felt this was one way to let his son know more about him. "I may say," he told Inglis, "that I have never had the time to become really acquainted with my son. He has been very busy always. I know that he is getting together this record out of his devotion to me, which I deeply appreciate."

The son was touched by this when he heard of it. He and his father had always had a close and beautiful relationship, he said, but he felt it was difficult for parents to realize their children had grown up and had opinions of their own. Less and less, he said, was his father "inclined to discuss subjects which he does not himself initiate." But Inglis's work provided a kind of meeting ground for father and son. When Inglis told Rockefeller that Ida Tarbell's history had used facts that disproved her point, Rockefeller exclaimed: "I wish that you would tell that to my son, if you see it so clearly, as I have no doubt you do, how often this woman puts in her book the facts which utterly destroy her contention. I have never told him these things."[2]

The son agreed. To the superficial reader, Miss Tarbell's arguments seemed convincing and her book had a great influence in forming public opinion, he said, but a critical study of it would not back up her inferences and conclusions. He hoped that Inglis might tackle this problem. "To be able to take the words out of her own mouth and prove the case against her is of the utmost value, and I am so glad that Father is pursuing this study with you with his customary patience and thoroughness," he wrote to Inglis.[3]

As the result of Inglis's careful gathering of material from J.D.R. Sr. over the next five or six years, Ivy Lee put together factual material which brought a change in the biographical sketches and obituaries that the press kept on Rockefeller. The Associated Press, in 1923, let Lee go over its file obit of Rockefeller before it was sent out to all its member newspapers.

"With the assistance of Mr. Inglis," Lee told Rockefeller, "we have carefully gone over this material and you will note the form in which it has now gone out to the Associated Press. You understand that the article was written by the Associated Press and the only respect in which we attempted to edit it was to correct it as to the facts, but we did not attempt to guide the article in its presentation.[4]

Now armed with the facts that had been extracted by Inglis, Lee was able to get most other newspapers and wire services to change their Rockefeller obits to omit the inferences of the Tarbells and Lawsons and include instead the conclusions of Inglis.

Altogether it took Inglis almost ten years to amass his material and write his biography of Rockefeller. During that time he was in the employ of Lee but his salary was paid directly by John D. Jr., the substantial figure of $8,000 a year. When Inglis finally turned in his manuscript, John D. Jr. in typical fashion treated it with the thoroughness of a professional publisher. On Lee's advice he turned the manuscript over to Ida Tarbell for her criticism. He also sent copies to William Allen White and others of similar standing, who could criticize it from a journalistic point of view. Another copy went to George Vincent, president of the Rockefeller Foundation, for judgment from the view of the Rockefeller interests.

Reaction to the Inglis manuscript was mixed. On the one hand, it had some positive influence on Miss Tarbell. She read it conscientiously, and John D. Jr. invited her to be his guest at lunch to discuss it. This and the point of view which Inglis presented made some impression for she shortly thereafter sat down and wrote a favorable article about the Rockefellers for the magazine *Success*. But other readers of the Inglis manuscript felt he had gone too far in the opposite direction, committing the same kind of errors as the earlier Miss Tarbell, except that his distortion was in favor of Rockefeller. White advised that the manuscript be shelved, as did Vincent. Lee concurred. John D. Jr. sadly cancelled the project and took Inglis off the payroll.

The biographer was jolted by this development. He tried to get a job in some other capacity with the Rockefellers but with little luck. He was given small tasks here and there, but nothing permanent. While Nelson Rockefeller was at Dartmouth, he reported back to his father one of his history lessons on the formation of Standard Oil. It was, said J.D.R. Jr., a "warped and erroneous view," and he detailed Inglis to go up to Dartmouth and give a lecture to Nelson's history class on the truth about Standard Oil. But there were few of these jobs.

Inglis turned instead to freelance writing and made a moderate success. He might have done very well, because many magazines were anxious to sign him up for the inside story of the Rockefellers. But since he had obtained his material under contract to the Rockefellers, they owned the rights to the story. And most of the time they refused to give Inglis permission to publish articles, fearing his one-sided view, even though on the favorable side, would do more harm than good in the public eye.

Rockefeller was obviously important biographical material. Other writers and publishers were interested and some of them went ahead with biographical projects despite the fact that they did not have access to primary sources. Two journalists got to work on such biographies in the late twenties—John K. Winkler, whose book, *John D. Rockefeller: A Portrait in Oils*, was published by the Vanguard Press in 1929; and John T. Flynn, *God's Gold: The Story of Rockefeller and His Times*, published by Harper and Brothers in 1932. Both of these books followed the earlier Tarbell thesis and were critical of Rockefeller in the muckraking tradition.

Early in 1929 Ray Long, editor of *Cosmopolitan*, a Hearst publication, decided to print a chapter of Winkler's biography as an article in his magazine. When Ivy Lee learned of this he contacted Long and got a press proof of the article in confidence. It was, Lee told J.D.R. Jr., "obviously an article that ought not to be printed. Its chief offense is the spirit in which it is written and the various innuendoes which are made."

But Lee told Rockefeller it would be a "great mistake to intervene in any way or to seek to prevent the appearance" of the book or the magazine article. He said he understood that Hearst had never asked Long to leave anything out of his magazine and it would be very unwise to ask him to do so. "Besides," he said, "even if it were done, the facts of the situation would get abroad through the journalistic world and it would surely become known that such an article had been killed through our influence.... I should not imagine that Winkler would like anything better.... It would advertise his book beyond his dreams."

Winkler had sought no information from the Rockefellers or the Lee office in writing his biography. "The fact that he did not ask us," Lee told Rockefeller, "constitutes ample proof that he wanted to write a book of gossip that would be merely spicy reading rather than a contribution to history." Lee felt that the position of the Rockefellers in mid-1929 was already of such dignity and character that an irresponsible publication would be subjected to so much criticism it would excite public sympathy for rather than hostility to the Rockefeller name. "Winkler's book is just about twenty years too late," he told J.D.R. Jr.

Indeed, Winkler's book created a small flurry of interest but eventually was ignored. Flynn's 1932 book lasted a little longer. Neither carries much weight with today's historians. But the publication of Winkler's book brought Lee back to the project that had been dropped with the end of the Inglis work. "We ought to take up seriously at the earliest opportunity," he wrote to John D. Jr., "the matter of putting into definitive form the authorized biography of your father."[5]

Lee thereupon began a search for an adequate biographer that was to take the next five years. He canvassed writers, editors, scholars, historians, university officials, and publishers for possibilities. Wherever he went around the world he was apt to have one eye out for good biographers, and he sought advice at every turn.

Editors and publishers were quick to suggest their favorites. Arthur Brisbane of Hearst, a long-time friend, proposed popular Dutch historian Hendrik Van Loon. Ellery Sedgwick, editor of *Atlantic Monthly*, suggested Henry James (the biographer, not the novelist). George P. Brett, president of Macmillan, suggested Walter C. Langsam, Columbia history professor. M. Lincoln Schuster, then of Appleton-Century, liked Stuart Chase, popular author-economist.

Those close to Rockefeller had their own ideas. Raymond Fosdick suggested Frederick Lewis Allen and Walter Lippmann. Abraham Flexner, director of the Institute for Advanced Study at Princeton, put forward Henry S. Commager, then a professor at New York University and Evarts B. Greene, a Columbia professor. John D. Rockefeller Jr. himself favored two University of Chicago teachers, William T. Hutchinson and William E. Dodd (later a formidable antagonist of Lee's).

Lee wanted to make sure that the man would be a biographer with an outstanding reputation. At first he strongly favored Charles A. Beard, who was gaining fame among historians for his economic interpretation of the Revolutionary period, but Beard was developing hearing problems that would have made the job difficult.

Lee next suggested James Truslow Adams, but Adams declined, not wanting to get involved in the Rockefeller controversy. Lee thought perhaps someone like Wallace B. Donham, the Dean of the Harvard Business School, might be appropriate, but on further consideration it was decided he was not enough of a historian.

On his trips abroad Lee got in touch with foreign biographers. Emil Ludwig had perhaps the most celebrated reputation as one of the "new wave" of biographers for his work on Napoleon. Lee cleared the way for Ludwig to come to the United States, interview Rockefeller, and see if he would be interested in a book. Ludwig ended by writing a magazine piece on the old gentleman and returned to his other work. Lee also contacted Philip Guedalla, John Buchan, and Lord Charnwood, all with international reputations. All were interested in the project and were willing to negotiate. But Lee thought he had found the perfect choice in the British Parliament: Winston Churchill.

Churchill was then finishing his biography of the Duke of Marlborough. He had several meetings with Lee to discuss the proposed biography, and, although he was deeply involved in his own work, Lee reported back to Rockefeller Jr. that the project had "really got hold of Churchill's imagination." Indeed, Churchill finally agreed to do it. But he told Lee that he was planning a monumental history of the English speaking peoples, which he would have to postpone to undertake the Rockefeller book. Churchill said the biography would take him at least two years. Therefore, he would have to have a guaranteed advance in royalties of at least £50,000. He suggested that the money be paid by the publisher, not Rockefeller, so the book would not appear to be subsidized.[6]

Lee had an innate ability to spot a man of destiny, and he felt that nothing could have been better for John D. Rockefeller Sr., under any circumstance, than to have Winston Churchill as his biographer. But when he reported Churchill's demands to J.D.R. Jr., he was flatly turned down. After all, £50,000 amounted to a quarter of a million dollars, and this was in the depression years.

Throughout the search for a biographer the matter of payment was a constant thorn in the proceedings. Rockefeller practically insisted that no payment or guarantee be made. The only thing guaranteed was access to John D. Rockefeller Sr., and to his papers, and the complete cooperation of the Rockefeller staff. Ivy Lee was more flexible. He felt that some kind of guarantee would have to be made to a good writer and publisher, but great discretion would have to be used and by all means no idea of a subsidized work could be considered. On the other hand most of the writers and publishers thought only in terms of a subsidized publication.

It was the payment of a biographer that was one of the last problems Lee tackled. Sedgwick told him he had an idea for its solution. Just two weeks before Lee died, he went up to Boston to discuss it with his friend. Sedgwick suggested that the *Atlantic Monthly* undertake to pay the biographer for chapters of the finished book which would appear as a magazine serial. Rockefeller could then guarantee an advanced sale of the book to the Atlantic Monthly Press, which would publish the biography in book form. In this way Rockefeller money would never get directly into the hands of the biographer. Lee thought it was an admirable plan, but Rockefeller rejected it.

Meanwhile, John D. Rockefeller 3rd, then a young man recently out of college, had become involved in the search for his grandfather's biographer. He wrote letters to the presidents of Dartmouth and Yale and asked for suggestions. Ernest M. Hopkins of Dartmouth referred the matter to Professor James McCallum of the history department. McCallum vetoed several earlier suggestions and then said with some hesitancy he would suggest the name of Allan Nevins. "My hesitancy," he wrote to J.D.R. 3rd, "is not caused by any doubt regarding his ability but solely because the biography which he might write would not be entirely acceptable to the family."[7]

This caught the interest of the Rockefellers and they looked into the background of Nevins. He was then a professor at Columbia, fairly young (44), had taught at Cornell and Illinois, had been a newspaper writer for the *New York Times*, and had already won the Pulitzer Prize for his biography of Grover Cleveland. And he had written a subsidized biography of Henry White, an American diplomat. But in his book on Cleveland, Nevins had referred to "the history of Standard Oil and its sordid record of business piracy." This could mean that Nevins was already prejudiced against Standard and Rockefeller, but it could also mean that he would not be a Rockefeller mouthpiece.

In all discussions of the biography thereafter, the name of Nevins kept cropping up, always, it seemed, as the best possible alternative to whatever other writer happened to be under discussion. James Angell, president of Yale, said Nevins was the best person for the job. M. Lincoln Schuster thought Nevins a likely prospect. Others disagreed. Flexner said Nevins was less brilliant and less able than either Guedalla or Buchan and proceeded to suggest Carl Becker; Alfred Harcourt thought Nevins was "rather dull." But John D. Rockefeller 3rd felt that the Columbia professor offered real possibilities.

The death of Ivy Lee in November of 1934 brought the search for a biographer to a climax. The Rockefellers did not want all the work to be in vain. Thomas Ross, who had been Lee's partner before Lee died, wrote a memorandum summarizing the results of the five-year investigation. The most important element in the biography was the writer, said Ross. He should not be over 50, should have demonstrated that he could write objectively, be preferably a "liberal conservative" in philosophy, with experience as a biographer and hopefully with interest in Rockefeller, be an American historian with an academic rather than journalistic background, an understanding of economics, and a capacity for imagination and interpretation.

The publisher should be any one of the four or five top houses. But the feeling was that this biography was too important and would arouse too much public interest to warrant giving in to a request for a subsidy. If the right author could be found, the undertaking should be an unusual publishing opportunity; and, if the author himself wanted an advance, the publisher would have to give it to him. Among the publishers, however, there remained a feeling that some backing would be needed, and Ross suggested a triangular relationship between the family, the author, the publisher, and the Lee offices, with serialization in a magazine such as the *Atlantic* or *Saturday Evening Post* as an alternative to outright guarantees.

Finally the list of authors was narrowed to those who were out of the running, those who still had some possibility, and two who had the inside track. Definitely out were Philip Guedalla and John Buchan for, even though they were world-known biographers, as Europeans they did not have a substantial acquaintance with the American scene. Lord Charnwood, out too, had written biographies of Americans—Lincoln and Theodore Roosevelt—but they had meager sales, perhaps due to his "uninteresting style."

Of the other names that remained on the list, biographer Henry James was out only because he had been at one time associated with the Rockefeller Institute. Robert Coffin, head of the English Department at Wells College, was lacking in economic background and his biographies were marked by "incapacity for accurate historical research" and "flippancy of style." Merle Curti, then of the Smith College History Department, was not a biographer and was inclined to be "rather dry and documentary," and Harvey Cushing, whom John D. Jr. felt wrote "exquisitely," was out because his background was too completely apart from business life.

A group of Pulitzer Prize winners was also suggested but of these the following were turned down: Hamlin Garland, then 74 and considered too old and too much of a novelist; Emory Holloway, who had written a literary biography of Walt Whitman, but was not enough of an economist or historian; Marquis James who had written about Sam Houston, but was "markedly lacking of knowledge of historical background"; and Charles Edward Russell, the man who had originally hired Ivy Lee as a *New York Journal* reporter. He was considered because of his biography of Theodore Thomas, but he was turned down because of his socialistic books, *Lawless Wealth* and *Stories of the Great Railroads*.

Several other authors were still considered possibilities. Mark Anthony DeWolfe Howe, closely associated with the *Atlantic Monthly* and Harvard and author of many American biographies of the period, headed this list. Burton J. Hendrick, winner of three Pulitzer Prizes, was considered, although he wrote in a "heavy uninteresting editorial style." R. L. Duffus, a long-time reporter for the *New York Times* and a freelance writer, was a possibility because of his recent book on the Santa Fe Trail which "caught the historical significance of the trails," but he lacked experience in biographical writing. Arthur Pound was in the running because he had written many excellent industrial histories, but this very fact was the principal objection because of the "danger of implication." Frederick Allen, who had recently published his popular *Only*

Yesterday, was a possibility but his "detached air of amusement" did not recommend him for consideration.

The field was finally narrowed down to two men. Henry Fowles Pringle was the first. Ironically, he had been the author of a very sarcastic article about Ivy Lee in the twenties. But that never stopped Lee from considering him. In fact, it may well have been one of the reasons for his high place on the list. In addition, Pringle had recently written a series of important biographies of Alfred E. Smith, Theodore Roosevelt, and William Howard Taft. The Al Smith biography had been written during the campaign for the presidency but was "so honest that it has never been discredited as a 'campaign document.'" This was appealing to the Rockefellers.

The light, however, finally centered on Allan Nevins. Ross's memo said that his biography of Henry White was "delightful," and quoted the reviews which said it was a "vital and scholarly contribution." And "this was a subsidized biography!" More important was his work on Grover Cleveland. "There are one or two references to the oil industry and particularly to the Standard Oil Company which reveal Mr. Nevins as perhaps a 'liberal conservative' rather than an out-and-out conservative," wrote Ross. This book, more than his others, made the Lee office feel that Nevins was the best qualified author. "Nevins stands far above all others who have been considered as a possible author of the 'life.'"[8]

Within a few months the Rockefellers agreed and Nevins accepted the offer. In five years he turned out a two-volume history of John D. Rockefeller that moved every other Rockefeller biography off the shelves and ultimately changed the attitudes of historians and scholars. What had not reached the crowd through the mass media ultimately filtered down from the ivory tower.

[1] John D. Rockefeller Sr. to Ivy Lee, Oct. 30, 1915, Rockefeller Archives, New York.

[2] William O. Inglis to John D. Rockefeller Jr., Jan. 31, 1918, Rockefeller Archives, New York.

[3] John D. Rockefeller Jr. to William O. Inglis, Feb. 19, 1918, Rockefeller Archives, New York.

[4] Ivy Lee to John D. Rockefeller Jr., Jan. 8, 1923, Rockefeller Archives, New York.

[5] Ivy Lee to John D. Rockefeller Jr., May 10, 1929, Rockefeller Archives, New York.

[6] Biography File, Rockefeller Archives, New York.

[7] Ibid.

[8] Letter of Thomas Ross to John D. Rockefeller Jr., Jan. 19, 1935, and memorandum of Thomas Ross to John D. Rockefeller Jr., Feb. 5, 1935, Rockefeller Archives, New York.

15: POLICIES FOR THE PEOPLE

JOHN D. ROCKEFELLER, JR., FORTUNATELY, was a man of good intentions who believed in Lee's formula: if you are going to tell the truth to the people, you have to have a good truth to tell. However, Rockefeller learned quickly that charity for one might very well antagonize another. Lee was the man to provide advice on the public reaction to the Rockefeller activities and to help gain understanding for those activities.

Lee's early recommendations had proven successful—the publication of a concise account of all Rockefeller philanthropic work around the world, with facts, figures, and illustrations that showed the dramatic impact of the Rockefeller charities, whether founding universities, strengthening medical school curricula, or stamping out hookworm disease in the deep South.

But equally important was material that demonstrated what the Rockefellers were thinking and how well their ideas agreed with prevailing public attitudes. Following the Colorado strike, J.D.R. Jr. gave speeches around the country on "The Personal Relation in Industry." In these he argued that cooperation was necessary between worker and management, and that labor and capital were partners in building America. By 1919 these ideas were so closely associated with Rockefeller that labor leader Samuel Gompers told Ivy Lee the younger Rockefeller "has grown both in comprehension of fundamental problems and in the esteem of the people, during the past few years."[1]

Lee persuaded Rockefeller to collect six of his speeches, including two he had made in Colorado after the Ludlow affair, together with a copy of his "Plan of Representation of Employees in the Coal and Iron Mines of the Colorado Fuel and Iron Company," to be published as a book under the title, *The Personal Relation in Industry*. Rockefeller insisted that the book be printed by a commercial publisher as a regular venture and that he be given royalties just like any other author. Lee suggested Boni and Liveright, who were willing to handle the book. But Rockefeller objected to the house because it had published a book that was the subject of an obscenity suit, one of several such cases in the twenties. "There is no question," Lee told him, "that they are publishers of a number of novels representing what you and I would consider the less desirable tendencies in modern fiction, but I rather imagine we would find such books on the list of nearly every publisher."[2]

Boni and Liveright published the book in 1923. It was widely reviewed and quoted, and some of the speeches were even reprinted in such unlikely places as college freshman English anthologies. The book undoubtedly had an effect in showing a different side of Rockefeller's thought, and even made money for its publisher and author. "You may want a little pin money for Christmas," wrote Ivy Lee to J.D.R. Jr., "so I have much pleasure in enclosing herewith Boni and Liveright's check for $591.90 as the royalties on your book."[3]

In time Rockefeller became known as a new voice in industrial relations. Editorials appeared praising him for his strong stand; cartoons pictured him walking arm in arm with a laborer in overalls while Mr. Moneybags Capitalist stood off in the background in consternation. At times John D. Jr. felt that possibly he was expressing too much sympathy toward labor and he would pull back, but both Mackenzie King and Ivy Lee bridled at the prospect.

As an example, during the mid-twenties, Lee strongly favored the Watson-Parker Bill which abolished the Railroad Labor Board and set up a system of mediation, arbitration, and fact finding. The measure abandoned definitive prohibition of strikes and was in general based on the theory that railroad managers and employees were friends and might be expected to iron out rather than fight out their troubles.

The Watson-Parker Bill was endorsed by the labor unions. The only opposition during a final hearing came from a representative of the Western Maryland Railroad, which the Rockefellers controlled. "I confess to a certain amount of both surprise and mortification," Lee wrote to Rockefeller, "that your representative...had taken such a reactionary stand and had placed himself in opposition to a sincere effort on the part of the railroad executives of the country to arrive at an understanding, rather than keep up a conflict with employees." Lee said that he knew that the principles of the bill were in accord with the spirit of Rockefeller's views about labor and capital, and the attitude of the Western Maryland was "singularly inexplicable."[4] Rockefeller agreed and sought to change the railroad representative's position.

But Lee also advised publication of material dealing with conservative principles and ideas in which Rockefeller believed. In 1922, for instance, one of the planks in the platform of the Labor Party in England called for a capital gains tax. "I believe we are going to hear from it very actively in this country," Lee told John D. Jr. "It seems to me we ought to be distributing literature now tending to show the fallacies of the capital levy idea and thus prevent the idea getting any currency."[5]

For the most part, however, Lee helped to liberalize Rockefeller's policies in the field of industrial and labor relations and this did much to promote public goodwill toward the Rockefellers.

The same diligence was needed to direct their benefactions, which frequently caused public problems. As the Rockefellers gave more money away, more people wanted a part of it. Many of the requests were channeled through Ivy Lee because they had public implications; some of these were vetoed politely by Lee without being sent on for further consideration. One that received substantial deliberation and caused sizable public problems was a request for funds to build a museum in Egypt.

Through a University of Chicago professor of Egyptology, Dr. James H. Breasted, Rockefeller became interested in giving money to help preserve Egyptian antiquities. In the mid-twenties, the decision was made to set up a $10 million fund to build and maintain a museum in Cairo. But Rockefeller insisted that, to insure the money would be used properly and not simply find its way into Egyptian pockets, he would give it only on condition that the museum be controlled by an international commission of archeologists. King Fuad of Egypt resented this as American interference in Egyptian affairs and both sides entered into negotiation to solve the affair.

In the middle of the discussions, Breasted in Cairo somehow released a statement to the press that the gift was a *fait accompli*, putting the Rockefellers in the difficult public position of going along with Egyptian demands or backing out of the affair ungracefully. When the story reached the United States, the Associated Press and the *New York Times* both called Lee to verify the story, and after he had made the situation clear, they agreed to withhold it.

Then United Press and International News Service got the story, however, and Lee felt compelled to release the A.P. and *Times* from their commitment. He asked all the papers to play the story with every reservation from the Rockefeller point of view, and they generally followed his request. Rockefeller, at Lee's instigation, later wrote to Kent Cooper and John H. Finley, heads of the A.P. and

Times respectively, that this was "in keeping with the best traditions of fine journalism."[6]

The premature announcement brought an unexpected reaction from the public. Newspapers around the country pointed out that if the Rockefellers were going to give money to museums, there were a lot of museums nearer home than Cairo which might well deserve their attention. Lee told Rockefeller that the editorials "express the point of view of the low-brow man in the street," but he urged that "when we make public the announcement of this gift, we should very definitely try to meet the point of view of this type of mind."[7]

Actually, premature leakage of the Cairo news might have been advantageous in the long run, Lee felt, because it not only showed public reaction to the proposed museum before the actual deed was done, but it also created an atmosphere of public interest that would allow the Rockefellers to explain their cause. "There is an opportunity," Lee wrote to Rockefeller, "when making the final announcement to give out a lot of information concerning Egyptology and the general problem centering around this museum."[8]

The Lee office never had to send out such information, however, because King Fuad would not give way in his demands that he have complete control over the museum. This and the negative American reaction led Rockefeller to withdraw the offer.

The fact that the American people expressed themselves on the Egyptian museum undoubtedly helped turn Rockefeller's mind in the direction of a museum to preserve American antiquities, specifically the restoration of Williamsburg. Within a few months of his withdrawal from the Egyptian project, Rockefeller was actively engaged in negotiation with Dr. William A. R. Goodwin, Rector of the Bruton Parish Church in Williamsburg and the man behind the restoration plan. This was perhaps the most ambitious reconstruction project ever undertaken in America, and one that has had wide public appeal.

The chief problem, once Rockefeller became interested in the restoration, was to keep his involvement secret during the delicate process of buying up the houses and land of Williamsburg, lest some opportunist should take advantage of the situation. As it was, when Dr. Goodwin began purchasing property, public curiosity was aroused. Goodwin finally went to the editors of the newspapers in the area to request their cooperation. He issued a frank statement saying a group of persons were interested in preserving some of Williamsburg's historic sites but warned that this interest would be dissipated if the people of the area did not cooperate.

At this, John D. Jr. sent Goodwin a letter demonstrating that the lessons of Ivy Lee had been well learned. "I have never seen any publicity in regard to a project so wisely and skillfully handled.... You have taken the public into your confidence, been completely frank with them, thus disarming suspicion and capitalizing curiosity."[9]

Lee prepared for the eventual announcement by having a release written with all the facts about the project, leaving a blank for the name of the donor. At the moment when Goodwin finally made a public announcement of Rockefeller's backing of the Williamsburg restoration, the Lee office simply inserted the Rockefeller name and issued the complete story to the press.

Lee continued as public relations counsel to the Williamsburg project after it got under way. He suggested the printing of a book about the project which "would place on record in the newspapers, libraries and universities of the country...an idea of what this scheme all means."[10] He suggested as the author a reporter from the *New York Times*, Henry Irving Brock, a Virginian who was interested in Williamsburg. Curiously, two years later Brock wrote a different book, called *The Meddlers*, in which he castigated Ivy Lee for interfering in public affairs.

Lee also proposed that a quarterly be published in Williamsburg, dealing with colonial American history in a scholarly vein, which eventually became the *William and Mary Quarterly*. One of Lee's staff members, Bela W. Norton, a former assistant editor of the *New York Post*, eventually went to Williamsburg as public relations director for the entire restoration program.

One Rockefeller project that was started for benevolent purposes and ended with vast public relations headaches was Rockefeller Center. Like many proposals with which Lee was identified, the Center was not his invention but he served as a catalytic agent to spur germination of the plan. Otto Kahn, a patron of the Metropolitan Opera, told Lee he felt that the Opera House in New York had outlived its usefulness and suggested that a worthwhile civic contribution could be made by building a new opera center. Lee discussed the idea with the Rockefellers, who had long shunned real estate investments but saw the public benefits of such a contribution to city life and art.

From this basic idea ultimately came a series of real estate projects financed by Rockefeller and centered on a few blocks in midtown Manhattan. Instead of opera and high culture, however, the Center became the mecca for the popular arts, dominated by RCA, NBC, RKO, the Music Hall, and an ice-skating rink. This, as it turned out, was a much better reflection of John D. Rockefeller Sr. and Jr., who were not great opera connoisseurs but strong believers in wholesome amusement and high grade recreation. The Center was deeded to Columbia University and thus ultimately served a nobler purpose.

The original name of the Center was the Metropolitan Square Corporation, but the popular term became Radio City, after RCA and NBC became an important part of it. John R. Todd, in charge of building the Center, asked Lee to come up with a name for it and he "cudgelled" his brain. He turned down "Radio City" as "catchy," valuable only from the standpoint of amusement rather than renting. He preferred a distinctive name which would be regarded as an asset to everyone taking space in the area.

Rockefeller did not want to have his name connected with the project, but Lee finally said, "It is unquestionable that the natural name for the district would be something like "Rockefeller Center."[11] And that was the name chosen.

Just a few months after the commitment had been made on the project in 1929, the stock market crashed and the country entered the depression. As the economic crisis of the nation worsened, the Rockefeller monoliths began to rise, almost as if oblivious to the problems of the people. The Center reaped editorial scorn and public criticism. The nature of the news stories about it did not help. Obviously the news was that this was a project of greatness—largest floor space, largest theater, and largest mortgage, among other items.

Thomas M. Debevoise, legal counsel to John D. Jr., wrote Lee that if this kind of news was not stopped, "the only conclusion the public can possibly reach is that Mr. Rockefeller and his people have the biggest heads in the world. Can't you use your benign influence to stop this?"[12] Lee refused to employ censorship; facts were facts, and he could not wave a magic wand to change them.

In the case of Rockefeller Center, contracts were made, steel girders riveted, and concrete irremediably hardened. But most policies were not that irrevocable, and it was by guiding the Rockefellers into changing their policies that Lee was able to improve their public image.

During those depression years, for instance, Lee often counseled the Rockefellers to invest publicly in the stock market and put some of their millions into circulation as evidence of their faith in the American economy. When the banks began to fail, Lee urged Rockefeller to personally subscribe to millions of dollars' worth of stock in new banks on a matching basis with the Reconstruction Finance Corporation. This kind of action, he wrote to Rockefeller, would "create a very beneficial effect throughout the country."[13] This sort of policy would certainly help to offset any bad public effects from the building of Rockefeller Center.

The Rockefellers sometimes agreed to changes in their policies only very slowly. It was with great reluctance that they altered their stand on the Eighteenth Amendment prohibiting the sale of alcoholic beverages. Reputedly, the elder Rockefeller and his son never tasted a drop of liquor in their lifetimes. Their mothers were among the militant women of the nineteenth century who in Baptist abstinence went to saloons to pray for drunkards. The family used the full force of its influence to support the prohibition proposal and get it passed into law in 1919.

From the moment of its enactment, however, the Eighteenth Amendment aroused more public antipathy than any other Constitutional change in the nation's history. During the wild twenties the Rockefellers' support for prohibition caused them to be denounced as "stuffed shirts"; it also played into the hands of those critics who saw prohibition as the source of a new wave of crime and violence. Other Rockefeller advisors joined Ivy Lee in urging a withdrawal of support for prohibition.

By 1926 Rockefeller Jr. withdrew his backing from the Anti-Saloon League, and in 1932, after much soul-searching and discussion, publicly announced that he favored repeal of this Amendment. The statement got front-page headlines across the nation, attracted worldwide attention, and undoubtedly had an impact on the resulting legislation of 1933. Ivy Lee and his staff undertook an editorial study of public reaction to the announcement and found that an analysis of 4,509 editorials in the United States and Canada showed a nine-to-one ratio of public agreement with the Rockefeller change.

Of all the public actions of the Rockefellers in the twenties and early thirties—charities, foundations, museums, centers, prohibition—none was as delicate a problem or had more public impact than the Rockefeller association with the Teapot Dome scandal. The position that the Rockefellers took in the Stewart Case rising out of the scandal probably did as much as anything to establish their courage and integrity in the public mind.

The Teapot Dome corruption came to light as the result of Senator Thomas J. Walsh's investigation of the lease of government oil fields in the Elk Hills and Teapot Dome reserves of Wyoming to private individuals for their own gain. The Senate hearings were held intermittently in the mid-twenties and during that time Secretary of the Interior Albert B. Fall was fined and imprisoned, Secretary of the Navy Edwin Denby resigned under pressure, the whole of the Harding Administration was rocked, and the crisis continued into the Coolidge period.

Deeply involved was Colonel Robert W. Stewart, chairman of the Board of Directors of Standard Oil of Indiana; and the Rockefellers, as stockholders of the company, were incriminated by association. John D. Jr. was called to testify before the Senate hearings, although he was only indirectly responsible. To avoid the criticism of "absentee capitalism," however, Rockefeller tried to contact Stewart, but found he was out of the country. Even when the Senate subpoenaed Stewart for an appearance, he refused to oblige.

Finally, however, Rockefeller succeeded in reaching Stewart, who maintained that his implication in the Teapot Dome transfer of oil reserves was just a good business deal that allowed him to buy oil for the company at far lower rates than usual. Rockefeller could not change Stewart's mind but he insisted that the Standard executive go before the Senate committee. When he finally did so, Stewart's testimony left no doubt in anyone's mind that his actions were based strictly on getting the greatest profit for the company and for himself no matter at whose expense.

Press comment increased and public criticism mounted. Ivy Lee arranged for John D. Rockefeller Jr. to go on the Colliers Radio Hour on February 12, 1928, and make a public statement about the affair. He said, in effect, that Stewart's action could not be tolerated. "Today," John D. Jr. said, "the vital matter to which business must need address itself is the reemphasizing of character and of high standards of business ethics, for upon such a foundation only can business be permanently successful." Rockefeller's speech evoked national praise. The *Louisville Courier-Journal*, expressing typical sentiments, said that his statement was a "refreshing breath of pure air in an atmosphere polluted by the contaminating effect of big business on politics."[14]

Rockefeller met with Lee and his other advisors to determine the proper course of action. By taking a strong public stand against the unethical practices in which Stewart had participated, Rockefeller implied that Stewart would have to be replaced as head of Standard of Indiana. Stewart refused to resign and a bitter proxy fight ensued. Stewart was strongly entrenched in a strategic position and had the support of powerful banking and business interests. The Rockefeller family held less than 10 percent of the stock out of more than 58,000 stockholders. Yet to the American mind

Rockefeller and Standard Oil were synonymous, and if one was guilty so was the other.

Rockefeller felt that not only his name but the ethics of American business were at stake. He set up a committee under his legal counsel, Thomas Debevoise, which included Ivy Lee, Winthrop Aldrich, Bertram Cutler, Colonel Arthur Woods, and Raymond Fosdick, with Charles Evans Hughes as the committee's counsel. Every day for two months the committee met in an effort to obtain proxies for the Rockefeller side.

The conservative stockholders felt that the financial standing of the company could be jeopardized by the removal of Stewart and the effects would be felt in all oil and related industries. But the reaction of the press and the public was strongly on the side of Rockefeller, and Lee urged him to continue the fight at all costs to his business associations.

At the annual meeting of Standard of Indiana on March 7, 1929, the issue came to a climax. When the vote was counted, Rockefeller had won by an eight-to-five margin. Rockefeller gave all credit for the victory to the committee, and later he rewarded Lee with a $10,000 check for his extra work on the campaign.

Throughout the proxy fight, Lee had provided the newspapers with dignified and low-keyed statements of the Rockefeller arguments and had the press firmly on his side in the campaign. He later wrote that he "felt all the time that our own statements and suggestions to the papers would gain in weight from under statement and conservatism, and that has been the spirit in which I have always answered newspaper inquires." On the other hand, he felt that the Stewart publicity had been "puerile and braggadocio," which had cost him much public sympathy.[15]

The press and the public, at the end of the Stewart affair, were very much on the Rockefeller side. By the middle of 1929 even the politicians thought that the public image of the Rockefellers was so favorable that it could be capitalized upon politically. Charles D. Hilles, of the Republican National Committee, suggested John D. Jr. as a candidate for mayor of New York. But when Lee's counsel was sought on the idea, he rejected the proposal. Political popularity and crowd popularity were two different things. "Great as my admiration for you is," he told Rockefeller, "I do not believe the time has yet come when you could be regarded as popular in the political sense."[16]

That time never came for John D. Rockefeller Jr., but it did come for his son Nelson. As John D. Jr.'s five sons grew into adulthood in the twenties and early thirties, they came into contact with Ivy Lee through their father's offices. After Nelson graduated from college and went to work for the Chase National Bank and Rockefeller Center, he became acquainted with Ivy Lee. He followed easily in his father's public relations-conscious footsteps, as an editorial in the *Yonkers Herald-Statesman* in 1932 demonstrated. Under the heading, "The New Generation," the editorial stated: "One reads with pleasure that a son of J.D.R. Jr. (Nelson) has accepted membership on a Mt. Pleasant Committee. It is pleasing to note on the part of the coming generation of younger Rockefellers this same spirit of civic cooperation and of understanding."[17] Nelson had sought Lee's advice on this activity.

Thus, over the years, the Rockefeller reputation had been transformed. The headlines and stories in the Nation's press had changed. Prior to 1915, they had charged: ROCKEFELLER, MAN OR MONSTER? — TAINTED MONEY! — THE CHURCH AND THE REWARD OF INIQUITY — ROCKEFELLER FACES JUSTICE. After 1915, with increasing regularity, the headlines read: ROCKEFELLER GIVES ANOTHER MILLION TO UNEMPLOYMENT FUND — ROCKEFELLER

FOUNDATION FIGHTS PELLAGRA IN GEORGIA — JOHN D. GIVES DIMES TO CHILDREN — HOW THE ROCKEFELLERS GIVE MILLIONS.

One writer, John T. Flynn, summarized the metamorphosis: "The figure of the striding, ruthless monopolist in high hat and long coat gripping his walking stick and entering a courthouse has been replaced by pictures of a frail old man, playing golf with his neighbors, handing out dimes to children, distributing inspirational poems, and walking in peace amid his flowers."[18]

Many writers have given Ivy Lee too much credit for the Rockefeller transformation. Many have attributed the vast Rockefeller foundations and charities solely to Lee's counsel. "On the advice of Lee," wrote Silas Bent, "the Rockefeller philanthropies were increased to an unparalleled scale."[19] But that is not wholly true. Indeed, the Rockefellers gave away an astounding $138 million in 1919, but they had been giving away money from the beginning. John D. Sr. had given away $13 million in 1905, $39 million in 1907, $71 million in 1909, $45 million in 1913, and $67 million in 1914, to say nothing of all the other years before Lee joined the family.

Many writers have said that Lee shaped all the Rockefeller policies after 1915. "What Lee proposed was really something new in the Rockefeller system—the study of public opinion," wrote Flynn. "It meant not merely placing the affairs of the corporation before the public in the most favorable light, but shaping the affairs of the corporation so that when they reached the public they will be approved."[20] That certainly was the basic advice that Lee gave. Other students of the Rockefellers, however, such as Allan Nevins, have maintained that Lee did relatively little beyond that, with the Rockefellers themselves carrying the burden for making their own decisions.

Curiously, writers antagonistic to the Rockefellers, such as Bent, Flynn, and Upton Sinclair, gave Lee credit for manipulations that changed the public attitude toward the millionaires; but writers sympathetic to the Rockefellers, such as Raymond Fosdick and Nevins, downgraded Lee's contribution. The truth is probably somewhere in between.

It would be totally wrong to think of Lee as the manipulator of the Rockefellers or as single-handedly responsible for the dramatic improvement in their relations with the public after 1915. Without doubt, he had great influence but he could have had no influence at all had the Rockefellers not been men of good intentions with a good story to tell. Lee is better described as a catalytic agent who got things moving. He advised the Rockefellers to give public expression to the ideas and convictions that were basically part of their nature. When the public expressed approval of these ideas and feelings, it only served to make them, especially John D. Jr., surer of their position.

Thomas Ross, Lee's long-time associate, said that the high regard and friendly attitude of the public "came out of Mr. Rockefeller's own understanding of his problem and genuine desire to serve the public and the community in which he had built his fortune. But it was the sensible counsel of Ivy Lee which furthered that purpose, plus the character and warm sympathy of John D. Rockefeller Jr., as he carried on the work begun by his father."[21]

Lee once explained to Martin Clement, president of the Pennsylvania Railroad, what he had done for the Rockefellers: "I just raised the curtains and let the people look in, and what they saw was not bad."[22]

[1] Quoted in R. B. Fosdick, op. cit., p. 168.

[2] Ivy Lee to John D. Rockefeller Jr., Aug. 23, 1923, Rockefeller Archives, New York.

[3] Ivy Lee to John D. Rockefeller Jr., Dec. 21, 1927, Rockefeller Archives, New York.

[4] Ivy Lee to John D. Rockefeller Sr., Mar. 4, 1926, Rockefeller Archives, New York.

[5] Ivy Lee to John D. Rockefeller Jr., Dec. 29, 1922, Rockefeller Archives, New York.

[6] John D. Rockefeller Jr. to Kent Cooper and John H. Finley, Feb. 20, 1926, Rockefeller Archives, New York.

[7] Ivy Lee to John D. Rockefeller, Mar. 9, 1926, Rockefeller Archives, New York.

[8] Ivy Lee to John D. Rockefeller Jr., Mar. 4, 1926, Rockefeller Archives, New York.

[9] Quoted in R. B. Fosdick, loc. cit.

[10] Ivy Lee to John D. Rockefeller Jr., June 22, 1928, Rockefeller Archives, New York.

[11] Ivy Lee to John D. Rockefeller Jr., July 13, 1931, Rockefeller Archives, New York.

[12] Thomas M. Debevoise to Ivy Lee, Jan. 23, 1933, Rockefeller Archives, New York.

[13] Ivy Lee to John D. Rockefeller Jr., Mar. 30, 1933, Rockefeller Archives, New York.

[14] Ivy Lee Papers, Rockefeller File, Princeton.

[15] Ivy Lee to Thomas M. Debevoise, Jan. 30, 1929, Rockefeller Archives, New York.

[16] Ivy Lee to John D. Rockefeller Jr., July 13, 1929, Rockefeller Archives, New York.

[17] Yonkers (N.Y.), *Herald-Statesman*, Dec. 10, 1932, p. 7.

[18] John Flynn, *God's Gold* (New York: Harper & Bros., 1932), p. 460.

[19] Silas Bent, "Ivy Lee: Minnesinger to Millionaires," *New Republic*, Nov. 20, 1929, p. 369.

[20] Flynn, loc. cit.

[21] Quoted in Averell Broughton, *Careers in Public Relations* (New York: E. P. Dutton & Co., 1943), p. 232.

[22] M. W. Clement to R. E. Hiebert, Apr. 19, 1963.

IV

THE CAPITALISTS
"Before the Court of Public Opinion"

16: COUNSEL FOR CORPORATIONS

WHILE UTILITIES WERE AMONG THE FIRST to face public relations responsibilities, and while the Rockefellers were foremost among leaders of American capitalism who accepted public relations principles and dramatically illustrated their efficacy, the growing American corporation was a generator of great public relations problems after World War I. Following his successes with the railroads and Rockefellers, Ivy Lee found himself in demand by corporate giants, and his independent firm of Lee, Harris, and Lee, founded in 1916, began counseling them on public problems.

Most of these problems resulted from mass production. In the fields where man once had tilled the soil with horse and plow, great machines now fertilized the loam, sowed the seed, and reaped the harvest. In the shop where craftsmen once had skillfully created products, long assembly lines now automatically manufactured and disgorged commodities in bulk. When mass production created a surplus in a competitive market, prices dropped below manufacturing costs causing recessions and depressions and driving producers into bankruptcy. One solution was monopoly; another was state control; both were autocratic. Instead of either, however, business in America in the first half of the twentieth century remained free and competitive largely as a result of public relations.

Even though businesses increasingly consolidated after World War I, they became even more competitive. In the automobile industry, for instance, where many hundreds of small producers existed before the war, during the twenties these merged into a few giants that ruled the field. Yet the competition was even fiercer, and to keep from driving each other out of business, some sort of liaison was needed to provide individual firms with information about the industry as a whole for the best interests of all. Ivy Lee proposed to serve corporations in this capacity, and he was instrumental in founding many industrial associations to provide such cooperation, among them the American Petroleum Institute, Copper and Brass Research Association, Anthracite Coal Operators Conference, Trans-Atlantic Passenger Conference, Cotton-Textile Institute, and others. Through such groups, business learned how to remain competitive yet cooperative.

Equally important, the basis of competition shifted. Mass production led to problems of mass distribution. If factories could produce more than people could consume, the burden must shift from manufacturer to distributor. But means other than price could be used to sell commodities. If cooperative endeavors among corporations stabilized prices to keep the members from driving each other out of business, competition could exist in color, style, design, durability, and quality. Competition shifted from the assembly line to Madison Avenue, where experts became engaged in analyzing the needs of the market, researching product promotion and publicity, and finding better ways to sell one's wares than had his competitors.

By the late twenties even Henry Ford had to abandon his puritanical, nineteenth-century dictum: "The customer can have a Ford any color he wants as long as it's black." The man who sold the cheapest car on the market had to have more than a low price to stay in the field. There was a new need to understand what made people buy, aside from price. Someone was needed who could advise on tastes and attitudes of the crowd. Today this aspect of public relations has become a science of its own, with sociologists and psychologists who clinically dissect society, not only to map its anatomy and chart its heartbeat, but to probe more deeply into its subconsciousness for hidden motives.

As one of the few in America who provided these kinds of services for big business before the thirties, Ivy Lee moved into the center of influence in corporate life. By 1923 *The Open Road* magazine carried an article, "Opportunities in Publicity," which began by describing Lee: "In a handsomely appointed office on the thirty-first floor of a New York City building sits a man who wields an influence exceeded by few men in America."[1] The author, Carl H. Getz, was a former journalism professor who had been an eyewitness to the exercise of that influence as a member of Lee's staff.

Getz described Lee as a man in the center of many great American corporations, providing counsel on the handling of their problems before the court of public opinion. At one moment, Getz said, he would be at the council table of the railroad executives faced with a strike; at the next he was conferring with cement manufacturers under indictment for antitrust violations; he was in Philadelphia advising operators during a coal strike; or in Paris directing American-Cuban sugar producers in their efforts to get a more equitable tariff; or in Washington giving counsel to petroleum industry chiefs under investigation by a Senate committee. The list of his activities, said Getz, could be extended almost indefinitely.

From its inception in 1916, the Lee, Harris, and Lee firm, unlike the 1904–08 partnership of Parker and Lee, had no difficulty attracting clients, undoubtedly as a result of Lee's work for the railroads and Rockefellers, strengthened with publicity given by the Walsh Committee. During World War I, Ivy took time away from the firm to serve the Red Cross, which brought him into contact with new leaders of American business. After the war he reevaluated the situation, decided to dissolve Lee, Harris, and Lee, and organized a new structure in which he could be more completely in control. He called the firm "Ivy Lee and Associates" and moved his headquarters a bit further uptown to a suite of offices at 111 Broadway. The firm existed under that title from 1919 to 1933.

The clientele of the firm grew to be enormous. Some, like the Pennsylvania Railroad and the Anthracite Coal Operators, were almost lifelong clients. Others were brief customers. During the twenties and early thirties, Lee's office represented nearly every facet of big business both in America and abroad: public utilities, banks, shipping, coal, oil, metals, sugar, tobacco, meatpacking, breakfast cereals, soap, cement, rubber, chemicals, investment companies, broadcasting, motion pictures, foundations, universities, charities, religious activities, political candidates, and the capitalists themselves.

Obviously, Ivy Lee could not handle all of the activities himself and his staff grew accordingly. The office was organized much like a legal firm with associates assigned to various clients. An office manager oversaw the details of the operation, with special personnel for accounting, printing, distribution, library and files, telephone, and clipping, as well as a battery of secretaries and two messenger boys. A large library was maintained with newspapers, magazines, and a clipping morgue much like a newspaper's.

The office routine was elaborate enough to require a manual. Lee was at the head of the organization chart and was consulted on all questions of policy. Thomas Ross was chief assistant, and both were backed by an advisory committee composed of Daniel Pierce,

W. W. Harris, and Lee's brother Wideman. The manual stressed the two-way nature of the public relations function which Lee saw as the role of his firm. "It should be clearly understood," he said in the manual, "that the work of the office has a dual reaction of supreme importance."[2] Decisions affected not only the client but also the public. Ivy Lee and Associates stood independently between the two.

As time passed, the firm engaged less in publicity and more in thinking and planning. Lee encouraged clients to set up their own internal publicity staff and to depend on him and his men for the larger framework of ideas from which to base public policy. "I started out thirty years ago as a straight publicity man," he later told a reporter. "Now the amount of publicity I send out is negligible. Most corporations have their own publicity departments. I rarely see their publicity. It isn't my business. My job is assisting in dealing with the public."[3]

At the inception of any venture, Lee required his staff to make a thorough investigation of the problem and the interest to be represented before the public. He instituted the practice of having his associates prepare memoranda for a client on subjects related to their interests; these would point out the significant developments and the long-range plans that might be made. For example, an analysis of the problem of a telegraph company revealed that the public was not using its services fully or investing money in the stock because of its association with "bad news" that telegrams usually brought. The Lee firm recommended that an advertising campaign be launched to use telegrams for festive occasions such as birthdays and anniversaries, not just for emergencies, to "put some joy instead of gloom into telegrams." Such analysis eventually resulted in the famous singing birthday greetings and telegrams with colorful flowers bedecking the borders.

Lee's staff dug beneath the surface of public opinion. Why did workers want higher salaries? Why did people dislike millionaires? These were merely symptoms, and he wanted to understand the deeper, more significant causes. The firm's shift in emphasis in the twenties anticipated the movement in public relations away from publicity and promotion and toward sociology and social psychology. As the thirties came on, the principle that "the public be *understood*" became as important as "the public be *informed*."

Lee was at his best as a counselor on public attitudes. One of his staff members described him as a man at whom the big men of the world could throw ideas, like balls, and see how they would bounce. George Murnane, a banking and investment executive from the twenties through the fifties and a close confidant of Lee's, called him "a man to think against." George Washington Hill, fabled president of the American Tobacco Company, hired Lee's firm primarily to get the benefit of Lee's thinking. He paid a $40,000-a-year retainer, and once said that $10,000 was for the publicity efforts of the staff but the remaining $30,000 was to be able to talk with Ivy Lee.

Lee's ability to reflect the attitudes of both the man on the street and the man of influence can be seen at its best in his work for the Waldorf-Astoria, built in the late twenties and early thirties as the most exclusive hotel in New York. He was hired as public relations counsel for the project, partly because of his association with famous personalities, such as Lady Astor and Charles Lindbergh, whom he could bring into the hotel picture for promotional purposes. But his understanding of the common man prompted him to bring the other side of the picture into focus, too. He told Lucius Boomer, president of the hotel corporation: "I for one hope that gold-plated door knobs will not be used, and even if it is found wise to use them, I hope they won't be called gold-plated.

A thing of that kind gives the impression of unnecessary luxury—luxury that gives no added comfort but is simply something to talk about."[4]

The shifting emphasis on providing public relations counsel reduced but did not eliminate the production of printed material. "The kind of work I do happens to make my office a clearing house for all kinds of information," he told writer Silas Bent. "One of my vivid memories of my father was his habit of culling from newspapers, magazines, books—in fact from every possible source—information of likely interest to his friends. He was constantly sending them clippings on every conceivable subject."[5] Lee made a science out of this. The clippings were assembled and printed for his mailing list under various titles: *Notes and Clippings* from 1918 to 1921; *Public Relations* from 1921 to 1925; and *Information* from 1925 to 1933. They were widely distributed and became well known.

Frequently, of course, items in the clip sheets concerned Lee's clients. Bethlehem Steel would be mentioned in one issue. F. Edson White, president of Armour and Company, would be quoted in another. A paragraph would be devoted to Charles Schwab. An article about the Copper and Brass Research Association would express optimism about new uses for copper. A news item might point out how the miners' refusal to arbitrate was one of the reasons for the winter's strike. Another article would be headed, "Carriers in Better Favor with the Public."

As they progressed, the clip sheets contained less plugging of products, people, or companies, and more expression of Lee's ideas: the value of public relations, the necessity of frankness and open dealings, the strength of public opinion, the virtues of capitalistic democracy. Many items concerned the broad ideas behind the problems of his clients. Lee felt that his job was not to promote products and companies so much as to improve the entire public atmosphere in which products were sold and companies operated. When he worked for the Pennsylvania, for instance, his efforts advanced the cause of all railroads. When he spoke for the Rockefellers, he was an advocate for all capitalists.

Just as Lee had little trouble getting clients, so he had no problem filling out his staff. Talented and experienced men came to him from high positions in the newspaper profession. Others were experts in business, labor, industrial relations, or international relations. Some were promising young men out of Princeton and the Columbia School of Journalism, often drawn by the glamor attached to Lee's work. Some stayed only briefly; others spent the rest of their lives with the firm. Frequently Lee sought out associates because of their particular talents or connections and, according to Sydney Pierce Hollingsworth, one of his staff, if he wanted them badly enough he induced them with high salaries. Already in the early twenties the staff numbered twenty-seven and it continued to grow until the depression.

Always loyal to his family and friends, Lee generally had a few of each on his staff. Wideman left in the early twenties, perhaps to get out from the shadow of his older brother. He became vice-president and later president of the George L. Dyer advertising agency, and he set up his own company in 1931. He was replaced by Lee's youngest brother, Lewis, who eventually became director for the Greater New York Fund. Ivy later brought his two sons into the firm after their graduation from Princeton, James Wideman II in 1930 and Ivy Jr. in 1933. Brother-in-law Lewis Bigelow was on the payroll, as was John Mumford, whose friendship went back to early reporting days at the turn of the century and who was almost a member of the family.

But chief assistant Ross remained the heir apparent through the twenties and early thirties. He had worked his way through college by handling night reporting assignments for the *Brooklyn Eagle*, and after graduation had become a full-time reporter for the *New York Morning Sun* and later the *Herald-Tribune*. During the war he had served as a second lieutenant and upon discharge, contacted his former editor at the Sun, W. W. Harris, then the middle member of Lee's firm. He became an associate in 1919, and stayed on as the dependable, down-to-earth manager who kept the office functioning smoothly while Lee was making contacts and influencing people all over the world. In 1933 Ross was made partner and the name of the firm was changed to Ivy Lee and T. J. Ross, with Lee continuing to be the dominant member until his death in 1934. The name of the firm was retained until 1960, when it became T. J. Ross and Associates; it has continued to be one of the leaders of the profession.

While Ross, Pierce, and Harris were the mainstays in the early twenties, men like Joseph Ripley, Harcourt Parrish, Burnham Carter, and Lee's sons were the chief partners in the first part of the thirties. Ripley, still with the firm in 1965, had worked his way up from sports reporter and sports editor to city editor of the *Dover Reporter* in Ohio. He went to New York in the twenties to serve as managing editor and then editor of *The American Press*, a trade publication serving small newspapers. In that job he had prepared an article about Ivy Lee and had written other items about press relations that attracted Lee's attention. One day Ripley got a phone call from Lee. "Joe, haven't you got your belly full of that paper yet?" Whereupon Ripley gave in to the attractions of public relations.

Parrish had served his apprenticeship as a reporter for the *Louisville Courier-Journal* and the Associated Press in New York where he met Ivy Lee. He worked for the firm on foreign accounts, the Rockefeller account, a Charles Lindbergh effort, and with

Melvin Alvah Traylor during the 1932 Democratic presidential nomination.

Carter joined the firm after teaching at the Taft School in Watertown, Connecticut. When Harry F. Guggenheim, a Lee client, was appointed ambassador to Cuba in 1929, Carter was chosen to go along as his secretary. He later worked on the I. G. Farben account and eventually left to devote his time to novels and short-story writing, subsequently becoming National Director of Recordings for the Blind.

Other members of the staff came from a variety of backgrounds and went on to various destinies. Victor Knauth was an Associated Press correspondent in Moscow where Lee had met him. Always interested in Russian affairs, Lee felt he could use Knauth's considerable experience and knowledge to advantage in handling international relationships. But Knauth, who later expressed gratitude to Lee for picking him up out of the lap of Bolshevism and putting him on top of Wall Street, spent most of his time with Lee writing material for Rockefeller Center and American Tobacco. One of his jobs was to serve as liaison between the tobacco and sugar people. Knauth later became editor and publisher of *Omnibook*, next a newspaper publisher, and then owner of radio stations in Connecticut and New York.

Foster Rhea Dulles, cousin of the later Secretary of State John Foster Dulles, joined the firm early in the thirties after many years as a reporter for the *Christian Science Monitor*, *New York Herald Tribune*, and *New York Evening Post*. He wrote articles for banking clients and for an anti-inflation campaign, and became a short-term partner in the firm after its reorganization in 1933. Dulles went on to become professor of history at Ohio State University and a widely read author of books on American history and foreign affairs.

Some of the staff members came to Lee almost by accident. Deane Malott joined the firm in the mid-twenties on a temporary loan basis while he was associate dean of the Harvard University School of Business. Harvard had hired Ivy Lee to undertake a fundraising campaign, and Malott was detailed to the Lee office to serve in a liaison capacity, but he stayed on and handled other jobs. He later became chancellor of the University of Kansas and president of Cornell.

Another who came by accident was Van Viault. Once when Lee was looking for an international trade expert to accompany him overseas, he approached Commerce Secretary Herbert Hoover, who recommended the Department of Commerce's Bureau of Foreign Trade. They recommended Viault, who was given the job and remained Lee's consultant on foreign affairs even after becoming a successful Manhattan attorney.

Among others who came and went was Bela Norton. He had been assistant editor of the *New York Post*, joined Lee in the mid-twenties, worked on the Rockefeller account and political affairs, but left Lee's staff to become director of public relations for the Williamsburg restoration, and eventually was appointed vice-president for public relations of Bowdoin College. Marvin M. Black joined the staff as a special writer and handled a variety of assignments for both the Pennsylvania and American Tobacco. He later became a professor of sociology and director of public relations at the University of Mississippi. Graham Parker, who joined the firm shortly after college to study European economic and industrial topics, went on to become an industrial and technical consultant with offices around the world.

Lee obviously had to turn much of the writing over to his staff. He always wanted to be the author of books but never had time and finally resorted to hiring ghostwriters for himself as he had been at times for others. He wanted particularly to write a book about publicity and public relations, especially after his chief rival, Edward Bernays, published *Crystallizing Public Opinion* in 1923.

To write the book, Lee hired Gilbert Seldes, a newspaper reporter and editor who had turned to freelance writing and in 1924 had published his popular book, *The Seven Lively Arts*. He was given access to Lee's material and put together a manuscript; but the finished product was undoubtedly too much Seldes and not enough Lee and it never reached the printed page. Not too happy with the arrangement anyway, Seldes went on to other jobs, notably as an executive for CBS (one of Lee's later clients), and later as dean of the Annenberg School of Communication at the University of Pennsylvania.

In the early thirties Lee had a number of manuscripts for book publication in preparation by members of his staff. One was on Russia, another on European memoranda that he had been collecting, a book on capitalism, and several new attempts at publicity books. He hired Orton Tewson in 1933 to write a book for him on one of his pet projects: Gothic cathedrals. But none of these was ever published, possibly because Lee himself was so particular about writing that he was difficult to please and frequently felt that he could have done the manuscript better himself if he had just had sufficient time.

One story that is told shows Lee as a perfectionist: Dudley Parsons, who was manager of public relations during the thirties for the New York Trust Company, a Lee client, recalls an incident when one of Lee's staff members submitted an unacceptable article for the *Index*, a bank publication which Lee's office helped to prepare. "The staff was quite in awe of him," notes Parsons.

"He displayed considerable side and, like the banker of his day, was quite unbending.... There was a bit of to-do about the poorly written manuscript—the Lee office never admitted mediocrity—and Ivy finally wrote it himself. He turned his office upside down, had all the boys rushing about looking up statistics and facts and turned out a reasonably good article in one day."[6]

Lee, wrapped up in his business, felt he should be treated with professionalism, that everything should be on a business basis. He was plagued with people who would seek his advice, and then be angered that Lee should charge them for his ideas. Doctors, yes; lawyers, yes; but for what Lee dispensed? Why? To Lee, however, the idea that he write out his views free was just as illogical "as though I were a professional lawyer in New York...and was asked to give my views on a legal problem free of charge.... You can imagine how promptly I would do so."

After he had become famous, he often received letters from his father with requests that he give some business advice to his father's acquaintances. One such request, shortly after he set up his firm in 1916, elicited a sharp reply from son Ivy. "I have put Mr. Oscar Johnson on the mailing list," Lee wrote, "but he should not expect a memorandum full of advice. It would be worth his while to employ me or someone else to make a study of the situation and make recommendations. You will understand that I am doing that for a good many people, and that I shall set a pretty stiff fee for my services, but I see no reason why I should send even a suggestive memorandum to Mr. Johnson on that subject when he has asked me for nothing."

"You will understand," he told his father, "that I am fully occupied with work of the greatest importance for some of the largest interests in the world and cannot take the time to give a snap opinion on a matter of this kind, where I am not definitely retained." But after a few more sentences, he realized how that sounded and added: "I don't want you to think that I know it all, but I do feel that from now on all such matters as this ought to be taken up as a business proposition."[7]

---

[1] Carl Getz, "Opportunities in Publicity," *The Open Road*, Feb. 1923, p. 2.

[2] *Organization for Conducting the Business of Ivy L. Lee and Associates*, p. 3., Ivy Lee Papers, Princeton.

[3] Quoted in Wayne W. Parrish, "Ivy Lee, 'Family Physician to Big Business,'" *The Literary Digest*, June 9, 1934, p. 30.

[4] Ivy Lee to Lucius Boomer, July 2, 1952, Ivy Lee Papers, Princeton.

[5] Silas Bent, op. cit.

[6] Dudley Parsons to R. E. Hiebert, Apr. 16, 1963.

[7] Ivy Lee to his father, Apr. 1, 1916, Ivy Lee Papers, Princeton.

Ray Eldon Hiebert

17: STEEL: ARMAMENTS FOR BETHLEHEM

As CORPORATIONS GREW and their problems multiplied, the chances for misunderstanding increased. One of the industries that most needed public understanding during Lee's career was steel. Steel was necessary to arm the nation for war, but it was also vital for the plowshares of peace. A company that had a reputation for being only an armaments producer would have trouble getting peacetime contracts, while the reverse could be true in time of war.

The European conflict, drawing steadily closer to the United States in 1914, alerted industrialists to prepare for wartime demands. The Bethlehem Steel Corporation anticipated a new need for a product it could manufacture and invested more than $7 million in an armor-plate factory. At the same time, however, the Congress of the United States was becoming concerned over the ability of the nation to take an adequate stand on the growing European hostilities. Accordingly, in 1916 a bill was proposed for the appropriation of $11 million to build a Government armor plant.

The steel companies, especially Bethlehem, felt that the construction and operation of a Government-owned armor plant would destroy the value of the three privately owned armor-plate factories then in existence in the U.S. Prior to that time the Government had always advertised for bids for armor plate, the contract then being divided among the three plants, thus assuring continued operation of all three.

The proposed bill called for a Government plant with a 20,000-ton capacity. Such volume would more than supply the armor for the program in the proposed Naval Appropriations Bill, eliminating private facilities as sources for Government contracts.

"Not only will a private industry then have been crippled, but an important reserve factor in national defense will have been destroyed," said Ivy Lee.[1]

The publicity expert made that pronouncement because Bethlehem had called him in to see what he could do about the problem. What Lee advised proved to be a large step for the steel company. It had been one of the most recalcitrant in its dealings with the public, while its chief competitor, U.S. Steel, had long since instituted a public relations policy under its chairman, Judge Elbert H. Gary.

Lee urged Bethlehem to abandon its "public be damned" attitude and tell its story to the people. But, he advised, "it is impossible to tell it to enough people by word of mouth, so you have to tell it with printer's ink." And, "you must, of course, deal with the newspapers. Take them into your confidence, not merely as newspapers, but as representing the public."[2] The papers, he said, "are more delicately adjusted to sense the feeling of the people than any other institution."[3] Lee demanded that the company make its relations with the newspapers "absolutely frank and candid . . . so that both sides know exactly what is being done."[4] The Bethlehem executives decided to take Lee at his word and turned over to him its publicity problems.

On April 13, 1916, just two weeks after Lee, Harris, and Lee had officially opened its doors on Broadway, the firm placed nationwide advertisements telling the world that Bethlehem Steel had seen the light. "We have allowed irresponsible assertions to be made for so long without denial that many people now believe them to be proven facts," the advertisement read. "We shall make the mistake of silence no longer. Henceforth we shall pursue a policy of publicity. Misinformation will not be permitted to go uncorrected. It is and has been the policy of our company to deal with the

American government in the frankest and most liberal manner. We expect henceforth to place the details of all those relations before the American people."⁵

With that announcement, the company began an all-out campaign to tell the people about its problem with the proposed Government armor plant. The campaign began in Washington. Each day a statement was prepared and sent to members of Congress arguing the point that Bethlehem Steel had charged the Government a low price for armor in the past and had derived little profit from that branch of its operations. The company was so certain that it could do better than the Government that it offered to accept any price which the Federal Trade Commission would decide to be fair to the Government and the company alike. And therefore the proposed Government armor plant would waste $11 million of the public's money, according to the Bethlehem argument.

These statements were also sent to all the newspapers, not for publication but for the information of the editors. Space was then purchased in the Washington papers to carry the statements as display advertisements. Lee told Bethlehem officers that advertising should not be overlooked as a means of telling one's story to the public, as advertising had many advantages in that the publicist could command his own location in the paper, lay out his own typographical display (always important to Lee), and write his own material, especially headlines. "In this way," he said, "you can command the attention of the people at least for a fleeting moment. And unless you can get the attention of the people away from the great mass of things which are claiming their notice nowadays, there is really not much object in having the thing printed at all."⁶

Lee decided that telling the story in Washington was not sufficient; the people themselves must be informed. So he and

Bethlehem launched what *Editor & Publisher* called "the biggest publicity campaign ever undertaken anywhere in the world." The technique was to prepare ads for about 1,000 daily and 2,500 weekly newspapers throughout the country. These told Bethlehem's side of the armor story in a new way. "This campaign is really the first of its kind," Lee told an *Editor & Publisher* reporter. "I believe that this departure from its former policy by the Bethlehem Steel Company marks the beginning of a new era in the conduct of American corporations, particularly in their relations with the public and the Government. I am confident that the campaign will have far-reaching effects, even beyond the determination of the case at issue."[7]

The ads themselves were forerunners of today's institutional advertising, presenting a rational, straightforward argument. Lee insisted that such advertising "be marked by its simplicity and dignity rather than by its ornateness or freakishness.... Like all really good publicity," he said, "the advertisement must be based on an honest case and breathe the spirit of sincerity and truth. If it be merely 'clever' it will fail. There is no hocus-pocus or mystery about good publicity or good advertising.... It is neither subtle nor mysterious nor clever. It is honest, direct, and simple."[8]

The new Bethlehem policy brought praise from the press. Reflecting the attitude of newspapermen, *Editor & Publisher* expressed the feeling that "this change of attitude toward the public on the part of one of the largest corporations in the land cannot fail to be welcomed by both the newspapers and the public...and cannot fail to be of inestimable benefit to that company in all its future public relations."[9]

The nationwide campaign was delayed for a few days by the tension in relations between the U.S. and Germany caused by the torpedoing of the Sussex. But when the crisis eased, the campaign went ahead. The bill, however, which had been voted on favorably by the Senate before the campaign began, was sent to the House of Representatives in June while the campaign was in progress. The House, too, gave it favorable passage. On August 29, 1916, President Wilson signed into law the $11 million Government armaments proposal as part of Naval Appropriations Bill for fiscal 1917.

That act appeared to render vain all of Ivy Lee's strenuous work. But within months the country was in a world war, long before the Government could complete its plant, and the three steel companies had more armor contracts than they could deal with. The campaign which Lee had waged had made Bethlehem Steel known for a new honesty, forthrightness, and efficiency, and it had no trouble winning its share of the war contracts. Its chairman, Charles Schwab, whose name had been signed to all of the ads, became one of the best known executives in America. During the campaign, Lee had become a close friend and confidant of Schwab's. Toward the end of the fourth month, Lee realized that he had been so busy with the work that he had not thought about a fee. One day, Schwab called him into his office and said, "How do you pay for your groceries?"

Lee answered, "Sometimes I solicit contributions from my friends."

"I just wanted to say that you've done a good job for the Bethlehem Steel Corporation. We should like to make it worth your while, and we are ready to pay anything you ask. How much is it?"

"Putting it that way makes me reluctant to name any figure," Lee said. "I should prefer to have you name it.

"But I don't know anything about your business and what you ought to get," Schwab said. "I'll have to leave it entirely with you."

"Probably you have a figure in mind which you think would be fair," Lee said. "I, too, have such a figure. Write yours on a piece of paper, and I'll write mine. We'll split the difference." When they compared their notes, Lee had written $10,000 and Schwab had written $20,000. They settled, of course, on the difference.¹⁰

During the war, Schwab became widely known as a hard-driving, fast-talking corporation executive who got things done for the war effort. After the war, Lee served him as personal advisor, even on matters other than publicity. With his characteristic exuberance, Lee pointed out to Schwab many opportunities for the company. The story is told that Schwab one day broke in on Lee's advice and said that he already knew of more things that needed to be done than he could do. What he needed was not advice but some way to do all the things he had to do. Lee thought a moment and then gave Schwab a hint, a simple technique that every reporter knows when he organizes a news story. Each day, Lee said, write down all the things you have to do and then number them according to their importance. Start doing the important ones and work down to the unimportant. If you don't finish, you will at least have taken care of the major jobs. Schwab apparently profited so much from this advice that he sent Ivy Lee a check for $25,000 some time later.

Lee became fascinated with Schwab whom he regarded as "one of the most attractive personalities this country has ever known." He helped prepare his speeches, and he once told how such speech conferences went. Schwab would have an idea (he was never lacking in ideas, Lee said), then he would call in Lee and say: "I have to make a speech." He would "ramble all over the map, murdering the King's English," Lee said, and then say: "This in a general way is the point I want to make. Now, won't you get up something to give to the newspapers that will put the point in concrete language, so that

I can give it as the substance of what I am saying, and then I will say it in my own way?"

At the meeting where the speech was to be delivered, Schwab would rise to give his speech. "Gentlemen," he would say to his distinguished audience, "before I came here tonight, I had three written speeches to deliver. One of them I wrote myself, another Judge Gary wrote, and the third was written by my friend here (pointing to Lee). But I am going to throw them all away and speak to you from the heart." With that the crowd would clap approvingly, and Schwab would then proceed to make the speech that Lee had written.[11]

The war led to enormous corporate expansion of Bethlehem Steel. The company began to buy out other firms and expand its horizons, acquiring Cambria Steel, Lackawanna, Midvale, and others. The intention was to modernize the plants in the postwar years and build Bethlehem into an efficient and modern corporate giant. But after the war the company did not have enough capital to revitalize all the plant and equipment it had acquired, so it went to the bankers for help. Eugene Grace, president of the company, sought $30 million for improvements.

But the bankers turned Bethlehem down. The reasoning, according to Ivy Lee, went like this: "Mr. Grace, during the war the Bethlehem Steel Corporation did some very wonderful things. Mr. Schwab touched the public imagination as few men ever touched it. But you had so much interest in the military lines that you were regarded as a war baby. The people have an idea that your money was made in war machinery, in guns and ammunition. They have read of the Washington Conference, which calls for a great deal of disarmament. Moreover, the people have understood that you build warships and that you have navy yards, and they know that the shipbuilding business is at a very low ebb. Everybody knows that you are a great man; but people have those ideas in the backs of their minds, and therefore you have not today sufficient public friendship to create the confidence which you ought to have for an issue of securities."[12]

Thus Bethlehem had a new public relations problem. Rather than prove to the public that it was capable of producing war armaments, the company had to prove that it had changed from an armaments manufacturer to a producer of goods for peaceful consumption. The Lee office again played an important role in this shifting of image. First, Lee and his colleagues began circulating information about the smoothness of the labor relations at Bethlehem, on the theory that no company faced with labor troubles could successfully appeal to the confidence of investors.

The Lee office also told the facts about the products Bethlehem was manufacturing. It pointed out that only 7 percent of the company's capital investment was in shipbuilding plants and less than 1 1/2 percent in armament facilities. In newspaper articles and bulletins distributed to bankers and investors, Lee attempted to show that Bethlehem's shipbuilding machinery had been recreated into a great ship-repairing industry which was yielding large returns to the company, and that the plants which had been devoted to the manufacture of munitions were now being devoted to making cars, locomotives, harvesters, and other implements of peace.

Perhaps the most valuable contribution which Lee and his staff made was in connection with the company's twentieth anniversary, an event that would give opportunity to review the past twenty years of the company and show that it was a manufacturer of peacetime products. It could further be shown this was not merely a postwar development but a policy that had been instituted twenty years before, when Schwab first took over. As a result of the anniversary publicity, Grace received letters from bankers all over the country congratulating him on the progress of his company. Shortly thereafter, Bethlehem Steel Corporation was able to sell $30 million worth of bonds to carry out its plant and equipment modernization and expansion.

During the twenties and early thirties, international conferences on armament and disarmament were common. Because he represented the Rockefellers, who were known to be pacifists, and because he represented the Schwabs of Bethlehem Steel, who built naval ships, Ivy Lee was frequently charged with distributing antiwar literature with one hand and prowar literature with the other. After the Geneva Arms Conference in 1927, which deadlocked over the question of naval cruisers, Lee was accused of being paid "something like $50,000" by the Council of American Shipbuilders for promoting greater naval allotments. He was also charged with aiding Great Britain in naval armament promotion, but he denied that he was involved in such activities and repeated the denial under oath during a Congressional investigation in 1929.[13] This was part of the burden of trying to achieve public understanding for easily misunderstood corporate problems.

Throughout the period from before World War I to after World War II the Bethlehem Steel Corporation was constantly caught in the throes of a public opinion shifting from peace to war and back again. As a major supplier of the armaments of war, Bethlehem had to be ready to deliver the goods when the people demanded them. But when the battles were ended, it had to shift to peaceful purposes without missing a beat. By adopting Ivy Lee's philosophy, Bethlehem learned the importance of understanding the crowd and getting the people to understand steel production. That understanding was undoubtedly one of the reasons for the corporation's growth into one of the top steel manufacturers in the nation.

[1] *Editor & Publisher*, May 27, 1916. See also June 17, 1916.

[2] Ivy Lee, *Publicity for Public Service Corporations*, pp. 19, 25.

[3] Ivy Lee, "The Technique of Publicity," *Electric Railway Journal*, Jan. 6, 1917, p. 16.

[4] Ivy Lee, *Publicity for Public Service Corporations*, p. 26.

[5] Quoted in Ivy Lee, "Enemies of Publicity," *Electric Railway Journal*, Mar. 31, 1917, p. 599.

[6] Ivy Lee, *Publicity for Public Service Corporations*, pp. 26–27.

[7] *Editor & Publisher*, May 27, 1916.

[8] Ivy Lee, "Advertising in Publicity Work," *Electric Railway Journal*, Oct. 6, 1917, p. 618.

[9] *Editor & Publisher*, May 27, 1916.

[10] Quoted in Wisehart, op. cit., pp. 126–127.

[11] T. J. Ross to J. W. Lee II, Mar. 13, 1950, Ivy Lee Papers, Princeton.

[12] "Publicity and Corporations," *Mr. Lee's Publicity Book*, p. 15, Ivy Lee Papers, Princeton.

[13] *New York Times*, Oct. 2, 1929, p. 24.

This Blank-Stoller photographer caught exactly the right expression to project the image of Ivy Ledbetter lee as the "Father of Modern Public Relations."

Ivy Lee with his family shortly after the turn of the century. Front row, left to right: Louis H. Lee (brother); Mrs. James W. Lee (mother); Dr. James W. Lee (father); Kate Lee Trueblood (sister); Wilbur Trueblood (Kate's husband). Back row: Ivy Lee; Cornelia Bigelow Lee (Ivy's wife); Mortimer Burroughs (Laura's husband); Laura Lee Burroughs (sister); James Wideman Lee Jr. (brother); Florence O'Day Lee (James's wife); Alice May Lee Hoxie (sister); and Robert Hoxie (Alice's husband).

During the "Ludlow Massacre" hearing in Congress, Lee waits outside Senate hearing room in Washington, D.C., to testify before the Federal Industrial Relations Commission on his relationship to the Rockefeller interests during the labor troubles in the Colorado mine fields. (Courtesy Brown Brothers, New York.)

A. Cotton Bedford, president of Standard Oil of New Jersey, with Lee, who served as his public relations counsel and speech writer, as they were planning the American Petroleum Institute in 1917.

Ivy Lee in his office at 61 Broadway (above). Taken about 1918, this photo typifies the volume of work Lee could dispatch in one day.

Rare photograph of the billionaire, John D. Rockefeller Sr., taken with Lee (right) at Rockefeller's Pocantino Hills mansion. Men in foreground are unidentified.

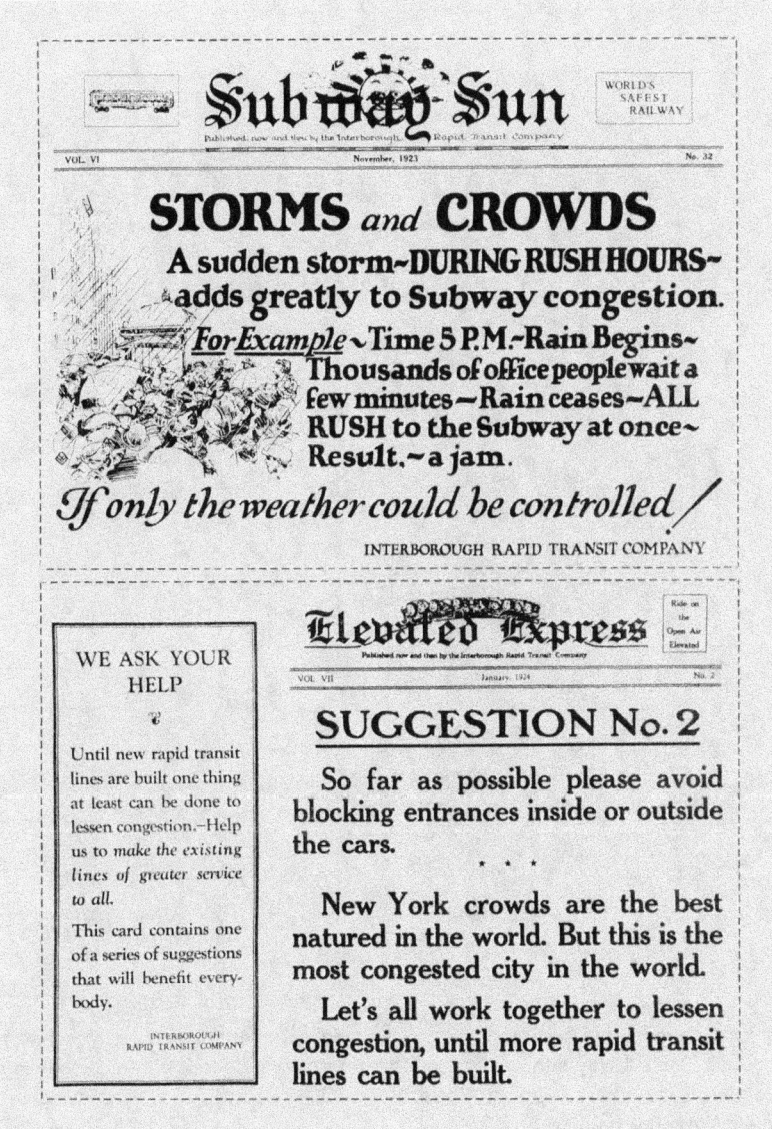

Lee's **Subway Sun** and **Elevated Express**, newspaper-style posters for subway stations and trains, contained no direct advocacy of the management's position but subtly suggested ways the passengers could improve service. The spirit of sharing problems and solutions did much to increase goodwill toward the company.

The fight to raise subway fares inspired much editorial comment expressed in both words and cartoons. The **Subway Sun** was a natural target for John Cassel, whose cartoon (above) appeared in the **New York Evening World**, March 17, 1921, and T. E. Powers, (upper right) in the **New York Journal**, Jan. 15, 1921.

Lee's dramatic rise to mastery in the profession of public relations provoked an entirely different kind of cartoon. Kessler's "rags-to-riches" angle appeared in the **New York Evening Graphic**, Aug. 26, 1921.

The "clip sheet" which Lee helped popularize as a public relations tool. This issue publicized a number of his clients: Armour & Co., Standard Oil, the subways, and foreign loans. He later changed the title, **Public Relations**, to **Information**.

PUBLIC RELATIONS

Issued by
Ivy L. Lee and Associates
61 Broadway
New York City

FEBRUARY 23, 1925

JOHN SIMON GUGGENHEIM MEMORIAL TO SUPPLEMENT RHODES SCHOLARSHIPS

Students Beyond Rhodes Age Limit Provided for in New Endowment Which Admits Men and Women of Any Race, Creed or Color; Rhodes Scholars Prove Value of Study Abroad by Their Achievements

A preliminary gift of $3,000,000 for the endowment of the John Simon Guggenheim Memorial Foundation Fellowships was announced today by Simon Guggenheim, former United States Senator from Colorado, and his wife.

In a statement explaining the purposes of the Guggenheim Fellowships, Simon Guggenheim said:

"I want to supplement the great Rhodes Foundation by providing a similar opportunity for older students of proved ability, and for women as well as men. Furthermore, I want to make it possible for these persons to carry on their studies in any country in the world where they can work most profitably."

Outstanding Features of Rhodes Foundation

The Rhodes scholarships, which for the last 21 years have afforded American students an opportunity to study at the University of Oxford, were founded under the will of Cecil John Rhodes, the South African statesman and millionaire, who died in 1902. Rhodes founded his scholarships for the purpose of promoting friendly understanding between the English-speaking countries of the world, believing that this was the best way to secure peace and the advancement of civilization. The means which he chose for such ing toward this end were to bring together at the University of Oxford representative young men from the United States and from all the British Dominions in order that they might live together for three years and come to understand each other and the young Englishmen who would in the next generation be leaders in thought and in public life.

There are always, in accordance with the terms of the Rhodes Will, 190 Rhodes scholars at Oxford, of whom 96 come from the United States. A Rhodes scholarship is tenable for three years and carries a stipend of £350 per year. Candidates, here, must be citizens of the United States, unmarried, not younger than 19 nor older than 25 years of age, and must have completed at least the sophomore year in college. They are selected on a three-fold basis which takes into account (1) qualities of manhood, force of character and leadership, (2) literary and scholastic attainment, and (3) physical vigor as shown in outdoor sports and in other ways.

No restriction is placed upon a Rhodes Scholar's choice of study. He may read for the Bachelor's degree at Oxford in some one of the various Honor Schools or become a candidate for one of the research degrees of B.Litt., B.Sc., or Ph.D. The largest single group at Oxford have taken up the study of law. Other subjects studied by the American Rhodes Scholars in the order of the number of men going into them are: Modern History and Economics, the Humanities (including Classics, Philosophy, and Anthropology), English Language and Literature, Theology, Mathematics, Physics, Chemistry and Engineering, Modern Languages, Physiology and Medical Studies, Geology and Forestry, and Music.

In their examinations at Oxford the American Rhodes Scholars have averaged better than the whole group of Oxford Honors men though slightly below the group of students from the great boys' schools of England, Eton, Harrow, and Rugby—called, strangely enough to American ears, "Public Schools"—who have won scholarships in the Oxford Colleges by open competitive examination. It has been observed that the Rhodes Scholars do better in subjects which do not depend upon preparatory school work while the Englishmen do better in those subjects which depend upon preparation in the English Public Schools.

Value of Foreign Study to Americans

There are now about 500 ex-Rhodes Scholars living in the United States. Nearly one-third of them have taken up education as a career. The next largest group is law, and the other careers chosen by the men, arranged according to the number of men in each, are: business, social and religious work, government service, scientific research, literary and editorial work, and medicine.

As a whole the group has justified the value of training at Oxford as a preparation for success in the United States.

Aims of Guggenheim Fellowships Are Outlined

The purposes of the John Simon Guggenheim Memorial Fellowships are:

To improve the quality of education and the practice of the arts and professions in the United States, to foster research, and to provide for the cause of better international understanding.

A bill for a special charter for the Foundation will be introduced in the legislature at Albany, N. Y., tonight by Senator Courtlandt Nicoll and Assemblyman Phelps Phelps.

The Foundation is a memorial to the son of Senator and Mrs. Guggenheim, who died on April 26, 1922. The Foundation offers to young men and women world wide opportunities under the freest possible conditions to carry on advanced study and research in any field of knowledge, or opportunities for the development of unusual talent in any of the fine arts including music.

No age limits are prescribed. Appointees, however, must be old enough to have shown marked ability in their particular subject. It is expected that ordinarily they will not be younger than 25 or older than 35 years.

The fellowships are therefore intended for students somewhat older than those to whom the Rhodes scholarships are open, including young professors on sabbatical leave, holders of fellowships from individual colleges and those who have won distinction in graduate study. Only those candidates will be appointed who have evinced some highly important piece of work and who show exceptional aptitude for research, or who demonstrate ability in some one of the fine arts.

These fellowships differ from the Rhodes scholarships, furthermore, in being open to women as well as men and being available for study in any country in the world.

The amount of money available for each fellowship will be approximately $2500 a year, but may be more or less, depending on individual needs. While appointments will be made ordinarily for one year, plans which involve two or three years' study will also be considered and in special cases fellowships will be granted for shorter terms with appropriate stipends.

The first national awards will be made for the academic year 1926-1927. It is the purpose of the Foundation after the first year to maintain annually from forty to fifty fellows abroad. The fellowships will be open to men and women, married or unmarried, of every race, color and creed.

There is no restriction of the subject to be studied or the place where study is to be pursued. The fellowships are open only to candidates engaged in research work along academic or artistic lines but also to those interested in the workings of foreign systems of government, in the study of social or business conditions or in productive scholarship in the fields of the various learned professions, art and music being especially mentioned as among the subjects contemplated.

The principal obligation imposed on the holders of fellowships is that they shall produce contributions to knowledge in their special subjects and, secondly, that they shall make the results of their studies publicly available. Where necessary and deemed wise the Foundation will give financial assistance towards publication.

Senator Guggenheim Tells Aims of New Foundation; Hopes to Supplement Work of Rhodes Foundation and Aid Older Students.

Concurrent with his announcement of the establishment of the John Simon Guggenheim Memorial Foundation, Simon Guggenheim made the following statement:

The establishment of the John Simon Guggenheim Memorial Foundation is the culmination of a plan that Mrs. Guggenheim and I have cherished for some time to create a worthy memorial to our boy, whose death, in 1922, was an inexpressible sorrow to both of us. If he had lived, he would have continued his education in one of our great American Universities, and then upon his graduation there, he would have embarked upon a course of graduate study abroad, just such as we are now endeavoring to make possible for others under this Foundation.

Ever since Cecil Rhodes founded the Rhodes scholarships I have watched the development of his plan with unusual interest. It has now been in operation 21 years, has attained its majority, and has more than justified the vision of its founder.

I want to supplement the great Rhodes Foundation by providing a similar opportunity for older students of proved ability, and for women as well as men. Furthermore, I want to make it possible for these persons to carry on their studies in any country in the world where they can work most profitably.

With the progress of our country it is inevitable that our interests should reach out over the world. My father and my brothers and I have participated in this modern trend in our business relations. My family came to this country originally from Switzerland and were once engaged in business there. Since then we have had large interests not only in many of our own States, but in Alaska, Mexico, South America, Asia and Africa. I have been deeply impressed therefore with the importance of a world wide viewpoint and with the necessity of a better international understanding.

I am also deeply interested in art and music, and my wife and I had always hoped that a similar interest would have developed in the boy we lost so that these things also might have had a part in his further education. For these reasons and many others I have endeavored to establish this new Foundation on the broadest possible base.

It is a matter of satisfaction to me that the income of the Foundation will be spent on men and not on materials. I have noticed that it has always been an easy matter for educational enterprises to secure money for buildings; but money in the place where this Foundation proposes to use it is apparently hard to get.

It has been my observation, from the outside, that just about the time a young man has finished college and is prepared to do valuable research, he is compelled to spend his whole time in teaching. Salaries are small; so he is compelled to do this in order to live, and often he loses the impulse for creative work in his subject, which should be preserved in order to make his teaching of the utmost value, and also for the sake of the value of the researches in the carrying on of civilization. I have been informed that the sabbatical year is often not taken advantage of because professors cannot go abroad on half salary and it is for this reason that we have provided that members of teaching staffs on sabbatical leave shall be eligible for these appointments.

In working out the details of our plan I have been singularly fortunate in securing the thoughtful consideration and assistance of a large group of leaders in the many fields of education, of art and of science in this country. To each of these men and women I am deeply grateful for the interest which they have taken in the Foundation and for the invaluable assistance which they have given. The plan as finally adopted is not the thought of a moment, but is the product of many minds and of long and careful discussion.

I earnestly hope that the Foundation may be of permanent benefit to those appointed to the fellowships which it provides, and by means of their study and research, as well as through the contacts which they establish, to our entire nation and to the world.

Another issue of **Public Relations** publicizes his Guggenheim clients, this time on the establishment of Guggenheim Foundation Fellowships.

241

The Rockefeller interests got regular publicity in Lee's **Public Relations** clip sheet, including this material on building the Cathedral of St. John the Divine in New York.

Whenever possible, Lee shared his adventures with members of his family as on this Hollywood set in 1926, while Lee was public relations advisor to United Artists. Left to right: son James W. Lee II; Ivy's wife Cornelia Bigelow Lee; Miss Adelaide Carrier, Leavitt Corning, and Allan Kirk, all friends of the family; Ivy Lee; Miss Geraldine McAlpin, another friend; Edmund Lowe in the Marine uniform he wore as star of "What Price Glory"; daughter Alice Lee; and son Ivy Lee Jr.

As early believer in air travel, Ivy Lee often made flights to meet his many clients around the world in the days when few were brave enough to join him. His wife had the courage as did his sons James and Ivy Jr., shown boarding this passenger plane in Europe in 1928.

A typical publicity still (left) taken by Lee's photographers, Brown Brothers of New York, shows the photo-shy John D. Rockefeller Sr. on his ninetieth birthday cutting his cake — a picture that got worldwide publicity. (Courtesy Brown Brothers, New York.)

At the height of his success in the late twenties, Lee sits at his desk in his office at 15 Broad Street (below). One of the legends about him is that he cold quote without hesitation from hundreds of these volumes.

One of the last photos of Ivy Lee, taken in the early thirties as he walked through Central Park near his Fifth Avenue apartment. The public relations burdens of his many clients were beginning to take their toll.

18: ADJUSTMENTS IN OIL, COPPER, AND COAL

IVY LEE LIKED TO THINK OF HIMSELF as an "adjuster of relationships," and he provided this service for some of the biggest industries in the nation.

Early in 1917 he added another corporate giant to his growing clientele: the Standard Oil Company. When A. Cotton Bedford assumed the New Jersey company's presidency in 1916, he quickly showed a greater interest in public relations than had most of his predecessors. "I mean to keep my door wide open to every person having a legitimate call upon my attention," he said when he took office. He personally engaged Lee to serve him on a consulting basis. The move might have been suggested by John D. Rockefeller Jr., who maintained contact with the company even though he had no control over it. Standard Oil historians George Gibb and Evelyn Knowlton maintain that whether Lee's hiring came from Rockefeller or not, "it clearly derived from the precedent set by him in the Ludlow affair."[1]

When Lee joined Bedford at Standard the company was still one of the most hated corporations in the United States. Only a little more than five years earlier, Standard had been sued by the Government and broken up into thirty-three companies, of which the New Jersey corporation was the largest. The publicity department had only made matters worse for the company by bribing the press and keeping the truth from the public instead of taking the people into their confidence, telling them what they were doing, how they were doing it, and why.

Bedford, however, was eager to cultivate the goodwill of the public and asked for Lee's advice. Lee told him that he would be laughed off the stage if he made speeches in which he claimed that Standard Oil was a public good. He could not carry on in the tradition of subsidizing the newspapers to print complimentary stories. It would be useless for him to write and publish articles on his own, appealing to the public to change its view, for the public would not read them. The first step necessary, Lee said, would be for Bedford to set his house in order and then to associate himself with the most progressive groups in the oil business.

Lee told Bedford that Standard Oil must have the confidence of many groups, chief among them its competitors. As he saw it, the great fight of Standard Oil had been lost in that arena. The competitors had abused it, had succeeded in making the public believe that the company was corrupt and ruthless, and Standard had not replied. Lee advised Bedford to meet his competitors as a friend, joining with them in efforts to make business better and establish higher standards of ethics. The best way to start would be to identify himself closely with the United States Chamber of Commerce, the group of cooperating businessmen designed to express the business view to the government.

Bedford thereupon became an active Chamber of Commerce man. During World War I, he was chosen by all of his competitors as chairman of the "Committee on Mobilization" for the oil industry. After the war, he was asked to become president of the United States Chamber, and then chairman of the American Committee of the International Chamber of Commerce. He declined these two roles but did accept the job of vice-president of the International Chamber.

"Now realize," Ivy Lee said later, "what it means for the president of the Standard Oil of New Jersey, the lineal business descendent of John D. Rockefeller, to be asked to become the head of the association speaking for the united business men of the whole United States! It is a wonderful achievement, and it is the result of these indirect, and yet direct, methods of cultivating confidence in behalf of a corporation."[2]

Even more important, the war efforts of Bedford brought to the oil industry a new kind of efficiency through cooperation. Lee pointed out that "often throughout the war and afterwards, Mr. Bedford and the presidents of all the large oil companies in the country sat in the old Board of Directors' room of the Standard Oil Company, with the picture of John D. Rockefeller hanging on the wall, and discussed ways of cooperating, even by sacrificing their individual interests in behalf of the great work of winning the war."[3] Not a long step remained then to full cooperation for peacetime harmony and progress in the oil industry.

At the instigation of Ivy Lee, the American Petroleum Institute was founded by the same men and companies that had been represented in Bedford's Committee on Mobilization. Lee's firm served as public relations representatives for the Institute, which became a highly respected central clearing house for information on the oil industry and a central body for dealing with mutual problems of all oil companies. Bedford was again asked to assume leadership of the Institute, and this earned confidence and respect for Standard of New Jersey, not only among its competition but from the public at large.

By the mid-twenties New Jersey Standard was bigger than the original Standard Oil monopoly that had been split into thirty-three companies, but public confidence had replaced most of the earlier antagonism.

Bedford was promoted from president to chairman of the board, and Lee continued to write many of Bedford's speeches and provide personal advice on public relations until the oil executive's death in 1925. Thereafter, Lee served Standard of New Jersey only through his relationship with the American Petroleum Institute.

But meanwhile another Standard company was having problems: Standard of New York, or Socony-Vacuum. At Lee's urging, Bedford and the New Jersey company had adopted a plan of employee representation, insurance, and benefits. The Vacuum company had not done this and its unsatisfactory labor relations led to a major strike in 1924. Rockefeller Jr., who had been pleased with Lee's efforts for the New Jersey company, told the Vacuum directors, with whom he was very close and had a considerable amount of influence: "You'd better get that Ivy Lee fellow to help you out."[4] Vacuum did, and the Lee firm continued to advise the company for a long time thereafter.

While the war effort aided Standard Oil, it seriously damaged copper producing and fabricating concerns including those which dealt with copper alloys, brass, and bronze. Almost all copper operations during the war were devoted directly to the production of munitions. Copper that had formerly been used for manufacturing, building construction, and in other fields was replaced by substitutes such as aluminum which were not needed for armaments. When the war ended and the munitions factories closed down, copper miners and manufacturers found themselves without a market.

Ivy Lee was engaged to handle the publicity for some of the largest copper producers including the Anaconda Copper Mining Company and Phelps, Dodge, and Company. He became acquainted with Daniel Guggenheim and did work for the Guggenheims' extensive mining interests. The general nature of his counsel to these copper companies individually can be seen in his advice to Anaconda.

Anaconda's publicity problem was no longer local, he told John Ryan, Chairman of the Board, because the company's products went all over the nation and needed national publicity. He felt that there was a great deal of curiosity in the "picturesque nature of so many of [the company's] processes and products.... This inherent interest makes it possible to accomplish by means of publicity, results which other companies or industries are frequently forced to seek through institutional advertising. Anaconda is alive with news interest," he told Ryan.[5]

He suggested three continuing public relations efforts on behalf of Anconda. The first was publication of a monthly magazine similar to the *Lamp*, a conservative, thoughtful type of periodical which Lee had set up for Standard Oil of New Jersey. The second was a booklet describing the company specifically, including a table to trace all the company's various activities. The third was the publication of an annual report which would elaborate on the welfare of the employees of the company. Lee specifically recommended to Ryan that Anaconda should not "engage in any blatant publicity or undertake steps which would be cheap.... The idea in my mind is that a company whose interests are so extensive as yours should take steps to see to it that, in a careful, conservative way, the public understands the general character of its policies."[6]

Out of this sort of counsel for the individual companies, Lee came up with the idea for the Copper and Brass Research Association, which soon became the central body to serve the public relations needs of forty-two of the largest copper producers and manufacturers in the country. The purpose of the association was to pool resources of the copper industry to regain a proper share of the market for its products.

Under Lee's guidance, the association carried out an extensive campaign. An advertising program geared to the copper consumer was run in newspapers and magazines. Copper dealers were given material for distribution to the public. Architectural, manufacturing, and technical publications were used for advertising aimed at specific groups and potential users of copper. In addition to advertising, a large promotional campaign was waged. A monthly bulletin was sent to the construction industry. Newspaper mats were prepared, containing items on new uses for copper. Books and pamphlets were written and published for distribution to the public.

Most important, however, was the setting up of a technical staff of research men. Their job was to find new and wider uses for copper and to make extensive surveys into just what was being done by industry with copper and its alloys. The work of the research staff, in turn, frequently provided news stories about new developments and discoveries which were sent out as press releases to the newspapers of the country. The Copper and Brass Research Association created an entirely new way for industry to deal with its public problems. It in turn spawned a variety of similar research groups in such fields as corn, alcohol, chemicals, oil, timber, and other industrial areas.

The Copper and Brass Research Association ultimately helped to restore the industrial uses of copper after the period of neglect following the war. But from time to time, other public dragons rose up to threaten copper interests, and Lee's public relations men would come to the rescue.

A typical case happened in the mid-twenties when a Harvard pathologist, in a medical journal article probably inspired by concern for the effects of the bathtub gin mills of Prohibition, wrote that alcoholic liquids distilled in copper pots were poisonous. Moreover, the scientist contended, food prepared in copper kettles was deadly; a man who ate such food for eighty or ninety years would accumulate enough copper in his system to kill him. The article was authoritatively written and was based on exhaustive examinations of supposed victims of corrosive poisoning. It attracted the attention of the nation's newspapers which picked it up and gave it wide coverage.

The copper industry feared that all the good effects of Lee's work with the Copper and Brass Research Association had been lost. The leaders of the industry immediately got in touch with him and anxiously requested that something be done to answer the article or counteract its effects.

Lee advised that "it is perfect nonsense to talk about answering a thing like this except with the facts." He told the Association that the first thing to do would be to appoint another eminent scientist to review the studies to see if there was any error. If they could not correct the original study and get the Harvard people to revise their findings, Lee said, they should set up a research project of their own and attempt to find out whether the Harvard study was right or wrong. If wrong, the Lee group would have a weapon to neutralize public reaction.

But, Lee said, if all research corroborates the Harvard study, "there is only one thing to do: we have got to withdraw copper from these uses. New uses for copper would have to be invented where the corrosive effects would not be bad," he said. "There is not any propaganda at all to do in that matter until we get the facts. Do not let us ever for one moment budge from that position."[7]

The Copper and Brass Research Association accepted Lee's position. In the end they were able to prove the original study was erroneous and copper has continued to be a useful product for a variety of purposes in the twentieth century, including cooking.

World War I also brought new difficulties to the anthracite coal industry, one of Lee's first important clients. The operators called on him again in 1920, this time not because they had labor problems, as in 1902 and 1906, but because they were losing their market. Before the war, the anthracite industry had never lacked demand for its product; every ton of hard coal was sold as soon as it was taken out of the ground. Soft coal, which was considered an inferior product, was not so widely used in spite of a lower price because of antismoke ordinances. But the relaxation of many of these ordinances during the war had opened the way for increased use of soft coal. Oil, too, had made vast inroads on the hard coal market during the war, and by 1920 the anthracite business was in trouble. The operators called once again for Ivy Lee.

The industry was composed of 102 companies organized into the Anthracite Coal Operators Conference which Lee's firm represented. His office divided its job for the operators into three categories: public relations, labor relations, and customer relations. The most immediate problem was with the customers: getting them to buy hard coal again, instead of soft coal or oil. In this effort, Lee and his staff, particularly under Dan Pierce, pioneered with yet another communication device: the exhibit.

Five permanent shows were set up in central locations in New York, Boston, Philadelphia, Baltimore, and Washington. These exhibits, put together at great expense—$50,000 to $60,000 a year in the early twenties—drew large crowds. The shows were advertised in local newspapers and in circulars distributed throughout metropolitan areas. They contained dramatic and eye-catching demonstrations of the best types of anthracite burning apparatus for all uses, from office buildings to garages.

In addition to the five permanent shows, Lee and his staff devised a traveling show, carried by truck, which ran throughout the

New England and mid-Atlantic states. At its opening in each city, a meeting was held to which local architects, builders, coal dealers, contractors, and city officials were invited. Usually an imposing invitation committee was set up beforehand, often headed by the mayor of the city. The committee also engaged prominent local citizens to talk on the problems of heating and coal. These meetings generated local newspaper publicity, and this in turn called the attention of the public to the traveling shows.

Lee's firm operated a speakers' bureau, which at first consisted of one man who went around the country addressing clubs and neighborhood meetings. Then, sensing in the early twenties that radio would become a powerful medium of communication, Lee urged the anthracite people to give it a try. Every two weeks, his firm presented a radio speech about coal for WEAF, one of the original and most important New York stations. The response demonstrated the effectiveness of broadcasting. Even while a radio set was something of a luxury item, the coal talks on WEAF drew as many as three hundred letters a week.

The firm also prepared and issued a publication called *The Burning Question*, a "germ carrier," as Pierce put it, to answer questions about the use of coal and to show consumers that the industry was interested in their welfare. At a staff meeting, Pierce told about the typical contents of the magazine: it contained articles on "how to run a furnace, how dangerous oil is, what a menace to health smoke is—smoke being produced by our competitors and not by ourselves."[8] *The Burning Question* was only distributed to those requesting it, primarily through coal dealers who passed the names on to the Lee offices.

Here again, however, as in the oil and copper industries, communication was treated as a two-way street. The Lee firm often counseled the coal industry to adapt policies to public attitudes.

One of the chief difficulties of the industry at the time was that the operators had no control over coal once it left the mine. The producer could ship a ton of the best chestnut coal, perfectly prepared, accurately sized, and honestly billed. But once it got into the dealer's hands, it could be mixed with inferior pea coal, or even dirt and refuse, to stretch out the ton. The coal operators were the target of consumer criticism that should have been aimed at the dealers.

Lee, and Pierce who handled the account, urged the coal operators to do just what the apple growers had done—standardize their product, then refuse to permit any coal to be shipped that was not up to that standard. They should then stand behind that policy and refuse to sell coal to dealers who adulterated the product. There should be, they said, Certified Coal just as there was Certified Milk. They advised independent inspectors who could warn any dealer not following the standards. Only in such a way, said Pierce, could the producer, the operator, "escape from some of the odium that is now unjustly visited upon him because of the misuse of his product after it leaves his hands."[9]

These were methods by which Lee and his firm adjusted relationships between the public and oil, copper, and coal. The resulting harmony spurred those industries to new growth. As American population expanded, with increasing crowds coming into increasing conflict, such adjustments became necessary in every sphere of activity, from travel and entertainment to religion and politics. In one way or another, Ivy Lee became involved in all of them.

---

[1] G. S. Gibb and E. H. Knowlton, *The Resurgent Years, 1911–1927: History of Standard Oil Company* (New York: Harper & Bros., 1956), pp. 253–254.

[2] Ivy Lee, "Case Studies in Publicity," *Publicity, The Profession of Persuading the Public*, ms., p. 4, Ivy Lee Papers, Princeton.

[3] Ibid.

[4] J. W. Lee II in conversation with R. E. Hiebert, July 1962.

[5] Ivy Lee to John D. Ryan, Jan. 18, 1924, Ivy Lee Papers, Princeton.

[6] Ibid.

[7] "Transcript of Staff Conference, Ivy Lee and Associates," Jan. 24, 1925, pp. 36 ff.

[8] Ibid., pp. 77 ff.

[9] Ibid., p. 86.

19: COOPERATION IN FOODS, COTTON, SUGAR, AND TOBACCO

UNCONTROLLED MASS PRODUCTION early in this century led to difficulties for many commodities, not the least of which was food. The fecundity of American agricultural production generated problems for farmers that have not yet been completely solved; vast storehouses of farm surplus currently cost Americans several million dollars a day in storage charges alone. Small food packagers and distributors suffering from overproduction and vicious competition began in the twenties to merge into large corporations to cut costs and prevent bankruptcy.

Food suppliers were learning that customers in an affluent society were motivated by more than hunger when they bought food. To reach the consumer in such an environment, a new approach was needed.

Washburn-Crosby of Minneapolis, the huge flour milling firm which grew into General Mills, was one of the first to recognize the need for an advisor in public relations. Ivy Lee was selected and almost immediately suggested that they make their product *superior*, then give it distinctive packaging. This resulted in the famous "Gold Medal" flour which General Mills produced.[1]

He also suggested that the company look for new and better ways to get information about its products to its potential market. What was the market? Housewives who used flour and baking ingredients. How do you reach that audience? Perhaps through another housewife, someone who could reflect the interests of all housewives, someone in whom they could trust. Eventually, this was personified in the creation of Betty Crocker, whose name has since become a household word throughout America.

To increase consumption of General Mills breakfast cereal it was necessary to analyze the reasons for breakfast eating habits. Lee found that most doctors agreed a good breakfast was important for energy throughout the day. A promotional campaign based on that fact would have unusual appeal, Lee advised. This idea eventually led to "breakfast of champions" as the time-honored slogan of Wheaties.

In addition to better packaging and promotion to sell more products, Lee continually sought greater cooperation among the manufacturers. He was frequently called upon to provide public defense for the logic of a merger. One such case brought him to work for one of the largest meat packers, Armour and Company. In 1923 Armour bought the business and properties of Morris and Company, and the Secretary of Agriculture began an investigation of the firm because he felt that the merger was a violation of the Packers and Stockyards Act of 1921, a law meant to preserve competition among packers.

Lee began a publicity campaign for Armour which factually put forth the arguments why the Armour-Morris merger was a business necessity. He sent out a series of bulletins entitled, "The People Should Know the Facts." He said, "The house of Armour and Company wants the American people to understand its business and the conditions under which it is conducted.... There is no 'Beef Trust.' The production and sale of meat is extremely competitive."[2] The bulletins then gave the facts and figures to bear out the contention. After the Department of Agriculture hearings began, Lee had flyers printed containing excerpts of the testimony. The bulletins and flyers succeeded in helping Armour prove its case, and Lee's continued public relations counsel helped the company grow into a major meatpacking corporation.

One small job which Lee did for Armour and Company provides a good illustration of the fact that he was not interested in using publicity to hoodwink the public with half-truths, but rather in honestly explaining the whole truth to his clients and to the public, knowing that a client would win if he had a sound case. In 1932, when Armour and Company was arguing the "Packers Consent Decree" case before the Supreme Court, Lee was asked to prepare a public statement about Armour's position and he delegated to one of his staff members the task of preparing a preliminary memorandum of facts.

When Lee read the report he was severely critical of it. "It tends to veer towards being a brief for our side," he said. "It ought to be a little more colorless; while bringing out our position it ought to bring out the other side. Our strength is in presenting the whole story in an impartial way."[3] Lee was usually better able to be impartial and objective than were his staff members, who sometimes let themselves be swayed by the hand that fed them.

Lee recognized that monopolies were illegal, yet perceived that other means must be found to coordinate business and prevent chaotic competition. He favored the "industrial institute," such as the American Petroleum Institute, Copper and Brass Research Association, and others with which he had gained experience. As he stated the problem in the mid-twenties: "Competition is developing mass distribution with its economies of volume purchasing and volume merchandising, providing benefits to the consumer while at the same time imposing greater pressure upon the producer. Manufacturing margins have been growing smaller per unit. Turnover has been accelerated. 'Profitless prosperity' has been suggested as a phrase descriptive of much that is current. What shall the manufacturer do?"[4]

The answer, Lee suggested, was industrial association, a "cooperative activity" which would help the manufacturer "expand his markets, analyze his costs, and provide him with information to assist in determining a policy of profitable production." He told his clients that such an institute must be operated only with the highest motives and in the best public interest. Its administrator must be "a leader of broad vision who can bring to industrial problems a new perspective and guide the deliberations of his associates beyond routine conferences to a point where vital matters affecting the industry's internal mechanism and its broad public relations are viewed in a fresh and progressive light. At all time such an effort is to be maintained with scrupulous regard for the law as well as the interest of industry and the public."[5]

In 1926 Lee helped the textile industry found its first such association, the Cotton-Textile Institute, and within two years more than 450 cotton manufacturers throughout the country were members. Walker D. Hines, former Director General of Railroads and a friend of Lee's, was chosen to head the institute, and Lee advised him during the early years of the association. He urged other textile producers to set up similar cooperative groups in wool, rayon, and silk.

The success of the American cotton industry in the twenties had worldwide ramifications, and Lee saw that soon *international* industrial cooperation would be needed. Because of his special interest in world affairs and friendship with British industrialists, he transferred his cotton experience to British textile problems. India, a cotton producer and consumer, and England, the manufacturer, were both in difficulty because of new foreign competition, especially from America and Japan. Lee urged that the British get together to solve their problems, and one step in that direction was the formation of the Cotton Yarn Association in England in 1927.

This Association was an early effort to deal with international competition and aid British and Indian efforts to meet that competition by providing a better flow of information among the members. According to a statement publicized by Ivy Lee, the Association was formed with the object "of adjusting output to demand, of the grading of yarns, and of the establishment of a protective minimum price, trusting thereby to deal with the surplus capacity of the trade and eliminate those sellers of yarn in the market who, by force of circumstances, have been obliged to dispose of their output without reference to price." However, the statement asserted that "this association disavows all intention of forming a monopoly to raise prices to an attractive level or of bolstering up weak and over-capitalized concerns where reconstruction is already overdue."[6]

International cooperation was not always easy to achieve, but perhaps Lee's greatest accomplishment in this regard was his work carried out on behalf of the sugar industry. Early in the twenties the New York-financed Cuba Cane Sugar Corporation became his client, as later did C. Czarnikow, Inc., a British-based Cuban sugar manufacturer. Throughout the twenties accelerated world production caused sugar to glut the market. Increased competition among export countries resulted in dropping prices. The manufacturers could not sell without a loss, and in Cuba much of the produce could not be sold at all, piling up a surplus of more than a half-million tons of sugar a year by the end of the decade. Sugar cane plantations were idled, refineries closed, and workers laid off. The depression had hit.

Lee saw that cooperative efforts might stabilize the sugar market. He worked closely with Thomas L. Chadbourne, a noted New York lawyer who represented Cuban sugar interests, to set up the International Sugar Council, composed of representatives from leading sugar export countries: Cuba, Java, Germany, Czechoslovakia, Poland, Hungary, and Belgium. These members named Frank E. Powell, retired head of the Anglo-American Oil Company and one of Ivy Lee's closest friends, as chairman of the Council. This group met in conference in 1930 to approve a plan put forth by Chadbourne calling for cooperative efforts to stabilize sugar prices throughout the world.

This proposal was a sort of capitalistic five-year plan, perhaps partly inspired by Lee's knowledge of Soviet industrial measures. The plan asked that each exporting country segregate its unsold surplus sugar stock, reduce export and production over the next five years by the amount of current overproduction, and put back on the market one-fifth of the current surplus each year for five years. At the end of five years, the surplus would be abolished, prices and production stabilized, and cooperation achieved among the countries to maintain levels and avoid future chaos.

Lee said that the "Chadbourne plan represents the most ambitious and far-reaching scheme yet developed to liquidate the over-production of one of the great staples.... Yet it must be clear that only by making [great] sacrifices completely and unreservedly can stabilization be made effective. 'Laissez faire' and the survival of the fittest may mean ruin to large numbers with no consequent benefits to anyone."[7]

Lee devoted a great deal of his time and energy promoting the Chadbourne plan among the member countries and getting them to make the necessary sacrifices for success. He found that achieving cooperation among countries was even harder than among corporations. Germany was the first to balk, but in spite of the confusion in Berlin, its cooperation was finally achieved. It was Cuba, for whose interests Lee had originally worked, that proved most difficult and, in the last minute, almost stabbed Lee and the proposal in the back.

Cuba threatened to withdraw from the agreement because she felt that Java was favored by the quotas. Lee fired off an eighteen-page letter to the chief of the Cuban stabilization group. The missive was calm on the surface but blistering underneath, arguing that anything jeopardizing the agreement would destroy not only Cuban sugar but the world market. A little later he wrote to an executive of the Czarnikow company: "Personally, I am working very hard to get a new spirit in Cuba...[and] I am inclined to think that Cuba is gradually coming to her senses."[8]

The Sugar Council which agreed to the Chadbourne plan was cursed as an international capitalistic cartel instigated by New York bankers with Cuban sugar investments to keep prices high at the expense of the consumers. But the more important truth was that uncontrolled competition had lowered prices to such an extent that the industry was in chaos. The only alternative to cooperation was socialism. Chadbourne expressed the situation most clearly in a speech he gave at the University of Virginia which was widely publicized by Ivy Lee:

"There are but three possibilities before us," he said, "chaos, collective leadership or collective control—and the last means governmental control of industry, such as exists in Russia, which is no more or less than State Socialism. The advocates of unrestrained and unenlightened competition...and the advocates of the survival of the fittest are...the best friends of the Russian Bolshevik theory, while the advocates of collective leadership in each industry are the worst enemies of the Bolshevists. Self-interest is the greatest and best fulcrum the human lever can rest upon, but if it continues to be a planless, greedy, selfish, stupid self-interest, another fulcrum is certain to be tried."[9]

The Cuban revolution in the nineteen-fifties proved that Ivy Lee's efforts to preserve self-interest through cooperation and sacrifice were not, in the end, successful for Cuba or the interests that controlled the Cuban sugar market, and another "fulcrum" was tried. But to the extent that self-interest has been preserved in the non-Communist world, cooperative efforts such as those advocated by Lee and Chadbourne have proved to be a most important aspect of that continued freedom.

Cooperation was not only necessary within an industry but often useful among different industries. Ivy Lee's role between sugar and tobacco provides a good example. During the twenties Lee's firm directed the public relations account of the American Tobacco Company. Under its president, George Washington Hill, the company had a famous advertising campaign based on the slogan, "Reach for a Lucky instead of a sweet." The sugar interests that Lee represented protested loudly that American Tobacco's campaign was damaging to the sugar and candy industry. But Lee, as an intermediary between the two, persuaded the sugar people that the campaign was stirring public interest in both tobacco and sweets and would do more good than harm for both industries.

During the early thirties Lee persuaded Hill and American Tobacco to cooperate with other industries that promoted their products through coupons. The company joined the efforts of the tea and cocoa interests, among others, to fight an anticoupon bill that had been proposed in the British Parliament and was likely to have wide repercussions. Lee was delegated the role of intermediary again, and he consulted at great length with Parliament officials and party leaders in London in 1932 and '33, ultimately achieving a compromise that benefitted all the coupon industries. Thus cooperation, rather than competition, helped preserve a free operation.[10]

Lee's experience as an international mediator among Cuban sugar and tobacco interests aided him in an important job he did for American Tobacco to overcome anxiety about the proposed manufacturing of Havana cigars in the United States during the depression. Hill wanted to import Cuban tobacco in bulk and have the cigars made in a new factory in New Jersey to provide American employment and stimulate the economy. Lee saw potential repercussions not only in Cuba but every place where American Tobacco's Havana cigars were smoked. He told Hill that the groundwork for a change to American manufacture must be laid carefully, with information and explanations to all concerned. For instance, Lee drafted a letter for Hill to be sent to Cuban President Gerardo Machado, which said: "We can assure Cuba that under the new conditions the cigars which we shall sell, as grown and processed in Cuba and manufactured in the United States, will be a credit in every sense to Cuban tobacco which tradition has made so famous."[11]

For Lee, cooperation never meant killing competition but preserving it by controlling it. He felt that individual companies had to present their sales argument strongly and distinctively in order to compete. Distinctive packaging, advertising, and promotion was required. A common practice of earlier days had been the placing of similar advertisements in the same sections of newspapers and magazines. Lee advised Hill and American Tobacco to insist that Lucky Strike ads should not be placed next to those of other cigarettes so they would be set apart in the public mind.

George Washington Hill himself was not always given to open dealings, at least not with his public relations advisors. He frequently employed a number of advisors secretly to give him counsel on the advice of each other. After receiving an advertising suggestion from Albert Lasker, for instance, he would call in Ivy Lee to get his wisdom on the matter. "I know of no one's reaction to Albert Lasker's suggestion that I would rather have than yours," he told Lee.[12] After Lee had given his counsel, Hill would call in Lee's chief competitor, Edward Bernays, and ask What Bernays thought of Lee's reaction. Bernays tells the story of how he and Ivy Lee surprised each other meeting in Hill's reception room one day finding that they had both been working on the same public relations problem for the tobacco baron, unknown to each other. Perhaps the greatest single public relations achievement of Ivy Lee for the American Tobacco Company was his insistence on a profit-sharing plan for its employees. During the early days of the depression, with discontent among workers and unrest in the industry, Lee was able finally to persuade Hill to provide some sort of incentive plan for his men. This was the kind of advice Lee had long given to the Pennsylvania Railroad without success. When the plan was put into effect for American Tobacco, it won enthusiastic employee and public support and the publicity that resulted enhanced the reputation of the company. Hill gave Lee the credit and sent him an appreciative letter, thanking him "for your initiative in the Company's behalf."[13]

The American Tobacco Employees' Stock Subscription Plan, as it was called, did much to foster cooperation within the company, much as other measures Lee advised had helped to promote cooperation within and among many industries. Such cooperation proved to be an indispensable aspect of the continued success for business in an age of mass production. Ivy Lee's influence in the profession of public relations increasingly played a key role in that cooperation.

1. For a description of the work Lee did for General Mills (Washburn-Crosby), see *The Meaning of Publicity* (a ms. based on lectures at Harvard University, May 1924), Ivy Lee Papers, Princeton.
2. Ivy Lee, "The People Should Know the Facts," Armour File, Ivy Lee Papers, Princeton.
3. Memorandum from Ivy Lee to T. J. Ross, Feb. 8, 1932, Ivy Lee Papers, Princeton.
4. Ivy Lee, "Industrial Institutes: Coordinating Business Through Cooperation," Feb. 29, 1928, p. 1., Ivy Lee Papers, Princeton.
5. Ibid., p. 2.
6. Ivy Lee, "Three British Bankers Discuss the Decline in English Cotton Exports," a pamphlet dated Feb. 17, 1927, p. 4, Ivy Lee Papers, Princeton.
7. Ivy Lee, "The Effort to Restore Equilibrium Between the World's Production and Consumption of Sugar," a pamphlet dated Dec. 29, 1930, p. 3, Ivy Lee Papers, Princeton.
8. Ivy Lee to Dr. Viriato Gutierrez, Mar. 10, 1932, Ivy Lee Papers, Princeton.
9. Thomas L. Chadbourne, "Cuba and Sugar Stabilization," (speech at the University of Virginia, July 7, 1932), Ivy Lee Papers, Princeton.
10. Ivy Lee to Hon. Malcolm MacDonald, M. P., Mar. 4, 1932, Ivy Lee Papers, Princeton.
11. Draft of letter to President Gerardo Machado of Cuba, June 13, 1932, Ivy Lee Papers, Princeton.
12. George Washington Hill to Ivy Lee, Oct. 26, 1934, Ivy Lee Papers, Princeton.
13. George Washington Hill to Ivy Lee, July 22, 1933, Ivy Lee Papers, Princeton.

Ray Eldon Hiebert

20: ANALYZING ATTITUDES TOWARD TRAVEL AND AVIATION

BEFORE BUSINESS COULD PROPERLY INTERPRET ITSELF, it had to understand the public—to diagnose public attitudes, to recognize hopes and fears, to understand delusions and frustrations, to comprehend the needs and desires of the people. As an expert on the crowd, Ivy Lee's basic work was opinion analysis. He usually arrived at his conclusions intuitively rather than empirically, but because of his keen perception he was often right.

Some of his most interesting work concerned tourism, where he found prevailing misconceptions to be a deterrent to success, and aviation, where he found public fear to be a chief obstacle to good relations. Lee was at home in both fields; an inveterate traveler himself, he had first visited Europe and Russia as a young man in 1905, had lived in England from 1909 to 1912, had traveled extensively on the Continent for the Red Cross during the war, and had visited Europe frequently during the twenties and early thirties, often on flying trips in the small and shaky airplanes of the day.

In the twenties the steamship passenger companies did what most other American industries were doing: forming associations, alliances, and cartels to protect their own interests. The steamship companies formed the Trans-Atlantic Passenger Conference and appropriately asked Ivy Lee to serve as its counsel in public relations. The companies felt they had a public relations problem on their hands because they could not get the American people to go to Europe. What could be done about it?

Ivy Lee and his staff analyzed the problem and told the Passenger Conference that the American people believed Europe was a terrible place to visit. For one thing, there were many war veterans who had been to France, England, and Belgium for the first time in 1917 and 1918 and whose memories of Europe were anything but pleasant. They had seen the Continent during wartime, from crowded troop ships and trains rather than from comfortable liners and Pullmans, had lived in barracks and tents rather than hotels and inns, and had eaten in mess halls and chow lines rather than sidewalk cafes and elegant restaurants. Even when the doughboys had gone on passes to cities and villages, they had found a wartime blight on everything.

After the war, Americans continued to get an impression of a devastated and starving Europe from stories in their newspapers and magazines. These were usually part of the reports from correspondents who, naturally, were concentrating on the political and economic affairs and were not concerned about the leisure activities of the Continent. As a result, the image remained of people in a state of unrest, of food that was scarce, hotel accommodations that were poor and difficult to obtain, hot water that was nonexistent, and tourist sights that were destroyed.

Lee told the Passenger Conference that there was no point in arguing about the image of Europe in America. Further stories would come in over the wires to negate all the advertising and promotion which the steamship lines might undertake to get people interested in travel. Instead, he laid out a plan for getting at the heart of the trouble. First, he said, the European correspondents who sent news about the Continent to America were not aware of interest in tourist information. And second, the sources of tourist material—hotels, railway companies, travel agencies, and business groups—were not supplying the writers with the facts and figures to whet the public appetite.

Lee wanted to stimulate the correspondents to write more about facilities in Europe and wanted to activate the tourist businesses to provide more information for writers. He had a list prepared of the eighty most important foreign correspondents in Europe and of more than 700 various news sources for travel and tourism. His first letter to the correspondents said frankly that "The Trans-Atlantic Passenger Conference...some time ago asked me to investigate the origin of the impression in some quarters in America that travel in Europe involves many difficulties, inconveniences, and annoyances." He added that there was great interest in the United States in travel conditions and enclosed reprints of articles in American newspapers and magazines to prove it. He attached a list of the principal sources of travel news in Europe, "with the idea that from these sources correspondents may obtain information of a news character dealing with such subjects as transportation, hotel and resort activities, athletics and art exhibitions."[1]

Lee stationed one of his staff members, W. R. Hereford, in Paris to serve as a central medium for gathering and passing along information about European travel. The correspondents were invited to contact Hereford on any questions they might have. As another of his colleagues, Jack Leighton, told the staff: "Any one of the correspondents who is hard up for a story or wants to get the truth about something, merely has to look up his list or contact Hereford to learn where to go for travel news."[2]

Lee next wrote a letter to the 700 news sources, in French, German, and Italian. It emphasized three points: first, that the current news in America about European travel was discouraging; second, that only by supplying the news correspondents with the facts about Europe could travel be shown in a favorable light; and third, he offered advice and assistance on the kinds of information that would be of interest to the American public and their correspondents. Finally, he attached a list of the eighty writers.

The Lee firm dispatched two other men to Europe in addition to Hereford to follow up the suggestions. They traveled to various hotels, resorts, museums, theaters, travel bureaus, and railroad offices, giving suggestions on how each might provide the press with current news stories whenever anything of interest came to their attention—new plumbing in a Paris hotel, a new railroad train to the Riviera, or a new golf club in Bavaria.

This was followed by a personal letter to all American ambassadors, consuls, and commercial attachés, as well as the principal European legations and commercial attachés in the United States, and the larger European and American banks. To these he emphasized the economic, political, and international advantages of greater European travel. He sent his European contingent to visit government offices to encourage spending on travel promotion for economic stimulation.

Finally, Lee recommended that the Trans-Atlantic Passenger Conference set up a permanent bureau in New York for providing travel information. He advised that a periodic news sheet be issued, "News for the Globe Trotter," which would be sent to all newspapers, and to all travel magazines and institutions. A secondary news service, he said, should then send to selected news publications all press releases and photographs about new situations as they developed. He recommended establishment of subsidiary offices in Chicago, San Francisco, and other principal cities, to which people interested in travel could go directly for factual information of all kinds: villas for rent in Cannes, doctors for children in Tours, American schools in Italy, or the cost of a six-week trip in the British Isles.

Through these techniques, as Leighton phrased it, "anybody who has any interest whatsoever in encouraging American travel in Europe has at his disposal the ways and means of getting over to this country, through the regularly organized news channels, information favorable to American opinion on conditions of travel in Europe.... In this way, we expect to make a net which will drag into it all information about travel conditions over there."[3]

The techniques were successful. Today publicizing the attractions of travel is a large industry in itself, having reached a high level of sophistication in European countries that thrive on tourist spending. Even the United States government has employed Lee's techniques. They were put into effect in America in 1961 by the United States Travel Service to stimulate Europeans to cross the Atlantic from the other side.

Lee's interest in travel led him into an altogether different public relations activity on behalf of the Guggenheims. Through his work as public relations counsel for the Copper and Brass Research Association, he met Daniel Guggenheim and his son, Harry F. Guggenheim. The son was the kind of man who interested Ivy Lee—a handsome, dashing, young millionaire who, like John D. Rockefeller Jr., was devoted to causes and activities far beyond the usual concerns of the wealthy scions of the day. During World War I, for instance, the younger Guggenheim had served as an aviator with the fledgling U.S. Navy aviation corps and had become an air enthusiast.

In 1925, after many discussions over what activities the elder Guggenheim should support with his money, he was persuaded by his son and Ivy Lee to establish a school of aeronautics at New York University. As a matter of fact, said Harry Guggenheim later, Lee "became so enthusiastic about aviation as a new great potential industry for America and as an outlet for American youth that he urged me to look into and recommend to him the establishment of more schools of aeronautics like N.Y.U. At that time," said Guggenheim, "I couldn't go so far." But after many further conferences and discussions with the Guggenheims, Lee convinced them that they should establish a fund for the promotion of aviation.

"This was the genesis of the Daniel Guggenheim Foundation," according to Harry Guggenheim.[4] He became its president and Lee served as its public relations counsel. From that position Lee advised as well on many other Guggenheim enterprises and personal matters.

The Guggenheim Foundation's major purpose was to sponsor programs to stimulate interest in aviation through education. The Lee office turned out press releases, booklets, pamphlets, and brochures. Many of these were based on studies of aerodynamics and similar subjects supported by Guggenheim Foundation funds. One of the principal concerns of aviators as well as average citizens was the vulnerability of man in flight. During the twenties aeronautical engineers made significant strides toward greater safety in airplanes, largely stimulated by grants from the Guggenheim Foundation. Yet the chief deterrent to increased air travel remained the general public's fear of flight. All the engineering advances in the world could not make frightened travelers climb into planes.

For Ivy Lee the problem was one of public relations, and the first solution was humanizing and dramatizing airplane flight. But how? One answer came in 1926 when one of his distant cousins, Naval aviator Richard E. Byrd, made the world's first flight over the North Pole. Here was a dramatic illustration of the safety and usefulness of airplanes.

Lee arranged to have Byrd fly his Polar plane around the country under the sponsorship of the Guggenheim Foundation so that the man in the street could thrill firsthand to the marvels of the new air age. Byrd later wrote to Lee that he was "delighted beyond measure when I learned that you were to handle the publicity in connection with the flight of our Polar plane around the country." The tour was so popular, however, that it became impossible for Byrd to fill the demand for lectures in cities where the plane stopped. But "under any circumstances," he told Lee, "I am glad to do my bit by donating our plane to the cause of aviation."[5]

A few months later, in 1927, daring young Charles Lindbergh flew his small monoplane solo over the Atlantic Ocean, and Ivy Lee realized immediately that an even more important aid in resolving aviation's public relations problem had been provided.

This transatlantic feat made Lindbergh the greatest hero of the crowds that the twentieth century had yet known. His name became a household word throughout the world; his deed had been a convincing demonstration of the safety and dependability of the modern airplane. Lindbergh was a living symbol of everything that the Guggenheim Foundation had attempted to promote.

This flight, the greatest publicity generator the aviation industry could have desired, was effective precisely because there was not a bit of fraud or hoax in the deed or the man who did it. Lee and Lindbergh came together almost by accident. The manufacturers of the "Spirit of St. Louis," the Ryan Airlines, had foreseen the publicity potential of the proposed flight and had hired a publicist, Harry A. Bruno, who specialized in aviation and was himself a pilot. Bruno had represented Byrd's North Pole flight in 1926, and later served as the public relations counsel for the Bremen Flyers, the Graf Zeppelin and Hindenburg flights, Wiley Post and Harold Gatty's round-the-world flight, and Jacqueline Cochran's speed flights.

It appeared that Lindbergh himself had expected he might receive some publicity from the flight he was planning. Some time before takeoff from the Long Island field, he had gone to a clipping bureau in New York City and, according to Lee, told them that he was going to get involved in a situation that might get a few stories in the newspapers and he would like to have clippings sent to his mother in Detroit. He left a thirty-five dollar deposit, signing an agreement that this would cover the first several hundred clippings but anything beyond that would cost him ten cents for each clipping. When he returned to New York in triumph he was told that clippings were coming into Detroit at such a rate that the post office had to set up a special section for Mrs. Lindbergh's mail. And the clipping bureau handed the nation's hero a bill for more than four thousand dollars. That, at least, was the story later recounted by Ivy Lee.[6]

Lindbergh thought he was being used and was furious. But recognizing the bad publicity potential, he went to see Ivy Lee to learn what could be done about it. Lee was able to settle the matter with the clipping bureau before it got into the courts or the newspapers. Meanwhile, he arranged with Lindbergh to make a nationwide tour similar to Byrd's under the auspices of the Guggenheim Foundation.

The tour proved to be a monument of public education in aviation. It began on July 20, 1927 and ended on October 23, after taking Lindbergh and the "Spirit of St. Louis" to every major city and over hundreds of small towns and villages across the United States. The tour was carefully laid out in advance, with precise timing and exact information given to the local papers. As proof of the dependability of airplanes, the flight arrived late only once—at Portland, Maine, because of fog. Throughout the tour literally millions of awed Americans saw the silver bird in flight. Along the route people stood to watch the plane, and Lindbergh circled over the hamlets where he could not land.

All of this, of course, was newspaper material. For almost a year, from May 21, 1927, when he landed at Le Bourget Aerodrome in Paris, until April 30, 1928, when the "Spirit of St. Louis" made its last stop at Bolling Field in Washington and was presented to the Smithsonian Institution, Lindbergh dominated the news. At every landing, Lindbergh was presented with the key to the city or a memorial scroll. And after the tour, honorary dinners and the presentation of honorary degrees were all thoroughly covered by the press. Every time the hero spoke, he told of the wonders of flight. Everything that was written and spoken about the nation's hero was a public testimonial to the durability and safety of aircraft in the new age of aviation. No other method of conveying its message so effectively to the crowd could have been devised by the Guggenheim Foundation.

Lindbergh and the "Spirit of St. Louis" not only provided vast public relations benefits to the aviation industry, they also contributed to the improvement of international relations, with Ivy Lee no doubt serving as catalyst. In July 1927, shortly after his return to the United States, Lindbergh was invited to fly to Ottawa by Canadian Prime Minister Mackenzie King, former colleague and long-time friend of Lee's. This visit helped make Canadians more "air-minded" and certainly aided Canadian-American understanding.

Later that year, in December 1927, Lindbergh flew to Mexico on a similar mission. Mexican-American relations were strained at the time. A short while earlier, Lee's Wall Street friend, Senator Dwight W. Morrow, had been appointed Ambassador to Mexico. At Morrow's suggestion, and perhaps again with a prod from Lee, Lindbergh flew to Mexico City. He was received with acclaim and undoubtedly the goodwill which his visit aroused helped smooth ruffled Mexican-American relations.

Lee's friendship with Lindbergh and Morrow had some catalytic effects on domestic as well as international relations. The Morrows lived in the same apartment house as the Lees. Lindbergh frequently had breakfast with the Lees and perhaps there learned to know Ann Morrow, who later became his wife.

Not all of Lee's public relations activities turned out so successfully. Lee was not a man to accept any job that came his way; according to staff member Victor Knauth, he turned down many available accounts because they did not seem solid, honest, and thoroughly substantiated. Occasionally, however, his personal interests led him astray. His enthusiasm for travel and for aviation involved him in at least one highly unusual and certainly unsuccessful project.

The race during the twenties to establish regular trans-Atlantic passenger flights, led to a wild scheme to build flat-topped ocean freighters to serve as landing strips in the middle of the ocean.[7] The freighters were to ply the Atlantic at evenly spaced intervals so passenger airplanes could land and refuel on their way to and from Europe. Lee was excited by the idea and hurried to consult with engineers, admirals, and aviators. A group of serious investors sponsored the plan and Lee was hired to gain public support for Government and financial backing.

Part of this job was to get the Government to double ship-building subsidies to aid the shipyards that would construct the flat-topped floating aerodromes. During the Coolidge Administration, Lee and his staff lobbied successfully in Congress to get Government subsidies raised from $125 million to $250 million, which provided the necessary conditions for construction to begin. In the meantime, the Administration changed and before any actual work got under way, the stock market crashed. The entire idea of floating stations sank and the investors were drowned out in bankruptcy.

This defeat was a small one when compared with other public relations ventures which Lee guided to success. His analysis of public opinion and attitudes enabled him to find methods to interest Americans in foreign travel and to overcome their fear of flying. Since the twenties Americans have increasingly traveled abroad and have increasingly flown in airplanes, until today they are the most travel-minded and air-minded people in the world. Ivy Lee played a small part in making them that way.

---

[1] "Memorandum to Trans-Atlantic Passenger Conference," Ivy Lee Papers, Princeton.

[2] "Transcript of Staff Conference, Ivy Lee and Associates," Jan. 24, 1925, p. 57, Ivy Lee Papers, Princeton.

[3] Ibid., P. 61.

[4] Harry F. Guggenheim to R. E. Hiebert, Nov. 15, 1962.

[5] Richard E. Byrd to Ivy Lee, Oct. 9, 1926, Ivy Lee Papers, Princeton.

[6] Recounted in speech before the Columbia University School of Journalism, 1932, Ivy Lee Papers, Princeton.

[7] Victor Knauth in conversation with R. E. Hiebert, July 1962.

21: MASS ENTERTAINMENT: UNITING THE ARTISTS

ACHIEVING COOPERATION AMONG THE "CHIEFS" of big business was one of Ivy Lee's accomplishments, but he also helped promote cooperative efforts among the "Indians" of the entertainment world, especially in the growing fields of mass communication where artistry and individuality could be easily crushed by the gigantic machines that made mass amusement possible. Lee worked for greater honesty and sincerity in Hollywood publicity and promotion. He advised motion picture actors, producers, and distributors in their mutual efforts to be independent. He aided individual authors and composers in the battle for their rights in the booming new business of broadcasting.

After World War I the entertainment industry, particularly motion pictures, reflected the worst aspects of the unrestraint of the twenties. To be important a thing had to be *big*. The movies became one of the biggest and least restrained elements in American civilization, and almost everything connected with it was inflated, materially and psychologically. Companies, studios, productions, theaters, salaries, sales, and advertising all took on gigantic proportions. In order to maintain such a scale, the movie makers had to turn to bankers and investors to meet their expanding needs. Wall Street became the most important backer of the film business. And as a result, Ivy Lee provided public relations counsel to some of the biggest movie moguls of the day.

One of Lee's first picture clients, acquired not long after the war, was Famous Players-Lasky. This company had resulted from a merger between Jesse Lasky's Feature Player Company, a vaudeville outfit that had turned to motion pictures, and Adolph Zukor's Famous Players Film Company. Lasky had formed his group with a stage director and playwright named Cecil B. DeMille and a glove salesman named Samuel Goldfish (later changed to Goldwyn). DeMille had taken the actors to an orange grove outside Los Angeles where he made the first Hollywood movie, "The Squaw Man." It was successful, but the Lasky group felt that merger with Zukor would support greater production. Zukor had built his company in New York out of the penny arcade business. Between the Zukor branch in New York and the Lasky branch in Hollywood, Famous Players-Lasky gained control over the industry. Eventually out of this combination came Paramount, Metro-Goldwyn-Mayer, and United Artists.

Zukor climbed on the throne about 1920 and remained there for several decades. Much like Rockefeller in the early oil business, he made an effort to bring big corporation efficiency to the industry. He bought out good small companies, forced weak companies out of business, and eventually gained control over exhibition and distribution as well as the production of films. While creative people, actors and directors, were absorbed with the artistic problems of making a movie, Zukor was concerned with business. One by one he signed talented performers to long-term contracts and gained control over their work. Within four years after he had left the penny arcades, he had made Famous Players-Lasky a $25 million combination, the largest producer and distributor of motion pictures in the world, and had more than half of the best-known screen performers on his payroll. With the production and distribution corralled, he began to force exhibitors to take only his films by threatening to allow them none or all.

World War I brought world leadership to the American movie business in the wake of the destruction of the European industry.

But in the rush to take advantage of the situation, Zukor and his few competitors had to go to Wall Street for money to expand. Zukor got the Irving Trust Company to extend credit for the increasingly large movie production outlays. And then the Wall Street house of Kuhn, Loeb, & Company agreed to underwrite film production. But the banks and investment firms insisted on supervision to prevent extravagance and insure greater profit for each movie.

In the meantime sentiment against Zukor was rising in the industry. He was threatening to destroy the independence of exhibitors, attempting to establish a movie monopoly, and allowing Wall Street to dominate the creation of motion pictures. The resentment his activities created could only hurt further investments and turn future investors away. Ivy Lee, who advised Kuhn, Loeb & Company and was a long-time friend of Otto Kahn, its chief, was recommended to Famous Players-Lasky as public relations counsel. What Lee had done for the Rockefellers and Schwabs he could do for the Zukors and DeMilles.

Famous Players-Lasky had, of course, their own publicist, the famous "king of sensational hoaxes," Harry Reichenbach. He had come to the attention of the movie people through his work in publicizing the painting "September Morn." He had hired a crowd of ragamuffins to ogle the nude portrait in the window of a Fifth Avenue art store. He then phoned the New York Society for Suppression of Vice and said the picture was corrupting the city's youth. The battle that resulted was front page publicity around the world and when the picture was sent on a nationwide tour, it made a fortune for its owners. This was the kind of promotion that Reichenbach brought to the movies, specifically to Famous Players-Lasky.

The sensationalism and exaggeration in movie publicity did little to help Zukor's case. When Lee came into the film business, he told his clients that "the main difficulty with motion picture publicity is that everybody in the business and the public likewise has a background of best-and-biggest-in-the-world advertising methods which have been extremely pernicious to the best interests of the business. No other industry has been so flagrant a sinner in this respect," he said. Lee engaged, rather, in issuing sober statements explaining Zukor's operations and attempting to show that Zukor was not destroying the exhibitors or building a monopoly but rather creating a new and vital industry. But in all of the work, Lee told his clients, "there must be sincerity and honesty at the very basis of the whole operation, else one can never get anywhere at all."[1]

Meanwhile the movie industry had developed other public relations problems. The stars, in particular, flouted public opinion; they were earning hundreds of thousands of dollars a year and, newly ensconced in the canyons of Hollywood Hills, were entertaining themselves in magnificent manner, caring little what the press or the public thought. To the people, the orange groves of Hollywood increasingly became a garden of uninhibited revelry.

As the prototype of the film-land profligate, the public seized upon the motion picture comedian Fatty Arbuckle. Overnight he had become an international star, and, in the tradition, threw a bacchanalian party at the St. Francis Hotel in San Francisco. But a girl died at the affair; there were allusions to intimacies and rape, and Arbuckle was indicted for manslaughter. Although he was never convicted, the case was a sensation in the press and solidified the growing public antagonism toward Hollywood.

Famous Players-Lasky had Arbuckle under contract, and he had just finished making three important comedies that were certain to be box-office bonanzas for the company. Lasky wanted to release the pictures and leave their reception to the people. But public relations counsels prevailed. The company lost money, but as DeMille later put it, "it could have lost much more if the public had not only rejected the Arbuckle films but boycotted Famous Players-Lasky for releasing them."

Shortly after the Arbuckle scandal a Famous Players-Lasky director, William Desmond Taylor, was murdered in Hollywood, apparently by a movie actress. And then a Famous Players-Lasky star, widely loved romantic actor Wallace Reid, died from drug addiction. These incidents got wide coverage and further aroused public indignation. In addition, a rash of sensational films, often bordering on the lewd and bawdy in an effort to attract larger audiences, drew the wrath of pressure groups which were gaining increased support from the movie-goer. One town in Massachusetts banned all movies. Demands were insistent for federal censorship and regulation of the films. Litigation and dissension within the industry itself also put the movies in a bad light. "The nation's box-offices," said Lasky later, "were beginning to reflect our loss of goodwill." The situation was not far different from that faced by the railroads and public utilities only a short time before. Again, Ivy Lee's counsel could help.

"With the very real Arbuckle and Taylor affairs as a basis," wrote DeMille later, "much of the press, many pulpits and organizations, and a goodly part of the public went into full cry." The movie director reflected, in an almost perfect paraphrase of Ivy Lee, that "it would have been useless to point out that, then as now, the overwhelming majority of the thousands who work in the motion picture industry were sober, hardworking men and women, devoted to their families, and as moral as any comparable cross section of America. That is never news. What the press screamed and the pulpits thundered was the lurid conception of Hollywood as a citadel of sin, and the entire motion picture industry was tarred with a brush wielded in broad strokes by righteously indignant but none too discriminating hands."[2]

The film industry reacted finally by putting Ivy Lee's philosophy to work in what proved to be one of the classic public relations solutions of the twenties. The producers decided to set up machinery for cleaning their own house, and then provide the necessary ingredients to make the fact newsworthy. The result was the Motion Picture Producers and Distributors Association, which was given the authority to set up and enforce a code of practice. To make the proper impact on the press and public, Hollywood wanted to get the biggest man it could. It reached into President Harding's cabinet, inducing Postmaster General Will H. Hays to take the job as president of the association at $100 thousand a year. He was installed in December 1921 to become liaison between public and movie industry.

The Hays office did not do much to make movies better. The Code of Motion Pictures prohibited such things as filming the udder of a cow or the inside of a bathroom. But it did keep federal censors from Hollywood's door and provided the machinery to answer and neutralize press and public criticism of movie morals. It thus directly kept Hollywood prospering on Wall Street as well as in the neighborhood theaters.

Ivy Lee was never employed directly by the Association or by Hays to serve as public relations advisor, but he had much indirect influence. He did provide counsel to some of the biggest men in the industry such as Zukor, Lasky, and DeMille and he maintained a close personal relationship with Hays, whose office was set up in New York. They lunched together occasionally and exchanged ideas and opinions.

Hollywood was, however, still an industry that was harming itself by its excesses. Zukor, in particular, was ruthless in his drive to create an efficient machine. In the fifteen years that followed his merger with Lasky, DeMille, and Goldwyn, he eliminated each of these men from the company one by one until he stood alone at its head. The people who made the movies, actors and directors, felt increasingly suffocated by the hand of big business and the banker.

In the mid-twenties, four of the biggest creative personalities at Famous Players-Lasky broke away to set up their own company, United Artists; they were David W. Griffith, Douglas Fairbanks Sr., Mary Pickford, and Charlie Chaplin. As one studio executive put it, "The lunatics have taken over the asylum." Hiram Abrams became head of United Artists, but his chief problem was that he could not sell his films to theaters, even independent exhibitors, because of block booking by which Zukor and the industry moguls could force all theaters to carry only their films.

Ivy Lee, perhaps feeling sympathetic to the independents and rebelling from the ruthlessness of Zukor, ended his association with Famous Players-Lasky and became public relations counsel to newly formed United Artists. He advised independent producers to communicate with independent exhibitors and make their common cause known. He told Abrams to send out leaflets giving his views on trends in the industry and showing why the independents had a common interest in maintaining an open market. He urged the publication of "sensible" magazine articles calling for reform in the industry.

Lee asked Abrams to address his remarks to the movie-going public, not the businessmen. "Exhibitors," he said, "will read these remarks, addressed ostensibly to their patrons, and the remarks will mean more to them, in a way, than if they were addressed directly to the exhibitors; for the exhibitors are constantly trying to read the minds of their patrons, and the ideas which are supposed to be reflected in the minds of their patrons naturally react upon the minds of the exhibitors."3

Lee told Abrams that "putting him over" on the pages of newspapers all over the country would not do much good. "That has been done before in the case of movie actors and movie magnates *ad infinitum*. It is the little drop of water constantly falling on the stone that will wear away the desired groove." He suggested two efforts. One was to discuss trends and problems in a short but serious weekly essay that could be syndicated to the newspapers. "People would look for this weekly material as a relief from the pyrotechnics of their own local movie editors," he said, "and newspapers would print it because the people would look for it."4

A second channel for United Artists would be for Abrams to express himself in small sheets or program notes that could be given out by the theater manager to his audiences. These should contain historical or literary "highbrow" aids to an understanding of the film and some discussion of matters in the industry. But Lee warned that such publications should avoid typical statements as: "To reproduce the city of Rameses required 555,000 feet of lumber." At the same time, he said, the program notes could and should be in the nature of "dealer helps," encouraging the audience to patronize the theater in which they were seeing the particular picture.5

Lee rarely went to Hollywood but maintained liaison with the film industry through its offices in New York. He remained close to the entertainment world, providing advice to other media as well, including CBS radio. He numbered among his close friends and confidants such leaders in the popular arts as Irving Berlin, Cecil DeMille, Jerome Kern, and David Sarnoff. But Lee was never a member of the exotic clan of show business press agents. He was more interested in getting the crowd to understand the problems of entertainers than in 'merely drumming up crowds to watch entertainers perform.

A typical example of his approach is provided by his work for the American Society of Composers, Authors, and Publishers, for which he served as public relations counsel in the early thirties. ASCAP had been organized in the twenties to combat the practice of using the works of authors and composers on radio programs without paying royalties. The association forced broadcasters to pay for every song or record under ASCAP control. The broadcasters, smarting from the increased restrictions under which this placed them, filed a suit against ASCAP for antitrust violations, claiming the association had gained control over the public performance of every popular song from "I Love You Truly" to "Fun to be Fooled."

As *Broadcasting* magazine stated it, Lee was hired by ASCAP to "justify its demands for tributes from radios, theaters, hotels, hot dog stands, and others who allegedly publicly perform music for profit."[6] This was an exaggeration, but Lee did undertake to justify ASCAP's position and carried the case directly to the people. In an effort to show the American public the worth of composers and authors, Lee's firm issued information demonstrating that American music was not only popular in the United States but throughout the world. He had a 35-page booklet prepared about the effect of American jazz on world music.

A pathetic incident aided Lee's campaign. James W. Blake, who had written "The Sidewalks of New York," was discovered living in destitution in a New York slum at the age of seventy. His story aroused the interest and sympathy of the public and the press, influencing ASCAP to provide care for Blake and put him on a lifetime retirement fund. The incident was newsworthy and provided a dramatic front-page illustration of the good that ASCAP was doing in its efforts to save composers and authors from exploitation by radio. These endeavors before the court of public opinion helped ASCAP win its case in the court of law.

Mass entertainment mushroomed into one of America's biggest and gaudiest industries following World War I. The swiftness with which it grew, the technical complexity of its operations, and of course the built-in problems of artistic temperament and relentless publicity upon which its prosperity depended, imposed on the industry massive organizational and public relations problems. Indeed, the industry not infrequently found itself teetering, like the hero of one of its own horse operas, perilously on the brink of destruction. It was perhaps more the inherent vitality of all show business and the public's omnivorous appetite for its products that saved it in the end, rather than shrewd management or brilliant public relations.

During this period, however, Lee made significant contribution to public relations policies of the mass entertainment industry. Through his association with many of its most influential leaders during this golden age of development, he exerted an influence for responsibility, open dealing, and greater honesty in communication with its audiences. Some of his advice, such as his caution about superlatives in advertising claims, seems to have made little impression on the industry, as any daily newspaper today attests. But here his advice, sound as it might be when offered to management of railroad or public utility, was counter to the basic and tradition-hallowed characteristics of show business. A world dedicated to the supreme importance of illusion is naturally disinclined to put much stock in the efficacy of truth.

But Lee's influence upon the industry's public relations policies and methods is discernible still. And it is suggestive that perhaps the most unrestrained tribute to Lee was paid by one of the giants of mass entertainment: "Because of his concepts," Cecil B. DeMille wrote of Ivy Lee, "the art of communication between man and man took a great step forward. So the world remembers him."[7]

---

[1] Ivy Lee, "Case Studies in Publicity," p. 13–14.

[2] Cecil B. DeMille, *The Autobiography of Cecil B. DeMille* (Englewood Cliffs, N.J.: Prentice-Hall, 1959), pp. 238–239.

[3] Lee, op. cit., pp. 12–13.

[4] Ibid., p. 13.

[5] Ibid., pp. 13–14.

[6] *Broadcasting*, July 1, 1934.

[7] Cecil B. DeMille to Mrs. Ivy Lee, Nov. 19, 1956, Mrs. Lee's personal papers.

Ray Eldon Hiebert

22: BANKS: RISING FROM THE FALL

THE YEARS BETWEEN 1920 AND 1930 have been given many names: Jazz Age, Lost Generation, Dry Decade, Roaring Twenties, and Age of Business. The last epithet was most appropriate for the world of Ivy Lee. Industrial charts rose sharply to new peaks in American history; businesses consolidated at record rates, yet, unlike in earlier decades, few objected, partially because of a business-oriented administration in Washington but also because many businessmen had increasingly taken the public into their confidence and formed policies acceptable to people.

In this period much of business progressively pursued the kind of management that Lee advocated. The basic idea was well stated by Franklin D. Roosevelt: "If every family owned even a $100 bond of the United States or a legitimate corporation, there would be no talk of bolshevism, and we would incidentally solve all national problems in a more democratic way." This idea gained steadily in the twenties as American corporations began operating on a platform of people's capitalism. By the end of the decade many American products were made in safe, well-lighted factories by employees enjoying a wide range of benefits from sanitary cafeterias and recreational facilities to free legal service, medical clinics, group insurance, and profit-sharing plans.

Before the twenties came to an end, political and social observers acknowledged the change. Walter Lippmann wrote: "The more or less unconscious and unplanned activities of businessmen are for once more novel, more daring, and in general more revolutionary than the theories of the progressives." And Lincoln Steffens, one of the fiercest of muckrakers, wrote: "Big business in

America is producing what the Socialists held up as their goal: food, shelter, and clothing for all."[1]

Yet the fantastic success of big business and the improved welfare of society did not mean that all was well, and in the last few weeks of the decade, the entire system came crashing down on Wall Street. As early as the mid-twenties Lee had seen dangerous trends on the horizon. A wave of get-rich-quick schemes, unsound practices, easy credit, thoughtless speculation, dishonest promotion, and false advertising threatened the foundations of business. Some corporations, abusing the spirit of Lee's publicity, tried to develop an image as a facade to hide behind. They extended their operations and their credit with words alone and were caught wanting. Lee always advised his clients that words were nothing without deeds. But as the Jazz Age waned, much of American business seemed caught in a vicious cyclone of words to cover up inadequacies in action.

Unsound policies and poor public relations affected all of America, resulting in a blighted national image. A half-year before the stock market crashed, Lee had written publicly for the *Atlantic Monthly* about the "Black Legend" of America, a perceptive analysis of the shortcomings of our society in the roaring twenties. This had become a land, Lee wrote, of "high buildings, mass production, standardization, materialism, hustle, self-assertiveness, vulgar wealth, mob-mindedness, electric signs, big headlines, ubiquitous advertising, the deification of self, of big business, and the machine." It was time for America to reassess the principles under which she operated and to bring her policies into line with the thinking of the world. It was time, Lee said, for Americans to accept what he called the "statesmanship of business."[2]

The American businessman of the twenties, Lee observed, has increasingly become the object of distrust and antagonism to the rest of the world. "When our official spokesmen talk of America's 'moral obligations' in places like Nicaragua," he pointed out, "the foreigner retorts that there isn't a pin to choose between that phrase and the older, franker term—imperialism." Lee felt that the real problem in America was "the immense financial power of the United States, its enormous industrial strength, its commercial aggressiveness."

In 1929, American business had an obligation to the world, just as in 1909 it had had an obligation to the people. Unless we accept that statesmanship, Lee said, the menace would grow. "Americanization as an influence, probably unconscious on our part, in peaceful penetration, now becomes 'American Imperialism' threatening the peace of the world, with a sinister and concerted plan, the conscious authors of which are variously represented to be our politicians, our Wall Street magnates, or our industrialists—or all three in unholy alliance."

The dilemma, said Lee, was summed up in a German newspaper editorial in the *Kolnische Zeitung*: "To whom does the world belong?" the editorial asked. "To the new mechanized civilization of America or the old culture—which opposes the conquest of spiritual things to that of material things."[3] But for Lee the answer was simply that America need not be merely materialistic and mechanized; it could be great both materially and spiritually. But in the rush of the Age of Business, responsible policies were often not followed. The result, Lee felt, was certain to be a collapse of some kind.

Lee actually predicted the stock market crash a few years in advance. He invested in stocks from time to time although never systematically (once when an investment paid a handsome dividend he bought a new library for his home, but he frequently gambled on the wrong issues). He planned to watch the market carefully for the crash, buying short immediately afterward and advising his friends and clients to do the same. He felt that such buying would bolster the market and restore a bullish trend. But it did not work that way.

Lee was in Russia in autumn 1929, traveling across the Steppes by train to Vladivostok on his way to an international relations conference in Kyoto, Japan. He knew things were coming to a crisis and he wanted to keep up with the information daily so he could provide necessary advice to his clients. He had his office send daily cablegrams to the train depots along the way. Suddenly, in the middle of the wilderness of Russia, the cables stopped coming. Lee was ready to fire his entire staff. But when he reached his destination, he was met by a huge Russian officer who grinned proudly as he held forth a fistful of cablegrams which he had faithfully saved for Mr. Lee. In the middle of the pile was one that told about Black Friday. It was of course too late for Lee to do anything.

Business's greatest decade in the history of capitalism had ended in its worst debacle. For Lee the stock market crash and the depression years that followed created one of the greatest public relations problems ever faced by capitalism. As never before, the economic collapse brought the soundness of free enterprise concepts into question. The situation provided an opportunity for those on the left of the political spectrum to argue for increased socialistic or even communistic measures and those on the right to argue for fascism. Lee had always agreed that greater control was necessary in American capitalism, but the controls he advocated were aimed at saving free enterprise rather than moving toward state or party dictatorship. He felt that business needed to shore up the holes through which the radicals were now infiltrating.

Lee felt that by putting his ideas into action and using his influence he could help restore public respect for American business and keep the economic system free. To urge a more diplomatic and responsible position of "statesmanship," he took up the gauntlet and entered into public debates on the question of capitalism versus socialism. It took some courage, for advocates of capitalism were not always well received in those days. During one debate at a symposium on capitalism at Columbia University, one student got up and shouted at Lee: "Call off your injunctions and your state militia and we'll beat you to a frazzle." Lee answered calmly that he was gratified to learn that someone thought he had "enough power to do away with injunctions and to stop action by militia."[4]

In these debates Lee argued that while the capitalistic system was not perfect in any absolute sense, the "profit motive" was the best energizing force that he knew of. He felt the evils that existed in America were "not inherent" in any capitalistic system. "Slavery," he said, "was a capitalistic evil in its time, but it was eliminated." He believed that child labor, white slavery, and other evils could be eradicated without doing away with capitalism. "Human society," he said, "has an outstanding capacity to reform itself."[5]

In a debate with Norman Thomas, leader of the American Socialist Party, he answered the criticism that capitalism was defective, "had advanced faster than the ability of the human intelligence to cope with it." Therefore, one of its greatest defects lay in the fact that it had not been planned but had merely grown up, but he felt it would continue to progress. He thought its greatest virtue was its power to "stimulate human enterprise by recognition of the right of private property and the profit motive as a basis for industrial activity." He urged that "this stimulus must be retained and restrictions must be placed on the use of capital so as to obtain, at the same time, the utmost good for the community as a whole."[6]

At no other time did big business have greater need for Ivy Lee's advice on public relations and his ability to communicate than during the dark days after Black Friday. In addition to debates and speeches, he took a prominent position in public discussions on economic affairs. In November 1930, for instance, the Economics Club of New York put Lee on a program to speak on economic recovery along with Dr. Hjalmar Schacht, president of the German Reichsbank; T. W. Lamont, president of J. P. Morgan and Company; Kent Cooper, general manager of the Associated Press; John E. Edgerton, president of the National Association of Manufacturers; J. D. Mooney, president of General Motors export division; and General Pershing.

That the business world respected Lee can be seen in a letter from B. C. Forbes, editor and publisher of the *Forbes Magazine*, a business publication. Forbes wrote on June 6, 1930: "Have you anything in your mind that you could jot down something about so that I might be able to quote it or discuss it in these days when live news—at least of a cheerful nature—is kind of scarce."[7]

Lee worked with leaders of the world in combatting the depression. He met with men such as John Maynard Keynes, noted British economist, to discuss the problem. He helped Keynes circulate a report made for the Prime Minister on the U.S. economic situation in 1931. He interviewed bankers and economists throughout Europe on the international gold situation and the problem of balance of payments, then he prepared and distributed widely a comprehensive memorandum on this aspect of the international crisis.

He carried the crusade directly to the President of the United States. He disagreed with the silent and hands-off policies of Coolidge and Hoover and was not afraid to tell them so. In 1930 he wrote to Hoover: "My reading of the trend at the moment is, I regret to say, to the effect that you as President at the present time do not arouse either the enthusiasm or the interest of the people.... Other Presidents who have aroused violent criticism in the U.S. have done so primarily because of what they did. The chief criticism which is being made of you...arises out of the things which you apparently do not do."[8]

Hoover's total answer was, "I greatly appreciate the frankness of your letter of May 27th. The matter you raise is indeed one of extreme difficulty."[9] Lee wrote many letters to Hoover between 1929 and 1938, most of them on the state of business, public opinion, and the war debts problems. Whether Hoover was actually influenced by Lee's point of view would be difficult to prove. Interestingly, however, the two bold actions which Hoover took during his administration agreed with proposals which Lee had made. They were the war debts moratorium and the federal credit agency for emergency loans to assist business, the Reconstruction Finance Corporation, at the head of which Hoover placed an old friend of Lee's, Jesse Jones, a banker from Texas.

Of all the elements of business in the twenties, the banks were the closest to the center of the fault that produced the jolting earthquake of 1929. They were frequently guilty of departing from sound commercial practices in the speculative orgy of the twenties. They suffered heavily from the crash, with more than 5,000 failing between 1930 and 1932. Bank investigation, legislation, controls, and restrictions were the imminent results. Ivy Lee, however, with his philosophy of business statesmanship, did much to preserve a degree of free enterprise by persuading some banking leaders to see the need to clean their own houses.

Since his early days as a Wall Street reporter, Lee had been close to banking and investment, adding some of the biggest banks and most important brokerage houses to his list of clients in the twenties and early thirties. These included the New York Trust, National City of New York, Bankers Trust, Liberty National, and the largest bank in the world at that time, the Chase National. He worked for a long list of brokerage firms at one time or another; his firm prepared a newsletter for Dominick and Dominick, worked on international loans for such companies as J. P. Morgan; Blair; Speyer; and Chandler. He gave public relations counsel to companies such as Dillon-Read; Kuhn-Loeb; Lee-Higgenson, and others. He counted among his closest business associates such men as Dwight Morrow of J. P. Morgan, Otto Kahn of Kuhn-Loeb, and Winthrop Aldrich of Chase National.

One of the projects Lee initiated for the New York Trust Company was a monthly magazine, something like the old *Literary Digest* except on banking and economic terms. According to Dudley Parsons, now president of his own public relations firm and in 1930 assistant credit manager for New York Trust assigned to work with Lee: "The idea was to impress the bank's public and create publicity through printing three to six articles monthly on topical subjects of specifically economic interest, plus selected statistical tables." The Lee firm did not always undertake to conduct original research upon which to base the articles but sometimes it popularized material already available. According to Parsons the bank on occasion insisted on rewriting the final draft, restoring a stilted style to lend "dignity and an air of authority" to the publication. Even so, the publication had a wide circulation and received good publicity, helping achieve Lee's purpose to inspire confidence in New York Trust.[10]

Lee aided the Lee-Higgenson brokerage house to float an issue for the Household Finance Corporation, feeling that Household Finance was an agency close to the people and if confidence could be restored in it, the entire world of finance would benefit. He felt the same way about Rockefeller. Immediately after the crash in 1929 he persuaded the elder Rockefeller to issue a public statement to the effect that "my son and I have begun to buy selected stocks." He felt that the public had great confidence in the financial acumen of the Rockefellers and would follow their lead and buy again, thus helping to bring the country out of the depression. It did not work that easily.

Lee also urged the Rockefellers to put their personal fortune to work to provide backing to established banks threatened by failure and to provide credit to bring new banks into existence. He worked with Jesse Jones to this end. Serving as a liaison between the RFC and John D. Jr., he advised that they jointly underwrite a new bank in Cleveland, the First National, similar to the Detroit bank which had been subsidized jointly by the RFC and General Motors.

"Mr. Jones observed, in talking with me this afternoon," he told Rockefeller, "that the RFC is going to see to it that the bank is set up on a gilt-edge basis, and that therefore there would be no possibility of loss through subscription to the stock." Lee told Rockefeller that "in view of the long association of your father and yourself with Cleveland, this might be an action on your part which would be greatly appreciated in Cleveland."[11] But Rockefeller rejected the proposal.

Lee apparently realized in advance that the banks might be closed after Franklin Roosevelt came into office. Shortly before the bank holiday, he sent his eldest son to withdraw one week's payroll and two hundred dollars in cash from the firm's bank. He also kept his office open around the clock in case the clearing house called for help. When the banks closed, the clearing house did ask Lee's office to prepare a statement and release it to the press to let the people know what was happening in the banking world.

The public was already getting a good deal of information on the deteriorating bank situation as a result of disclosures made by the Senate Banking and Currency Committee. The investigation had been started by President Hoover in 1932 as a measure to check speculative manipulation. Led by its counsel, Ferdinand Pecora, a cold and methodical inquisitor, the committee one by one examined Wall Street leaders and banking executives, men such as A. H. Wiggin, Clarence Dillon, Thomas Lamont, George and Richard Whitney, Charles Mitchell, J. P. Morgan, and many others.

The hearings demonstrated that many of these men understood little about their public relations responsibilities. For example, Richard Whitney, president of the New York Stock Exchange, was among those most severely exposed by the Pecora investigation yet he was most reluctant to change his ways. When Ivy Lee contacted him to suggest changes in New York Stock Exchange policies that would improve its public relations, Whitney fired off a letter declaring firmly: "I feel that we must follow along the very definite course of action that we have outlined for ourselves.... I must be candid in reiterating that our line of procedure is very definitely outlined for the present as well as the future."[12]

Another whose policies were severely criticized was A. H. Wiggin, chairman of the Chase National Bank, for which Lee had worked. But from the beginning Wiggin had not understood the wisdom of Lee's advice. Once during one of the many mergers that had made Chase the world's largest bank (the joining of Mechanics and Metals), Wiggin had refused to give out information about the merger.

A reporter finally reached the bank chairman and told him that he had the facts and if Chase National would not give him further details or confirm the merger, he would submit the story as he had it. Wiggin was furious and called Lee, demanding that he contact the publisher and kill the story. "I won't do anything of the kind," Lee retorted.[13] He told Wiggin to issue his own statement so the story could be told in his own way and not leave any misunderstanding. But Wiggin did not see the efficacy of Lee's counsel.

When Wiggin was called before the Pecora committee, he was easily debunked on the witness stand and was ultimately forced to resign his position. The investigation, getting headlines across the country, made it clear to many people that many banks practiced the suspect policy of taking in money for savings and then investing it on wild, speculative schemes. When the schemes failed, the banks closed and the people lost their money. Many sellers of securities misrepresented their wares; many commercial banks had gone into stock jobbing, and many private banks were floating securities with one hand while accepting savings deposits with the other. One banker who unexpectedly suggested a solution was the man who succeeded Wiggin at the head of Chase National, Winthrop Aldrich. As a brother-in-law of John D. Rockefeller Jr., he knew Ivy Lee intimately and agreed with his basic public relations principles.

When Aldrich became president of Chase National Bank, he and Lee agreed that "planned publicity" used to cover up banking sins would never cure the unpopularity of bankers nor heal the source of the trouble. Rather, Lee advised that Aldrich must bring his policies into line with the necessities of the times, make his own house clean first, his actions sound, and then open the channels of communication to tell the man on the street about it.[14]

Before Aldrich's turn came to testify at the Pecora committee, he and Lee and other advisors analyzed the problem. If the savings deposit aspects of banks were separated from the speculative investment aspects, much of the trouble would be cured.

Accordingly, Aldrich proceeded to separate the commercial and investment banking operations at Chase National and set up procedures to guard against misrepresentation of securities. Working night and day from the time of the subpoena to the date of his appearance before the Pecora committee, he and Lee prepared a lengthy memorandum which spelled out the steps that the Chase National had already taken to reform its banking procedures and made recommendations to the committee on the type of banking legislation that should be proposed. Many of the ideas expressed in the memorandum were Lee's. During the preparation, according to both of Lee's sons, he could often be heard conferring with Aldrich by phone late at night, often quoting whole sentences and paragraphs of the proposed report verbatim, without turning on the light.

The report was printed for distribution preceding Aldrich's appearance before the committee, and he suggested he could "save the committee's time" by reading a prepared statement before submitting to direct examination. The committee agreed and while Aldrich read the report, an aide distributed the printed document to committee members and the press. The Aldrich statement came as a pleasant surprise. It revealed that the president of the Chase National Bank had already taken the reform steps that the investigating committee was preparing to recommend. The members had nothing further to say to Aldrich. Not only was he completely exonerated—his testimony influenced the banking legislation that was ultimately adopted.

The Aldrich statement was at first interpreted as a Rockefeller assault on the House of Morgan, but there was little to support this. On March 29 Roosevelt in a message to Congress called for a banking law based on a concept that Aldrich had already put into action, namely on "the ancient truth that those who manage banks, corporations and other agencies for handling or using other people's money are trustees acting for others." Although legislation had been proposed that would have put extreme restrictions on the banks, in June 1933 Congress passed the Glass-Steagall Bill which divorced commercial banking and investment banking in the manner suggested by the Aldrich report, but allowed the banks to continue as private agencies.

In time this turned out to be one of the best pieces of legislation for banking reform ever passed. Instead of curtailing free enterprise, it made the banking business more responsible and successful. Throughout the rest of the thirties there were fewer banking failures than during any one year of the twenties, and financial institutions were much more on guard to keep their houses honest and their actions above public suspicion. Aldrich himself later said that Ivy Lee "deserves great credit for having made an important contribution to the development of high ethical standards in the American business community."[15]

---

[1] Quoted in William E. Leuchtenburg, *The Perils of Prosperity, 1914–32* (Chicago: Univ. of Chicago Press, 1958), P. 202.

[2] Ivy Lee, "The Black Legend," *The Atlantic Monthly*, May 1929, pp. 579–580.

[3] Ibid.

[4] *New York Times*, Dec. 29, 1927, p. 7.

[5] Ibid.

[6] Ibid., Mar. 27, 1933, p. 16.

[7] B. C. Forbes to Ivy Lee, June 6, 1930, Ivy Lee Papers, Princeton.

[8] Ivy Lee to Herbert Hoover, May 5, 1930, Ivy Lee Papers, Princeton.

[9] Herbert Hoover to Ivy Lee, May 28, 1930, Ivy Lee Papers, Princeton.

[10] Dudley L. Parsons to R. E. Hiebert, Apr. 16, 1963.

[11] Ivy Lee to John D. Rockefeller Jr., Mar. 50, 1933, Rockefeller Archives, New York.

[12] Richard Whitney to Ivy Lee, May 4, 1932, Ivy Lee Papers, Princeton.

[13] Recounted by Ivy Lee in a speech at the Columbia University School of Journalism, 1932, Ivy Lee Papers, Princeton.

[14] Winthrop Aldrich to Ivy Lee, 1932, Ivy Lee Papers, Princeton.

[15] Winthrop Aldrich to R. E. Hiebert, Apr. 8, 1965.

23: AUTOS: FAITH INSTEAD OF INFLATION

THE DEPRESSION WAS A TIME OF questioning old methods which seemed to have failed and of searching for new ideas that would succeed. Roosevelt's New Deal proposals for improving the financial situation included banking reforms, better supervision of security and commodity exchanges, and, increasingly, a policy of inflation. Ivy Lee saw the need for reform and regulation but believed that inflationary measures would only weaken the credit system on which capitalism was based. The debtor naturally demanded cheaper currency, but Lee was convinced that only by stabilizing the currency could investors have the faith to put their money to work to create new capital and get the economy moving again.

As the new Democratic Congress came into power in 1933, the old Populist-Greenback-Silver sentiment suddenly found new expression. Business feared that the dollar would be devalued to such an extent that the worth of loans and mortgages would be wiped out. In the first months of 1933, before Roosevelt took office, Lee sent Victor Knauth on a tour of the heartland of America to take the pulse of the average citizen on the inflation issue. Knauth, an experienced reporter, toured Illinois, Iowa, Nebraska, Kansas, Arkansas, Tennessee, and Georgia, interviewing bankers, journalists, farmers, and men on the streets, sending back to the Lee office reports of what he learned.

"I find no interest whatsoever in the crop allotment plan and practically none in inflation," he told the Lee office. He determined that the average farmer felt the gold content had been too low when he had placed a mortgage on the farm ten years earlier, that the gold content was now too high, and that this situation could be corrected legally and honestly. He ascertained that the farm problem was twofold: the farmer had to pay both taxes and mortgages and where the mortgages were high, the strain could be eased by reducing mortgage payments, and where taxes were high, the same could be done by reducing tax payments.

Most of all, Knauth discovered, the people wanted Roosevelt to take matters into his own hands and do something, rather than let things slide as previous administrations had done. "The general feeling seems to be that, if Roosevelt will get up on his hind legs and roar, things will pick up, and if he fumbles the ball and gets into the sort of indefiniteness and delay and passing of the buck which we've had up to now, then we'll find we aren't yet half way into our troubles," Knauth wrote. Even bankers like Melvin Traylor told Knauth that business was ready to go ahead if the businessmen could "get reassurance that there's a strong guy in Washington."[1]

The Lee office kept busy writing, printing, and distributing information sheets, bulletins, and pamphlets on the financial crisis, describing Lee's reading of public opinion, explaining the point of view of the business world, and attempting to restore some faith in the capitalistic system. One of Lee's interesting efforts at building public confidence was the printing and distribution of a pamphlet called *History Repeats and Depressions Do Pass*. This was a reprint of a chapter from *A History of the Thirty Years' Peace—A.D. 1816–1846*, written in 1877 by Harriet Martineau. Miss Martineau had described the period of prosperity that followed the end of the Napoleonic Wars in 1815, culminating ten years later in an orgy of speculation. The result was a serious depression but as Miss Martineau had put it, "the depression did pass away. Our ships were once more abroad upon the sea; and the clack of the loom and the roar of the forge were again heard in our town."[2]

In his introduction to the reprint of the Martineau work, Lee said that "the pages read as though they were descriptions of our times.... They teach a lesson of optimism." He also quoted John D. Rockefeller's message to the public on his 93rd birthday (undoubtedly Lee-prompted): "These are days when many are discouraged. In the ninety-three years of my life, depressions have come and gone. Prosperity has always returned, and will again."[3]

By these and other activities Lee endeavored to stimulate and encourage public optimism, faith, and confidence in the hope that the depression would end and the new Administration would not take measures so drastic they would imperil the entire free enterprise system.

No industry in America was more desirous of public faith than the youthful automobile industry. No business was more closely wedded to the free enterprise system under which the assembly line had been given birth. None was more anxious for the return of a sound economy in which every man would be solvent enough to have a Model T in his garage, as well as the proverbial chicken in his pot. The twenties had seen automobile ownership extended to the masses, bringing greater change to the entire transportation system than in any other decade. Yet the depression seriously brought to question the continued success of the auto industry.

Through a set of fortuitous circumstances, the kind that often gave Lee opportunities of which he was keen enough to take advantage, he came to be an influence in the auto industry at this time. His relationship began with Walter Chrysler. The Kuhn-Loeb banking firm had handled the financial dealings when the Dodge Brothers were absorbed by Chrysler in the twenties, and Otto Kahn had brought Lee to Chrysler as public relations counsel.

A close relationship developed between the two men because each admired the abilities of the other and found an interchange of ideas most stimulating. When Lee rented a summer house in Glen Cove, he would occasionally go into the city with Chrysler on the industrialist's boat, both conserving time by discussing their problems. (Lee never wasted a minute because he had so many projects in progress. He often gave "business" breakfasts in his Fifth Avenue apartment, which became important occasions for conferences and councils.)

One of the Chrysler problems on which Lee worked was the loss of foreign sales. The American auto industry during the twenties had cornered a good share of the world market, including Russia. But as the Soviet Union began to build its own factories, Chrysler's trade in Russia dropped drastically, with no sales at all by 1930. Lee drafted a position paper for Chrysler on Russian recognition, arguing that America's closing of the diplomatic doors had only forced Russia to set up her own facilities and in the process destroyed a good deal of American business with Russia.

As the depression deepened, the assembly lines in Detroit slowed to a near halt. Workers were laid off while production and plant improvements were curtailed. But Lee's optimism and analysis of the economic situation made Chrysler feel that the depression was on the wane and business should begin getting ready for a rising market, particularly in the automobile industry. In the depths of the depression in 1932 Chrysler called his board of directors together and said: "Gentlemen, Ivy Lee tells me that the depression won't last long, so I'm going ahead for the future. We must begin our plans for a rising market."[4] This opened the way for other manufacturers to follow in restoring auto production.

Chrysler made the audacious suggestion that the company spend millions of dollars on new assembly plants and equipment and undertake retooling for an entirely new automobile that could be produced and marketed on a mass basis. The result was the

Plymouth, which could compete with Ford and make possible a car in every garage.

At a time when men were taking salary cuts or being laid off, when they were not buying new automobiles and failing to keep up payments on their old ones, such a suggestion seemed ridiculous. But the market did improve, and the Chrysler Corporation was the first to be able to raise its sails effectively when better winds blew, as a study of production statistics for the industry substantiates, partly because Lee convinced Chrysler that the depression was ending when others did not think so.

With new investments in plant and equipment in 1932 and 1933, Chrysler became more apprehensive about the inflation policies of the new Administration. Businessmen feared that Roosevelt would flood the market with paper currency and devalue the dollar, aiding the man on the street to pay his debts but wiping out creditors' investments. Roosevelt's actions in 1933 all pointed in that direction and business was alarmed. The Emergency Banking Act of March 9, the executive order curtailing the export and forbidding the hoarding of gold, the Farm Relief and Inflation Act of May, the refusal to discuss currency stabilization at the London Economic Conference that summer, and the raising of gold and silver prices in the fall—all of these added to business apprehension that Roosevelt would permit inflation to get out of hand and bring financial ruin to the creditor.

The situation was indeed a delicate one. The condition of the country made it obvious that something needed to be done, and Roosevelt was trying to do it. Merely criticizing his actions was not enough. The United States Chamber of Commerce had issued a harsh public denouncement of Roosevelt's policies, but the Chamber in turn was attacked by the public and the Administration for its archaic attitudes and for having no positive policy to offer as an alternative to Roosevelt's at a time when things could not go on as they were.

Lee recognized the need for positive action, and as a preparatory step in that direction he urged Chrysler to bring the automobile industry together and form a committee of industrial leaders who could be articulate on economic questions. After all, as Lee later told Roosevelt, the auto industry "has very wide ramifications through its dealer organizations, its contacts with motor-car owners, service stations, et cetera. It has been felt that if this constituency should be educated to sound thinking along economic lines, it would be helpful."[5]

Such a committee was organized in 1932 through the National Automobile Chamber of Commerce. It was composed of Walter Chrysler, Thomas Chadbourne, Ivy Lee, and Alfred P. Sloan Jr., president of General Motors. Sloan told Lee that the industry's views should be reconciled and coordinated. It would be "difficult enough to get an intelligent consideration" of the auto industry's views in Congress, which must deal with national movements. "Even if we approach it in a coordinated, intelligent and aggressive manner, if various bodies approach the matter independently, then the only inference that can be made is that the constructive forces in the country do not themselves know what they want and Congress is very likely to do nothing or do as it pleases."[6]

Lee agreed with Sloan, but he emphasized that it would be fatal to launch a program which would be offensive to the President or which could be interpreted by the public as directed against the President's program, monetary or otherwise, the mistake which the Chamber of Commerce had made. Rather, Lee said, before he recommended any program at all he wanted to be certain that the President approved of it, and if the President would not approve of any plan, it would be unwise to recommend it. Lee proposed that the auto industry, through its dealers, service stations, and contacts with owners, issue a series of pamphlets dealing with all aspects of the money question—Government credit, the significance of inflation, and such matters—but only with Roosevelt's understanding and approval.

Accordingly, Lee made arrangements to exchange ideas with the President. He first met with James Harvey Rogers, one of Roosevelt's principal monetary advisors at the time. Rogers endorsed the Lee idea and took it to the President, who invited the public relations counsel to come to Washington and discuss it with him personally in the White House. On December 8, 1933, they met in Roosevelt's office.

"The motor people have constituted me as a kind of miniature 'brain trust' to prepare a program of action," Lee said, bringing a guffaw of laughter from the master brain truster. Lee told Roosevelt that the auto industry wanted to start a program of educating the people on "sound money" but that phase had many definitions and he would "appreciate any suggestions that occur to you as to appropriate lines we might follow that you feel would be most helpful." He said he did not want to repeat the kind of criticism that the Chamber of Commerce was making.

Roosevelt answered that the trouble with the Chamber of Commerce criticism was that "it simply wasn't carefully thought out. The idea you are working on is a first-class one."

As to inflation, the President said that he did not intend to have any. "I have depreciated the value of the dollar, but there has been no inflation. We are going back on the gold standard. It will be a bullion standard, but it will be based on gold. These principles are fundamental with me. I may have to fight to maintain them, but I am going to do it.... What the automobile industry ought to do is to support me and my program in getting the widest possible distribution of purchasing power. The industry ought not to go ahead with the old ballyhoo about two cars in every garage, but try to get one car in a great many more garages."

Lee agreed, saying that this was precisely what the industry sought, but that it widely misunderstood Roosevelt's basic desire for sound money, as did the people themselves. If he believed in sound money, he should tell the people so. Roosevelt understood the uncertainty that the people felt about his program, he said, but it stemmed from his inability to "tell the people the reasons for the whole of my policy."

He told Lee in confidence that he wanted to come to stabilization as quickly as possible but this required an agreement with Great Britain. The trouble was that Great Britain would not discuss the subject. A week earlier, the President said, he had sent out a "feeler" to the Bank of England suggesting that both the pound and dollar be devalued at 40 percent gold content and that both go back on the gold standard, restoring the old parity of one pound sterling to 4.86 dollars. But the British, with other troubles, including the franc, turned Roosevelt down. "Now you can see why my tongue is tied," the President told Lee. "Unless I am prepared to face serious international embarrassment, I simply cannot tell the people the whole story."

Lee said the auto industry feared that when Congress came into session there might be a feeling that Roosevelt's program had not gone forward fast enough, causing a movement to push inflation and make the permissive features of the Thomas amendment (which gave the Administration an unwanted power to inflate the currency with paper money) compulsory. "I hear reports around Washington that Congressmen floating in for the new session are talking inflation on every side...that if a vote was taken in Congress today it would be for inflation," Lee said.

"You are absolutely correct," the President said. "That is a very real danger, and is not one to be minimized in any manner. I believe Congress is going to let me do what I want to, at least for a year, but the pressure is very great."

What, Lee asked, did Roosevelt feel about the possibility of the right to issue Thomas notes (paper money) being taken out of his hands and made mandatory by Congress?

"I think it is a very real possibility," the President said. "Ivy Lee, I would issue Thomas notes today but for the fact that I am certain once I began to issue them Congress would enlarge the issue and possibly make it mandatory, and we would be on the way to real inflation. So take it from me, I am in favor of a balanced budget, amortization of our national debt, and I am sticking to an absolutely sound money policy."

Lee suggested that the auto industry undertake to create a sentiment which, if the issue arose between Roosevelt's sound money policy and those in Congress who wanted the printing of paper money, would marshal the opinions of the people more strongly behind the President than might otherwise be the case. "That is very worthwhile," said Roosevelt, "and I would welcome it."[7]

The Lee plan to educate the public to sound money thinking probably had some influence on the eventual stabilization of the economy. Reducing the gold content of the dollar did not prove to be as effective as New Dealers had once believed. Roosevelt never seriously undertook the proposition of making silver one-fourth of the monetary stock, as had been proposed by senators from the silver states. Gradually, more credence was given to the explanation of the nation's failure to respond quickly as due to the fact that nine-tenths of the nation's business was conducted by credit rather than currency, and the need was for faith in the credit system rather than inflated money. By 1936 the Roosevelt Administration had completely reversed its earlier policies on inflation and cheap money and sought to stabilize prices.

The auto industry ultimately pulled out of the depression and made steady gains as the thirties progressed. Chrysler Corporation helped lead the way, following sound public relations policies with Ivy Lee's firm as its chief counsel.

---

[1] Victor Knauth to Harcourt Parrish, Feb. 13, 1933, Harcourt Parrish Papers, University of Virginia.

[2] Ivy Lee, *History Repeats and Depressions Do Pass* (New York: Industries Publishing Co., 1933), p. 22.

[3] Ibid., p. 3.

[4] Letter from J. W. Lee II to Howard G. Stevenson, Sept. 24, 1948, Ivy Lee Papers, Princeton.

[5] "Confidential Memorandum: Conversation Between Ivy Lee and Franklin D. Roosevelt," Dec. 8, 1933, p. 2, Ivy Lee Papers, Princeton.

[6] Alfred P. Sloan to Ivy Lee, Nov. 9, 1932, Ivy Lee Papers, Princeton.

[7] "Confidential Memorandum," op. cit., pp. 2 ff.

RAY ELDON HIEBERT

24: POLITICS: THE FAILURE OF MODERATION

WHILE IT MIGHT SEEM THAT techniques of public relations which Ivy Lee developed and used with such effectiveness in business would be well suited to American politics, he was not nearly so successful in that field. Nevertheless, he entered the political arena five times, never as a candidate himself but as an advisor to or publicist for the aspirant. In his politics he was consistently a Jeffersonian rather than Hamiltonian, a Democrat rather than Republican, but a conservative Democrat who disagreed with the radical New Deal of Franklin Roosevelt as much as he disagreed with the *laissez faire* policies of Coolidge or Hoover. But while measures for cooperation and conciliation strengthened business, compromise and moderation were not typical of the political scene.

Lee had first been introduced to politics in the Citizens Union campaign to elect Seth Low as a Fusion ticket mayor of New York in 1903. He had subsequently joined George Parker to work for the election of Judge Alton B. Parker against Teddy Roosevelt in the 1904 national presidential campaign. He returned to politics on the national scene in 1924. The Republicans were again in the White House, but the incumbent candidate, Calvin Coolidge, was a vastly different political racehorse from Teddy Roosevelt—in fact, he was Roosevelt's political opposite, rarely raising his voice against big business or for anything else. The Democrats, sharply divided by Robert LaFollette's Progressive Party, took 103 ballots to nominate John W. Davis, a compromise candidate after William G. McAdoo and Alfred E. Smith brought the convention to a deadlock.

Davis, a former West Virginia Congressman, was a partner in one of the most influential Wall Street law firms, Stetson, Jennings, and Russell (to which Grover Cleveland had once belonged) and was counsel for the J. P. Morgan Company. He was an internationalist who had served as Ambassador to Great Britain from 1918 to 1920 and in 1919 had helped President Wilson prepare the Peace Treaty at Versailles. He was, like Judge Parker, a courteous, courtly man. (The King of England had called him "one of the most perfect gentlemen I have ever met.") And he was an ardent Jeffersonian.

With such a background, Davis and Ivy Lee were in complete agreement on politics, and were, in fact, personal friends. Lee was called in to serve as special advisor on matters of publicity and public relations. Like Lee, Davis did not believe in dependence on government but on men. But, also like Lee, he did not believe in the unbridled stampede of selfish interests. In fact, he had once declared the Antitrust Act to be "the deliberate effort of conservative, clear-thinking men to place some reasonable check on that liberty of combination which, if permitted to the 'logical extreme' would in the end imperil liberty itself."

The 1924 political battle was as unusual as the 1904 campaign. The Republicans held their peace, except for an occasional outburst at LaFollette as a "tool of Bolshevism." The Progressives joined the liberal and left-wing press in criticism not of Coolidge but of Davis as the "Wall Street lawyer" who was controlled by financial interests. Finally, Davis's party itself was weak and indecisive; at the Democratic convention, no meaningful platform had been written.

Lee helped Davis with his campaign, providing speeches, press releases, and printed material, and in spite of party weaknesses, they came up with a significant program. The race which Davis ran was later characterized as "energetic, truthful, and well-bred." *World's Work* said that Davis "tackled the issues with considerable vigor.

His speeches have confirmed the impressions of his ability and his grasp on public questions." Deviating from the "party line," Davis took a strong stand against the Ku Klux Klan, proclaimed his "ringing" support of the League of Nations, and issued a "pledge of a liberal program for the benefit of the people."[1]

But the Progressive-Democrat split hurt the Davis campaign, and Coolidge won the election easily. The Republicans, trading on the prevailing complacency created by the boom years of 1924 to 1928, stayed in power with Hoover, but the crash of 1929 and the depression that followed dealt a disastrous blow to Republican chances in 1932 and did much to bolster the liberal element in the Democratic party. When the political star of New York's Governor Franklin D. Roosevelt began to shine brighter as a result of his "New Deal" proposals, some of the moderates in the Democratic party such as Davis grew wary of the gathering influence of the Socialists and Communists within the councils of the liberal wing of the party. As a result, one of Ivy Lee's most interesting political maneuvers occurred.

In an effort to head off the growing popularity of Roosevelt and come up with a candidate who would bring moderate rather than drastic reforms to the country, Lee and his firm undertook to "make" a candidate. The man who was chosen was an almost exact copy of Judge Alton B. Parker and John W. Davis. He was Melvin Alvah Traylor, president of the First National Bank of Chicago. He was a handsome, youthful-looking, courteous, soft-spoken gentleman, an expert on livestock, loans, and international banking. In 1929 he had been the American representative at the organization of the International Bank at Basel. He was a Democrat, an internationalist, a man who believed in government reform while holding fast to a sound money policy. He urged stronger measures to cure the depression while he clung to a basic faith in property and free enterprise.

Since Traylor was from Chicago and was free of Wall Street connections he would not suffer by association as had Davis. But to make sure from the first that the public would not associate the banker with the stock market, his campaign was launched with an article in the *American Magazine*, November 1931: "When the old machine begins to creak," read the article's lead referring to the Democratic Party, "it's time to throw a monkey wrench. In this case Mel Traylor threw one that made Wall Street gasp." He was described as a "back country boy" who used to sell monkey wrenches and subsequently had risen to become a power in American finance. He understood the money problems of the country, of the common man—and had nothing to do with the stock exchange.[2]

That approach seemed successful and a mild interest in Traylor was kindled. The Lee firm put the machinery of publicity into gear. First of all, political analysis showed that Speaker of the House John Garner of Texas had the conservative backing in the party, while Roosevelt had the support of the liberals. If the two factions deadlocked as they had in 1924, Garner could throw the nomination to a moderate candidate similar to the manner in which Davis had gotten the bid after the McAdoo-Smith deadlock. Accordingly, Ivy Lee in early 1932, many months before the Democratic convention in Chicago, took his campaign for banker Melvin Alvah Traylor to Texas, whose delegates controlled the crucial vote.

He put two of his top men on the Traylor project; Harcourt Parrish went to Texas to direct the campaign on the scene, and Bela Norton operated out of New York. Lee believed that Traylor, who had been born near Lincoln's birthplace, was another "honest Abe," a quiet but brilliant man of the people, a common man, not exactly a rail-splitter but a grocery clerk and salesman who had worked hard and reached the top, and in the national crisis was the man who could best lead the people.

The Lee campaign went slowly, never touting Traylor as a presidential candidate but rather as a man who had new and worthwhile ideas on the depression crisis. These were, above all, "homespun" ideas. Parrish, operating especially in Texas and Kentucky, put out clip sheets for the country newspapers which contained folksy sayings by Traylor about the economic situation. He put out broadsides that were mailed to the people; pamphlets on weightier subjects, such as taxation and government spending, were sent to the leaders of the community.

Norton passed Lee's commands on to Parrish, who put them to work in the field. The gist of the campaign can be seen in a paragraph of Norton's instructions: "One other matter which Mr. Lee suggested was that you include the homespun quotes in one of your early clip sheets. This feature has gone so well in the country papers that we would like to get it into the hands of the first-class dailies because it fits in very nicely with the objective you have already been emphasizing—that our man is not available as a candidate. What you have done in that direction has been very helpful and we want to keep it up. By including these brief excerpts—and any others that you may have come across that you think suitable for this summary—we will keep building him up in a way that will show he is the only man and the right man for the job."[3]

Pictures were taken of Traylor visiting his birthplace in Breeding, Kentucky, a backwoods "bend in the road." He was photographed sitting on the porch of the country store, leaning on a rail fence, talking in the midst of the tobacco-chewing, unemployed mountaineers and farmers—pictures certain to get good space in the newspapers. Articles appeared in national magazines such as the *Review of Reviews* and the *Mid-West Review*. The articles were reprinted and sent out to the Lee mailing list. Before midyear in 1932 a New York Life Insurance booklet on "Great Personalities" appeared; it was devoted to four people: Helen Keller, Herbert Hoover, Eddie Rickenbacker, and Melvin Alvah Traylor.

By the time the Democratic convention began in late June, the unknown banker was, according to the *New York Times*, "a potential Presidential candidate. In the upper brackets of the Democratic party, his name was linked with those of FDR, Al Smith, Newton Baker, and Albert Ritchie of Maryland." But Roosevelt had too much strength.

For the first three ballots, it looked as though Garner might be able to prevent Roosevelt's getting the required two-thirds majority; then Garner could build up his own strength by slowly stealing Roosevelt delegates. This, at least, was what Ivy Lee hoped for, believing that the resulting deadlock would provide the opportunity for moderate Traylor to step forth. The deadlock did not come about; Garner, reportedly on the advice of William Randolph Hearst, threw his Texas block to Roosevelt. But, the *Times* said later, "before FDR's followers swept the convention the Chicago banker loomed as a strong possibility."[4]

Immediately after his defeat at the Democratic convention, Traylor wrote to Lee: "You have brought me to an honor greater than I ever anticipated.... I can only hope that the future will not rob me of the intimate association I have enjoyed with you in the last few months."[5] He sent a couple of wry notes to Parrish, who had worked so hard in his behalf. "Confidentially, they were good enough to offer me the job of Treasurer but I could not conscientiously accept," he wrote. However, he did feel that some good had come out of the campaign. "We feel that the publicity we have received makes it a little more difficult for these fellows to put over their stuff," he said of the New Dealers.[6]

Traylor died a little more than a year later, in early 1934, and his obituary in the *Times* was testimony to the effectiveness of Lee's publicity. "At the beginning of the year 1932," wrote the paper, "Melvin Alvah Traylor was known merely as the competent president of the First National Bank of Chicago.... A few months later, however, [he] was a national figure and a sudden aura of color helped his personality. Most surprisingly the unassuming banker's personal character became public property. And from coast to coast he was called the 'new Abe Lincoln,' 'the barefoot boy from Kentucky,' 'the hillbilly,' and the 'grocer's clerk.' [He] was dragged from dignified seclusion and held up to his country as just plain Mel, America's 'homespun' son."[7]

Ivy Lee learned in four political defeats that courting the crowd and winning in politics were two different things. Just before Lee died he helped elect W. Warren Barbour to the U.S. Senate from New Jersey in 1934, but for the most part Lee was not successful in helping candidates win election.

Lee's greatest achievement in politics came shortly after his unsuccessful attempt to nominate Traylor—and ironically the opportunity came *after* the candidate had been elected. New York City politics were at a low ebb in 1932. Mayor Jimmy Walker had resigned under pressure after scandals had rocked his administration from 1929 to 1932. Increased costs of government and diminishing revenues due to poor business conditions had put the city in a nearly bankrupt position. The banks were reluctant to loan money to the city for its needs at the very time when other sources of revenue were drying up. Relief payments and the city payroll were eating up the city funds. Cutting down relief would have caused an angry uproar, and cutting down the city payroll would have only enlarged the unemployment problem. The job was to win the confidence of the people and of the bankers.

Into this situation Tammany put the only man who was not tainted. Surrogate John P. O'Brien was a good-natured, likeable man rather than an intellectual. He won the election, but immediately became the object of scathing ridicule and indignation. The press, which had treated Walker kindly, criticized O'Brien, describing him as a buffoon who was simply a tool of Tammany Hall. In this situation, it was probably John Curry, the Tammany boss, who saw the need for Ivy Lee. From January 1933 to January 1934, when Fiorello LaGuardia was sworn in as the new mayor of the city, Lee served as a close advisor and counselor to Mayor O'Brien.

Some observers have said that Ivy Lee was mayor in all but name during that period. Lee wrote most of the mayor's speeches and public statements and advised on his policies. According to Peter Grimm, who was involved in city politics at the time and was later chairman of a New York real estate firm: "Lee's role in the O'Brien administration was that of advisor and assistant on all matters that Phillip Dunn [an attorney] and Curry did not feel competent to settle without outside help."[8]

A radio speech which Lee wrote for O'Brien gives the best indication of the stand which O'Brien took; it emphasized the kind of politics which Lee always believed made for the best public relations. There were four objectives he had adopted for the city government, said O'Brien: (1) that he would conduct the affairs of the city honestly and efficiently; (2) that the services of the city would be performed with utmost economy; (3) that he would make every effort to protect the credit of the city; and (4) that relief for the needy of the city would continue.[9]

One of Lee's first acts was to prepare and release to the press a detailed statement explaining the ways and means by which the mayor would save some $115 million in the city budget by pruning such funds as education and hospitals. He reduced salaries by $20 million without eliminating jobs, thus keeping as many people employed as possible. The press publicized this action as proof that he was obediently keeping Tammany men employed.

Lee countered this with a speech which the mayor delivered at the Board of Trade explaining with detailed facts and figures just how many men on the city payroll were appointive employees and how many were civil service employees, giving the salaries of each. Within a few weeks, the mayor gave another speech in which he carefully explained his budget cuts in education. This was followed by a statement on relief for the poor, plans for a transit unification, a speech on unemployment relief and welfare, a speech on the German anti-Semitic troubles that were plaguing the city. Soon after these were delivered, the mayor authorized a dock project to create new jobs and Lee promptly spread the news about this action. The city administration created a new Central Department of Purchase to tighten up the city's expenditures. And finally, O'Brien proposed new methods of securing revenues for the city, including auto taxes, taxi-fare taxes, bridge tolls, inspection and license fees. The press loudly condemned the auto-tax plan and the mayor publicly rescinded it.

But Lee meanwhile was conferring with the bankers, helping them recognize that the O'Brien administration was making a real effort to put the city on a sound financial footing again. Lee served as liaison between the administration and the bankers in drawing up the so-called "Bankers' Agreement," whereby the banks would loan money to the city under very restrictive conditions: for instance, the city could not raise real estate taxes for three years. The loans which the banks made available kept the city from bankruptcy. As historian Charles Garrett points out, the O'Brien Administration deserves credit for the Bankers' Agreement: "In the light of the circumstances at the time...it is hard to see what other course the city administration could have pursued."[10]

The O'Brien administration, according to Garrett, boasted a number of significant accomplishments, including changes in governmental machinery that did much to eliminate graft, corruption, and irresponsibility and open the way for real reforms in the city. Ivy Lee, with his counsel and his machinery for communicating to the public the truth of the situation, greatly aided the O'Brien administration. As Grimm put it, Lee "was of immense assistance to Mayor O'Brien and largely because of that assistance the mayor left a record of great accomplishment in a much troubled time."[11]

LaGuardia's subsequent victory, however, like FDR's, was indicative of the political atmosphere in America—an atmosphere not conducive to political moderation, while Lee *was* a moderate. His heritage was Jeffersonian. Lee believed in the individual rather than Government, and he believed in the right to property. But he also believed that the acquisition of property brought with it social responsibility. He recognized the increasing importance of greater federal planning and control to protect the individual from his own excesses and preserve his rights and property. As a conservative Democrat, Lee believed in intelligent, sincere, responsible government. America, swinging from strong conservatism to ardent liberalism during Lee's politically active years, did not often vote for the middle-of-the-road democracy he advocated.

---

[1] Quoted in Irving Stone, "John W. Davis," *They Also Ran* (Garden City, N.Y.: Doubleday, 1943).

[2] *The American Magazine*, Nov. 1931.

[3] Bela Norton to Harcourt Parrish, Apr. 11, 1932, Harcourt Parrish Papers, University of Virginia.

[4] *New York Times*, Feb. 15, 1934.

[5] Melvin Alvah Traylor to Ivy Lee, July 5, 1932, Ivy Lee Papers, Princeton.

[6] Melvin Alvah Traylor to Harcourt Parrish, July 25 and Aug. 3, 1932, Harcourt Parrish Papers, University of Virginia.

[7] *New York Times*, Feb. 15, 1934.

[8] Peter Grimm to R. E. Hiebert, Apr. 10, 1963.

[9] A nearly complete file of Lee's speeches, press releases, and memos to the mayor exists in the Ivy Lee Papers, Princeton.

[10] Charles Garrett, *The LaGuardia Years* (New Brunswick, N.J.: Rutgers University Press, 1961), pp. 142 ff.

[11] Peter Grimm to R. E. Hiebert, op. cit.

25: RELIGION: DIVIDED PROTESTANTS

IN SPITE OF THE FACT THAT IVY LEE once told his father that everything he did was for a fee, he often worked for causes without charge if he believed in them. Many of these were religious because Lee was basically a deeply spiritual man, practicing his profession with the same devout fervor that his father had brought to the Methodist ministry. Their professions were not vastly different; both were, after all, concerned with and involved in the occupation of influencing others. Even their techniques for doing so were frequently similar.

Not all Lee's charitable work was for religious activities. He provided public relations counsel for educational endeavors, including fundraising for Georgia Tech, Princeton, and Harvard. Lee maintained that the only time in his life he ever asked the newspapers not to print a newsworthy item was during his work on a Harvard campaign. George F. Baker had given $5 million to the university and the Associated Press had learned of the story. But Lee asked the A.P. to withhold publication because public knowledge of the bequest would seriously hinder potential for further donations to the Harvard fund. The Associated Press agreed with Lee and complied.[1]

Lee did voluntary fundraising for the United Hospital Fund, the Henry Street Settlement, the Episcopal Fund, and others. He served voluntarily as a trustee of the Neurological Institute and director of the Metropolitan Opera Company. He was a member of the New York Bicentennial Commission and briefly served as chairman of the National Washington Portal Committee until someone pointed out that these two groups were in competition with each other. He was chairman of the executive committee of the English-Speaking Union and chairman of a national committee in charge of raising a million dollars for the American Historical Association's research fund.

He used his offices to aid the fundraising for construction of two New York religious edifices, St. John the Divine and the Riverside Memorial Church, and his interest in Gothic cathedrals proved immensely helpful in these ventures. He did publicity work for John D. Rockefeller Jr.'s Park Avenue Baptist Church and directed the publicity of the Layman's Foreign Mission Inquiry Board, a group of distinguished Protestant laymen led by Harvard philosopher W. E. Hocking. This group made an effort to revaluate the mission program of the Protestant church in the twentieth century, leading finally to the publication of an important book, *Re-Thinking Missions* (Harper & Brothers, 1932). Lee's publicity effort in this behalf had much to do with the success of the group.

Through his association with Rockefeller, also a deeply religious man, Lee was led to using his publicity talent to bring crowds into church. When the Park Avenue church was founded in 1922, Rockefeller went to Lee and asked him to help out with publicity. "We are anxious to do everything we can to make the Park Avenue Baptist Church a real factor in the life...of the community and...of the city," he told Lee. One of the things he suggested was that Lee publicize a series of organ recitals to get people to come to church.[2]

Lee opened publicity channels and got stories into the *New York Times* and the *World* giving the organ recital lengthy treatment and generous headlines. Within a week Lee gave Rockefeller a folder full of clippings, and the news that the first concert had attracted more people than could be accommodated. Two weeks later Lee advised Rockefeller that the channels of publicity ought to be closed for fear of flood—it had been necessary to turn away immense crowds each Sunday and Lee feared that the people unable to get in might feel more ill will than if they had not even heard of the church. "I think it would be advisable," he told Rockefeller, "simply to send the program for each Sunday to the religious and music editors."[3]

But in his work with religious endeavors Lee was not as interested in gathering a crowd as he was in getting the crowd to understand what it was being gathered for. This can be seen best in his work for the cause of Harry Emerson Fosdick. Lee had changed his religious affiliation from Methodist Episcopal Church South to the liberal Presbyterian group in the North. In his work with Raymond Fosdick in the Rockefeller offices he had come to know Raymond's minister brother, a Baptist who in the early twenties was preaching at the Old First Presbyterian Church in New York. At this time the Protestant church was seriously shaken by what Fosdick called "the Fundamentalist controversy," an outgrowth of a split in the church that went back to nineteenth century Darwinism. On one side were, the fundamentalists who believed in a strict Biblical interpretation, and on the other were the radicals who were ready to throw out the trinity and become Unitarians or throw out God entirely and become atheists. As Reinhold Niebuhr put it: "That part of the church which maintained an effective contact with modern culture stood in danger of capitulating to all the characteristic prejudices of a 'scientific' and 'progressive' age; and that part of the church which was concerned with the evangelical heritage chose to protect it in the armor of a rigorous biblicism."[4]

Like Ivy Lee's father, who had believed in a middle position between the evolutionists and the biblicists, Harry Emerson

Fosdick stood in the middle of the fundamentalists and radicals. In a now-famous sermon preached in 1922, "Shall the Fundamentalists Win," he pleaded for tolerance, for a church broad enough to take in both liberals and conservatives. He described the honest differences of opinion that divided the two groups over such questions as the virgin birth of Jesus, the infallibility of the scriptures, and the second coming of Christ. Instead of further antagonism, he called for conciliation and understanding.

These ideas, of course, were basic to Ivy Lee's public relations point of view. Lee seized upon Fosdick's sermon as a perfect statement of principles in which he believed. He deleted a few introductory and concluding sentences and had the sermon printed with a new title, "The New Knowledge and the Christian Faith." He sent it out to his mailing list with a commendatory message calling attention to its importance. The sermon, wrote Fosdick later, "might have had no unusual result had it not been for Ivy Lee."[5]

Fosdick's widely circulated sermon did not at first bring about harmony and goodwill. To the contrary, it caused an explosion of controversy in which the fundamentalists were pitted against the modernists. It made headline news, prompted vehement editorial invective in the Protestant press, and incidentally filled Fosdick's church to overflowing, even though as the fight raged Fosdick was ultimately forced to resign his pastorate at the Old First Church. "As the months passed," he later wrote, "the controversial uproar grew even louder and more obstreperous across the country. The headlines screamed and even the Episcopalians entered the fray."[6]

In answering one of Fosdick's antagonists, Ivy Lee said: "I am...a firm believer in the Christian religion, and am convinced that the only safety of the world lies in the triumph of the Christian Church. Doctor Fosdick's sermon was sent out by me, not because of my belief or disbelief in any of the dogmas which are discussed in his sermon; but because of my profound conviction that the spirit of tolerance manifested by Doctor Fosdick is the spirit which the church must manifest if it is to attract, rather than drive away from its influence, a great mass of men."[7]

This is a good example of Lee's idea of public relations, based simply on the idea that in a democracy nothing can succeed that does not have the acceptance of the public. An idea must be understood before it can be accepted. When there is a conflict of ideas, those ideas which are best understood succeed the best. If the ideas on both sides are equally understood, they can be tolerated, the conflict can be neutralized, and society can continue to progress in peace and harmony.

Lee told Rockefeller that "the most striking fact to me about the distribution we made of Dr. Fosdick's sermon on Fundamentalism was the apparent surprise manifested in so many quarters that such a sermon could be preached. As Dr. Alexander said to me the other night, 'that sermon got to the back woods.' It seems to me" he told Rockefeller, "that what is necessary in the present situation is to get to the back woods just the kind of preaching that Dr. Fosdick is doing."

Lee gave a great deal of thought to what could be done about Fosdick's sermons and finally approached Rockefeller with a recommendation to underwrite the printing and distribution of the sermons to 125,000 Protestant clergymen in the United States. Earlier he had suggested that Princeton undertake to print copies of a lecture series which he sent to alumni with excellent results. He advised that Fosdick's sermons should be given similar treatment, in a simple and inexpensive typographical form.

Lee suggested to Rockefeller that the distribution could be done in the name of a committee of Christian laymen, although he said he was prepared to make a "strong argument in favor of the excellent results which would be obtained by the distribution of these sermons by you yourself in your own name. At first, of course," he told Rockefeller, "there would be some criticism and the cry of Rockefeller money being used 'to break down the pillars of the church' would be raised. But if Dr. Fosdick's sermons do not fortify the foundations of the church, I am a very poor judge of the significance of preaching."

Lee told Rockefeller that he was convinced that distribution over a period of months would carry such conviction and constitute such a constructive contribution to the situation that the result "would be not alone profound thanks to you for having done this, but, what is of far greater importance, the building of a firmer and stronger foundation upon which the work of the church in this country might proceed."[8]

Rockefeller chose not to become involved in further controversy. However, as the fury increased and Fosdick was forced out of his pulpit at the Old First, Rockefeller invited Fosdick to become the minister at Park Avenue Baptist. Fosdick objected to the fact that full membership at Park Avenue was available only to those who had been baptized by immersion. But the Park Avenue ministry was only a temporary position while Rockefeller could build the Riverside Memorial Church as the temple of liberal Christianity, where Fosdick was ultimately installed for a lengthy tenure.

Lee, meanwhile, continued to print and distribute on his own those of Fosdick's sermons which he felt were particularly important. He sent out the sermon on "Faith" and Fosdick's famous "Farewell" sermon when he left Old First, as well as his first sermon at Park Avenue, "A Church That Abraham Lincoln Could Join." By the time he sent out the "Farewell" sermon in 1925, Lee could already report to Fosdick a change in attitude. "I am getting an immense number of letters from laymen," he wrote to Fosdick. He said that the letters from the laity were the most striking and most favorable and would do the minister's heart good. "I wish I could get this sermon to ten million laymen," he said.[9]

In the end, by raising the conflict to the level of public discussion, Lee did much to bring about understanding of Fosdick's point of view and increased harmony within the Protestant church. The fundamentalist-modernist controversy ultimately became a secondary question to that of the triumph of the Christian church as a whole. Fosdick later said of his relationship with Lee: "I warmly appreciated his support and am endlessly grateful to him for the encouragement he gave me.... I know from a very heartening experience that he was a man of courage and conviction, and a faithful friend to me."[10]

---

[1] John Mumford, loc. cit.

[2] John D. Rockefeller Jr. to Ivy Lee, Dec. 28, 1922, Rockefeller Archives, New York.

[3] Ivy Lee to John D. Rockefeller Jr., Jan. 23, 1923, Rockefeller Archives, New York.

[4] Quoted in Harry Emerson Fosdick, *Living of These Days* (New York: Harper & Bros., 1956), p. 144.

[5] Ibid., p. 146.

[6] Ibid., p. 152.

[7] Ivy Lee to Rev. G. W. McPherson, Sept. 11, 1922, H. E. Fosdick's Personal Papers.

[8] Ivy Lee to John D. Rockefeller Jr., Oct. 16, 1924, Rockefeller Archives, New York.

[9] Ivy Lee to Harry Emerson Fosdick, Apr. 23, 1925, H. E. Fosdick's Personal Papers.

[10] Harry Emerson Fosdick to R. E. Hiebert, Apr. 11, 1963.

Ray Eldon Hiebert

26: BIG MEN: A NETWORK OF INTERESTS

IVY LEE, WROTE BRITISH WRITER TERENCE O'BRIEN in 1935, "stood at the center of a network of powerful interests." He "had friends and connections in many spheres of life [including] Europe, Soviet Russia, and the Far East. He acted, internationally as well as in America, as a link between people whose business (and sometimes cultural) activities converged." Lee was a diplomat carrying on negotiations through endless personal conferences and high-level missions, a business statesman for the interests he represented. "It stands to reason," wrote O'Brien, "that if he simultaneously represents Mr. A, a steel magnate, Mr. B, a banker, and Mr. C, the president of a railroad corporation, there will be many occasions upon which his knowledge of the interests and policies of any one will, without his committing any breach of faith, be extremely useful to the other."[1]

Through his association with big men, Lee constantly served as an intermediary, promoting a series of relationships and sometimes even marriages among his clients. Early in his London career Lee developed an intimate friendship with an American oil executive, Francis E. Powell, who became chairman of the Anglo-American Oil Company in 1912. In America, Lee's association with the Rockefellers brought him into contact with A. Cotton Bedford, chairman of Standard of New Jersey. Lee brought these two men together through the International Chamber of Commerce, for which Bedford served as vice-president while Powell served as president of the American Chamber in London. By 1930 Standard of New Jersey merged with Anglo-American of London, with Ivy Lee no doubt serving as silent matchmaker.

Oil and sugar interests were brought together in an unusual way through Powell and Lee. The Anglo-Standard merger took place at the time Lee was working on the sugar stabilization problem, and Powell, retiring from his oil position, was a logical choice to be made chairman of the International Sugar Council. Lee's earlier role with the sugar interests had brought him into association with Cuban affairs and tobacco concerns, and he served as an intermediary between them. Working with Thomas Chadbourne, legal counsel to Cuban sugar, Lee met Paul Hahn, young attorney in the Chadbourne-Stanchfield-Levy firm. When Lee was working for American Tobacco Company, Hahn became assistant to George Washington Hill and eventually became president of the company. While Lee was working for both tobacco and sugar interests which had deep involvements with Cuba, a longtime Lee friend, Harry F. Guggenheim, was appointed American ambassador to Cuba. Later Chadbourne got involved with Lee in a committee serving the automobile interests.

As the Rockefeller association brought Lee into a large circle of influence, so did his relationship with the Guggenheims, which gave Lee an affiliation with the aviation industry and brought him into contact with people like Lindbergh. At the same time, Lee had a wide association with the important men of Wall Street, which led to his work with the motion picture industry, the automobile industry, politics, and others. Lee's relationship with Otto Kahn and John D. Rockefeller, for instance, resulted in the spark that produced Rockefeller Center. His friendship with Dwight Morrow, another Wall Street leader, resulted ultimately in holy matrimony for Anne Morrow and Charles Lindbergh.

Lee not only served as an intermediary for his clients but for many acquaintances, all of whom benefitted his customers. Although he never worked directly for General Electric, he maintained a close working friendship with Owen D. Young, its chairman. Also, he never served as counsel for Sears, Roebuck, but he was a friend of General R. E. Wood and William Rosenwald, its president and chairman. The list of big men with whom Lee interacted could go on at great length. He became a sort of industrial go-between for oil, sugar, tobacco, copper, aviation, the stock market, movies, politics, railroads, millers, public utilities, department stores, and even religion.

Early in his career Lee recognized that these contacts enhanced his ability to acquire new clients. In one letter which he sent out in the hope of getting new business, he said: "As you know, the nature of my work has brought me into contact with a great many men and situations which are of public interest. The gentlemen to whom I refer are not necessarily clients of mine nor are the events and facts which lie behind them always related to publicity.... [But] the basic thought which I have in mind is that I and my staff have a body of information that, within definite limits, might be of some service to you and your organization."[2]

Lee's respect for the great men of his time never waned. Even as an adolescent he kept scrapbooks with prized autographs or letters from famous people. While still in his teens he wrote to famous people and was frequently pleasantly surprised to receive a reply. In his early years he corresponded with a variety of no-table individuals including Luther Burbank, horticulturalist; Bliss Perry, philosopher; William H. Crocker, San Francisco businessman; William C. Redfield, congressman; J. Ramsey MacDonald, then a Member of Parliament; Theodore Roosevelt, Woodrow Wilson, and Andrew Carnegie. Ultimately, he was able to put this enthusiasm for people to work in his public relations, not only on a personal basis but through the mail. He developed a mailing list of the thirty thousand most influential men in the world, which ranged from occupants of the White House to Bolsheviks in the Kremlin. Because he had actually met and talked to the owners of many of the names on his list, he could be reasonably sure that his mail to them would be read with interest.

During his travels Lee constantly sought out people for their opinions—big men who influenced opinions and little ones who reflected them. He talked with cabinet officers and prime ministers, bankers and economists, journalists and industrialists, always taking the pulse of public opinion. He was often successful in securing interviews with leaders who were customarily unapproachable: Nitti and Mussolini in Italy, Cuno and Stinnes in Germany, Rykov and Radek in Russia.

He scored a major scoop in 1923 by getting a private conference with Benito Mussolini, the new Italian prime minister. He found Mussolini in "a large, plain, almost bare room in the Chigi Palace, scorning the trappings of state." He asked the Italian leader why he had turned away from socialism, and Mussolini answered that the war and the Russian revolution had taught him that capitalism was the only way out for the Italians, an answer which, at the time, must have been gratifying to Lee. In the middle of their conversation, according to Lee, a messenger entered with word that Italian taxi drivers were threatening a strike. "Now that isn't right—here, in the middle of the season, with Rome full of tourists," Lee quoted Mussolini. "They'll give us a bad name before the world. Tell them I haven't stood for a strike since I took charge of things. Attend to it, will you, Joseph?" And with that, said Lee with considerable awe, the strike was called off.[3]

Lee also interviewed German Chancellor Cuno in 1923 and was entertained in the chancellery made famous by Bismarck. He found the five Cuno children's voices filled the air during all the "struggle of the German Prime Minister to maintain his government in a jangling world." The German industrial magnate, Hugo Stinnes, granted a rare interview to Lee. He was in one of his own hotels, which had conspicuous signs on the door, "French and Belgians will not be accommodated." Lee concluded, after talking to Stinnes, that "no sense of moral guilt for the war exists among the Germans…. There is no hope of goodwill in Europe unless the Americans can bring it."[4]

Lee sometimes gave dinners for important men to which he would invite leaders of business and press. He did much to make Sir Josiah Stamp well known in America as an economist by giving a well-publicized dinner for him in New York. And Lee in turn was invited to many important state dinners and other occasions where the notables of Europe would be gathered. Because he felt that his clients ought to understand the minds of the men who influenced Europe, he often sent memos to them after a dinner or an interview. In 1920, for instance, he went to a dinner in Paris which Marshal Foch attended. The next day he wrote about the event and circulated the memo to his clients. "The Marshal was very much of a man," Lee wrote. "He drank his claret and liqueurs, smoked three cigars, joked with ladies, and shook hands with me twice before the evening was over."

Lee often took note of advice great men gave on how to achieve success. Marshal Foch, he reported, felt that "the lucky man is always lucky because he always manages to be around when the luck is handed out. The successful man is he who plans for every conceivable eventuality and realizes all the time that something is going to happen which he has not expected," Foch told Lee. "The secret of successful organization is simplification. Nothing complicated is going to be a great success. My best ideas come in the morning when I am shaving. Cutting the beard from my face removes the cobwebs from my brain."[5]

On the Collier's Radio Hour in 1929 Lee gave a talk on the "big men" he had known, which he ended by saying: "I have mentioned these few men as typical of the statesmanship of Europe. As we know such men better we will understand their nations and peoples better—and over such a route we will find the way to international peace."[6]

Lee eventually became acquainted with many of the leaders of Europe. Among them were Dr. Eduard Benes, foreign minister and later president of Czechoslovakia; Count Bethlen, Prime Minister of Hungary; Baron Furakawa of Japan; T. V. Soong of China; King Boris of Bulgaria, and Hjalmar Schacht, president of the Reichsbank of Germany. The notable exception was Joseph Stalin. Lee once had an appointment with Stalin, but the Russian dictator kept him waiting three days and then failed to show up as he promised at a luncheon held at an estate thirty miles outside Moscow.

King Boris III apparently enjoyed Lee's friendship. The young King went out of his way to give a cordial welcome to the public relations counsel when he visited Bulgaria in the twenties. Some time later, while Lee and his family were vacationing on Long Island, he remembered that it was the King's birthday and called the local Western Union office to send a cablegram addressed to King Boris, Royal Palace, Sophia, Bulgaria. The operator thought it was a practical joke and refused to send the cable. After much persuasion, she reluctantly put it on the wires. Within a few hours, a cable came back from the Royal Palace in Sophia, addressed to Ivy Lee. It expressed thanks for the congratulations and was signed simply, "Boris."

Perhaps the world leader to whom Ivy Lee was closest was Mackenzie King, who served as Prime Minister of Canada during the years of Lee's greatest success, 1921 to 1930 (and again from 1935 to 1940). Lee and King had met while both worked for John D.

Rockefeller on the Ludlow crisis and subsequent industrial relations problems. King in turn asked Lee's advice after he became Prime Minister and dealt with the problems of Canada's nationalized railroads. Lee was influential in the 1922 appointment of Sir Henry Thornton to be General Manager of the Canadian Railways.

Lee had known Thornton as a one-time Pennsylvania Railroad executive. After Thornton was installed in office, King wrote to Lee that "no appointment made by any government in this country for years has been received with such general enthusiasm and approval as that of Sir Henry Thornton." King added that "we shall always recall the occasion as one of historical moment in the working out of Canada's transportation problem.... You certainly will realize how much I relied upon our friendship."[7]

Lee was interested not only in men of state but in philosophers and artists from whom he felt he could learn. He had a long interview with French philosopher Henri Bergson in Paris in 1919 in an effort to analyze prevailing attitudes of the French towards war and peace. He was an admirer of Jo Davidson, the sculptor; he talked with him on several occasions and even helped arrange for the Davidson statue of Walt Whitman to be placed in Central Park. He was a close friend of Lucretia Bori, opera star of the twenties.

Lee once berated an associate, Daniel Pierce: "Dan, you spend too much time with unimportant people." Pierce himself later said, "Ivy wears the fine clothes and gets around to all the swell places with important people and I am still in my short sleeves working to make good on his promises."[8] Seeking out the leaders did not mean fawning over them, however. Lee was always a man of his own mind. It was frequently said of him during the twenties that he was "one of the few men who could make millionaires wait for him."[9]

Just why important people sought Lee's advice was explained by John Mumford. He said Lee "knows more about the inside of more corporations than any one man in America. Big business from Maine to Texas goes to him with its troubles."[10] James L. Quackenbush, general counsel of the Interborough Rapid Transit Company, gave a succinct description of why business wanted Lee's advice. He was questioned by Samuel Untermyer, counsel for the New York State Transit Commission, on just what Lee was being paid for.

"Brains," answered Quackenbush.

"Just for holding them in his head?" asked Untermyer.

"No, for advising.... If I thought at the close of this session," said Quackenbush, "some statement should be made concerning the subject of our interesting discussion, I might get it up and ask Mr. Lee to revise it and see whether he thought it was [prepared] in a fashion that would carry what I was trying to convey to the public generally."[11]

Lee did not always tell his clients what they wanted to hear. His usual advice, said Mumford, was that "secrecy was the parent of suspicion.... He told them the biggest thing he could do for them was to correct their policies and attitude toward the public rather than get partisan stuff printed for them as news.... Most of them shook in their shoes at this new teaching." One who shook, for instance, was George Washington Hill, head of American Tobacco Company, when Lee advised him to give his stockholders a complete report on the company's secret bonus system.

Lee's son James felt that men sought out his father because he understood them and spoke their language. He could talk easily with top men of industry, finance, or state about their ideas and problems, possibly because he was a voracious reader and readily absorbed knowledge in many fields for future reference; also because he possessed a genius for thinking in the same terms as another. One of his associates, Victor Knauth, said that Lee was a very wise man. His opinions were usually right, and "he knew what motivated people. He could clarify other people's thoughts for them."

Another of the reasons for Lee's success was that he had an almost uncanny knack for being prepared in advance. He was able to predict how events would turn out and was ready to take advantage of them. For instance, when Wendell Willkie suddenly came into national prominence in 1939 as the surprise Republican candidate for president, the Lee-Ross firm had in its office a complete file on Willkie which Lee had prepared before he died. Lee had noticed the young Indiana lawyer during his work for the Public Utilities Executive Committee in the early thirties, had recognized him as a man with great potential, and had proceeded to gather information about him.

Lee predicted Hoover's election to the Presidency some eight years before it occurred. He saw in a young lawyer on Wall Street, James V. Forrestal, a man who would make an important contribution to America. Another young man that impressed Lee was a big, rough West Pointer by the name of Jack Schwab (no relation to Charles). Lee helped him get a job on the Pennsylvania Railroad, where he rose to become vice-president of the line.

In the mid-twenties, Lee saw the young John Foster Dulles as a man with a bright future. Dulles was a lawyer for the firm of Sullivan and Cromwell, which handled international financial accounts, and he and Lee worked together on several international stabilization loans, Lee once undertaking a public relations job for Dulles himself.

During the widely publicized trial of Harry M. Daugherty, United States Attorney General implicated in the Teapot Dome scandal, Dulles had served as a government witness against Daugherty. During the trial, defense attorney Max D. Steuer had characterized Dulles as "a scoundrel and unfit to practice law." The statement was quoted prominently by the press. But Steuer later sent Dulles a letter of apology saying he had been led by false impressions and false beliefs. Lee sent copies of this letter and a press release to newspaper editors and editorial writers all over the country and achieved wide publication of the retraction.

Henry Luce came to Lee in the early twenties with an idea for unusual kind of news magazine. Lee encouraged the young man and predicted that the proposed *Time* magazine would be a success. Ten years later, however, when Luce asked Lee about his idea for a business magazine he was going to call *Fortune*, Lee advised against it, saying that business in the early thirties would not support such a publication. In spite of this wrong analysis, Luce retained a great respect for Lee and urged him to write a series of articles on capitalism and democracy for his new business magazine. Lee never found the time.

Benjamin Javits, brother of Jacob who later became a Senator from New York, once came to Lee with an idea for organizing the people of America who own a stake in its economy—the policyholders, stockholders, and homeowners. Lee helped the young attorney organize these people into the United Shareowners of America, Inc. The objectives of the society were to counterbalance the power and influence of labor, reduce corporate and individual taxes, protect the value of the dollar, reduce the national debt, limit the government's role in business, and preserve the basic economic freedoms and opportunities guaranteed in the Constitution and Bill of Rights.

Javits is still president of this national organization which has many prominent men and women on its National Policy Advisory Committee. He found Lee a "fascinating person and a good friend...one of America's industrial statesmen." In 1957 he wrote to

Ivy Lee's widow: "Your husband, who was a very dear and old friend of mine, helped me on the road to whatever small measure of success the Javits family has achieved."[12]

Lee had many important friends in the mass media, even though media representatives were often quick to be critical of his efforts. He quickly assessed the future importance of the motion pictures and radio and was close to such pioneers as Cecil B. DeMille and David Sarnoff, men who saw the new media as keys to mass entertainment and persuasion. Sarnoff wrote to Mrs. Lee after her husband's death that he "valued his friendship and admired him greatly as a man for many years." The radio executive told how he once attended a conference with Lee. In the middle of it, Lee leaned over and told Sarnoff that he had to leave for a few hours because it was his day for registering to vote. Sarnoff asked if he could accompany Lee because, he later said, he would "rather spend three hours in Lee's company than to remain at the conference, however interesting the others who were present might be."[13]

Lee worked with many prominent newspaper people, men such as Roy Howard of the Scripps-Howard chain; Arthur Brisbane of the Hearst papers; Kent Cooper, head of the Associated Press; John Finley, editor of the *New York Times*; columnists such as David Lawrence, Lowell Thomas, and George E. Sokolsky. Sokolsky and Lee met in China while the public relations man was on an international relations tour. The two differed strenuously on the Soviet Union; Sokolsky felt it should be abolished, not recognized. But they respected each other's opinions and were both completely frank about them. Sokolsky reflected the feeling of most newsmen who knew Lee well when he said there was nothing underhanded about Lee's methods and that "one could depend upon him without question.... He would not have permitted himself to be in a dubious position."[14]

Lee was interested in what important people were reading, and on one of his summer travels, he made a point of asking the famous men he met about their current book favorites. He published the results in the October 20, 1928, issue of *Information*. The names of the books that were being read in 1928 are no longer important, but the people to whom Lee put his question are interesting, for they show the range of his acquaintances. There was Sir Josiah Stamp, eminent British economist, author, railroad president, and longtime Lee friend; H. G. Wells, whom Lee admired; Montagu Norman, Governor of the Bank of England; Lionel Curtis, Honorary Secretary of the Royal Institute of International Affairs and Fellow of All Souls' College, Oxford; Sir Ernest Benn, London publisher; and J. L. Garvin, distinguished editor of *The Observer*, among others.

Lee was interested in learning just what it was that made a man popular. One figure who intrigued him was T. E. Lawrence, the legendary "Lawrence of Arabia," who in the twenties was almost worshipped as a god by many people. Lee got to know Lawrence through Lionel Curtis, who was Lawrence's residuary legatee. Lawrence, in turn, had great respect for Lee. He felt that Lee's May 1929 article in *Atlantic Monthly*, "The Black Legend," was "first-rate stuff" and had high praise for Lee's book on Russia.

Lee wanted some of his friends to meet Lawrence, then an enlisted man in the British Air Force going under the name of T. E. Shaw. Lawrence wrote that he would do anything he could to oblige Lee but warned him of the "social prejudices against fellows in the ranks of the services."[15] Lee was one of the few men allowed to read the original version of *The Seven Pillars of Wisdom* during Lawrence's lifetime. Lee told his family that it had been the greatest piece of English prose he had ever read.

Lee's personal library, a large portion of which was later given to Princeton, contained more than ten thousand volumes. His office walls were lined with book shelves filled not with collector's items but practical books on economics, politics, labor, history, biography, public affairs, writing, and semantics. His fantastic memory enabled him during a discussion to go to the shelves, take down a volume, and turn to a precise reference to support his point.

As his practice grew he needed to be closer to his work, so the Lees moved to a Fifth Avenue cooperative apartment at 4 East 66th Street which Dwight Morrow, who also lived there, had urged him to purchase. According to social scientists in the employ of the Social Register Association, this address was just two blocks from the exact social center of New York. Lee had no need to be concerned with his social status, for the family moved quite naturally in circles that would not have admitted most of his colleagues of earlier generations. His wife did charity work for the Opera Society and took part in other socially prominent affairs; in 1926, his daughter Alice was formally presented at the Court of St. James.

He belonged to a long list of clubs in almost every major capital of the world: University, Princeton, Metropolitan Clubs of New York; the Rittenhouse Club of Philadelphia; the Travellers Club of London; the National Press Club of Washington, and many others. According to his son, he made a science out of joining the right club in order to meet the people who could bring him into contact with potential clients. When he saw a public relations problem, such as an approaching congressional investigation, he frequented the same club as the person who was the object of investigation; Lee would get the man into a game of bridge and then drop a remark or two about the coming investigation on which he had some ideas.

Lee often provided his services without discussing specific terms of his fee, and sometimes agreed to a small fee with the hope that it could be raised as his work proved successful. Money, after all, was not the most important goal. Getting a new client, working on a vital project, or influencing others—these were much more significant to Lee. After his death the firm lost two accounts, one because the immediate job was completed and the other, according to Harcourt Parrish, "because we shocked them by asking $20,000 whereas they thought they would have to pay about $6,000. Ivy Lee did that, you know—worked for an undetermined amount and then argued himself into a good fee."[16]

As his practice increased, Lee gave up his suite of offices at 111 Broadway and took for his operations the entire thirty-fourth floor of the Equitable Trust Company Building at 15 Broad Street, not far from where he and George Parker had first started. According to one New York reporter, it was "one of the most luxurious and restful offices in the city." This was probably one of those exaggerations that became so typical of writing about Ivy Lee.

The walls in the reception room were covered with photographs of the "big men" of the day, all inscribed to Ivy Lee. In addition to the Rockefellers, Chryslers, and Schwabs, the gallery included pictures of Jerome Kern, Owen D. Young, Irving Berlin, Hjalmar Schacht, Winthrop Aldrich, Clarence Mackay, Viscount Matsudaira, and dozens of others.

The main office where Lee met his friends, colleagues, and clients was a room about twenty by twenty-five feet containing a big desk, and a few gold-brocaded and enameled Chinese cases containing art objects; these walls were hung with finely tinted etchings of Amiens, Rheims, Bourges, Westminster, and other great Gothic cathedrals.

Behind this main office was a smaller room with one small desk where he could get away to do his serious work. Here, surrounded with the book-lined walls accented with busts of Marshal Foch and Henry P. Davison, he sat in a straight-backed chair and, in his decorous way, never put his feet up on the desk.

Still in his early fifties as the Age of Business climbed toward its pinnacle in the nineteen-twenties, Ivy Lee had put himself squarely into the middle of the circle of influence of his day. From this position he was able to win wide respect for the new profession of public relations.

---

[1] Terence O'Brien, "Propaganda as a Private Industry," *The Listener*, Jan. 30, 1935. p. 195.

[2] Draft of letter to potential clients, Office File, Ivy Lee Papers, Princeton.

[3] *New York Times*, May 27, 1923, p. 6.

[4] Ibid.

[5] Memo to Lee's clients, 1920, Ivy Lee Papers, Princeton.

[6] "Transcript of Lee Address on Colliers Radio Hour," Jan. 18, 1929, Ivy Lee Papers, Princeton.

[7] Mackenzie King to Ivy Lee, Oct. 9, 1922, Ivy Lee Papers, Princeton.

[8] Quoted in Berlin, op. cit., p. 115.

[9] Quoted in S. P. Hollingsworth, "Pioneers—Blair, Barnum, and Lee," "Publicity," ms. in Red Cross Archives, Washington, D.C.

[10] Mumford. loc. cit.

[11] "The Difference Between 'Public Relations Advisor' and 'Press Agent,'" *Printers Ink*, June 1927, p. 10.

[12] Benjamin Javits to Mrs. Ivy Lee, Jan. 1, 1957, Papers of Mrs. Ivy Lee.

[13] David Sarnoff to Mrs. Ivy Lee, Nov. 14, 1934, Ivy Lee Papers, Princeton.

[14] George Sokolsky in conversation with R. E. Hiebert, Oct. 1962.

[15] T. E. Shaw (Lawrence) to Ivy Lee, May 27, 1929, Ivy Lee Papers, Princeton.

[16] Office note, Harcourt Parrish Papers, University of Virginia.

V

FOREIGN INTERESTS
"At the Council Table of the World"

27: RED CROSS: HUMANIZING AMERICA

WORLD WAR I USHERED INTO MODERN CIVILIZATION the conflict of words. For the first time in history, propaganda became a major weapon and was used on a mass scale. America was made conscious of the strategy early in the battle when the Germans and the British made strenuous efforts to influence American opinion. As early as 1914 a *New York Times* editorial had declared: "This is the first press agents' war." But it was also the first war in which public relations, as opposed to press agentry, was put into practice—primarily through the American Red Cross.

With the declaration of war in April 1917, President Wilson recognized the importance of the Red Cross to the nation's effort and, as titular head of the organization, exercised his right to reorganize the relief association for greater effectiveness. On May 10 he announced establishment of a War Council to take charge of all Red Cross efforts. Henry P. Davison, a partner of J. P. Morgan and Co., was chairman; other members named were Edward N. Hurley, former chairman of the Federal Trade Commission; Grayson M-P. Murphy, vice-president of Guaranty Trust Co.; Charles D. Norton, vice-president of the First National Bank of New York; and Cornelius N. Bliss Jr., a leading New York businessman. William Howard Taft and Eliot Wadsworth, peacetime head of the Red Cross, were named as ex officio members.

Acknowledging that "the utmost publicity should be given to the activities of the Red Cross...," the office of Assistant to the Chairman of the War Council was created "to have special authority, under the direction of the chairman, over matters relative to publicity."[1] On May 10, 1917, Ivy Lee was officially appointed to serve in that capacity. As Davison's personal advisor and right-hand man, he played a significant part in making the Red Cross a successful adjunct to the entire war effort. He left in the hands of his associates many important clients, including Interborough Rapid Transit Company, the Bethlehem Steel Corporation, Standard Oil of New Jersey, and the Rockefeller interests, and turned his complete attention to the Red Cross.

When the War Council met in May the first order of business was the raising of funds to carry on military and civilian relief programs throughout the world. Wadsworth told the gathering that "great sums of money" would have to be obtained. He was thinking of five or ten million dollars. Some of the bankers cautiously suggested a goal of perhaps twenty-five to fifty million. But Henry P. Davison went before the Council and said, "I think we might ask for one hundred million." In something of a state of shock, the members agreed but said it would take time. To which Davison retorted: "Gentlemen, I'd rather raise a hundred million dollars now than two hundred million next fall." The Council finally agreed to accept the goal and a date was set one month hence, June 18–25, 1917, to be named "Red Cross Week" for the purpose of raising the hundred million.[2]

Working closely with Davison, Seward Prosser, chairman of the Bankers Trust Company, and Charles S. Ward, fundraiser for the YMCA, Lee immediately put into motion the machinery for a nationwide publicity campaign. They had only a few weeks, but they spent literally night and day on the project. Lee stayed in the Davison house in Washington where he directed publicity, wrote speeches, drafted magazine and newspaper articles, pamphlets, brochures, and leaflets, laid out advertising and posters, and oversaw the entire promotional operation. He called on the experience and the personnel of his own firm, including his associates John Mumford and Bronson Batchelor.

"Whenever possible," wrote G. R. Gaeddert in the official Red Cross history, "the public's attention was focused on the Red Cross." Under Lee's direction, every newsworthy item was put into a press release. When a Red Cross unit arrived in England on May 18, for instance, it not only got front page headlines but it also provided an opportunity to explain what the Red Cross was doing in England. This kind of activity, begun during the fundraising campaign, was continued at full pace throughout the rest of the war.

Prominent men from all walks of life—business, government, the arts—were brought in to participate in Red Cross activities, taking part in everything from parades to high-level policy conferences. All such activities got news space: a Washington conference was held to brief top Red Cross leaders on relief needs around the world—Herbert Hoover discussed the needs of Belgium, General John Pershing talked about those of France, Sir Ian Malcolm spoke on Great Britain, and Frederick Wolcott of the Rockefeller Foundation discussed the situation of Poland—ex-President Taft and War Secretary Newton Baker exhorted the workers, who then returned to their posts and in turn exhorted their colleagues.

In a full-page appeal which Lee wrote for *The American Press*, a publication for newspaper publishers, he said: "This is the biggest philanthropic job in the history of the world—the most far-reaching enterprise for the relief of the sufferings of mankind ever planned." He felt that the campaign could prove to be the greatest example of generosity ever displayed by any nation, if the American people could be informed about it. "The people can be depended upon to respond to just the extent to which they know the story," he told the publishers, "and upon the press alone can dependence be placed to carry the story to the people."[3] (*The American Press* commented editorially that it was altogether fitting that Ivy Lee should be publicizing the Red Cross for he "ranks at the very top of that small but influential bank of men who have been the pioneers in replacing the press agent and his dark lantern methods with the light of sound publicity.")[4]

Divisions and teams organized to spread the word were often headed by the most prominent individuals in the community, men like J. P. Morgan and F. A. Vanderbilt and women like Mrs. E. H. Harriman. Benefit entertainments were offered, even by such groups as the U.S. National Lawn Tennis Association which turned its profits over to the campaign.

Lee and his banker colleagues persuaded corporations to declare extra dividends in behalf of the $100 million fund. Cleveland H. Dodge pledged $1 million on condition that twenty-four other individuals or corporations match his gift. United States Steel declared a dividend that brought in nearly $6 million; the Rockefeller Foundation contributed $5 million, and the Ford Motor Company a half a million.

Less affluent people, too, gave generously—many washerwomen donated a day's work; a woman in Ohio supplied a hen and twelve eggs, which were promptly auctioned off for $2 thousand; countless workmen gave several days' wages. Gaeddert described how the "campaign director found on his desk fifty cents in silver and a note scrawled on a telegraph blank: 'To the Red Cross from a Messenger Boy.' It was placed beside the five million dollar check from the Rockefeller Foundation."

Each city and state was given a quota to fill, and on the morning of June 18, teams throughout the forty-eight states got off "at the crack of the starter's pistol," with team captains contending for first place, city vying with city, state with state, and division with division. News releases were sent out three or four times a day, with the picture changing each hour and the country's headlines reflecting the latest results in the race. Sunday, June 24, was a day of rest, except for the churches, and hundreds of them turned their collections over to the drive, while their Sunday School students went out gathering funds.

By the end of Sunday the total was just below $80 million, some $20 million under the goal. Monday, the last day of the campaign, was announced as General Pershing Day, and it dawned amidst great anxiety at Red Cross headquarters. In the most spectacular bid for public attention yet, a stunt was planned that was similar to one used later by Ivy Lee and Charles Lindbergh to promote aviation. A beautiful young Chicago aviatrix, Miss Katherine Stinson, was hired to fly an airplane solo from Buffalo to Washington, stopping at Rochester, Syracuse, Albany, New York, and Philadelphia. She brought the last-minute pledges and reports from those cities and the flight drew crowds of thousands along the way.

After a feverish night of figuring the totals, Davison released a statement on Tuesday morning, June 26, that the goal of $100 million had not only been reached but had been oversubscribed by nearly $14 million. "Nothing which has happened before shows so clearly," Davison said, "that the great heart of the American people is in this struggle with determination that our own men shall be cared for, that everything that can be done shall be done to hearten and to aid the suffering people among our Allies, indeed that nothing shall be left undone to *win this war*." He also announced that henceforth the Red Cross would provide for "the care and safety of our soldiers and sailors wherever they may be," and would take over the administration of all relief work in France and the other Allied countries, including Russia.[5]

Lee's successful planning and publicizing of the fundraising campaign led to his being asked to serve as Director of Publicity for the entire Red Cross. He worked closely with Davison, and later said of him that he was "unquestionably the greatest businessman with whom I have ever come in contact. His enthusiasm as well as his vision made him so." Such vision ultimately enabled Davison to bring a complete reorganization to the Red Cross, making it a meaningful instrument of quasi-governmental power. He gave Lee the authority to make sweeping changes in the organization and effectiveness of the public relations and promotion department.

For more than a year, between July 1917 and August 1918, Lee worked to create a powerful publicity organ within the Red Cross. He brought specialists and professionals from a wide variety of fields, including a "first-class advertising man as head of our Advertising Bureau" and a top *New York Tribune* women's reporter, Miss Anne Pierce, "to supervise what we say concerning the work of women." He created a Magazine Bureau to handle relationships with magazines throughout the country; he created a Bureau of Relations with Church and Labor Organizations, and a Bureau of History, putting in charge his long-time friend and colleague, John Mumford, who wrote most of Davison's book, *The American Red Cross in the Great War*," published by Macmillan in 1919.

Lee installed publicity departments in each foreign as well as American division of the Red Cross; each, under Lee's advice, started its own division bulletin and operated its own speaker's and motion picture bureau. He reorganized the Motion Picture Department and began the preparation of a comprehensive film to cover all Red Gross activities. And he reorganized the Speaker's Bureau, setting up an elaborate campaign that utilized teams of "Four Minutemen" who, with lantern slides and motion pictures, traveled around the country. He told Davison that "our speaker's bureau has a very ingenious program for selecting a group of men from the convalescent hospitals and training them to become Red Cross speakers so they can go around the country and speak for us in uniform."

He organized the Red Cross "relationship with the press of the country so that every class of newspapers and publications will have regularly fed to it a quantity of material specially adapted to its own requirements, thus insuring attention to labor papers, farm publications, church journals, and house organs of business concerns. We shall give to the newspapers some kind of a story practically every morning and every afternoon," Lee said. As each of the stories was released, it was put into "information sheets" and distributed to all chapters. The stories were also put into small poster form and mounted on the bulletin boards of post offices, banks, railroad stations, churches, and all the store windows of the United Cigar Stores, Woolworth Stores, and others.

Lee advised that a great deal of attention should be paid to carrying on a regular campaign of education among Red Cross workers on the why's and wherefore's of all they were doing. "If the Red Cross is to realize its mission, it must be not only a great relief organization but a great social and moral force, including the gospel of service and sacrifice and basing its program upon an appeal to the reason as well as the emotions of its workers and members," he said. All of these things would make this a very large program "which needs to be put over in the biggest possible way." If the plan was successful, it "would mean a great wave of Red Cross enthusiasm sweeping over the country, based on complete accounting by the War Council for all that it has done and resulting in the inoculation of the American people with a spirit, and a knowledge behind the spirit, which would be the best possible guaranty for the future success of our work."[6]

A membership campaign was launched in December of 1917 and, as a result of extensive publicity and promotional activities directed by Ivy Lee, membership was increased in one week by twelve million, or 200 percent. In May of 1918 a second war fund drive similar to the 1917 all-out effort, was launched, and again its goal was $100 million. At the end of the week the total subscription had reached $180 million, 80 percent over the quota.

The collection of so much money, of course, led to some charges of abuse. From the first, Lee recognized this possibility and reiterated his usual policy of openness and frankness. "We are going to spend a great deal of money," he told the Red Cross officers. "It is going to come from the people. We must take the people into our confidence and keep them there." He wrote an article for the *Review of Reviews* to tell the nation "how the Red Cross money is spent." All expenditures, he said, were being subject to the constant and continuous scrutiny of auditors under the direction of the War Department, "so that every dollar contributed will be carefully accounted for. Reports in great detail are being constantly made to the people, and it is the policy of the War Council to conduct all the affairs of the Red Cross during the war as an open book."[7]

In a personal memorandum to Davison, Lee said he was hopeful that no impediment would be encountered in arranging to publish the complete War Council minutes in pamphlet form, with a complete statement of all contracts involving the payment of a thousand dollars or more, a statement of all salaries, and a complete copy of the comptroller's report giving all details of the financial operations. He recommended that such a document be given to each chapter, each library in the country, every large contributor, and to the chairman in each community where a campaign for funds was waged.[8]

Knowing the value of personally carrying the message to the public, Lee induced Davison to tour the country making speeches to raise funds. This, said Mumford later, was a task "about as easy for Davison as carrying off the Woolworth Building, for he was no speaker." But Lee was a polished orator, and he accompanied the War Council chairman on a nationwide tour. Lee wrote Davison's speeches, listened to them with a practiced ear, and then between stops coached Davison on his strong and weak points. By the end of the tour, according to Wideman Lee, Davison was also an accomplished speaker.

Ivy Lee urged Davison to make a personal tour of Europe, to "get its spirit and news meaning, so that you can come back after having cabled over considerable material from the other side, give out a big interview on your arrival in this country and then make a quick tour of division headquarters, addressing large meetings at all the thirteen cities in quick succession. We would," he told Davison, "plan to take no chances with these cities but would send an advance man to all to work up the meetings in a direct way and thus make sure that a fixed impression is left behind with the audience."[9]

Lee himself visited the European front several times, touring the war-torn areas with Davison or inspecting the lines on his own. Granted the rank of Major in the Red Cross, he wore the uniform of the Red Cross with the Sam Browne belt during these visits. When he returned to the states and proudly wore this uniform to a meeting in Riverdale, a regular Army Major threatened his arrest for impersonating an officer, and he reluctantly returned to civilian dress. "But," he told an audience at the Rockefeller Foundation, "the uniform of the American Red Cross carries a message in Europe today that it is impossible to describe."[10]

Lee's European schedules were overfilled. "You will get some idea of my rush time from the fact that I am dictating this letter while taking my bath," he wrote to his father from Paris. "Ever since I arrived here last Saturday, I have been in a whirl. The days are not really long enough to do the things that I want to do and should do. Paris is full of people that I know, many of them intimate friends of mine."[11]

Lee talked with many of the important people of Europe—Clemenceau, the Queen of Belgium, and other notables—to get endorsements for the Red Cross work. He also conferred with such diverse acquaintances as General Atterbury of the Pennsylvania Railroad, Samuel Gompers, and General Pershing. Pershing told him: "There is no question whatever that the Red Cross has saved the day, tiding over the period while we were getting ready to become an effective military force." On the side, the General of the Armies asked Lee to prepare a public statement for him, as long as the publicist was at hand.[12]

Lee was himself interviewed by a French journalist for *Le Petit Parisien* who wrote: "He is still a young man, with forceful features, of few words but to the point. You can feel that he is a man of as much method as decision, as much order as precision. He is clear in his undertakings and has proven himself well-informed in all."[13] Lee duly sent translations of the French news article to United States papers.

From the front lines Lee wrote his father: "I am having a marvelous experience. I have been under fire at least a half a dozen times since I have been over here and the sensation is not pleasant.

I went through two terrible air raids, one at Chalon and the other at Compeigne.... At Chalon...three bombs fell within one hundred yards of where I was, absolutely helpless and unprotected. I cannot give you more details but I will be able to tell you some thrilling experiences when I get home."[14]

These experiences of actual war provided Lee with renewed enthusiasm for his articles and speeches when he got home. Ultimately he asked to resign from the Red Cross to accept a commission in the army. This desire may have been partially motivated by some dissension that had developed when the Red Cross hired William Allen White to serve as a publicity consultant. Lee felt he was doing a satisfactory job and was insulted at the idea of White being brought in to tell him what to do. Red Cross officers immediately did all they could to mollify Lee and finally shelved White in his favor. At the same time, Secretary of War Newton Baker turned down Lee's request for a direct commission, saying: "Will you not...remain at your present post in the consciousness that in your work you are serving the Armed Forces and the cause for which they are fighting as directly as if you were carrying a gun."[15]

Tired from the constant traveling and from carrying the heavy burden of Red Cross work, Lee took a vacation in 1918 and devoted his attention to the war efforts of some of his own clients. Among other things, he helped A. C. Bedford of Standard Oil organize the National Petroleum War Service Committee; then assisted John D. Rockefeller Jr., who was chairman of the United War Work Campaign. Lee served as Chairman of the Publicity Department, and Rockefeller later thanked him for his "valuable contribution. I felt your leadership of this important department was essential to the success of the campaign."[16]

Lee served throughout the war on a voluntary basis, and even offered to provide the services of his office and to pay his own expenses incurred in connection with Red Cross activities. These amounted to more than $18,000. "You have been kind enough a number of times to suggest that I ought to render a statement of my expenses," he told Davison, "but I have felt a great deal of pride in the fact that I was enrolled in the Red Cross as a volunteer, and my opinion still is that working under you and with the other members of the Red Cross, not alone toward winning the war but toward the greater object of relieving human suffering the world over, has in itself been sufficient compensation for whatever it has cost me. I feel sure, therefore, that you will see the situation from my viewpoint and will excuse me from rendering any account to the Red Cross for either services or expenditures during the war."[17]

After the Armistice, Davison asked Lee's help in connection with the International Red Cross Commission to Europe. In this capacity he continued as a consultant to the Red Cross for the remainder of his life. His expenses were paid, but he donated his own time in public relations services for fund drives and for emergency relief campaigns during floods, droughts, and depression periods.

Traveling for the Red Cross in Europe, Lee saw an entirely new field of endeavor for public relations—the promotion of peace and harmony among nations and peoples. In an address before the Rockefeller Foundation, Lee described small scenes that symbolized the effect of the Red Cross. At a Rome railroad station, he and Davison watched as young teen-aged Italian draftees were being sent to the front. Their fathers, mothers, sisters, and brothers were all standing around, hugging and kissing the boys before the train left. "Mr. Davison and I stood on the outside, and you couldn't do it without crying," Lee said. "I saw Mr. Davison with great big drops falling down his face—we didn't have anything to say to each other. About that time one of these youngsters looked at me, saw this Red Cross uniform and called out, 'Viva la Croce Rossa Americana.' As soon as he said that the whole crowd broke into cheers for the Red Cross."

While visiting a bread line in Chalon, Lee and Davison were impressed with the way in which a Red Cross lady was distributing food tickets. The men said "Merci" to her in so charming a way and there was such a radiant smile on her face that Lee remarked: "When I was on the Pennsylvania Railroad I used to dream of the time when we could induce a ticket agent to sell tickets in that spirit. Mr. Davison and I went and stood behind the case to see the effect of it on the men. These men would come up, put down their 75 centimes, and the lady would give them their change and her demeanor brought forth a perfectly beautiful attitude on their part."

At a Belgian school for refugee children, Lee related, "the thing that made the greatest impression on me was that the children seemed to want to feel the touch of a human hand. Two or three of them would try to grasp your hand at once. They would cling to you and pull your coat just to feel the presence of a friend, of an American. That word 'American' had a meaning to those people that I almost wonder sometimes if it has to us."[18]

Lee began to see how the Red Cross was more than an agency of relief during wartime; it was a public relations program for the American people, just as the Rockefeller Foundation was for JDR. He had no doubt that the Red Cross campaign was changing the image of America in the eyes of foreigners. The Red Cross "gave the world an entirely new vision of the essential meaning of American life and character," he said. "Through carrying a message of relief and mercy, as an expression of the sacrifice and sympathy of the American people, it let our Allies know that this is not a mere money-making nation," he wrote in the *Review of Reviews*. On another occasion, he said, "The Red Cross is taking to Europe an expression of America as she really is, not as Europe had always supposed her to be in the past—a nation interested primarily and largely in money-making—but a nation of ideals and sympathy and love of peace."[19]

Lee increasingly recognized that "through promoting better understanding between ourselves and all the Allied nations," the Red Cross could "lay a foundation for an enduring peace after the war." He advised the Red Cross to cooperate closely with the League of Nations, recommended that the association build its headquarters in Geneva near the League headquarters, and suggested the appointment of an official board composed of distinguished international personalities to spur the organization's effort to extend its activities around the world.

He went to Geneva during the League of Nations debates and helped insert into the covenant the important Clause XXV which called for members of the League to promote the development of Red Cross organizations devoted to peaceful activities. He told a *New York Times* reporter that Clause XXV was "the most promising assurance of the future usefulness of the Red Cross."[20] In April 1919 he attended a world conference of medical and public health leaders in Cannes, France, and aided in the establishment of the League of Red Cross Societies, which was officially founded on May 5, 1919. The League has continued ever since to give worldwide assistance and guidance in the medico-social field.

World War I brought international application of the publicity and public relations techniques that Ivy Lee practiced. Woodrow Wilson, an advocate of frankness, openness, and publicity, appointed George Creel as head of the new Committee on Public Information. Creel, a Colorado newspaper man who at one time attacked Lee's methods in the Colorado strike, came to Washington and put into effect in the national interest the same techniques which Lee had used in that strike. He launched nationwide publicity campaigns to win the support of the American public to the war effort, to increase enlistments, to promote war bond sales, to save food, to hate Germans, and to support the other ideas and actions necessary to win a war. Creel set up speakers' bureaus, published tons of pamphlets and other written materials, and carried out an advertising program more massive than any ever seen before.

In the words of historian Eric Goldman, the propaganda campaigns of World War I were "brilliant: publicity for publicity."[21] Words could be used to break strikes, win rate increases, create public sympathy, and to fight and win a war. It was not long, however, before the slogan "words won the war" became "words won the war but lost the peace." Observing this turnabout during the twenties, Lee increasingly devoted himself to the problem of using words to regain international peace, harmony, and goodwill.

---

[1] Quoted by Jeannette H. Wade in "Historical Sketch, Department of Publicity," ms. in Red Cross Archives, Washington, D.C.

[2] G. R. Gaeddert, *History of the American Red Cross*, ms. in Red Cross Archives, Vol. IV (World War I, 1917–18), see chapter on "Campaigns."

[3] Ivy Lee, "An Appeal for the Red Cross," *The American Press*, June 16, 1917, p. 3.

[4] Ibid., p. 4.

[5] Gaeddert, op. cit.

[6] Ivy Lee to Henry P. Davison, Aug. 27, 1918, Red Cross Archives, Washington, D.C.

[7] Ivy Lee, "How Red Cross Money is Handled and Spent," *Review of Reviews*, Dec. 1917, p. 615.

[8] Ivy Lee to Henry P. Davison, Aug. 27, 1918, p. 5, Red Cross Archives, Washington, D.C.

[9] Ibid., p. 6.

[10] Ivy Lee, "Address Before the Rockefeller Foundation," May 17, 1918, Red Cross Archives, Washington, D.C.

[11] Ivy Lee to his father, Feb. 15, 1918, Ivy Lee Papers, Princeton.

[12] Ivy Lee to Grayson M-P. Murphy, Mar. 7, 1918, Rockefeller Archives, New York.

[13] *Le Petit Parisien*, Feb. 19, 1918. Translation in Red Cross File, Ivy Lee Papers, Princeton.

[14] Ivy Lee to his father, Mar. 29, 1918, Ivy Lee Papers, Princeton.

[15] Newton Baker to Ivy Lee, Oct. 28, 1918, Red Cross Archives, Washington, D.C.

[16] John D. Rockefeller Jr. to Ivy Lee, Nov. 29, 1918, Rockefeller Archives, New York.

[17] Ivy Lee to Henry P. Davison, Dec. 12. 1918, Red Cross Archives, Washington, D.C.

[18] Ivy Lee, "Address Before the Rockefeller Foundation," loc. cit.

[19] Ivy Lee, "How Red Cross Money is Handled and Spent," op. cit, p. 615.

[20] *New York Times*, May 11, 1919, Sec. II, p. 2.

[21] Goldman, op. cit. p. 11.

28: PROBLEMS OF INTERNATIONAL PROPAGANDA

THE TWENTIES WERE YEARS THAT seemed to be characterized by a reactionary nationalism without parallel in our history; but, quietly and under the surface of public opinion, the United States made considerable progress in breaking down its policy of isolation. Ivy Lee was in the forefront of a group of top industrialists who differed with the narrow nationalism that was predominant among small businessmen. Instead, Lee and his advisees were internationalists who eventually brought about American global commitments, participation in a parliament of world governments, and a vast program of international public relations.

Lee was always an international partisan. From his father he had acquired a love of travel and an interest in other countries. Even before he attained success in publicity, he visited Europe, Russia, and Panama. He first went to Europe in 1905 and toured Russia on the eve of the 1905 Dumas revolution. He wrote a series of travel articles about England and Russia for religious publications and for the North American News Alliance and worked in Russia on a job for the Harriman railroad interests. Russia aroused his lifelong curiosity, and studying it became a hobby that he pursued for the rest of his days. By 1909 he had gathered a personal library of eighty books on Russia, which he gave to Princeton University upon leaving for a new assignment abroad that year.

From 1909 to 1912 Lee engaged in a new activity that increased his interest in international affairs. He went to Europe and set up branch offices for the investment firm of Harris, Winthrop, and Company in London and Paris, negotiating with offices in

Copenhagen and Berlin. The experience not only made him familiar with the field of investment banking but also led to his absorbing interest in European culture. In England and France he became fascinated with Gothic architecture, a subject that at first had bored him. In a moment of inspiration he saw how cathedrals were extensions of the minds and emotions of the people who had built them and who worshipped there. To understand the Gothic cathedral was to understand a good part of the European mind. More and more he began to see the importance of what anthropologist Edward Hall later called "the silent language," the communication of a people through its culture.

Later, as his firm grew, he took on more of the international problems of his clients. Even when he brought associates into his firm, he retained for himself primary jurisdiction, over matters which dealt with public relations beyond American borders. He became a member of international institutes, a frequent speaker on international questions, an advisor and confidant to international figures.

After World War I Lee devoted himself to international affairs with more regularity. Red Cross experiences undoubtedly made him conclude that those ideas and concepts of communication he had utilized for that organization could be applied on an international scale. These ideas and concepts were never systematically formulated by him, but they evolved out of his work and can be traced through his speeches, articles, and public statements until his very last year when, just four months before his death, he made his most complete and significant thesis on international public relations.

From the first, Lee considered that the proposed solutions to the problems created and revealed by the war failed to recognize economic realities. The Versailles Treaty, he said, foisted upon the world a disease because "in the framing of that treaty too much consideration was given to political boundaries, to questions of self-determination and racial ambition, to an effort to get people established with sovereignty over them in accord with their national traditions and national aspirations."[1]

The concept of war debts and reparations was particularly onerous to Lee. "Some of our leaders," he said, "tell us that if Europe does not pay her war debts American taxpayers must pay them. A study of the facts may reveal what it has cost the American taxpayer to have the purchasing capacity of the countries of Europe dried up."[2] For that reason, America needed to participate at the council table of the world, but her chair, the most important in the world, was vacant. "We are," Lee said, "vital to the very safety of civilization, and if we fail, civilization fails."[3]

He understood clearly what many others did not understand until after World War II: that a healthy world is vital to a healthy United States. Americans had a definite interest in preventing the collapse of Germany, he said, in helping Austria to her feet, in keeping France from crumbling, in rallying to the support of Italy, even in preserving a vital Russia. America's refusal to join the League of Nations was "one of the tragedies of civilization," a blot on the American image abroad. He later quoted the Bishop of Aberdeen on the anomaly of the American character: "The Americans are a strange people. They invented the Treaty of Versailles and refused to sign it. They invented the League of Nations and refused to join it. They invented the cocktail and refused to drink it."[4]

Speaking to a group of bankers in Philadelphia in 1922, Lee used an analogy to put the League of Nations problem in sharp focus. "Suppose," he said, "that one of the great banks of New York was subjected to a run, and financial disaster should threaten the country. Suppose that J. P. Morgan and Company and the Federal Reserve Bank and all the other bankers should get together around a council table and decide that they would stand by that tottering bank. Do you not think," he asked, "that the very fact that the Federal Reserve Bank and J. P. Morgan and Company were in that conference would be sufficient to make unnecessary the providing of any financial assistance for the bank? Suppose," he asked finally, "the largest bank of all should stand aside in a credit crisis, and fail to give its advice and the results of its experience and the strength of its position to saving the institution—what would you think of such a bank after such a moral failure?"[5]

Through this period, Lee kept an observant eye on the world situation. Upon returning from Europe in 1919 he wrote a lengthy article for the *New York Times* on conditions abroad. Europe, he said, was tired. It was materially and spiritually exhausted, yet needed to get to work. But "the greatest cloud that hangs over Europe is Bolshevism."[6] By 1920 Lee was seeing the situation with prophetic insight. "There can be no peace in Europe," he told a reporter, "until the situation in Russia and Germany has been cleared up." And he had already begun to see what the approach to the problem must be. "Russia," he said, "can never be beaten by fighting. The only thing for the Allies to do is to acknowledge the Soviet government and let in the sunlight. That will kill it."[7] It was the same advice he had once given the railroads and the Rockefellers.

Lee was attracted to the British. "Wherever one goes in Europe now he finds an Englishman doing the work of the world in saving civilization," he said in 1920. But this magnetism lost some of its power with time, and he became more and more convinced that America and not Britain would be the savior of civilization. "Europe looks to us to bring the breath of spring," he said in 1922. "A new spirit must come over [Europe]. We in the United States must implant that new spirit." Lee, saw, as most Americans in the twenties did not, that American destiny was firmly involved with world destiny, that Americans could not ignore what happened in Europe, Asia, and the other continents. "The world of today is profoundly an economic unit," wrote Lee. "No part of the world can do business without reference to its relations to the other parts."[8]

International-minded industrialists shared Lee's economic point of view; American capitalists were investing heavily abroad; the United States had become the world's chief creditor and international trader—yet the people and the politicians and even the intellectuals preferred a policy of isolation. Lee used almost every device at his disposal to arouse public and official interest in what he called a constructive world outlook. Speeches, letters, pamphlets, and statements to the press flowed from his office.

In 1926 he undertook to sponsor a greater internationalism in the academic atmosphere. He offered to send a Princeton professor, to be chosen by the university, to Europe to see what was really happening. Princeton president John Hibben suggested Walter Phelps Hall, a history professor, but Hall declined. He gave the excuse that he was writing a book and raising a young family, but underneath might have been the fear that he would be accepting tainted money that would force him to color his impressions in favor of the big business interests which Lee represented. But Lee, according to Hall, emphatically declared that he was offering his own money, not Rockefeller or Pennsylvania Railroad funds. And, he emphasized, Hall was free to say whatever he wanted to say about Europe, and to write whatever he wanted to write. The history professor finally accepted the offer, went to Europe and wrote an eye-opening book which was dedicated to Ivy Ledbetter Lee.[9] Lee also sent to France a Hotchkiss School instructor and a cousin, Cornelia Ledbetter, both French teachers who had never been to that country.

An even more important instrument for strengthening ties between nations was the English Speaking Union, which Lee helped to found in order to solidify relations between the United States and Great Britain. While in London with the Red Cross during the war, Lee had met regularly with Sir Evelyn Wrench, a noted British journalist in charge of the British Foreign Office's American Information Department. Sir Evelyn had the basic idea for the English Speaking Union as an organization to promote goodwill between the countries. With the advice and counsel of Lee, the Union was set up after the war and became an important institution for British-American alliance. It sponsored meetings, conferences, and lectures, all of which promoted the cause of better relations between the countries.

Lee served as public relations counsel to the Union on a voluntary basis until his death. This connection brought a public relations crisis in the early twenties when the Irish attacked Lee as the emissary of Rockefeller who, the Irish critics contended, was using the English Speaking Union as a propaganda platform for British oppression. There was no logic in the charge, but the name of Rockefeller added emotional appeal to the struggling Irish seeking freedom from the British. The Union eventually set up offices in the United States to avoid Irish criticism.

Sir Evelyn discussed every problem with Lee. He was impressed with "the way Lee grasped things," "his common sense," and his "great flair for promoting good will." He later said that Lee, perhaps more than any other in the twenties, made an impact on Europe as a well-informed American. After the war, Sir Evelyn returned to his job as editor of *The Spectator*, running the English Speaking Union on the side. He brought Lee in as consultant to *The*

Spectator, and Lee later wrote a series of articles for the British magazine. "I never learned more from any other American," Sir Evelyn said later.[10]

The English Speaking Union was just one of the many channels through which Lee worked for greater international understanding. He took part in many international conferences, the most notable being the Institute of Pacific Relations, for which he was an American delegate in 1927 in Hawaii and 1929 in Kyoto, Japan. In 1927 he addressed the Institute in Honolulu on the subject of "International Communications." The nations of the world, he told the conference, must "get matters of importance into print" in the newspapers, and to accomplish this they must develop an appetite among the reading public by telling their story in human terms. In 1930 he conducted a round table on Russian affairs at the Williamstown Institute of Politics at Williams College. The consensus of the round table, which Lee chaired, was that the Soviet Union should be recognized by America. This in turn set off a new wave of criticism against Lee, and against Williams College as well.

Ivy Lee's most important statement on international relations came on July 3, 1934, in a speech he made in London before a group of persons concerned with international affairs. Entitled "The Problem of International Propaganda," it set forth his principles in their most systematic form. The problem, he said, was that if people assert their sovereignty, which he felt they were doing around the world, then "truth alone can endure." And a complete knowledge of the truth will make people understand each other. He quoted the French proverb: "*Tout comprendre, c'est tout pardonner.*"[11] Achieving understanding between people in the thirties, however, called for different methods from those used to get people to adopt new attitudes during World War I. "Healthy contacts between nations are not promoted by the methods of war propaganda or those of any form of underground or indirect propaganda in time of peace," Lee said. "Something new is necessary in an era of progress."

For one thing, Lee felt, the world was not all black and white. Propaganda in international relations, just as public relations in business, must be a two-way street, a matter of giving and receiving information. He quoted J. L. Garvin, editor of the *London Observer*: "Tragedy is the conflict not of right and wrong but of right and right," and thus, he said, "the most tragic fact of our time is the failure of nations to understand one another's best sides." Lee agreed. He thought the United States could no longer afford to follow Teddy Roosevelt's dictum: "Speak softly but carry a big stick." It was now necessary to speak loudly and clearly, without carrying any sticks at all behind one's back. Lee felt that the body of scientific knowledge being accumulated on mass psychology might contribute to the task of establishing peaceful relations throughout the world but could not provide the complete solution.

Research in mass psychology had revealed possibilities of developing effective methods of moving the hearts and stirring the minds of collective man. But Lee felt that while these methods could be used effectively within a nation, there were limitations upon their use between nations. He pointed out that as men grow more sophisticated, better educated, more aware of the fact that their emotions are being subjected to vivisection and conscious stimulation, "they insist more and more upon knowing the facts, and reaching conclusions of their own which do not flow from their emotions, and which are not made for them by others." But as man evolved, newer and better techniques for national communication with the masses would also evolve, finally affording "opportunity for intelligent and reasonable intercourse between peoples."

Lee felt that one of the great difficulties in getting intelligent opinions from the masses on matters of great importance lay in the fact that these matters were not sufficiently dramatic to capture mass attention. One reason for the failure to make progress in disarmament discussions was that the subject was so technical and so difficult to present to the people, thus "people generally do not seem interested in it, and consequently do not become excited about it or place the weight of their influence behind enlightened efforts to deal with it."

The dilemma of international relations he presented eloquently in the question: "In the presence of this vast power of the multitude, bound as we are by so many shackles of custom and tradition in the intercommunication between nations, apparently thwarted by the interplay of conflicting interests and sinister ambitions, how can the peoples of the world make their thoughts, aspirations and longings known to one another to the end that they will trust one another, believe in one another, and be willing to cooperate in creating a new world worth living in? Certainly no more vital question could be raised."

The measures Lee suggested to help resolve international misunderstandings were much the same as the suggestions he had made to the railroads and the Rockefellers. First of all, a great advantage would be registered in the relationships of nations if in each country the government would become aware of press relations. The governments must understand that "correspondents of foreign newspapers were there to ascertain facts and facts alone, and to ascertain them promptly and accurately." Therefore, "the wisest and most enlightened government" is the one which most effectively assists the press "to obtain quickly, accurately, and authoritatively the information their newspapers seek to publish for their readers."

The language in which these facts were couched for the press also needed revision. "The ponderous Johnsonian language and the subtleties of phraseology so characteristic of diplomatic communications are utterly lost upon the masses of the people who read them in the newspapers." We should not get rid of lawyers and diplomats, Lee said, but we should get rid of the "wig and gown spirit" and persuade foreign officers to talk to each other in the language of the people.

He recommended the establishment of an International Affairs College to educate statesmen in the same way that the War College prepared soldiers. Not only should such a college instruct potential statesmen in the use of the language of the people, but it should foster closer contacts among people. Governments should develop international contacts, cultural exchanges, and international associations of artists, scholars, and scientists as well as statesmen. All of these ideas expressed by Lee in 1934 have by now been implemented by the American government.

Lee's final contention was that governments should make effective use—openly, vigorously, and with regard for every psychological consideration—of three media for carrying the messages so important to international understanding. Governments should understand that these media cannot be used effectively except at enormous expense, for which they should be prepared.

The first and always most important medium was the printing press. The great trouble in most countries, Lee said, was that governments relied on the printing presses of other countries to tell their stories for them. The United States gave press releases to Washington correspondents for the Agence France-Presse and then hoped that its story would make its way to the French people through French newspapers. Why not "openly print documents, books, pamphlets, posters or other material designed to tell their story to other peoples." As long as the source of this material is fully disclosed, he insisted, there would be nothing dishonest about such an effort.

Paid advertising could also be an effective way of telling one's story to other people. Lee cited the case of Russia's repudiation of and refusal to pay the Czarist debts; to the average Russian there was a good reason for this action, but such an attitude was not acceptable to other peoples and stirred up international antagonism against the Soviet Union. "Why then," Lee asked, "should not Russia, in paid advertisements inserted in the press of all important countries, set forth its attitude on the question of its debts? The advertisements might be signed by Stalin himself, for that would ensure attention. Such advertisements would be read and if the argument was appealing, it would gain support. The millions such an adventure would cost might mean the addition of billions to the Soviet national income," he said.

The motion picture was the second important medium. How interesting and effective it would be, Lee said, if Italy should present its problems to the whole world in the form of a motion picture, or a series of motion pictures, and if at the very beginning of each picture Mussolini himself would sign a message saying that this, frankly, was Italy's own interpretation of itself; such frankness would be refreshing.

Radio was the third important medium that could be exploited to advance international communication. The same techniques Franklin D. Roosevelt used on radio to win support for his new programs could be used for international understanding. Lee suggested that if King George of Great Britain would speak to the American people about the problem of war debts or naval armaments, "the whole American people would listen not only with great interest, but respect." But, he warned, "they might not listen at all if a lesser figure were to undertake the task."

Lee realized that all of these proposals did violence to the diplomatic protocol under which heads of nations were expected to speak only to one another. However, he urged, if the people do rule, then protocol is an "outworn tradition" and governments should seek to make use of some new "direct and common sense procedure where other processes have clearly proved ineffective."

The essential evil of any propaganda, he maintained, and its only menace, was not in the effort to disseminate ideas, but in the failure to disclose the source of the information. As long as every statement was signed, the people could judge it for what it was worth.[12]

These proposals for international public relations in the thirties were ahead of time. By the end of the forties, alter a second World War and the development of nuclear weapons that could destroy mankind, the need for world understanding had reached its crucial climax. In that crisis, many of Lee's proposals were put to work. The United States Information Agency, founded after the war, was and still is devoted largely to the kind of practices in international communication which Lee advocated in 1934. By 1962 Russia was following one of Lee's most radical suggestions—placing advertisements in Western newspapers. The text of Premier Khrushchev's speech to the Supreme Soviet on December 12, 1962, was inserted in the *London Daily Express* as a two-page paid advertisement. The paper announced that the Soviets were buying further space for the future.[13]

---

[1] Ivy Lee, *The Vacant Chair at the Council Table of the World* (Philadelphia: privately printed, 1922), p. 10.

[2] Ivy Lee, "Commencement Address at Elon College," *New York Times*, May 27, 1931, p. 9.

[3] Ivy Lee, *The Vacant Chair*, op. cit., p. 9.

[4] Ivy Lee, "The Black Legend," op. cit., p. 578.

[5] Ivy Lee, *The Vacant Chair,* op. cit., p. 20.

[6] Ivy Lee, "A Tour Through Europe Since December," *New York Times*, May 18, 1919, Sec. IV, p. 8.

[7] *New York Times*, Aug. 22, 1920, p. 13.

[8] Ivy Lee, *The Vacant Chair*, op. cit., pp. 10, 19.

[9] Berlin, op. cit., p. 126.

[10] Sir Evelyn Wrench in conversation with R. E. Hiebert, Nov. 1962.

[11] Ivy Lee, *The Problem of International Propaganda* (New York: privately printed, 1934), pp. 3 ff.

[12] Ibid.

[13] Associated Press dispatch, Dec. 20, 1962.

Ray Eldon Hiebert

29: LOANS FOR FRANCE, POLAND, AND ROMANIA

IVY LEE AND THE MEN OF FINANCE with whom he worked were ahead of public opinion in their conviction that a sound world economy was the best possible assurance for a growing America. The man in the street, still under the illusion that he could isolate himself from the world's difficulties, rejected all offers to invest in foreign loans. He could not understand that the devastated countries of Europe needed capital to rebuild their economies and get a sound footing once again; that a strong European economy was vital not only because it would lead to increased American trade, but because it would be the best bulwark against the radical political forces of fascism and bolshevism and would help secure free enterprise everywhere.

In order to raise the needed capital, a climate of opinion had to be created in which Americans felt safe investing in bonds to help stabilize the currencies of European countries. The situation was ripe for Ivy Lee's public relations counsel. At that time the loans were put up by a syndicate, but the syndicate closed as soon as the issue was disposed, leaving the small investor, the person who bought the issue, to worry about his returns. With no further information on developments, the small investor naturally lost confidence in the issue and refrained from further investments of that type.

"One of the necessities of our foreign investment business," Lee advised his clients, "is going to be that a government which makes an issue must assume the responsibility of informing American investors concerning that issue, after the issue has been made." This was a job that his firm could undertake for foreign governments. He told his overseas banking friends that "publicity in relation to investment banking is a far wider matter than merely advertising these investments. It concerns itself not only with creating an atmosphere which will be favorable to the success of these issues, but equally with maintaining these issues in the confidence of the public."[1]

Lee first entered the field of publicity for international finance in 1920 when he undertook a promotional effort for the investment firm of Chandler and Company, which had sponsored the "Chandler Plan" to stabilize the German economy. Soon after that, J. P. Morgan and Company asked him to handle the preliminary publicity leading to the flotation of a $100 million loan to the French government. With only two weeks to prepare publicity for the issue, Lee and his staff went to work immediately, turning out pamphlets, documents, newspaper articles, and other publicity materials aimed at showing why people should invest in French loans. Two weeks later, when the issue was offered, it was a great success, and J. P. Morgan and Company immediately announced that another such issue would be made six months later.

"If we are going to have another issue in six months," Lee told the Wall Street firm, "let's begin now with our publicity so that we'll create a different atmosphere for the issue." But the Morgan people said that they could not sign any agreement until a contract had actually been made, and that would not be done until immediately before the loan issue. Lee took his idea directly to the French embassy, advising them that the logical thing to do would be to persuade the French Government to pay for sending a man to France who would "keep a string of information coming from France to the American people."

But the French minister responded that "we should like to have it done, but propaganda is politically unpopular, and we cannot charge as expense of the loan any item which is incurred prior to the time that the loan is authorized."

Since neither the investment bankers nor the French government would finance such a publicity campaign, Ivy Lee offered to undertake the work and pay for the expenses out of his own pocket, "on the moral assurance that when and if the loan is authorized, I shall be employed to do the work." Some of the members of the Morgan company felt it was a rash offer because the money expended by Lee might never be recovered, But he went ahead on his own, forming a separate company for this purpose which he called the U.S.-France Financial News Corporation, and for the next six months he privately financed his own publicity campaign for the French loan. When the issue was made, he was paid for the work and the second $100 million loan was also successful.

"That sort of thing has to be done," he told his clients. "Those who handle a loan must create an atmosphere, whether it concerns a local investment or an international investment, if that issue is going to be successful. Favorable atmosphere is not created by the distribution of mere statistical facts. The spirit of the borrowers has an enormous amount to do with the impression made upon the public." For example, in advising on a foreign loan for Hungary, Lee said it would be difficult because too many people in America "had a mental picture of the [Hungarian] people as a wild, Bohemian lot, instead of the agricultural, sane, and highly cultivated people that they really are." Lee said that instead of sending statistical tables or tax receipts, the Hungarians should do whatever they could to impress the Americans that their country was thoroughly stable and highly civilized.

Lee cited the advice given to the Argentine Republic as an example of what he meant. When Argentina wanted to issue securities in America, its officers found investors unenthusiastic because "many unenlightened people were inclined to think that, in South America, there was a lack of social stability." The Argentines were advised that one of the best ways to interest the public in their government would be to send a polo team to this country to compete with America's players. "The vital idea," Lee said, "is that polo is not played except where there is a very high degree of civilization and a stable society.... The galloping gentleman would tell the story more convincingly than any amount of statistics or mere statements as to the true conditions."[2]

From the mid-twenties until the stock market crash in 1929, Lee spent much of his time working on foreign loan publicity arrangements, traveling to foreign countries, developing contacts, making friends, attending conferences, and giving lectures. During this time he gained two accounts, Poland and Romania. In both cases he was able to persuade the governments to spend money in advance of the loan flotation and to station one of Lee's men in each country to insure a steady stream of information about the country and the imminent loan.

In connection with the Polish and Romanian loans Lee worked closely with three men, two of whom later loomed large as influences on international relations in the twentieth century. The first was John Foster Dulles, then an international lawyer representing American banking interests with the Wall Street firm of Sullivan and Cromwell with whom Lee frequently conferred on international problems and particularly on loan publicity. The second was Jean Jacques Monnet who later became the "father" of the European Common Market, an idea that would have appealed to Lee. Monnet was then a partner in the American banking firm of

Blair and Company, working on stabilization plans for Polish and Romanian currencies. A third man with whom Lee conferred was Frank Close of the Bankers Trust Company on Wall Street, which with the Blair firm handled the Polish and Romanian loans.

Lee depended heavily on these three for advice in the precarious business of negotiation with foreign governments. When he finally secured a tentative commitment from the Poles in Warsaw, he cabled his office to get in touch with Close, Monnet, and Dulles and informed them that he was "quite willing to undertake any plan they outlined, upon terms they are prepared to recommend as fair and practicable, the chief aim being to accomplish the results they are seeking."[3] Lee was able to work out an arrangement for world publicity with services in London, Paris, and New York, and to arrange for a full-time representative in Warsaw, at a fee of $50,000 a year, including services and expenses.

Lee worked during the summer of 1927 on the publicity arrangements for the Polish loan and proposed a detailed release schedule to be timed carefully over a ten-day period from September 26 to October 5, 1927. The statements were to be issued by the Finance Minister in Warsaw and released simultaneously by the Polish embassy in Washington and Bankers Trust Company in New York. The first statement announced the agreement, and the purpose, significance, and effect of the loan.

The lead of Ivy Lee's initial release read: "The Government of Poland announces today the signing of an agreement with an international syndicate of bankers, headed by the Bankers Trust Company of New York for a stabilization loan in the amount of $60,000,000.... The Government believes that this loan will give a new impetus to the economic development of Poland itself and will strengthen the position of Poland's international credit."

Lee outlined five subsequent press releases to follow on September 27 and 30 and October 1, 3, and 5. The second statement, Lee advised, should announce the Polish government's cancellation of a $15,000,000 loan it had made earlier in the summer. The third should announce adoption of the stabilization plan summarizing budgetary and administrative features. The fourth should name and explain the duties of an American advisor who would supervise the loan (this was an important consideration that Lee insisted was necessary for American investors' assurances; the man named was Charles S. Dewey, an American financier). The fifth release should announce the revaluation of the Polish zloty and explain currency and monetary changes that were to be made. The sixth and final release should announce the public offering of the Polish bonds.[4]

The Polish government agreed to the publicity plan, but since there was no contractual agreement about the fee, it was steadily lowered from $50,000 to $25,000, then to $15,000, and the firm was finally paid only $7,500. And the Polish liaison officers grumbled that that was too much. Lee finally fired off a letter to Harcourt Parrish, his representative in Warsaw, "The Polish government got the benefit of all the work done during the summer without charge for it.... I am telling you this so the Poles may realize that they have got an unusual bargain in their present contract and that it would not have been made on such a basis except as a favor to the Bankers Trust Company who wanted me to do the job. If any contract is made beyond September 1st, it is going to have to be upon a still higher fee."[5]

The news coming out of Poland was not favorable, and this reduced the potential for public investment in Polish loans. For one thing, the countries surrounding Poland were constant sources of unsympathetic news because they were unhappy about the territorial adjustments made after the war. The Polish government added to the bad public impression by imposing strict censorship whenever anything went wrong. This simply exaggerated whatever unfavorable aspects the situation might have had. Finally, little complete and accurate information, favorable or unfavorable, was coming from the country.

Parrish had been sent to Warsaw as a major effort to improve the publicity for the Polish loans. A former Associated Press reporter, Parrish would be "a man on the ground and in touch with local conditions" who could provide "a steady stream of usable material."

Lee's chief assistant, Tommy Ross, instructed Parrish: "Do not hesitate to use the cables, and above all do not hesitate to write things yourself even though it may be a bit of local color that seemingly has no economic or financial value. Our job is to tell the facts constructively...and the field is just about as big as all outdoors. We shall have no difficulty in utilizing anything that your sense of news values or magazine interest prompts you to send—including photographs."[6]

But sending information was just one phase of the operation. The other half of Parrish's job was to make contacts in Warsaw with bankers, finance ministers, economists, consuls, journalists, and anyone who might shed any light on the country's financial situation that could be used to promote the sale of loan bonds.

After a year of that kind of work for the Polish loans, Lee was able to sign up Romania for the same sort of service in 1928. Parrish was transferred to Bucharest to provide information needed to publicize the Romanian loan issue. The situation in Romania was even more uncertain, politically as well as economically, than in Poland. A good deal of unfavorable news was coming out of Romania on three particular issues: (1) facts about corruption in the Romanian government, especially rumors about the licentiousness of Prince Carol; (2) reports of growing anti-Semitism in the Balkan state which aroused the fear of American bankers that the issue would not be bought by Americans, particularly not by American Jews; and (3) reports of a growing Nationalist Peasant Party, communist in sympathy, which made investors fear that in case of a coup by the Peasants, their loans would not be honored by the new party in power.

Lee told Parrish, "What we want of course is the facts and the truth insofar as Romanian affairs are concerned."[7]

Parrish, after a lengthy silence, wrote a long and rambling letter to the office in which he said: "I doubt whether I can obtain the truth. I can get official statements, but if I were to write the truth it wouldn't be publicity for a loan of one dollar." He found that, concerning Prince Carol, "the general opinion is that he's pretty much of an ass in all respects." And the Liberal Party's prime minister, Bratianu, "stays in power only because he lets the boys graft."

On the Jewish question, Parrish reported that there was a great deal of latent anti-Semitism, but he was inclined to feel that nothing serious would come of it. In fact, he found very little worth writing about at all. "Romanian history is singularly uncolorful and the Romanian himself," Parrish wrote, "is a repulsive Gypsy.... As soon as I can possibly find the time I am going to write some views that will be favorable. I hope I can do it tomorrow."

In the end, the disillusioned Parrish insisted that "the loan should not be made unless there is strict American supervision." But he felt that the Bratianu government would never submit to any kind of control and said that Blair and Company should probably not undertake to float the loan at all.[8]

This, of course, did not leave much for Lee's publicity efforts. He was able to secure a statement from M. Julius Maniu, the leader of the opposition Nationalist Peasant Party, that reports of his willingness to repudiate a foreign loan, should he gain power, were completely false. Lee's office prepared a press release on this statement, adding that "whether these loans should be contracted by the government under the auspices of the Liberal Party or the Nationalist Peasant Party is solely a matter of internal partisan politics and has nothing whatsoever to do with Romania's debt policy as a government." The Lee statement concluded that Romania had always in the past been in a position to meet its foreign obligations readily.[9] Little else came out of Lee's office and the issue fell by the wayside.

As with much of Lee's international work on behalf of foreign clients, his job for Poland and Romania seemed to bring him nothing but headaches. He himself enjoyed visiting foreign capitals and meeting princes and royal courtiers. For a time he advised Ismet Pasha, the Prime Minister of Turkey. He was a close friend of King Boris of Bulgaria, of Thomas Masaryk, first president of Czechoslovakia, and his son, Jan, the diplomat, and he personally met many others.

But the most persistent criticism of Lee's work in the twenties concerned his international dealings. His role as diplomat without portfolio and his motives for promoting international harmony and goodwill were the cause of doubt and distrust. It was hard for many people to understand the size of Ivy Lee's mind and vision. Like all people, he was not infallible; he made mistakes. But time and history have been able to show that his motives were honest and his instincts sound.

---

[1] Ivy Lee, "Case Studies in Publicity," *Publicity, the Profession of Persuading the Public*, mss. p. 1, Ivy Lee Papers, Princeton.

[2] Ibid., pp. 2, 3, 4.

[3] Ivy Lee cable to his office staff, June 19, 1927, Ivy Lee Papers, Princeton.

4 Ivy Lee to M. Jan Ciechanowski, Minister of Poland, Sept. 23, 1927, with "Schedule of Publicity" and releases attached, Ivy Lee Papers, Princeton.

5 Ivy Lee to Harcourt Parrish, May 5, 1928, Harcourt Parrish Papers, University of Virginia.

6 Thomas Ross to Harcourt Parrish, June 1, 1928, Harcourt Parrish Papers, University of Virginia.

7 Ibid., p. 3.

8 Harcourt Parrish to Thomas Ross, June 23, 1928, Harcourt Parrish Papers, University of Virginia.

9 Draft of release, Romanian Loan File, Ivy Lee Papers, Princeton.

Ray Eldon Hiebert

30: RUSSIA: A COLOSSAL AXE TO GRIND

On January 7, 1926, the Chamber of Commerce of New York passed a resolution urging that the United States should never recognize Russia as long as the Communist Party was in control of the country. To Ivy Lee, a member of the Chamber and a man closely identified with its philosophy, that resolution was a step backwards in international public relations. He felt, instead, that constructive action should be taken to stimulate understanding rather than promote ignorance.

He thereupon undertook to send out a series of letters over the next few months to various influential members of the Chamber to seriously pursue the problem of how to deal with the menace of communism. He wrote to William L. DeBost, chairman of the New York Chamber's executive committee; to Elihu Root, Wall Street lawyer and former Senator and Secretary of State; and to other prominent members. He also prepared and distributed widely through his mailing list two bulletins, "What Might Be Done to Clarify American Knowledge of Conditions in Russia," and "Solving the Russian Riddle: How Can Progress Best Be Achieved."

In accord with his general philosophy of frank and open dealing, Lee argued in his letters and bulletins that American businessmen ought to candidly explain their position to the Soviets and in turn make every effort to understand the ideas of communism. Closing the door and turning their backs on the problem would never solve it; instead, the Chamber should establish an advisory bureau in Moscow to exchange information about trade. He called for a closer cooperation with the International Chamber of Commerce and the American-Russian Chamber of Commerce.

He was not afraid of Soviet propaganda, he said. "My own observation of the operation of propaganda has been that nothing so quickly exposes error as to bring it out into the open."[1] He had once told a conservative vice-president of the Pennsylvania Railroad that the best thing he could do for his company would be to become a steady reader of *The Call*, a socialist newspaper, and *The New Masses*, a communist magazine. Lee himself read these publications regularly, along with many others of all varieties, in order to understand what others were thinking.

Throughout the early twenties, newspapers had curtly reported Ivy Lee's statements on international affairs. But his letters and bulletins on Russia became page-one news partly by accident. On March 27, 1926, during the middle of Lee's crusade to achieve greater understanding of Russia within the Chamber of Commerce, the *New York Times* published a major story reporting that Standard Oil and Vacuum Oil, two companies which Lee had advised, had just completed negotiations in Russia for the purchase and distribution of Soviet oil in exchange for much-needed cash and loans worth many millions of dollars to the Soviet government. It appeared that the oil companies were out to make a profit even if they had to strengthen the communist regime to do so.

The next day the *Times* and other papers published page-one headlines on the Lee letters to Elihu Root and the Chamber of Commerce (which had been sent two to three months earlier). "Ivy Lee," said the *Times*, "the best known and most expensive of publicity agents, who among other activities is the advisor on public relations to the Standard Oil interests, has begun to display keen interest in the recognition of the Soviet government."[2]

The *Times* said that its information about the Lee letters had come from Miss Ruth Stout, editor of *The New Masses*. The implication was clear, and less subtle publications spelled it out. Ivy Lee was working for the recognition of the Soviet Union, contrary to the interests of American position, simply because recognition would promote the imperialistic schemes of Standard Oil and John D. Rockefeller.

Lewis Pierson, president of the United States Chamber of Commerce, wrote an open letter to Lee strongly criticizing his stand. Ralph M. Easley of the National Civic Federation, a conservative society for the promotion of better relations between capital and labor, took Lee to task for his position. Elihu Root told Lee that his position would lead "our government [to] accept the principles of the Bolsheviki as something 'equally as good.'"[3] Across a wide front, Lee was attacked and challenged for his Russian statements. The conservatives on one hand accused him of promoting communism. The liberals on the other cursed him for promoting Standard Oil profiteering.

Both sides misinterpreted Lee's action. To be sure, Lee was interested in the continued success of his clients and of free enterprise. The oil companies were involved in an effort to increase world trade, especially with Russia, but both Standard and Vacuum issued statements that they were neither directly nor indirectly interested in the letters sent by Lee. Rather, his work grew out of his conviction that constructive international policies of cooperation and trade would benefit American business as a whole, that understanding on both sides was necessary for success.

Later he told a Chamber of Commerce executive: "My only job in this situation, insofar as it is a job, is to protect my clients against Bolshevism. Many of my clients are asked to put up money to fight Bolshevism, and they ask my advice about it. I have not felt that I could give intelligent advice without making a first-hand attempt to study the thing and know its meaning. Now my philosophy is that you don't fight Bolshevism effectively by intensifying it. You don't protect a steam boiler from explosion by refusing to put a safety valve on the engine."⁴

In spite of the criticism and attacks on Lee from both sides during the late twenties and early thirties, he began a diligent effort to study Russia and communism, a topic that had been of great interest to him all his life. He visited Russia a half-dozen times, the most important trip occurring in 1927, when he undertook a brief but in-depth study of Russian life for the purpose of writing a book that would help explain the problem of Russia and communism in world affairs. His book, *USSR: A World Enigma*, was privately printed in July 1927 and was published publicly by the Macmillan Company in 1928, under the title, *Present-Day Russia*. "As a man distinctly allied with capitalism," Lee said in a foreword, "I wanted to go directly into what the whole Western World regards as the enemy's camp and if possible find out what he was up to."⁵

Lee's interest in the Soviet Union was not unnatural. There were many facets of Russian life and the Soviet experiment that were akin to his own convictions and ideals. He saw that Russia, like the United States, was a mass society, where public opinion was the key to power. He saw that the revolution was the result of an aroused public indignation at the excesses of the Czarist regime. Moreover, Lee felt that what had happened in Russia might have happened in the United States had not the development of public relations policies by big business led to measures of self-control that curbed the excesses of capitalism before the masses revolted.

Lee was fascinated with the Soviet experiment because it employed publicity and propaganda techniques on a mass scale to control public opinion for the benefit of those in power. Lee, of course, did not condone the Soviet's control of propaganda, for he believed that everyone should have the right to try to influence public opinion, but he was interested in it because it provided a dramatic demonstration of the power of propaganda in a mass society.

The visit described in his book, *Present-Day Russia*, took place in early May of 1927. He found a society still primitive but poised on the edge of great power. The machinery for vast propagandizing was already in place, and it intrigued him. He found pamphlets for foreigners in which Russian history had been already rewritten. He saw signs and posters and slogans already prepared. He found a new alphabet that made it easier for the common man to use the language. He found a new abbreviated vocabulary that reduced complicated terms to simple syllables for the benefit of the masses: Comintern for Communist International, Narkomindel for People's Commissariat of Foreign Affairs, and many others.

The printed word, with which Lee was always so concerned, was completely in the hands of the Party. Newspapers were state-owned and run by the Party or by the Government, and the news service, Tass, was under direct control of the Government. Wall newspapers, for those who could not buy or read their own copies, were ubiquitous and Government-produced. Books, magazines, and everything else obtained from the printing press were under strict Party control—even the printing of a streetcar transfer slip. Other media, too, were being developed for propaganda use—the radio, the motion picture, the stage. All means of getting information into the country—the foreign correspondent and foreign media—were carefully watched and censored. The people themselves were guarded in their communication with others.

"I was impressed," Lee wrote in describing his official interviews, "with the fact that in practically all my talks with Russian officials, one or two silent witnesses were present. Generally, stenographic notes were taken of the questions asked and answered. Often, these witnesses would, in the course of the conversation, pass a slip of paper to the cabinet minister, obviously making suggestions as to answers that might be made to questions."

In his interviews, Lee found that the leaders of the country were amateurs at government, for the most part honest, and essentially realists. He felt that they were groping for the best solution to the Russian problems, and sooner or later, he believed, they would find that to be capitalism. He quoted Leon Trotsky on the need to use foreign capitalists who had experience and money to build up the country. Karl B. Radek, the great revolutionary editor, also pointed with some optimism to capitalism. Although he did not want to accept Western capital, Radek told Lee, "If you don't want to drive Russia toward Asia, you will be well advised to attract it toward the West." Aleksei I. Rykov, then head of the government as Prime Minister, expressed a similar point of view.

Lee was scheduled to see Stalin, who as head of the Party was the real power behind the scenes, but Stalin failed to keep his appointment. Curiously, Trotsky, Radek, Rykov, and others with whom Lee spoke concerning cooperative East-West efforts were later purged by Stalin, who in his drive for personal power rejected the idea of peaceful coexistence. When Khrushchev de-Stalinized the Soviet in the fifties, he rehabilitated the very victims who in the twenties had discussed closer cooperation with Ivy Lee.

Lee found that the Russian people were often receptive to America and American ideas. He dined with Stanislavsky and Madame Chekhov and others outside the political realm and found sympathy for America, though little for Britain or France and none for Germany. When he told Madame Chekhov that he was returning directly to America, she responded, "Oh, happy man!" Her tone of voice, Lee said, spoke volumes.

He realized, however, that the Russians would not return to Czardom, that the revolution was an inevitable result of "the oppression, the persecution, the distress of the Czar's regime. The people's resentment against capitalism and imperialism is based on that experience," he said. He found the people themselves lovable. "And they are human beings—140,000,000 of them," he said, and quoting Edmund Burke, added: "You cannot indict a people."[6]

Lee found Russia and America similar in many respects; He said that "two fundamental processes seem to be irrepressibly at work in Russia and the United States. The United States started with complete individualism, every man for himself. There was no restriction upon each man getting all he could and keeping it. But in the course of time we have found it necessary gradually to restrict the power of the individual to get and keep all he can. We have had a great succession of laws and regulations, income taxes, employers' liability laws, labor laws, self-regulation of industry, all tending toward an effort to secure for society the greatest possible benefit from the efforts of the individual, always endeavoring at the same time to avoid repressing the energy, originality, and enterprise of the individual.... Russia, started at the other end. There was at first complete communism," but by 1930 Lee found the Russians gaining a little individual freedom.

He saw the revolution as the first step toward eventual political freedom for a land that had been under domination for thousands of years. Under the Czar, Lee said, the Russian peasant "had nothing to say about how he was governed, but today he has the first faint glimmerings of political consciousness. Theoretically he has a right to vote, and though in practice his right exercises but feeble influence, we must remember that it took from the time of the Magna Carta in 1215 to the abolishment of rotten boroughs under

Queen Victoria six hundred years later to establish real democracy in England."

The dilemma of the Soviet Union, said Lee, was the problem of how to speed the process of democracy, to draw Russia toward the West, to cure the disease of Bolshevism, to avert the menace of a revolutionary Asia. For Lee, the way to deal with this dilemma was not hard to find. How would human nature react, he asked, if the Russian people, instead of having to live on starvation wages, were able to earn enough to amass a little property? Would they want to hold on to that property or would they want to give it up? For Lee, there was only one answer.

In answer to the criticism that the businesses he represented were only interested in their own profit, Lee said: "Does anyone suppose that these intelligent businessmen would trade with Russia even to gain a few momentary profits if they thought that the prosperity of Russia would mean their own ultimate doom? Is it not indeed possible that these men of big business see that the best cure for Bolshevism is to enable the Russian people to gain some measure of better living conditions? Certainly the success of American corporations in developing contented employees has arisen from a conscious effort to lift the standard of living of the workingmen."[7]

"How has Bolshevism been virtually killed in the United States?" Lee asked. "Has it not been done by producing such a state of prosperity that everybody is at work at high wages, everyone has a chance to own some property, and having owned that property, he does not want to give it up? How had radicalism been driven out of the United States Steel Corporation? Has it not been done by making the workers stockholders and self-respecting citizens of the country? Is there not a law of biology upon which many physicians base their practice of medicine, namely that the purpose of medicine is to build up the body so that the body may fight off the disease?"

Lee felt strongly that by building up the Soviet economy the United States could help weaken Bolshevism. He did not advocate propagandizing the Russians. "The Russian people are entitled to do as they like, unmolested by us. But is not the supreme propaganda the propaganda of deeds rather than words?" The propaganda of deeds meant increased support for the present regime, although it was, he said, possibly the greatest gamble in history. "Have the possibilities of trade relations, of banking, or commercial contacts been explored and developed to the limit? Isolation has been tried, armed intervention by other nations has been tried. These have not cured the Bolshevik disease. What is left?"[8]

Lee pressed his fight for an open exchange of ideas as well as commerce. He wrote and distributed an open letter to Pierson and the Chamber of Commerce saying, "the fundamental suggestion is that American business should *establish a contact* with the Russian Government and seek to promote the development of business intercourse between the two countries."[9]

He wrote and printed a long letter to Secretary of State Frank B. Kellogg, calling, among other things, for a commission to deal with the Soviets directly and advise the President and State Department on Russian matters. Kellogg told Lee that "your observations are of interest and value to the Department."[10]

Lee worked closely with the American-Russian Chamber of Commerce, and many of his clients became members, including Chase National Bank, Standard Oil of New York, and Dillon, Read and Company. He worked with the American-Russian Chamber's board of directors, headed by the young W. Averill Harriman, a man who had a similar philosophy about Russia and was himself engaged in frequent Russian trade negotiations during the period.

The problem posed by the emergence of the Soviet Union could be solved, in other words, by the influence of capitalism, adjusting relationships through the wise counsel of public relations. What Lee really wanted, he said later, was "that the problem be faced realistically, that we find out what the facts are, that we adopt a spirit of friendliness toward these great peoples, not a spirit of what we would like, nor what we would think it ought to be, nor how we think men different from ourselves ought to act. Let's find out how they *do* act, how they *do* react, what are the circumstances behind their actions, and their reactions, in an effort to try and work out some *adjustment* between the rest of the world in this extremely complicated and difficult problem."[11]

But public relations was a two-way street, and Russia had to play the game fairly, too. It had, like Rockefeller, to "establish a reputation for good faith, and a desire to comply with every international obligation, no matter if that obligation is toward the capitalist world." Second, the Soviet Union must "take all possible steps to remove from within her borders any organization which seeks to upset the institutions of friendly nations *through violence*. No one," Lee said, "can object to arguments or to new light which may be shed upon the problems of mankind, but to bring about reform through violence is a negation of everything that civilization stands for."

In order to establish sound international relations, Lee maintained two things were essential: first, real freedom of thought, action, and belief must be established; and second, a system of justice must be set up, "based upon fundamental principles inherent in the very nature of liberty itself."[12]

Russia, of course, did not carry out her side of the program contemplated by Lee, but neither did the United States. And always a realist, Lee was not rigid in his views of the problem. By 1930 he saw that the Soviets were winning their battle. He told a *Business Week* reporter, after a 1930 trip to Russia, that the Soviet Union was politically confident, perhaps a little cocky. It was economizing to the very limit and had shown it could live without foreign capital. The five-year plan for industrialization, "Russia's biggest dream—her madness," was progressing, and she was looking forward to socialized farming. The newest Russian revolution, he said, was "Fordism...the holy doctrine of the day.... Within five years Russia will have the biggest tractor plant, the biggest paper mills, the biggest of many other industries in the world. And it is no dream. It is a fact."[13]

In spite of Lee's open and frank policies, his own position was often misunderstood and misinterpreted. His ideas about Russia were, to many men, as great an enigma as the Soviet Union itself. "What are you doing all this for?" asked C. W. Barron, editor of the *Wall Street Journal*. "Who is paying you for it?" "I am doing it for the same reason that you are raising Guernsey cows," Lee answered. "That's your hobby. Some people collect first editions, some people collect postage stamps, I collect information about Russia, That is the whole of my relationship to the problem."[14]

But many did not believe him. *Business Week* magazine said of Lee: "In instinct, doctrine, career, he is the ultimate, the absolute capitalist of them all. He is reputedly the subtlest of protectors of capitalists, their arch advocate, the veritable high priest of their whole controversial business—a professional director of public relations. That he of all men should have been for three neglected years the champion of the idea of a new business statesmanship in Russia is the anomaly, enigma, and mystery of cynical Wall Street."

To many it seemed that Russia had simply hired Ivy Lee as its propagandist. The Soviet Union was simply a client—this time one of monumental proportions. Ideals? "Sophisticated managing editors frankly do not believe a word of it," said *Business Week*. "It is impossible that Ivy Lee, aide to millionaires and millionairedom, should be serious in all this stuff about Soviet Russia. What a colossal axe he must be grinding!"[15]

Charges against Lee echoed through the halls of Congress. George Holden Tinkham, Representative from Massachusetts, told the House that international bankers, among them. Americans, were engaged in a "conspiracy" to compel the United States "to abandon its traditional policy of no foreign entanglements and force it into the League of Nations."

Tinkham supported a resolution calling for the investigation of expenditures of international bankers and others to influence American foreign policy. He told Congress that the first witness to be summoned should be Ivy Lee, "the representative of John D. Rockefeller." He declared that "the international Standard Oil interests, John D. Rockefeller, and their agent, Ivy Lee, now open propagandists against the interests of the United States, have no country, no flag, and no allegiance except the power of money, and what money can compel or buy."[16]

A year later, Representative Hamilton Fish Jr., chairman of the House committee investigating Communist activities, also singled out Ivy Lee for attack. He called him a "notorious propagandist for Soviet Russia."[17]

The strangest episode of the Lee-Russia affair was made known in the Senate early in 1929. A group of documents had apparently been smuggled into Mexico and from there had gotten into the hands of the United States Department of State, becoming the basis of a monumental smear campaign and Senate investigation. Among these documents were letters which showed that Senators William E. Borah, George W. Norris, and others were implicated in a massive bribery attempt by the Soviet Union. Norris, a progressive Senator who looked favorably upon Soviet recognition, and Borah, who as Chairman of the Senate Foreign Relations Committee had advocated eventual Soviet recognition, were both charged through the documents with receiving Soviet money for their advocacy, Borah as much as $100,000. Both men denied the charges vehemently.

Among the documents were several pertaining to Ivy Lee. Exhibit J, as translated from the French and introduced into the Senate hearings, went as follows:

> L'Ambassade de l'Union des Republiques Sovietistes Socialistes en France, Paris le 11 Septembre 1927.
>
> Please pay to Mr. Ivy Lee, or the person duly authorized by him, the amount indicated to cover all his expenses contemplated by the Special Account of Narkomindel No. 362. M.W.
>
> At the same time notify officially Mr. Ivy Lee, or his representative, that there has been put at his disposition a complementary credit provided for by his arrangement with Moscow.
>
> These complementary credits and the increase in the normal amount of the periodical payments should also be put to the special account of Narkomindel No. 361 M.W. concerning Senator Borah.
>
> Rykovsky
> Kempner

Banque Commercial Pour L'Europe du Nord, Paris[18]

This seemed to be fresh and concrete evidence for Lee's enemies that he was, indeed, employed by the Soviet government. He telegraphed the Senate committee as soon as he heard about the documents and asked to be permitted to appear and answer under oath any questions that the committee might ask. "Any report that I have ever received a penny of money from the Soviet government, directly or indirectly, is a complete fabrication," he said. "Evidently the same forgery mill which accused the chairman of the Foreign Relations Committee of the United States Senate of accepting a bribe from the Soviet government has thought it worth while to bring my name into the discussion."[19]

Senator Borah began a massive independent investigation to ascertain the origin of the documents. A. M. Kempner, the director of the Commercial Bank of Northern Europe in Paris, to whom the account was supposedly directed, was contacted and he denied all knowledge of the affair, "I heard of the existence of Mr. Ivy Lee for the first time today when I read his name in the newspapers," the French banker said.[20] It was, perhaps, fortunate for Lee that two Senators were involved, for they were as anxious to clear their names as he was his, and they had all the facilities of the United States government at their disposal for doing so.

The Senators were eventually able to prove that the documents were forgeries, the work of Russian refugees embittered against the Soviet government and anxious to destroy anyone who advocated American recognition of the Soviet regime. Senator David A. Reed reported that the Senate committee could get no corroboration for any of the material. The letter about Ivy Lee had not even been signed but only had a typewritten signature. "I have been hoping that this incident is closed," Senator Reed wrote to Lee. "Our committee is unanimously of the opinion that the whole affair is a cock-and-bull story and a fake."[21]

In the end, Lee maintained that the growing and prospering Soviet Union was gaining strength not through communism but through "Russianism." "Most activities in Russia today," he said, "existed in the time of the czars—secret press, secret police, lack of freedom." Communism was inherently weak because "its underlying assumptions do not provide for the dignity and independence of human beings." Capitalism, he said, was inherently strong because it does.[22]

Lee's work for Soviet recognition was effective at least in the eyes of the Soviets themselves. When the Democrats came into power and under more liberal atmosphere were able to get the American people to accept Soviet recognition in 1933, the Russians gave part of the credit to Ivy Lee. Upon notification of American recognition, one of the first things done by Maxim Litvinov, Soviet Foreign Minister, was to send a cable to Ivy Lee expressing appreciation for the part he had played in paving the way for a closer Russian-American relationship.

During the years of Stalin's power, the Soviet Union did little to make any exchange a two-way street. But under Khrushchev greater freedom for an interchange of ideas and opinions generated some encouragement that an "adjustment of relationships" between the countries would, as Lee hoped, eventually bring the colossus of Russia closer to the Western world and nearer to an atmosphere of peace and harmony for all.

[1] Ivy Lee to William L. DeBost, Jan. 7, 1926, Ivy Lee Papers, Princeton.

[2] *New York Times*, Mar. 29, 1926, p. 1.

[3] Elihu Root to Ivy Lee, Mar. 2. 1926, Ivy Lee Papers, Princeton.

[4] Ivy Lee to James S. McCulloh, Chairman, Executive Committee, New York Chamber of Commerce, June 6, 1931, Ivy Lee Papers, Princeton.

[5] Ivy Lee, *Present-Day Russia* (New York: Macmillan, 1928), p. 8.

[6] Ibid., pp. 46, 49, 149.

[7] Ivy Lee, "Introductory Remarks," *Proceedings of the Williamstown Institute of Politics*, Aug. 1–2, 1930, pp. 2, 3.

[8] Ivy Lee, *Present-Day Russia*, pp. 153–156.

[9] Ivy Lee to Lewis E. Pierson, July 5, 1927, Ivy Lee Papers, Princeton.

[10] Frank B. Kellogg, Secretary of State, to Ivy Lee, July 14, 1927, Ivy Lee Papers, Princeton.

[11] Ivy Lee, "Relationships to the Russian Problem," *Annals of the American Academy of Political and Social Science*, July 1928, p. 93.

[12] Ivy Lee, *Present-Day Russia*, pp. 152–153.

[13] "A Realist Looks at Russia," *Business Week*, June 29, 1930, p. 35.

[14] Ivy Lee, "Relationships to the Russian Problem," op. cit., p. 93.

[15] "A Realist Looks at Russia," op. cit., p. 35.

[16] *New York Times*, Feb. 22, 1929, p. 8.

[17] Ibid., Oct. 29, 1930, p. 14.

[18] Ibid., Jan. 11, 1929. p. 4.

[19] Ivy Lee to Senator David A. Reed, Jan. 16, 1929, Ivy Lee Papers, Princeton.

[20] *New York Times*, Jan. 12, 1929, p. 6.

[21] Senator David A. Reed to Ivy Lee, Jan. 16, 1929, Ivy Lee Papers, Princeton.

[22] *New York Times*, Feb. 24, 1931, p. 17.

31: GERMANY: AN EXPERIMENT THAT EXPLODED

IVY LEE HAD LONG BEEN INTERESTED IN Germany and the German problem, as he had been in Russia. In the early twenties he had seen that the Versailles Treaty would not create goodwill between Germany and the nations of the world, just as reconstruction programs had failed in the South after the Civil War. There are many similarities between the United States after the Civil War and Europe after World War I. As the North had tried to reconstruct the South socially, politically, and economically, so the Allies had tried to place the full guilt for the war upon Germany and were punishing her with reparations and debt payments. As the Bourbons of the postwar South had struggled to free themselves from the yoke of reconstruction, so the Fascists of postwar Germany were struggling to get out from under the heavy hand of reparations.

In much the same way that Henry Grady had sought a new relationship for the South, Lee sought the end of reparations and war debts payments, an expanded trade relations, and a spirit of equality toward Germany. A similar spirit of conciliation and cooperation had been fostered in Germany, despite the hardship of reparations, by such men as Gustav Stresemann, foreign minister from 1923 to 1929. But the Allies were determined that Germany should pay reparations totaling $81.5 billion. And the United States demanded that the Allies should pay their American debts. Even as Germany collapsed under the burden of the payments and as American sympathy was aroused by the German plight, the

American government refused to place any moratorium on Allied debts.

"How," Lee asked "can you expect France, Italy, and Belgium to be reasonable with Germany if we are not willing to be reasonable with France, Italy, and Belgium?"[1] Economically, the war debts payments and reparations were debilitating European trade and world markets, said Lee. Germany, unable to trade, was a bottleneck in the entire balance of payments and international trade system. Lee pointed out that when President Hoover placed a temporary moratorium on German war debts in June of 1931, the New York Stock Exchange improved by $10 billion in two weeks— ample proof, he said, that the war debts had weakened the market in the first place.

For Lee the failure of the countries of the world to solve their public relations problems was largely responsible for the depression. He pointed out in a speech at Depauw University in 1952 that in 1911 the United States produced sixteen million bales of cotton, and half of it was traded in England and Germany; in 1931, the United States again produced sixteen million bales of cotton, but England and Germany, unable to trade because of debt and reparation blocks, bought a much lower percentage of America's cotton. "Hence," he said, "the disastrous price of cotton which spreads its blight over all our Southern States." He pointed out that prewar England and Germany accounted for 40 percent of America's total exports. But "today the ability of either Germany or England to buy in our markets is steadily diminishing, and the unemployed men upon our streets, the idle machines in our factories, the empty freight cars on our railroads, the pitiable plight of our farmers tell part of the story."[2]

In July 1931 Lee wrote to President Hoover that he "threw his hat in the air" when the German moratorium was announced. But he was strongly convinced, he told the President, that such steps could only be "purely temporary, and that unless fundamental measures are taken to correct the situation at the earliest possible moment, we will be faced with an even more serious crisis in the not distant future." He urged Hoover to consider two further steps: first, to assume some kind of political relationship with the countries of Europe through the League of Nations or by implementing the Kellogg-Briand Pact, either of which would help give France a sense of security; and second, to face the problem of German reparations and interallied debts realistically, not only with a temporary moratorium.[3]

Since the League of Nations was a dead issue, however, there was little that could be done to give France a feeling of security. Hoover failed to go any further in the international situation so Lee, after a long discussion with Britain's Sir Eric Drummond in Geneva, proposed in September that a diplomatic approach be made to France, appealing to the best interests of all Europe. He gave the President a tactfully worded statement that he had worked out with Sir Eric: "You and ourselves," the note to France should say, "are the only people who can straighten this situation out." The note went on to suggest cancellation of all intergovernment war debts and a substantial reduction immediately in armament expenditure.[4]

But neither France nor the United States got together on the matter while there was still time, and the spirit of conciliation which Stresemann had fostered in Germany disintegrated after the economic depression hit Europe. When the last democratic cabinet of Heinrich Breuning called out in 1932 for a rejection of the humiliating Versailles settlement, it only awakened a surge of patriotic enthusiasm in Germany. Much as the post-Civil War South had turned to the Ku Klux Klan and southern demagogues, so the German masses, angry and recalcitrant, were ready to listen to fanatics like Hitler, betraying the democratic Weimar Republic and forfeiting their own freedom in the bargain.

The new Nazi government jolted the German people, their business, and industry. Especially anxious, of course, was the Interessen Gemeninschaft Farben Industrie, commonly known as I. G. Farben, or the German Dye Trust. It was one of the largest corporations in Germany, with subsidiary branches around the world. Its relations with its own government as well as the governments of the world with which it traded were of immense concern. Ivy Lee, on a minimal retainer of $3,000 a year, had worked for the American subsidiary of I. G. Farben since 1929, handling its public relations in America. The American corporation was a holding company with subsidiaries such as Agfa Photo. Its board of directors included Edsel Ford, Walter Teagle (president of Standard Oil of New Jersey), an officer of the City Bank of New York, and other prominent American businessmen.

Company officials, now realizing that Hitler's policies were making those relations worse than they had ever been before, invited Lee to broaden the scope of his relationship with the company to include the parent corporation in Germany; they raised his retainer for the American subsidiary to $4,000 a year and gave him an additional $25,000 a year for his work for the parent company. The directors of the company told him that they were "very much concerned about the German-American relations and the criticism being made" in the United States of Nazi Germany. They asked him to advise them "as to what could be done to improve those relations and to do so continuously." The new regime in Germany had also stirred up labor problems for the corporation, and knowing Lee to have had success with labor relations as well, they asked him for advice on that problem, too.[5]

Lee always insisted that he had "stipulated in the beginning that there should be no dissemination whatever by me of information in the United States. I very religiously adhered to that phase of the situation because I thought it would be futile and objectionable," he said. He also turned down the German company's request to provide labor advice because, he said, that would require knowledge of the internal affairs of Germany and of the German mind which he did not have. His relationship with the company was confined, he said, to advising the officers "as to what I considered to be American reactions to what has taken place in Germany and as to what, if anything, could be done about it."

In order to provide this advice he put several members of his firm to work for the new client. First, he had Burnham Carter abstract from American newspapers and magazines what was being said about Germany, and this, together with statements pointing out the significance of the information, was forwarded to the company in Germany.

He also sent his son, James Wideman Lee II, to live in Germany and study the situation and the German mind and to serve as a liaison, passing on Lee's ideas to the company officials in a more personal manner, and passing their ideas back to his father. One of his regular duties was to watch for German material that would help Lee understand shifts and currents in German attitudes, those of the masses as well as the leaders. Lee's son also served as liaison to the Solvay Company of Belgium and, through a contact with one of the officers of the German Railways, he became involved in a small publicity project on his own. Always interested in automobiles, he prepared a pamphlet for the German Railway on motor touring for visitors to Germany.

Lee himself visited Germany frequently in 1933 and 1934 for personal evaluation and to meet with the corporation officials. Lee's chief contact with the company was Dr. Max Illgner, managing director. To provide Lee with as wide a background as possible, Illgner arranged for him to meet such officials of the new German government as Joseph Goebbels, minister of propaganda; Franz von Papen, the aristocratic vice-chancellor; Baron Konstantin von Neurath, foreign minister; Karl Schmitt, minister of economics, and finally Hitler himself. The company officials wanted, as Lee said later, to have him "size up" Hitler. He talked with the dictator for half an hour, asked some questions about his policies, and told him he would like to understand him better if he could. This, said Lee later, brought out "quite a speech" from Hitler.

Basically, Lee's advice to the Germans was along the same lines as his advice to the railroads and the Rockefellers. "I have told them repeatedly," he said later, "that the only way for Germany to be understood in the United States was for responsible people in Germany to make authoritative utterances which would receive publicity in the normal way. Complete reliance should be placed upon that process." Lee told the Germans that complete frankness and openness was the only sound basis for public relations. If their policies were unacceptable to the people after they had been frankly and openly explained, then the Germans had better change their policies.[6]

For awhile after the Nazi government came into power, Lee had faith it would prove to be a temporary economic expedient restoring Germany to a sound footing once again. He felt that if the U.S. would deal fairly with Germany, she would deal fairly with America. For example, on September 7, 1933, John D. Rockefeller 3rd asked Lee to come to his office to discuss the important problem of a German building among the proposed international buildings of Rockefeller Center. A good deal of antagonism to the proposed building had been aroused by reports of violence as well as antireligious and anti-Semitic undercurrents in the Nazi movement.

Rockefeller feared a boycott. Lee told him that the fourth building should be reserved for the Germans, that there need be no fear of a boycott, that Hitler would do much to restore German confidence, and that a confident and successful Germany was a prerequisite to a healthy Western economy. He advised Rockefeller to postpone any negotiations on the German building until Hitler was better understood and American sentiment had calmed."[7]

Lee felt that the only way to enable Germany to be understood with any accuracy would be to establish closer and more authoritative relationships with the American press correspondents located in Germany. He advised that authoritative statements be given the widest possible publicity in Germany, and he also recommended that all significant statements be distributed in the United States, with proper identification as to its source. However, he refused to do this distributing himself.

In advising on the kinds of statements that would win sympathy in America, he sent this memorandum to the I. G. Farben officers: "Could not a suggestion be made that von Ribbentrop undertake a definite campaign to clarify the American mind on the disarmament question." He suggested devoting a series of press conferences to this topic, and recommended that von Ribbentrop speak over the radio to the American people about disarmament. He even suggested that von Ribbentrop make a visit to the United States to explain Germany's position personally to President Roosevelt, and to make addresses to such groups as the Foreign Policy Association and the Council on Foreign Relations.

The kinds of statements that von Ribbentrop should make were outlined in a lengthy memo: "The National Socialist government has repeatedly proclaimed its sincere desire for international peace.... It should be clearly understood that the German people have not been asking for arms, but for equality of rights.... This principle has been the basis of...negotiations with other nations. Specifically, Germany wants an army of 300,000 effectives for the defense of its long frontiers." This was followed by a series of facts and figures on guns, war planes, and tanks aimed at showing Germany's weakness and inability to defend itself.

In another statement Lee advised I. G. Farben to say that "Germany does not want armament in itself. It is willing to destroy every weapon of war if other nations will do the same. If other nations, however, continue to refuse to disarm, the German government is left with no choice except to demand an equality of armament. The German people are unwilling to believe that any people will deny them this right today."

The dispute over the Saar Basin was another public relations problem for the Nazi government. Lee suggested that Vice-Chancellor von Papen should do the same thing for the Saar question that von Ribbentrop should do for the armaments problem—make speeches on the radio, place articles in magazines, hold press conferences for newspaper reporters.

Public furor in other countries had been created by reports of the activities of Hitler's storm troops. Lee advised that the government issue a frank statement on this subject, including in it the information that the storm troops number about 2,500,000 men, were "between the ages of 18 and 60, physically well-trained and disciplined, but not armed, not prepared for war, and organized only for the purpose of preventing for all time the return of the Communist peril." In his memo outlining the suggested German statement, Lee recommended it add that, "In view of the misunderstanding in regard to these civil forces, however, Germany is willing to permit an investigation into their character by such international arms control organization as is eventually established."

Although it appears to be slightly contradictory, Lee also advised that "anything that savored of Nazi propaganda in this country was a mistake and ought not to be undertaken. Our people," Lee told the Germans, "regard it as meddling with American affairs; it is bad business." It was all right to make radio speeches and write magazine articles, but they must not savor of propaganda.

Other Nazi policies which aroused public resentment were the persecution of Jews, the treatment of churches, and the loss of freedom of the press and speech. Lee said later that, "in the first place, I have told them that they could never in the world get the American people reconciled to their treatment of the Jews; that it was just foreign to the American mentality, could never be justified in the American public opinion, and there was no use trying." He made the same kind of plea for the Nazi treatment of the churches and religion in general, as well as the problem of speech and press freedom.[8]

During the last year and a half of Lee's work with German business, the American Ambassador to Germany appointed by FDR was William E. Dodd, a professor of history at the University of Chicago and an ardent liberal who was unable to view Lee objectively. When they first met in Berlin on January 22, 1934, he remarked that "Ivy Lee showed himself at once a capitalist and an advocate of Fascism." Dodd said of Lee that "his sole aim was to increase American business profits," which he characterized as "strange work." Dodd adopted an attitude of complete incredulity when Lee "told stories of his fight for Russian recognition and was disposed to claim credit for it."

A week later Lee reported his activities to the Ambassador, who later recorded them in his diary. "He had seen Goebbels an hour, had talked freely with Dr. Karl Schmitt, Minister of Economics, and other key men. He had warned Goebbels to cease propaganda in the United States, urged him to see the foreign press people often and learn how to get along with them." The Ambassador also reported that Lee had urged Party leaders to abandon their propaganda in Austria. And when Dr. Schmitt and Dr. Hans Heinrich Dieckhoff of the Foreign Office had suggested expulsion of foreign press correspondents, "Lee said he warned the Foreign Office that such an act would ruin the Nazi movement."

A month later, Ambassador Dodd went to tea with propaganda minister Goebbels, the Papal Nuncio, the British ambassador, and other diplomats. At an appropriate moment, Dodd related, Goebbels arose and read a somewhat conciliatory speech to the diplomats and the foreign press. "It was plain," Dodd wrote in his diary, "he was trying to apply the advice which Ivy Lee urged upon him a month ago."[9]

Matters in Germany, however, grew steadily worse. How much of Lee's advice was taken is academic. The Nazis were pursuing diligently their own policy and plans. Hitler, no mean propagandist himself, knew that "the great masses of the people will more easily fall victim to a great lie than to a small one." He was also putting into practice another principle he had enunciated: "The importance of physical terror against the individual and the masses also became clear."

As Lee became increasingly aware of the violence and irrationality of Hitler's Nazi party, he began to advise the I. G. Farben company to break with the Nazis and return to sane policies in Germany. When he realized that this was impossible, he finally saw that he himself had made a great mistake. He broke off his relationship with the Germans and, according to records later subpoenaed by Congress, he was never paid his full retainer.

In one of his final reports to New York, James Wideman Lee II wrote from Berlin in July 1934 that "we are having serious and strenuous times here. One doesn't dare to believe anything even when you see it and feel it.... The upper classes who have tried to believe in National Socialism...are beginning to realize that discrepancies exist.... The middle and lower middle classes are all muddled. They believe they made the revolution. They believe in Hitler. They find they not only got nothing but that much is taken from them."[10]

Ivy Lee, too, had become disillusioned with German progress. He had believed so thoroughly in his principles that he felt they would lead to ultimate understanding, which in turn would bring about peace and freedom for all. For several years he had been talking about applying his principles of public relations to the solution of international problems. He thought that the German situation had given him the chance to try it. It was, in effect, an experiment, but an experiment doomed to failure from the start, not because Lee's principles of public relations were unsound but because the Nazis never did more than make a superficial pretense of adopting them. The experiment exploded in Lee's face.

His realization was a little too late to save his own reputation from the trap jaws of the Special Committee on Un-American Activities which had recently been set up by the United States House of Representatives. The great increase of propaganda activity, by both the Communists and the Fascists in the early thirties, had led to a special investigation. The chairman of the committee in 1934 was John W. McCormack, Representative from Massachusetts, and the vice-chairman was Samuel Dickstein, Representative from New York, called the "arch bloodhound" of the committee probably because of his zealous efforts to expose anti-Semitism in the Nazi propaganda investigations.

By the spring of 1934 the committee had gotten around to the activities of Ivy Lee and had subpoenaed him and his records for a secret hearing in New York on May 19. Realizing how easy it would be to misinterpret his position, Lee made an intense effort to prepare for the coming ordeal. He had his associates ask for all possible questions so that he would be fully trained for all eventualities. He knew just what he wanted to say and how he wanted to say it, and stayed up long hours working out his statement. He had often made similar preparation for press conferences or hearings for others. But this was the most important test of them all.

The committee met in New York in closed session. After a few preliminary questions, Lee made his statement. "I have often discussed with German officials, friends of mine, German relationships with the United States," he told the committee. "I have been very much interested in Germany for a great many years. Chancellor Cuno was a great friend of mine.... My German friends have often, long before the Hitler regime, discussed with me the problem of how to get Germany better understood in the United States." He went on to tell what his ideas were, and he answered questions on his relationship with the I. G. Farben Company. He maintained that he had never advised the German or Nazi government directly, that he had advised the company on recommendations it should make to the government, but for the purpose of strengthening the goodwill toward Germany that the company needed to carry on its business, not for strengthening the Nazi government itself.

He was asked if he had tried to secure any publicity in American newspapers and magazines in defense of Germany. "None whatever," he answered. "I have never discussed Germany with any American newspaper or any American newspaperman in this country. I have discussed the situation with some of the correspondents in Berlin, and I told them precisely what my relationship was, and what I was saying to those officials whom I met in Berlin. I also went around the last day I was there in June 1933, when I had had these contacts with the Nazi ministers and with Hitler, and called on the American Ambassador and told him the whole story."[1]

The committee members also questioned several of Lee's colleagues, including Burnham Carter, who had worked on the Farben account, and Dudley Pittenger, the firm's office manager and accountant who was questioned about the German corporation's payments to Lee. The committee was satisfied with the answers they got. They excused Lee and gave their attention to the activities of others, including another public relations firm, Carl Byoir & Associates, which had become even more deeply involved than Lee in German propaganda. The Lee testimony, for the moment at least, remained confidential; it was not given to the press or disclosed to the public.

The German campaign, however, was not finished for Ivy Lee. Within a few months, the results of the investigation would be made known in such a way that it would blacken his name throughout the country and write the last chapter to his life.

---

[1] Ivy Lee, *The Vacant Chair*, op. cit., p. 10.

[2] Ivy Lee, "The War Debts Question," *Information*, Mar. 4, 1932, p. 3, Ivy Lee Papers, Princeton.

[3] Ivy Lee to President Herbert Hoover, July 25, 1931, Rockefeller Archives, New York.

[4] Ivy Lee to President Herbert Hoover, Sept. 19, 1931, Rockefeller Archives, New York.

5 U.S. Congress, House, Special Committee on Un-American Activities, *Investigation of Nazi Propaganda Activities*, 73d Congress, 2d Session, Vol. 7, pp. 176 ff.

6 Ibid., pp. 176, 178, 189.

7 "Memorandum: John D. Rockefeller III Interview with Ivy Lee," Sept. 8, 1933, Rockefeller Archives, New York.

8 U.S. Congress, House, Special Committee on Un-American Activities, op. cit., pp. 178, 203, 205. See also *Business Week*, July 21, 1934, p. 24.

9 William E. Dodd, *Ambassador Dodd's Diary* (New York: Harcourt, Brace & Co., 1941), pp. 74, 75, 76, 83.

10 J. W. Lee II to Harcourt Parrish, July 22, 1934, Harcourt Parrish Papers, University of Virginia.

11 U.S. Congress, House, Special Committee on Un-American Activities, op. cit., pp. 178, 191 ff.

VI

FINAL TRIAL

"The Judgments of the People"

32: PROSECUTION BY THE CRITICS

As Ivy Lee's influence increased so did the number of enemies and attackers. John Mumford, his close friend and colleague who had worked as a reporter with him at the turn of the century, wrote that Lee had more enemies among "dangerous demagogues and corporation haters" than probably any man in America. He was called "poison Ivy," "the little brother of the rich," "the corporation dog-robber," "minnesinger to millionaires." Mumford called him the "physician to corporate bodies," the title Lee thought most appropriate.

He was investigated by governmental bodies: the Industrial Relations Commission, the New York Transit Authority, the Public Utilities Commission, the House Un-American Activities Committee, and others. He was denounced on the floor of Congress, especially by the adversaries of banking and corporate interests. Senator LaFollette referred to Lee's work as a "monument of shame."[1] Bills were introduced into Congress in an attempt to legislate the publicist out of existence. During the railroad rate debate, LaFollette submitted a measure to the Senate which would have made it a misdemeanor to attempt to influence the action of the Interstate Commerce Commission by writing letters, articles, or other forms of communication. The bill was declared unconstitutional, but the fact that it was introduced indicates the amount of concern with which Lee's work was regarded.

Shortly before America's entry into World War I, when Lee was advising on advertising for the Bethlehem Steel Corporation and the Interborough Rapid Transit Company, a bill to curb institutional advertising was introduced in Congress. This inspired heated debate and it appeared there was actually a chance of its being passed. Lee called for its defeat in print, saying: "Newspapers, advertising men, and all interested in the progress of democratic institutions—whose ultimate safety must depend upon a fully informed public opinion—should omit no opportunity to make it clear to public officers, commissions, even Congress, that the people want to know.... Every man is entitled to a full hearing, to his day in the court of public opinion."[2]

Severe attacks on Lee also came from progressives outside government, from liberals, socialists, and leftists. Lee's association with Rockefeller, particularly in the Ludlow affair, supplied most of their ammunition. His naive faith in the Colorado Fuel and Iron Company operators who gave him exaggerated and erroneous information, which he printed and published as the truth, opened the door for criticism.

Writing in 1915 in the socialist newspaper *New York Call*, Carl Sandburg lashed out venomously at Lee. Referring to his work in the Colorado strike, Sandburg called him a "paid liar" and asked "how shall the labor movement handle this form of human snake, and how meet the poison scattered by this subtle tongue?" Lee's activity in the Ludlow dispute, said Sandburg, was "dirty work. It was coarse. It was cheap. It was desperately bold and overplayed. It was done by the cunning, slimy brain of a cunning, slimy charlatan.... Ivy L. Lee is below the level of the hired gunman and slugger. His sense of right and wrong is a worse force in organized society than that of the murderers who shot women and burned babies at Ludlow."[3]

A little later, Chester M. Wright, also in the *Call*, said: "Let not this Ivy Lee tell you that Ludlow is white.... Be one of the 'crowd,' but help the crowd to stand erect in full possession of its own sense. At last the crowd will think right—and then the day of the class struggle will reach its eventide."[4]

Herbert J. Seligmann, writing in *The Masses* in 1918, said: "More systematic and perverse misrepresentation than Mr. Lee's campaign of publicity has rarely been spread in this country. The industrial struggle passes him by. He has hired himself out and the god of his employer is his god. In the service of his employer he enjoys believing evil of his opponents and then he publishes it."[5]

Upton Sinclair attacked Ivy Lee with passion, anointing him with the notorious nickname of "Poison Ivy" in his book about the press, *The Brass Check* (1919). In another book, *The Goose-Step* (1923), Sinclair devoted to Lee a part of his chapter on "Jabbergrab in Journalism." "Being curious to know what kind of ethics Mr. Pulitzer's school is teaching," Sinclair wrote, "I pick up a publication of the Alumni Association, *Clean Copy*. The title page contains a list of officers, and I note the chairman's name, and his address—prepare yourself for a laugh—care Ivy Lee, 61 Broadway, New York City! So we learn that the Columbia School of Journalism is preparing students to work in the offices of 'Poison Ivy'! Its standards are such that it is willing for an employee of 'Poison Ivy' to be chairman of its Alumni, and to advertise that fact in its paper!"[6]

Other writers in the same tradition struck out at Lee during the twenties: Silas Bent in *Ballyhoo* (1927), Henry Brock in *Meddlers* (1930), and John T. Flynn in his biography of Rockefeller, *God's Gold* (1932). Even the humorists got into the act. Robert Benchley, writing on "Moulding the Public Mind?" in the *New Yorker*, said: "Mr. Lee, for those of you who lead sheltered lives, has long been the press-agent *de luxe* for such radical organizations as the Standard Oil Company, and has devoted his energies to proving, by insidious leaflets and gentle epistles, that the present capitalistic system is really a branch of the Quaker Church, carrying on the work begun by St. Francis of Assisi."[7]

The legend of Ivy Lee found its way into fiction, as well. A central character of John Dos Passos' *The 42nd Parallel*, first of the *U.S.A.* trilogy, is J. Ward Morehouse, a money-grabbing, amoral publicist, supposedly modeled on Ivy Lee. Only one or two details actually fit a description of Lee ("Johnny graduated from high school as head of the debating team, class orator, and winner of the prize essay contest"), but blatantly false to the supposed model as it was, the characterization became widely accepted as a portrait of the public relations counsel. Dos Passos later insisted that the character was based on Lee.[8]

Samuel Hopkins Adams, an early muckraker turned novelist, undertook to satirize Lee in a character named Elie Ives. But Adams later acknowledged that by the time he completed the book, any resemblance between the fictional character and Lee was accidental.[9]

After Lee's death, a sympathetic radio dramatization of his life was broadcast by Emory University under the direction of Raymond B. Nixon, later professor of Journalism at the University of Minnesota and editor of *Journalism Quarterly*. "Release at Will," a play based on Lee's life, was written by Jack Seligman in the late thirties but never produced on Broadway.

Lee was not the only recipient of criticism; increasingly in the twenties all publicity agents were denounced in many quarters of journalism. James Wright Brown, head of the newspaperman's trade magazine *Editor & Publisher*, expressed the view of many newsmen in 1925 when he said: "The function of any publicity man is to emphasize favorable news for his clients and to suppress unfavorable news. Such a man renders no service to the public interested in the truth. Publicity is a blatant fraud upon the public, and the publicity agent commits an outrage when he colors news to suit his client's wishes."[10]

One of the chief objects of many a journalist's scorn was the press release, the "handout" or "canned statement," as it was called. Lee had helped to make the press release respectable by always insisting on giving the source of the statement. Instead of anonymous tips and the secret leaking of information, Lee's releases always clearly stated his name and the name of the client he was serving. He felt that the only evil in propaganda was the failure to disclose its source. Yet he was accused of being a newspaper "space-grabber" and the fact that he put his name on his statements simply gave his enemies an easy argument for criticism.

Henry Pringle, a reporter for the *New York World* and a firsthand observer of Lee's methods, described the handing out of the press release. When, for example, John D. Rockefeller Jr. issued announcements, one of Lee's secretaries at once telephoned all the city editors in New York and the chief editors of the wire services. At the designated hour, Pringle noted, a dozen reporters arrived at Lee's office. They were received cordially, handed typewritten statements, and asked if they had any questions; if there were any, Lee answered them diplomatically. He might express regret that Rockefeller was out of town, but he promised that all inquiries would be called to his attention. The reporters, said Pringle, then stuffed the handouts into their pockets, "one or two of them protesting *sotto voce* against the role of messenger boy," and left. Lee had told them no funny stories and had offered them no drinks, but he would, said Pringle, "that afternoon and the next morning receive his column or two of free space."

In spite of the newspapermen's objections to the news release, they succumbed to it quickly. After the release of a statement, the city editor of a New York morning newspaper sent one of his bright reporters to cover the news. When the reporter returned, the city editor asked what it was about and whether it was a good story. "Oh," said the reporter pulling a sheet of paper out of his pocket. "I don't know. I haven't read it yet."

The press also attacked the press conference, or mass interview, as a "journalistic atrocity." When the demand to see a Rockefeller or Schwab or Chrysler could not be denied, Lee invited all the reporters to come and ask their questions at one time." A formal statement was prepared and this was given to the reporters when they arrived. The reporters and the interviewee were introduced, and the questioning would begin. When an embarrassing question was asked, said Pringle, the public relations counsel would "cough slightly, smile politely," and regret that some matters must be confidential.

What the journalists objected to principally was the scantiness of the information gained whenever a large group asked questions. "Some jackass from the tabloids," Pringle said, would ask for the favorite recipe of the interviewee's wife, and the efforts of the more intelligent newspapermen present would be "buried under the avalanche of imbecility." When the ceremony was over, the reporters found they had "little to print but the statement handed them at the beginning of the session."[11]

Neil MacNeil, an editor of the *New York Times*, accused Lee of "giving the press only the facts he wanted it to have and only when he was good and ready."[12] For instance, he said, all inquiries to the Rockefeller homes and offices were automatically referred to Lee;

and most of the time Lee simply denied statements made about the Rockefellers. One irate city editor informed Lee that he would make a liar out of him by printing the facts together with Lee's denial. But the editor was never able to make good the threat.

Newsmen also criticized Lee for putting an embargo on the news. During the prolonged negotiations over the monumental real estate deal for Rockefeller Center they angrily accused Lee of blocking at every turn their efforts to get information. Rumors about the project spread throughout the city, but reporters said Lee did not want any publicity for the project until the negotiations were finished, so he refused to give out any official statements.

Lee answered this criticism once in a letter to Stanley Walker, the celebrated city editor of the *New York Herald Tribune*, who had written an article for *Harper's* magazine, "Playing the Deep Bassoons" (February 1932), a critical piece about publicists. "I am not aware of ever having been non-committal when anyone asked me about the Rockefellers," Lee said. "If a question is one that can be answered, I answer it. If it is a question that cannot be answered, I say that we have no comment to make." Lee told Walker that the only subject on which he usually refrained from making a comment was Rockefeller's investments, and he said it should be perfectly clear that such information, for the stability of the market, should not be made public. Walker expressed the sentiment that all publicity men had "as fantastic a code of ethics, as flimsy a sense of obligation to ordinary intellectual integrity, as the lawyer who will defend without pay any issue which he believes to be right, and the next day takes part in a blackmail game." Don't you think, Lee asked Walker, that a man interested in publicity could have just as much character and ethics just as noble as a conscientious newspaper editor?"[13]

Few men in the twenties or early thirties were able to single out Lee for his lack of ethics. He was the exception to the rule. "He never directs that a story must be published in a certain way," said Pringle. "He uses no personal influence to get space, and boasts that he has not been in a newspaper office four times during the past twenty years. Why is it then," Pringle asked, "that this amiable gentleman, who provides so many good stories, is so generally disliked by newspaper men?"[14]

The chief reason, said Pringle, was that Lee was a "buffer," and the press objected to the fact that a liaison was needed between them and the sources of news. However, it was this open role of intermediary between business, press, and public that was one of Lee's contributions to the American communication process in the early twentieth century. That such a buffer was sorely needed is made clear by an illustration used by MacNeil to show how Lee protected clients from the press.

During the Rockefeller Center negotiations, MacNeil related, a city editor finally decided to bypass Lee and go to Rockefeller directly. He gave a reporter a letter addressed to Rockefeller, mentioning all the favors that the newspaper had done for the millionaire in the past, and asking that he return the favors by granting the reporter a few minutes alone. For one reason or another, Rockefeller was completely unnerved by the experience and trembled so that he could hardly speak to the reporter. The reporter obviously did not get his information, and the city editor was undoubtedly forced in the future to put up with the intermediary role that Lee played.[15]

A good deal of the criticism of Lee was one-sided. George Creel, for instance, in his article on the Colorado steel strike, pointed out all the items which were false and ignored those which were true in an effort to make the reader believe that everything

Lee had written was false. Such distortion led to the exaggerations in the Lee myths. Lee encouraged many of the myths by his refusal to divulge a complete list of his clients' names. It reached a point where almost every time he opened his mouth to mention a name, he was charged with representing the person of whom he had spoken. Because he admired Billy Sunday and spoke of him favorably, the evangelist's name was included without question in most lists of Lee's clients. When he advocated recognition of the Soviet Union, it was said that the U.S.S.R. had hired him as her American press agent. Lee was accused of nefarious dealings with Standard Oil long after he had severed all connections with the corporation.

Many of these myths and much of the criticism they inspired grew out of misunderstanding, and for some of this Lee was to blame. Instead of answering his critics with defensive statements and denials, he relied upon constructive action, but the press never completely understood his policy of openness and frankness. For him the truth was a far more effective tool for influencing public opinion than falsehoods could ever be, but newspapermen, often cynical about motives, frequently missed Lee's point that in a democracy truth is the most powerful weapon. They refused to believe that he was truly dedicated to a policy of truth and constantly searched for the mysterious significance beneath the surface of his activities.

"He has long purposes," said Mumford, "but there's no mystery about him except what's inside his head." Mumford described a dinner for an important railroad official which Ivy Lee had given at the Metropolitan Club earlier in his career. Lee invited all the financial editors of the newspapers to attend the dinner, simply as a gesture of friendship. However, Mumford related, it was midnight before the guests stopped wondering when the lid was to be taken off and the ulterior motive for the feast revealed. "Some of them, I think," Lee told Mumford later, "are wondering yet."[16]

To the outsider, the businessman, or corporation official, the mystery of Ivy Lee was even greater. Not the least of the mystery to the innocent businessman, said Pringle, was Lee's ability to predict the manner in which a speech or a public statement would be featured in the newspapers. "He can forecast with uncanny accuracy whether it will get on the front pages and what the editorial comment will be," said Pringle. "He can even guess at the size of the headlines." But newspapermen such as Pringle knew "this clairvoyance is possessed by any good newspaper copy reader."

Misunderstanding remained even when Lee made an effort to dispel it. "Nothing is more ridiculous than the idea that anybody can get the papers to print what he wants them to print," he said. But still businessmen would come to Lee and say: "We went to you because they say you can get a thing on the first page of the newspapers." Lee's reply to them was: "I cannot do anything of the kind. If you want a subject to get on the first page of the newspapers, you must have the news in your statement sufficient to warrant it getting on the first page."

He once told of a group of conservatives who wanted to hold a public debate with spokesmen for liberal causes over the question of public ownership of public utilities and street railways; they asked Lee to see to it that the conservative side got a good showing in the newspapers.

"I have just one piece of advice to give you," Lee told them, "and if I should study the case and consider it from now until the day of your debate, the advice would not be different." He told them "to employ court stenographers to take down the debate, just as it is done at large political meetings, and thus give the newspapers, as it goes on, an authentic account of what takes place.

If that does not get publicity for the conservative side, it will be because the conservative side has not said anything that was worth publishing."

Lee had faith in the press even though the press did not always have faith in him. He believed in the necessity for a free and responsible press as the bulwark of democracy. The crux of the problem of a free press in the twentieth century was that it was increasingly difficult, if not impossible, to present a complete and candid survey of the newsworthy events of any given day, as Lippmann had pointed out in his 1922 book *Public Opinion*. Because there is so much news, the newspapers could not handle it all.

"News," as Lee defined it, "is that which the people are willing to pay to have brought to their attention; while advertising is that which the advertiser himself must pay to get to the people's attention."[17] Because many people are interested in baseball, it becomes news and gets a great deal of "free publicity" in the press. Not many people are interested in what Cadillac Motor Company is doing, so Cadillac must pay to bring it to the people's attention through advertising, or they institute policies and take actions that are so interesting and vital to the public that they become news. This is where Lee came in. He advised individuals and corporations on what policies would be sufficiently interesting and vital to the public interest to make news.

Lee told Stanley Walker that there was a need for "someone to assist corporations and large interests in so framing their policies that they would be in accord with an enlightened public sentiment.... If a man and his wife get along happily together, the fact has no news value. Isn't the same true of the activities of a great many corporations? If a man can help the corporation to conduct its affairs so that the public is quietly satisfied with the policy of the corporation, isn't he doing some service? Furthermore, isn't there real value in having men in corporations who understand the news value of various activities, of which, if the newspapers were not told about them, the public would be ignorant and valuable information would never see the light of day?"[18]

When it was suggested that news releases be outlawed, Lee called the proposal ridiculous. He told the American Association of Teachers of Journalism in 1924: "If I were an editor and had offered to me any kind of information, I would welcome it with open arms.... I would do anything I pleased with the material offered to me; but as to objecting to having information offered me, it seems to me that by so doing I should convict myself of stupidity." Lee offered as an analogy his wife going into Macy's and objecting because the store had displayed so many items to entice her to buy. She did not have to buy anything, he said, but it would be idiotic of her to say that therefore the store should not offer all the possibilities.

In answer to criticism that Lee was a buffer between the press and his clients, he said: "If the publicity man is a barrier against newspapermen getting to the sources of information, he has no right to be there. The publicity man has no right to deny you access to the real source of information. That does not mean," he maintained, "that you have a right to ask every man in a responsible position to give you a personal interview about any question that you may want to ask him. But it does mean that you are entitled to a first-hand answer to any legitimate question."[19]

In a speech to the Columbia School of Journalism in 1932 he touched the sensitive heart of the newspaper problem when he said: "You know, the press is sometimes a little naive, with all of its sophistication. If I send a printed statement to the press and they realize that I am trying to use them and to get them to print it, there is always a certain backwardness about using it. It has got to be compelling news. But if I or anyone sends them a document which represents an advanced proof of something which is going to be distributed anyway, and here is a chance for the papers to print it first, the newspaper instinct is immediately aroused, and it is amazing how often the newspaper will print material submitted to them in that form that they would not when sent in any other."[20]

Many members of the press, understanding the motivation as well as the injustice of much of the criticism of Lee, came to his defense. Walter M. Harrison, president of the American Society of Newspaper Editors in 1928, said "people used to sneer at or condemn the Work done by Ivy Lee…. I believe that today, newspapers recognize Mr. Lee's work as perfectly legitimate and usually helpful. That form of propaganda which takes the shape of reasonable arguments or of securing publicity for demonstrated facts is only helpful. When it attempts to distort facts or to substitute threats or cajolery for arguments, it becomes contemptible and should be ignored by the journalist to whom it is directed."[21]

"For all the snorting that the newspaper people did," said Victor Knauth, an A.P. reporter before joining Lee's firm, "they really respected him." Herbert Bayard Swope, the legendary editor of the *New York World*, said of Lee: "I wish all 'journalistic menaces' were as really helpful as he is."[22]

Numerous journalism professors also disagreed with the criticism of Ivy Lee. The head of journalism at the University of Minnesota, Ralph Casey, and the director of journalism at New York University, James Melvin Lee (no relation to Ivy though they were both Methodist ministers' sons), were typical of teachers who were friends of the public relations counsel. Even the Columbia School of Journalism, as Upton Sinclair had asserted, came under the influence of the "corporation dog-robber." Columbia's Dean

Carl Ackerman was a close friend of Lee who depended upon him for guidance. "I should like to have your advice before we go ahead," Ackerman wrote to Lee about a curriculum change.[23] Dr. J. W. Cunliffe, Professor at the Pulitzer School of Journalism, defended Lee and publicists in general, directing his criticism at the newspapers instead. "The fact is," he said, "the reporting organization has fallen down on its job. I do not say that it has been the fault of the reporters, but it has become incapable of dealing with the vast, complex, modern life of a great city."[24]

Nevertheless, the criticism continued to grow throughout Lee's lifetime. For the most part, the critics of Ivy Lee had a louder voice than the defenders, and across a widening front American suspicion of public relations flourished. In 1929, Lee expressed his own deep concern for his inability to win a better reputation for his profession. In a letter to his friend, Professor Herbert Adams Gibbons in Paris, he wrote: "A good many years ago I started on the work I am doing, feeling that there was a real field in it for usefulness. I know now that there is a great deal to be done that is useful. But of course a great many people feel that it is an undignified work that I am doing and not worthy of great intellectual effort. There is a great deal to be said on both sides. Of course in these matters one has to search his own heart and obtain his satisfactions from the result of such a searching."

Outwardly, the criticism of his profession seemed not to disturb Lee, but in his heart, he was hurt by it. He was particularly disappointed that his ideas were never given much credit because he was stereotyped as a press agent. He told Professor Gibbons that he found "the greatest difficulty in getting people to take anything I say as an independent expression of opinion. I am always merely a propagandist.... Sometimes in my low moments I have thought of throwing the whole thing overboard and taking a minor job as a newspaper editor. Even then I wonder if I would not still be suspect; whether I have not been so thoroughly tainted as a propagandist that people would always suspect that there was an angel in the closet telling me what to say and think."[25]

---

[1] U.S., *Congressional Record*, 63d Congress, 2d Session, 1914, Vol. LI, Part 8, p. 7736.

[2] Ivy Lee, "Enemies of Publicity," *Electric Railway Journal*, Mar. 31, 1917, p. 600.

[3] Carl Sandburg, "Ivy L. Lee—Paid Liar," *New York Call*, Mar. 7, 1915.

[4] Ibid. June 13, 1915.

[5] "A Skilled Publicity Man," *The Masses*, Aug. 1918.

[6] Upton Sinclair, *The Goose-Step* (Pasadena, Calif.: privately printed, 1923), Chap. LXVI.

[7] *The New Yorker*, Apr. 1926, p. 23.

[8] John Dos Passos in conversation with R. E. Hiebert, Feb. 1962.

[9] Samuel Hopkins Adams to Walter Oswald, May 21, 1951, Harcourt Parrish Papers, University of Virginia.

[10] *New York Times*, Dec. 31, 1925, p. 4.

[11] Pringle, op. cit. pp. 145–147.

[12] Neil MacNeil, *Without Fear or Favor* (New York: Harcourt, Brace & Co., 1940), p. 312.

[13] Ivy Lee to Stanley Walker, Mar. 7, 1932, Ivy Lee Papers, Princeton.

[14] Pringle, op. cit., p. 151.

[15] MacNeil, loc. cit.

[16] Mumford, op. cit., pp. 21–22.

[17] Ivy Lee, *Publicity: Some of the Things It Is and Is Not*, pp. 9–13.

[18] Ivy Lee to Stanley Walker, op. cit.

[19] Ivy Lee, *Publicity*, p. 31.

[20] Ivy Lee, "Address at Columbia School of Journalism," Dec. 13, 1932, Ivy Lee Papers. Princeton.

[21] "The Public Relations Man and The Editor," reprinted in *Occasional Papers*, p. 20, Ivy Lee Papers, Princeton.

[22] Inscription on photograph of Swope, Photograph File, Ivy Lee Papers, Princeton.

[23] Carl Ackerman to Ivy Lee, Sept. 20, 1934, Ivy Lee Papers, Princeton.

[24] Quoted in Lee, *Publicity*, p. 30.

[25] Ivy Lee to Prof. Herbert Adams Gibbons, Feb. 13, 1929, Ivy Lee Papers, Princeton.

Ray Eldon Hiebert

33: VERDICT FROM THE CROWD

As advisor to many far-flung operations, Ivy Lee was constantly on the go: to Philadelphia for a board meeting of the Pennsylvania Railroad; on to Detroit for an executive session at Chrysler; down to Cuba to talk over troubles in the sugar or tobacco interests; to Washington to confer with government officials; across to London to discuss problems of international propaganda; to Berlin, Paris, Moscow. Life was a perpetual crisis, a strike, a Ludlow affair, a Teapot Dome scandal, a revolution. The world needed his public relations counsel, and he had a burning conviction that he possessed the solution to most of mankind's problems.

Lee was an aggravating perfectionist, and the increased criticism of his work from 1915 until his death seemed to make him strive even more to be blameless. He grew more dependent upon his staff, but they never measured up to his skill and insight, and when things did not go right he himself took over. He tried to do everything and be everywhere; he had always lived his business, but increasingly it became a twenty-four-hour-a-day operation. His temper seemed to grow shorter and his exasperation with his colleagues mounted. At times he would abruptly summon his staff and demand to know why a certain letter had not been sent out as directed or why a detail had not been given attention, and climactically he would announce with a broken spirit: "I'm through. I simply can't go on. You fellows divide up the accounts."[1]

He had always been high strung, rarely taking time for relaxation. He did not enjoy sports or activities that were not intellectual. He had always suffered from headaches, apparently migraine; as a young newspaper reporter he discovered that by soaking his entire head under the water tap in the men's room, he could ease the pain enough to enable him to return to work. He continued to use this method, but the headaches increased as the pressures multiplied and criticism spread. After the stock market crash, his health deteriorated. In 1933, after a physical checkup, his wife was told that he was suffering from leukemia and had only a slight chance to live.

In the summer of 1933 Lee called his staff together in his office at 15 Broad Street for an important meeting. As Lee stood by, Thomas Ross announced that he would henceforth be a partner in the firm and the name would be changed to Ivy Lee and T. J. Ross. Through the years it had been Tommy Ross who had kept the staff together and his responsibilities had grown as Lee's health had failed. As *Time* magazine put it Ross was the "public relations man between Lee and members of his temperamental chief's office."[2] In reality Lee remained the legal owner and allocated the firm's profits, but the change gave Ross more authority to step in for the boss.

Ivy Lee, now fifty-six years old and at the peak of his career, had the reputation of being the number one public relations counsel in the world. In reality, however, he was on the edge of crisis. The apex of his life probably came when the House Un-American Activities Committee investigated his work for the German Dye Trust. He was not strong when he was called to testify in secret hearings in May 1934, and diligent preparation for the testimony further damaged his health. He knew that he had done nothing un-American, but he realized that his actions could be easily distorted by his critics and he wanted his position to be sound.

Lee was deeply hurt by the implication of the hearing for he felt that his policy of operating in the open before the world court of public opinion was in the interests of humanity. Even though the House committee cleared him of any guilt, the ordeal proved to be too much and his doctors ordered a complete rest. Without releasing the Lee testimony to the public, the Congressional committee granted him permission to leave the country and he returned to Europe for a few weeks to "take the cure" at one of his favorite spots, the baths at Baden, Germany.

By the summer of 1934 Lee and his colleagues were fully aware of the disastrous turn of events in Germany and were anxious to help the Dye Trust restore responsible government. They had already severed ties with their German client, but it was too late. Toward the end of June the American public learned the true nature of the Nazi regime. Hitler's storm troops and secret police had turned to violence. On June 30 the world was told of Hitler's "blood purges," with more than a thousand men slain for "political" purposes, including former Nazi party members and sympathizers who had spoken out against an insane Hitler. When news of these events reached America, public opinion turned against Nazi Germany with a surge of revulsion.

A week and a half later, early in July 1934, while the public was still aroused over the Nazi killings, the Un-American Activities Committee suddenly released the story of the Ivy Lee hearings. The timing was *disastrous*. Even though the testimony had led the committee to exonerate Lee, the transcript was easily distorted by newspapers eagerly seizing any fuel to stoke the flames of public antagonism toward fascist Germany. The revelation made blazing headlines: LEE GIVES ADVICE TO THE NAZIS—LEE'S FIRM REVEALED AS REICH'S PRESS ADVISOR—LEE EXPOSED AS HITLER PRESS AGENT.

Lee's reputation, which had been on public trial since the Ludlow affair in 1914, reached a new low. To the man on the street it was easy to think of Ivy Lee as the cynical manipulator of capitalists and fascists, of billionaires and war-mongers. With the

Great Depression at its worst, men who were taking wage cuts, seeking jobs, or standing in breadlines across the nations were receptive to any criticism of capitalism. To them the headlines had proclaimed Ivy Lee the mouthpiece of "Robber Barons," Rockefellers, and Wall Street. Now he was also the defender of Nazi atrocities and the spokesman of fascist fanatics. If the crowd had been asked to make a final judgment at that moment in July 1934, it would have returned a verdict of guilty.

In August Lee once more visited Ambassador Dodd in Germany, an event recorded in Dodd's diary. "Today the old man looked broken and in spite of talk about his cure I am sure his health is very poor." The Ambassador had only recently heard of the disclosures of the Un-American Activities Committee and wrote. "He has made his millions the last twenty years and now the world knows how it was done." He noted that "I talked frankly with him and he turned red in the face more than once." When Lee left, he asked "kindly" about Dodd's family in Austria. "It is only another of the thousands of cases where love of money ruins men's lives," the Ambassador wrote, concluding, "I cannot say a commendatory word about him to the State Department."[3]

Such misunderstanding was due to the characteristic lack that was Lee's liability throughout his lifetime: his inability to do for himself what he had done so well for his clients. He had no one to fight his case before the court of public opinion. He was rarely able to explain his work adequately or to gain understanding for the underlying principles by which he operated. He often admitted that he did not know what to call himself, and that what he did was an art that he could not explain.

When reporters reached him in Baden after the news of his I. G. Farben work had been made public, he pulled within his shell and refused to make a statement. When he returned to the United

States a few weeks later, reporters met him as his ship docked; he made only a brief comment about conditions in Germany and Europe and would not answer questions.

Lee resumed normal activities but his health did not improve. Meeting with the executive board of the Pennsylvania Railroad in the last week of October, he was suddenly unable to recognize the men sitting across the big oak conference table—men who had listened to his advice for so many years. At the age of fifty-seven he had suffered a cerebral hemorrhage.

A private Pennsylvania car took him back to New York where, against his wishes, he was taken directly to St. Luke's Hospital for a checkup. His mind cleared and he insisted that he go back to work, but a squadron of doctors consulted and diagnosed his illness as a brain tumor that was inoperable. Curiously, the doctors reported that the tumor had started approximately four months earlier, when the headlines were screaming about his association with Nazi Germany.

For a while he continued to carry on from his hospital bed, dictating letters and memos to his secretary. But on Friday, November 9, eleven days after he entered the hospital, and with his family at his bedside, Ivy Ledbetter Lee died.

Throughout Lee's illness John D. Rockefeller Jr. had kept in frequent communication with the hospital. The elder Rockefeller, now in his late nineties, was understandably less concerned. But when Lee died the press insisted on getting the reaction of world's wealthiest man whose image had been changed by Ivy Lee. Death had come late in the afternoon, and it was six o'clock in the evening when reporters reached the elder Rockefeller's home. They were told bluntly that Mr. Rockefeller could not under any circumstances be disturbed after six. The man for whom public relations had done so much still needed a good press agent. The one who had served his interests for twenty years was no longer available.

One of the ironic aspects of Lee's death was the fact that his office had no statement ready for the press. The man who had prepared so many press announcements for other men had none available on himself. "There was no obituary ready in the files of the vast organization he directed," wrote the *New York Times*. "His associates hurriedly assembled one and it was run off on the mimeograph machine which in recent years has been the source of so much information."[4]

Lee's funeral service at the Madison Avenue Presbyterian Church in New York was attended by some of the wealthiest and most influential figures in America. Among them were John D. Rockefeller Jr.; George Washington Hill; Frederick W. Williamson, president of the New York Central; Cornelius N. Bliss, director of the Radio Corporation of America; Edwin W. Freeman, of the International Sugar Council; Harry Guggenheim; William Chadboume; and about two hundred and fifty other friends, colleagues, and clients. There were no eulogies, but the Rev. Dr. George A. Buttrick closed with a short prayer. "We thank God," he said, "for his delight in friendly ways, his simple faith, his manliness, for his effective skill to interpret man to man, and for his longing and service for world peace."[5]

Eulogies came later from his clients. W. W. Atterbury, head of the Pennsylvania Railroad, said Lee's "brilliant mind" was "absolutely without prejudice." He had a knowledge of world events and causes, unique and unrivaled, obtained by a personal investigation and contact. His advice was invaluable."[6]

George Murnane, a banker with Lee-Higgenson, Bankers Trust, and later Lazard Freres and Company, whose association went back to the Red Cross days, spoke for the financial world when he said: "He was a man of high character who never undertook to publish anything that was not thoroughly substantiated; he had an enormous respect for the truth and was not apt to suppress anything. He was a man with a broad view, but realistic in his thinking. If you ever had a problem, Ivy Lee could convince you that the solution which he helped you arrive at was the right one."[7]

Harry Guggenheim attempted to clarify Lee's German association, feeling that the advice Lee had given I. G. Farben epitomized the philosophy that was "the basis of his great success in public relations.... At the beginning of Hitler's ruthless regime, Ivy sent word to Hitler that American opinion of him must depend to begin with on his own actions, and as long as he pursued his ruthless and inhuman course, there was nothing that anyone could do to improve the opinion America had of him."[8]

Nelson Rockefeller added his praise in a wire sent to the family on the night of Lee's death: "The country has lost a great leader."[9] Nelson's father, John D. Jr., who perhaps had benefitted most from his association with Ivy Lee, wrote later to Lee's widow: "From the early days of my contact with your husband it became clear to me that his point of view was the same as ours, that complete sincerity, honesty, and integrity were the fundamental principles which regulated his daily life and upon which his every action was based. What he did for us in the Colorado situation and in the general relations of our family and business interest to the public thereafter was of the greatest value. He was broadminded, far-seeing, sound in his judgments, wise in his counsel, and through these many years was one of my valued associates and advisors."[10]

Lee's colleagues regarded him in the same spirit. "Ivy Lee was the wisest man I have ever known," said Victor Knauth some years later. Thomas Ross said, "His courage, sincerity and clarity gave the firm a strength and understanding which made our personal association of the greatest importance to my own work in the field.... He was always frank and friendly, yet had the courage to disagree if necessary." On another occasion Ross pointed out that "Lee could be two different people. He was a difficult boss and task master, bearing down on imperfect work, a real perfectionist at the office. But at home he could be the sweetest, most gentle man in the world."[11]

Lee's courage and his sharp perception were perhaps his two most valuable attributes. "He possessed the rare talent," said Sydney Hollingsworth, a one-time member of his firm, "of furnishing to his companions a mind that was a sounding board and a springboard combined, from which the person could lead to dynamic and effective activity."[12] Pendleton Dudley, who followed Lee's example in the early years of public relations, said: "Undoubtedly, he was one of the key public relations pioneers. He was a catalyst. He got things going, got action started, made people think."[13]

His severest critics, too, recognized his contribution to business life in America. *Editor & Publisher*, which was highly critical of him in the twenties and thirties, said after his death that he "revolutionized the concept and scope of publicity" and "popularized the written handout." He was the first "to convince the American peerage of trade and industry that they could benefit by tight control of what the public learned" (but Lee felt businessmen must first control what they did). "He did not betray friendships," said *Editor & Publisher*, "for he did not cultivate the friendship of newspaper owners or workers to get his job done."[14]

One of the Ivy Lee myths that was shattered after his death was the widespread idea that he was a multimillionaire. His net estate, after payment of debts and taxes, was valued at less than $24,000.[15] Fortunately he had made an agreement with Ross in 1933 that either surviving partner should take care of the other's widow for five years. As a result, Mrs. Lee retained a major share of the profits of the firm until 1939, and for a time the Lee sons remained as partners.

Ivy Lee Jr. went on leave of absence to serve in World War II, and upon his return opened his own public relations office in San Francisco. James W. Lee II remained with the firm, chiefly in the Detroit office, until 1960, when he retired to become the owner and operator of Barrows House, a Vermont inn. At the time of his withdrawal from the firm, Mrs. Lee requested that her husband's name be removed from the Lee-Ross organization to become the sole property of Ivy Jr. who had made a name for himself in public relations in California.

During Lee's lifetime the practice of public relations passed through several stages of growth, at each of which he was in the forefront. At the beginning he was concerned with persuading business to open channels of communication between groups so they could relate themselves to each other and achieve understanding. A two-way flow of information was required—employees had to understand management, but management had to understand employees; business had to understand government, but government had to understand business; Americans had to understand the world, but the world had to understand Americans. Increasingly, business came to him not only for his skill in opening channels of communication but also for his critical judgment on affairs that touched public interest. If one opened the channels of communication, the information had to be acceptable. An intermediary was needed not only to communicate but to judge the acceptability of one's actions. To know what would be acceptable, one had to understand people, to analyze opinions, to foresee trends. Business increasingly turned to Lee for creative analysis which would determine acceptable actions and policies.

At one of the last staff meetings over which Lee presided, on October 4, 1934, just a month before his death, he expressed his ideas on the new creative role of the public relations counsel. "The need for our services," he told his colleagues, "is the same as the need an Atlantic liner has for a pilot when it comes up the Bay...to safeguard the ship and her passengers from some unusual situation, some unexpected currents, some new condition that only the pilot, trained and familiar with it in his day-to-day work, can meet." The contribution of the public relations counsel, he said, was to "bring an intelligent, detached, outside point of view, based on a multitude of experience and contacts, and a keen, up-to-date study of trends, of new forces, of new currents of opinion.... Our business is becoming potentially a miniature brain trust for the business we are working with," he said. He pointed out to his staff that creative thinking, along with sound judgment, was what each must develop. He wanted to instill in his colleagues a "spirit, a vision.... The greatest thing for the human mind is to let it roam; let it soar. Don't be afraid of an idea. Never mind whether it may be contrary to what the client thinks. Don't hide your ideas."[16]

There was something uniquely American about Ivy Lee and his conception of public relations. He held within himself the dichotomy of America. On one hand he was Jeffersonian, a believer in the people, in economic opportunity for all, in the rights of the worker and the property owner. On the other hand he was Hamiltonian, desiring to lead the masses to avoid anarchy, favoring a strong mercantile class, economic freedom to stimulate industry, sound credit, and financial integrity to spur investments. Ivy Lee was unusually able to contain this duality because of his background in the new South, where compromise between Southern agrarian and Northern merchant had been adopted as the solution to Southern problems. He grew up among men who used public persuasion to help bring about that compromise.

Lee was an American romantic and realist combined. Gilbert Seldes wrote after Lee's death that it had been his romanticism that was most impressive.[17] Lee believed in the goodness and rationality of mankind and had the optimism that man could achieve, understand, solve his problems, and progress. He had a romantic faith; a humble, open, straightforward innocence; generosity; devotion to family and friends; sincerity; and the seriousness of the aristocratic, Southern, Jeffersonian planter. But he was also a realist. His puritanism, his straight-laced honesty, his hardworking, hard-talking, self-promoting, dedicated, almost pompous certainty, and his courtly, clean-cut, gentlemanly demeanor were traits of the hard-headed, New England, Hamiltonian trader.

Ivy Lee's total Americanism was perhaps his tragic flaw. Lee, who understood America's great strength, was also victim of America's weakness, for it is a matter of symbolic irony that the Un-American Activities Committee hurt his reputation most. He accurately assessed modern America as a mass society where the crowd ruled supreme, where no action could be successful in the long run unless it was acceptable to the people. He devoted himself to the American idea that everyone has a right to influence everyone else, dedicated to the proposition that the people would subscribe to those ideas which were true. But it was not difficult for Americans to translate this into the typical American notion that public acceptance need not depend on any intrinsic value but only on how well the idea or item was sold on the marketplace.

Out of his appraisal of the dilemma of free enterprise and democracy at the beginning of the twentieth century, Ivy Lee helped to develop a new social mechanism to preserve an open and pluralistic society. In the words of Foster Rhea Dulles, who once worked for Lee and observed the American scene afterward as a scholar and teacher of American history, Lee's "influence on the whole strengthened certain aspects of American business and American life." But, Dulles added, the mechanism also "weakened the fabric of our society with its emphasis on the image rather than the reality."[18] Lee was concerned with opening channels of communication to provide information about the real reputation of his clients. Less ethical contemporaries used his techniques to create an image as a facade to cover the truth.

In a sense even for Lee the distinction between persuasion and understanding, between image and reality, between education and propaganda, public relations and publicity often blurred. The profession he practiced was an evolving one that had no boundaries. It still suffers from a lack of regulation, from an absence of professionalism, from a want of laws that would require licensing and an oath of allegiance to a code of ethics. Much that parades under the title of public relations today is nineteenth century press agentry in bankers' clothing. Only a handful of independent public relations counseling firms operate at the level that Ivy Lee thought the proper one for his profession. Much of the public relations field has not yet caught up with Ivy Lee.

As a result Ivy Lee and his present-day counterparts, while serving a useful function in society, still suffer from a widely held and deep-seated suspicion of being fixers, propagandists, and ghost thinkers. To the average American, Lee was a puppeteer for the millionaires, a man behind the scenes who pulled the strings that made the public dance. This idea was most prevalent among the intellectuals of the thirties and forties and was directly related to their loss of faith in free enterprise, in capitalism, in the people, and at times in democracy itself. One historian of that period, Alfred

McClung Lee (no relative), succinctly expressed the widely held opinion of Ivy Lee's counsel: "Niccolo Machiavelli could scarcely have given the modern princes more apt advice."[19]

To be sure, too much public relations is Machiavellian, concerned with maintaining power regardless of ethical considerations. Lee, however, was primarily interested in preserving freedom by considering the public ethics of one's actions. Instead of thinking of him as a puppeteer, it would be more accurate to regard him as a courtier to the crowd, a man who thought of people as something more than pawns to be manipulated. He regarded people as rational creatures endowed with inherent goodness and ability to make the right decisions if they were given complete and accurate information. He saw the crowd as a king, a rational being upon whom he ought to use the most flattering and persuasive approach—an open declaration of the facts.

Lee expressed his philosophy most succinctly at the Columbia University School of Journalism in 1921 when he said: "We live in a great democracy, and the safety of a democracy will in the long run depend upon whether the judgments of the people are sound. If the judgments are to be sound, they will be so because they have the largest possible amount of information on which to base those judgments."[20]

Lee not only provided the public with information about his client, he also represented that client before the court of public opinion. He felt that everyone deserves his day in this court as surely as in our legal courts. The traditional lawyer, operating within a framework of statutes and precedents, must persuade a jury of men and women thoughtfully selected for their objectivity; and his persuasion is guarded by a judge trained in the fine points of the law. On the other hand the public relations counsel practices before the court of public opinion without any of the traditional safeguards of the legal system. He is a defense attorney, speaking in a court that often has no judge, no legal precedent, and, too frequently, has no opposition.

Lee practiced before this court in an ethical manner because he was a man of high principle who had great faith in the soundness of the judgments of the people. Had he lived longer he might have become more cynical about the nature of man in a democracy. The depression, World War II, the nuclear age, and the successes of the communist world have increased the thoughtful man's doubts of the basic premises of Jeffersonian democracy. Yet in the mid-sixties one clear fact remains: the American man on the street still lives in an open society and plays a greater role in his affairs than any other common man in the history of the world.

Ivy Lee and public relations played a significant role in preserving the pluralism of American society by opening channels of communication and allowing opposing groups to understand each other. His practice has been abused, but those who are optimistic about man, as Ivy Lee was, can hope that a free and open society will in time devise controls of public relations without destroying its essential usefulness, in much the same way that it found means to curb the excesses of business without overthrowing the system. Instead of puppeteers manipulating the people, we might hopefully have more Ivy Lees, more courtiers to the crowd, so the judgments of the people would be based on accurate information and the verdict of the crowd would be sound.

---

[1] Pringle, op. cit., p. 151.

[2] *Time*, Aug. 7, 1933, p. 21.

[3] Dodd, op. cit., p. 155.

[4] *New York Times*, Nov. 10, 1934, p. 15.

[5] Ibid., Nov. 13, 1934, p. 17.

[6] Ibid., Nov. 11, 1934, Sec. II, p. 9.

[7] George Murnane in conversation with R. E. Hiebert. Aug. 1962.

[8] Harry F. Guggenheim to Mrs. Ivy Lee, Nov. 30, 1956, Mrs. Lee's personal papers.

[9] Nelson Rockefeller to Mrs. Ivy Lee, Nov. 9, 1934, Rockefeller Archives, New York.

[10] John D. Rockefeller Jr. to Mrs. Ivy Lee, Aug. 26, 1935, Rockefeller Archives, New York.

[11] Victor Knauth and Thomas Ross in conversations with R. E. Hiebert, Aug. 1962. See also Broughton, op. cit., p. 231.

[12] Hollingsworth, op. cit., p. 18.

[13] Pendleton Dudley in conversation with R. E. Hiebert, Aug. 1962.

[14] *Editor & Publisher*, Nov. 17, 1934, pp. 18, 26.

[15] *New York Times*, Nov. 30, 1935, p. 15.

[16] "Transcript of Staff Conference, Ivy Lee and T. J. Ross," Oct. 4, 1934, pp. 2–3, 10–12, Ivy Lee Papers, Princeton.

[17] *New York Evening Journal*, Nov. 16, 1934.

[18] Foster Rhea Dulles to R. E. Hiebert, Apr. 3. 1963.

[19] Alfred McClung Lee, *The Daily Newspaper in America* (New York: Macmillan, 1947), p. 454.

[20] Ivy Lee, "Publicity: A New Profession," Address at Columbia School of Journalism, Nov. 22, 1921, Ivy Lee Papers, Princeton.

APPENDICES

A NOTE ON SOURCES AND ACKNOWLEDGEMENTS

DEALING WITH THE HISTORY OF PUBLIC RELATIONS is difficult partly because the public relations advisor works with his clients behind the scenes to some extent, providing confidential counsel which he regards as private and privileged, much as a doctor's or lawyer's advice would be. Thomas J. Ross, Lee's partner, successor, and owner of their firm's papers, has over the years refused to open the files to scholars. "Our fundamental philosophy," Ross has written, "—and this was a philosophy of Ivy Lee himself—is that relations between the client and this firm are completely confidential, and neither time nor death nor anything else relieves the firm of its fundamental obligation to maintain the confidential nature of the relationship." Ross, Joseph M. Ripley, and other members of the former firms of "Ivy Lee and T. J. Ross" and "Ivy Lee and Associates," have been helpful in providing personal facts and opinions about Lee. But they have not broken the confidences of their clients by providing information about Lee's work or advice.

However, material shedding much more light on Lee's actual work on behalf of his clients has recently been made available from other sources. The key resource now accessible to scholars is the collection called the Ivy Lee Papers at Princeton University, donated by Lee's widow and two sons. Among other collections that contain valuable material pertaining to Lee and the history of public relations are the Harcourt Parrish Papers at the University of Virginia, the Guggenheim Collection in the Library of Congress, the Archives of the American Red Cross in Washington, D.C., and the Rockefeller Archives in New York, although the latter is not easily accessible.

Several theses have been written about Ivy Lee. The most useful is probably Arnold Berlin's, submitted to the School of Public and International Affairs at Princeton. The thesis was finished in 1947, when many of Lee's clients, colleagues, contemporaries, friends, and family were still alive, including his brother Wideman and even his mother. Berlin interviewed many of these people, no longer available, and their thoughts about Ivy Lee are preserved in this thesis.

Senator LaFollette unwittingly did scholarship on Lee a great favor when he reprinted in the *Congressional Record* (Vol. LI, Part 8, pp. 7736 ff.) a complete file on Lee's campaign materials for the railroad rate debate in 1913 and 1914. Frank Walsh performed a similar service when he subpoenaed Lee letters and papers in his role as chairman of the Senate Commission on Industrial Relations investigating the Colorado strike and the railroad rate debate (see *Final Report and Testimony*, Vols. VIII and IX). Further investigating committees have made other materials available. Chief among them are the New York State Transit Commission hearings on the subway fare increase in 1926 and 1927 (see *Recommendations of Special Counsel*, 1927), the Senate Public Utilities Investigating Committee in 1935, and the House Un-American Activities Committee in 1933 and 1934 (see *Investigation of Nazi Propaganda Activities*, Vol. VII).

I would like to express my appreciation and gratitude to members of the Lee family who aided this undertaking: his widow, Mrs. Ivy Lee of Wilton, Conn.; his daughter and sons, Mrs. Alice Cudlipp of Wilton, James W. Lee II of Dorset, Vt., and Ivy Lee Jr.

of San Francisco; his sister, Mrs. Kate Lee Trueblood of St. Louis; and a cousin, Fred Cooper of Georgia. They generously made themselves available for interviews or provided family records and papers.

Many friends and colleagues of Ivy Lee provided assistance of a wide variety, all of which was useful and deserves acknowledgement: Winthrop Aldrich, Edward Bernays, Marvin M. Black, Harry Bruno, Burnham Carter, William M. Chadbourne, Martin W. Clement, Kent Cooper, William L. Dempsey, Foster Rhea Dulles, Harry Emerson Fosdick, Raymond B. Fosdick, Maxwell M. Geffen, Peter Grimm, Harry F. Guggenheim, Robert Gumbel, Paul M. Hahn, Roy W. Howard, Benjamin A. Javits, Victor Knauth, Deane W. Malott, George Murnane, Graham Parker, John D. Rockefeller III, Gilbert Seldes, George E. Sokolsky, Sir Evelyn Wrench, Van Viault, and others.

Thanks is also due to many librarians at Princeton University, American University, University of Maryland, University of Virginia, Library of Congress, American Red Cross, and the New York City Library. A word of special appreciation is due to Joseph Ernst, Archivist of the Rockefeller Archives; William S. Dix, Librarian, Princeton University; Alexander Clark, Curator of Manuscripts at Princeton, and all in the Manuscript Division there.

I gratefully acknowledge the Foundation for Public Relations Research and Education, Inc., for its grant of funds enabling me to catalog and arrange the Ivy Lee Papers at Princeton University. Particular thanks is due to Milton Fairman, president; Pendleton Dudley, trustee emeritus; and Dudley L. Parsons, vice-president and treasurer, for their interest in this project.

A special word of gratitude is due to Dr. Carl Bode, professor of American Civilization at the University of Maryland. His understanding and encouragement have been of immeasurable value. To Professor Harry Lee of American University, my thanks for his stimulating criticism and editorial suggestions.

ACKNOWLEDGEMENTS, Second Edition, 2017

I want to express my gratitude to Shelley and Barry Spector, of the Museum of Public Relations, for valuing history, for understanding the unusual role public relations has played in the twentieth and twenty-first centuries, and for establishing a museum to acknowledge and commemorate the importance of that history.

I learned of their museum as I was getting ready to move back to California from my long-time home in Maryland. And it was like a dream come true to learn at that moment there might be a place that would value the items I had collected in the course of my effort to understand the place and role of public relations in modern history.

For me, that effort had started when I was looking for a research project that might lead to a PhD dissertation in American history. That was the beginning of this book.

NOTES

A word about footnoting might be helpful. I have endeavored to save the average reader from the agony of countless little numbers, the ibid., op. cit., and loc. cit., and in doing so may cause some misunderstanding on the part of the scholar interested in pursuing the source of some minor detail. For the most part, I have omitted citation of secondary material and other material where the source seemed readily apparent from the text. I have also endeavored to place the footnote at the end of all material cited from a single source, rather than at the end of the first reference. Sometimes the quotation may spread over several paragraphs, or even in a few instances over several pages, and on occasion interspersed with my abridgments, before the citation is given for the entire reference.

SELECTED BIBLIOGRAPHY

WORKS ABOUT IVY LEE

Beckett, Henry, "Ivy Lee, America's Most Highly Paid Publicist." *New York Evening Post*, Jan. 1929.

Bent, Silas, "Ivy Lee: Minnesinger to Millionaires," *New Republic*, Nov. 20, 1929, pp. 369–372.

Crowther, Samuel, "The Menace of Propaganda, An Interview with Ivy Lee," *Collier's Weekly*, Oct. 13, 1925.

DeBekker, L. J., "World's Greatest Authority Caught at His Own Game," *Success*, Jan. 1924.

Drutman, Irving, "The Voice of the People," *Town and Country*, Mar. 1941, pp. 65–67 ff.

Dudley, Pendleton, "Current Beginnings of Public Relations," *Public Relations Journal*, Apr. 1952, pp. 8–10.

Forbes, B. C., "Rockefellers Make Publicity New Watchword," *New York American*, Feb. 26, 1915.

Goldman, Eric F., *Two-Way Street: The Emergence of the Public Relations Counsel*. Boston: Bellman Publishing Co., 1948.

Hollingsworth, Sydney P., "Pioneers—Blair, Barnum, and Lee," *Public Relations Journal*, Nov. 1945, pp. 15–18.

"House of Rockefeller Learns To Talk Under Tutelage of 'Publicity Doctor,'" *New York Press*, Apr. 11, 1915.

"The Ivy League," *Newsweek*, Feb. 17, 1947.

"Ivy Lee: An Extraordinary Press Agent Gives Advice to the Nazis," *Newsweek*, July 21, 1934, pp. 24–25.

"Ivy Lee a-Visiting," *Time*, June 11, 1923, p. 10.

"Ivy Lee Explains His Press Agent Work," *Editor & Publisher*, July 2, 1927, p. 5.

"Ivy Lee's First Job Was Under Socialist," *Philadelphia North American*, Jan. 3, 1915.

"Ivy Lee Lessons Still Go Unlearned," *Tucson* (Arizona) *Star*, Sept. 19, 1963.

"Ivy Lee: Pioneer of Public Relations," *Scope*, July 1951, pp. 74–82.

"Ivy Lee Revealed." *Editor & Publisher*, Nov. 15, 1950, p. 6.

"Ivy L. Lee," *St. Louis Christian Advocate*, Feb. 1, 1916.

"Ivy L. Lee, Father of Public Relations," *Magazine Industry*, Apr. 1962, p. 3 ff.

"Ivy L. Lee, New York's Door Opener," *New York City Herald*, Feb. 25, 1917.

Leake, Grace, "Southern Personalities: Ivy Lee, Public Relations Counsel," *Holland's*, Oct. 1934, pp. 7 ff.

"Lee and Company," *Time*, Aug. 7, 1933, p. 21.

"Meet The Man Who Made Publicity a Profession," *Industrial Digest Magazine*, Nov. 1927.

Mumford, John K., *A Physician to Corporate Bodies*. New York: Industries Publishing Co., 1925.

———, "Who's Who in New York, Number 55," *New York Herald-Tribune*, Apr. 5, 1925.

O'Brien, Terence, "Propaganda as a Private Industry," *The Listener* (London), Jan. 30, 1935, pp. 195–196.

Parrish, Wayne W., "Ivy Lee, 'Family Physician to Big Business,'" *The Literary Digest*, June 9, 1934, pp. 30 ff.

Pearson, Drew, "Rockefeller's Flight to Fame Started by Father's Associates," *Washington Post*, Nov. 8, 1958.

Pringle, Henry F., "His Master's Voice," *The American Mercury*, Oct. 1926, p. 145–153.

"This Publicist Recognizes the True Relation of Capital to Labor," *National Magazine*, Feb. 1923, p. 418.

"Publicity Agent of the Coal Combine," *The Fourth Estate*, Nov. 2, 1907.

Ripley, Joseph M., "Ivy Lee Talks About Publicity and Newspaper Editors," *The American Press*, Dec. 1926, p. 1.

Sandburg, Carl, "Ivy L. Lee—Paid Liar," *New York Call*, Mar. 7, 1915.

Tully, Andrew, "Rockefeller Victory Got Assist From Ivy Lee," *Washington Daily News*, Nov. 7, 1958.

Watson, Max, "Interviews With Ivy Lee," *New York Evening Post*, Feb. 19, Mar. 11, 1921.

Wisehart, M. K., "How Big Men Think and Act," *The American Magazine*, July 1929, pp. 30 ff.

White, James T., "Ivy Ledbetter Lee," *National Cyclopedia of American Biography*, 1940.

Wright, Chester M., "Rockefeller's Barricade of Ink," *New York Call*, June 13, 1915.

BOOKS BY IVY LEE

The City for the People: The Best Administration New York Ever Had. New York: Citizens Union, 1903.

Facts Concerning the Struggle in Colorado for Industrial Freedom. Denver: privately printed, 1914.

Human Nature and Railroads. Philadelphia: E. S. Nash & Co., 1915.

Memories of Uncle Remus: Joel Chandler Harris as Seen and Remembered by a Few of His Friends. New York: privately printed, 1908.

Miscellaneous Publications (a bound compilation of fourteen of Lee's speeches and articles). Princeton: no date.

Occasional Papers (a bound compilation of three of Lee's articles). New York: privately printed, 1934.

Present-Day Russia. New York: The Macmillan Co., 1928.

U.S.S.R.: A World Enigma. New York: privately printed, 1927.

PAMPHLETS BY IVY LEE

The American Railroad Problem. London: B. F. Stevens & Brown, Publishers, 1910.

Bulgaria and the Proposed Refugee Loan. New York: privately printed, 1926.

The Crux of the Railroad Difficulty. New York: privately printed, 1916.

The Efforts To Restore Equilibrium Between the World's Production and Consumption of Sugar. New York: privately printed, 1930.

The European Crisis and America's Relation to It. New York: privately printed, 1923.

The Gold Clause. New York: privately printed, 1933.

History Repeats and Depressions Do Pass. New York: Industries Publishing Co., 1933.

Poland Under Pilsudski: Some Observations on the Economic Progress of the Polish Nation. New York: privately printed, 1927.

The Press Today: How the News Reaches the Public. New York: privately printed, 1933.

The Problem of International Propaganda. New York: privately printed, 1934.

Publicity for Public Service Corporations. New York: privately printed, 1916.

Publicity: Some of the Things It Is and Is Not. New York: Industries Publishing Co., 1925.

Public Opinion and International Relations. New York: Institute of Pacific Relations, 1927.

Railway Progress in the United States. London: B. F. Stevens & Brown, Publishers, 1912.

Sources of International News. Chicago: privately printed, 1933.

The Third Party A.D. 1924. New York: privately printed, 1924.

The Truth About the Asphalt Trust. New York: privately printed, 1906.

The Vacant Chair at the Council Table of the World. New York: privately printed, 1922.

ARTICLES BY IVY LEE

"Advertising in Publicity Work," *Electric Railway Journal*, Oct. 6, 1917, pp. 617–618.

"American Notes of the Week," *The Spectator* (London), Jan.–June, 1929, Jan.–June, 1930.

"Anomalies in American Politics," *The Spectator* (London), Aug. 24, 1929, p. 245.

"An Appeal for the Red Cross," *The American Press*, June 16, 1917, p. 3.

"The Art of Publicity," *Book of Business*, New York, 1920, Vol. IV, pp. 78–96.

"The Black Legend," *The Atlantic Monthly*, May 1929, pp. 577–588.

"A Business Statesman: An Intimate Portrait of Dwight D. Morrow," *New York Herald-Tribune*, Oct. 9, 1927, Sec. VIII, pp. 2 ff.

"Capitalism and Democracy: Their Virtues and Defects," *Information*, Apr. 13, 1933, P. 1.

"Commission Regulation of Utilities Is Itself on Trial," *Electric Railway Journal*, Nov. 10, 1917, pp. 859–860.

"Constructive Engineering Publicity," *Professional Engineer*, Dec. 1921, pp. 7 ff.

"Corporation Publicity," *The Free-Lance Writer's Handbook*, New York, 1926, pp. 196 ff.

"A Downtown Church in London," *New York Christian Advocate*, Jan. 20, 1910.

"The Duties of an Advisor in Public Relations," *Printers Ink*, July 7, 1927, pp. 73–80.

"Education in the United States," *The Spectator* (London), Sept. 7, 1929.

"Education Is the Best Antidote for Labor's Radical Tendencies," *Public Relations*, Dec. 1, 1922.

"Enemies of Publicity," *Electric Railway Journal*, Mar. 31, 1917, pp. 599–600.

"The English Lakes," *North Carolina Christian Advocate*, Oct. 5, 1905.

"Feature of the American Political Structure," *The Spectator* (London), Aug. 10, 1929, p. 185.

"Great Britain and Gold," *Information*, Oct. 5, 1931, p. 1.

"Higher Fares Benefit the Public," *Electric Railway Journal*, Sept. 15, 1917, p. 441.

"Hopeful Aspects of Russia," *North Carolina Christian Advocate*, Oct. 26, Nov. 2, Nov. 9, 1905.

"The How and Why of Publicity," *Electric Railway Journal*, July 14, 1917, pp. 52–53.

"How Facts May Contribute to the Maintenance of Industrial Stability," *Public Relations*, May 1, 1923, p. 1.

"How Red Propaganda Works," *The Chicago Rotarian*, Sept. 1920, pp. 125–126.

"How the Costs of Operation Are Steadily Mounting," *Electric Railway Journal*, June 30, 1917, pp. 1180–1183.

"How the Costs of Rendering Service Are Steadily Going Up," *Electric Railway Journal*, June 23, 1917, pp. 1139–1141.

'How Red Cross Money Is Handled and Spent," *Review of Reviews*, Dec. 1917. pp. 615–616.

"The Human Nature of Publicity," *Electric Railway Journal*, Aug. 4, 1917, pp. 181–182.

'Indirect Service of Railroads," *Moody's Magazine*, Nov. 1907, pp. 580–584.

"Interborough Solicits Complaints," *Electric Railway Journal*, Apr. 7, 1917, pp. 638–640.

'Interesting Meeting Held in London Church," *Atlanta Constitution*, Jan. 9, 1910.

"The Internal and External Problems of Russia," *Proceedings of the Williamstown Institute of Politics*, Aug. 1–2, 1930.

"Ireland and England," *North Carolina Christian Advocate*, Sept. 28, 1905.

"John Simon Guggenheim Memorial To Supplement Rhodes Scholarships," *Public Relations*, Feb. 23, 1925, p. 1.

"Law in the United States," *The Spectator* (London), Aug. 17, 1929, p. 216.

"The League of Nations: Pacific Relations," *The Spectator* (London), Jan. 4, 1930, p. 15.

"London in Easter Week," *North Carolina Christian Advocate*, Oct. 12, 1905.

"Making the Railway Gateways of the City Attractive," *The American City*, Sept. 1922. pp. 221–224.

"The Man Behind Steps Out: A Study in Public Relations," *Public Utilities Fortnightly*, Feb. 6, 1930, pp. 141–145.

"Men and Books in Europe," *Information*, Oct. 20, 1928, p. 4.

"Modern Lawyer," *World's Work*, June 1904, pp. 4873–4880.

"Moscow After Twelve Months," *The Spectator* (London), Oct. 26, 1929, pp. 575–576.

"New Center of American Finance," *World's Work*, Nov. 1902, pp. 2772–2775.

"News Versus Propaganda," *Information*, Nov. 8, 1928, p. 1.

"An Open and Above Board Trust," *Moody's Magazine*, June 1907, pp. 158–164.

"Personality in Publicity," *Electric Railway Journal*, Aug. 11, 1917, p. 223.

"The Place of Interstate Railroads in Reducing Food Distribution Costs," *Annals of the American Academy of Political and Social Science*, Nov. 1913, pp. 10–19.

"Preserving Peace in the Pacific," *Information*, Jan. 15, 1930, p. 1.

"The Problem of Russia," *Engineers & Engineering*, Oct. 1930, pp. 257–262.

"Publicity and Propaganda," *Readings in Public Opinion*, New York, 1928.

"Railroad Valuation," *Bankers' Magazine*, July 1907, pp. 81–94.

"The Railroads at the Parting of the Ways," *Money and Commerce*, July 5, 1924, suppl.

"Relationship to the Russian Problem," *Annals of the American Academy of Political and Social Science*, July 1928, pp. 93–96.

"Remedies That Would Wreck the Railroads," *Magazine of Wall Street*, Feb. 3, 1923, pp. 588 ff.

"Russian Communism," *Engineers & Engineering*, Sept. 1931, pp. 193–196.

"Savings Banks," *World's Work*, Sept. 1902, pp. 2488–2490.

"Say Agencies Vital to Business," *Advertising*, Mar. 26, 1925, p. 10.

"Some Facts in the World Crisis," *Engineers & Engineering*, Jan. 1923, pp. 1–3.

"Some Practical Aspects of the Railroad Problem," *Proceedings of the Academy of Political Science*, Jan. 1920, pp. 703–706.

"Storm-Tossed Russia," *St. Louis Christian Advocate*, Dec. 20, 1905.

"The Technique of Publicity," *Electric Railway Journal*, Jan. 6, 1917, pp. 16–18.

"This Hour of Bewilderment" (Commencement Address at Elon College), *Information*, May 28, 1931, p. 1.

"This Shrinking Planet" (Commencement Address at Vanderbilt University), *Information*, June 21, 1930, p. 1.

"A Tour Through Europe Since December," *New York Times*, May 18, 1919, Sec. IV, p. 8.

"The War Debts Question," *Information*, Mar. 4, 1932, p. 1.

"The Vacant Chair at the Council Table of the World," *Current Opinion*, Dec. 1922, pp. 763–766.

"Walks and Talks in London," *North Carolina Christian Advocate*, Oct. 19, 1905.

"What a Publicity Bureau Could Do," *Electric Railway Journal*, Aug. 18, 1917, pp. 265–267.

"Whole-Hearted Publicity," *Electric Railway Journal*, Aug. 25, 1917, pp. 304–305.

UNPUBLISHED MANUSCRIPTS BY IVY LEE

Constructive Publicity (four chapters), undated, Ivy Lee Papers, Princeton.

An Intelligent Citizen's Guide to Propaganda (seven chapters), undated, Ivy Lee Papers, Princeton.

Mr. Lee's Publicity Book (twenty-one chapters), undated, Ivy Lee Papers, Princeton.

The Meaning of Publicity (lectures given at Harvard School of Business Administration, six chapters), 1924, Ivy Lee Papers, Princeton.

Problems of Propaganda: A Challenge to Democracy (ten chapters and various notes), undated, Ivy Lee Papers, Princeton.

The Public Eye (various versions and titles, five to seven chapters), undated, Ivy Lee Papers, Princeton.

Publicity: The Profession of Persuading the Public (nine chapters), undated, Ivy Lee Papers, Princeton.

INDEX

A

Abrams, Hiram, 285–286
Ackerman, Carl, 427–428
Adams, James Truslow, 186
Adams, Samuel, 26
Adams, Samuel Hopkins, 65, 418
Aldrich, Winthrop, 24, 203, 300, 344, 448
Allen, Frederick Lewis, 184, 189
American Association of Teachers of Journalism, 426
American Petroleum Institute, 209, 235, 248–249, 259
American Red Cross, 5, 24, 346–355, 447–448
American Society of Composers, Authors, and Publishers, 287
American Society of Newspaper Editors, 427
American Tobacco Company, 24, 213, 217–218, 264–266, 332, 338
American Transit (Detroit), 132
Anaconda Copper Mining Co., 249
Angell, James, 187
Anglo-American Oil Co., 262, 331
Anthracite Coal Operators Conference, 209, 253
Anthracite Coal Roads and Mines Co., 79
Anthracite Coal Strike, 70–72, 108
Arbuckle, Fatty, 282–283
Archbold, John D., 159
Armour and Company, 24, 214, 258–259
Asphalt Trust, 456
Association of American Railroads, 138
Association of Railroad Executives, 132

Atlanta Constitution, 42, 50–52, 458
Atlantic Monthly, 184, 186, 189, 291, 342, 456
Atterbury, W. W., 119–121, 123, 126, 134–136, 355, 436

B

Baer, George F., 70–71, 79–80
Baker, George F., 324
Baker, Ray Stannard, 65
Baltimore and Ohio Railroad, 74, 130
"Bankers' Agreement," 321–322
Bankers Trust Co., 296, 347, 379–380, 436
Barbour, W. Warren, 319
Barnum, P. T., 27
Batchelor, Bronson, 348
Baumgartner, Hampton, 130
Beard, Charles A., 184
Becker, Carl, 187
Bedford, A. Cotton, 235, 246–249, 331, 356
Benchley, Robert, 417
Bennett, James Gordon, 64
Bent, Silas, 205, 214, 417, 452
Berlin, Irving, 286, 344
Bernays, Edward, 131, 137, 219, 266, 448
Bethlehem Steel, 24, 109, 214, 223–230, 347, 416
Betty Crocker, 257
Bickel, Karl A., 176
Bigelow, Lewis, 66, 215
Black, Hugo, 136
Black, Marvin M., 218, 448
Black Friday, 34, 293–295
"Black Legend," 291, 342, 456
Blair, Francis, 27
Blake, James W., 287

Bliss, Cornelius N. Jr., 346, 436
Bly, Nellie, 64
Bolshevism, 217, 290, 314, 365, 375, 387, 392-393
Boni and Liveright, 193
Boomer, Lucius, 213
Borah, William E., 396-398
Boris III of Bulgaria, 336, 383
Bourbons, 41-43, 401
Bowers, L. M., 142, 147-148
Brandeis, Louis D., 99, 106
Breasted, James H., 195
Brett, George P., 184
Breuning, Heinrich, 403
Brisbane, Arthur, 22, 143, 168, 184, 341
Brock, Henry, 198, 417
Brown, D. W., 145
Bruno, Harry A., 274, 448
Buchan, John, 185, 187-188
Bureau of Railroad Economics, 132
Burning Question, The, 254
Byrd, Richard E., 273-275

C

C. Czarnikow, Inc., 261-263
Cable, George Washington, 42
Cake, J. L., 80
Canfield, Dick, 61
Carl Byoir & Associates, 413
Carnegie, Andrew, 45, 333
Carter, Burnham, 216-217, 405, 448
Carter, C. F., 143
"Casements, The," 164
Casey, Ralph, 427
Cassatt, Alexander J., 88-89
Chadbourne, Thomas L., 261-263, 308, 332
Chadbourne, William, 448
Chadbourne Plan, 262-263
Chamber of Commerce of New York, 385-386
Chandler & Co., 376
Chandler Plan, 376

Chaplin, Charlie, 285
Charnwood, Lord, 185, 188
Chase, Stuart, 184
Chase National Bank, 299, 300-301, 393
Chrysler, Walter, 24, 305-308, 420
Chrysler Corporation, 24, 305-308, 312, 431
Churchill, Sir Winston, 24, 213, 264-266, 332, 338, 436
City for the People, The: The Best Administration New York Ever Had, 67, 454
Clark, J. I. C., 159
Clement, Martin W., 120, 126-127, 206, 448
Cleveland, Grover, 25, 53-55, 77-78, 187, 190, 314
Cloisters, The, 50
Close, Frank, 379
Coal Operator's Committee of Seven, 80
Code of Motion Pictures, 284
Coffin, Robert, 188
Colorado coal mines strike, 21-23, 30, 140-149 153-154, 160, 416, 447
Colorado Fuel and Iron Company, 97, 98, 99, 102, 298
Commager, Henry S., 184
Commission on Industrial Relations, 105, 141-142, 149, 152, 447
Committee on Public Information, 359
"Common Sense," 26
Coolidge, Calvin, 313
Cooper, Kent, 105, 141-142, 149, 152, 447, 448
Copper and Brass Research Institute, 24, 209, 250-252, 259, 71, 272, 385
Cosby, Capt. Arthur, 67
Cosmopolitan, 183

Cotton-Textile Institute, 209, 260
Cotton Yarn Association, 260
"Courtier to the crowd," 10, 34, 57, 443
Creel, George, 359-360, 422
"Crisis Papers," 26
Crystallizing Public Opinion, 219
Cuba Cane Sugar Corporation, 261
Cullom Committee, 86, 88
Cummins, Albert B., 103-104
Cunliffe, J. W., 426
Cuno, German Chancellor, 334, 412
Curry, John, 320
Curti, Merle, 25, 188
Cushing, Harvey, 189
Cutler, Bertram, 203

D

Daugherty, Harry M., 339
Davis, John W., 24, 313-316
Davison, Henry P., 24, 346-348, 350-354
Debevoise, Thomas M., 199, 203
DeBost, William L., 385
"Declaration of Principles," 80
Delaware & Hudson Railroad, 94
DeMille, Cecil B., 280, 283-286, 288, 341
Democratic Party, 75, 315-316, 318
Denby, Edwin, 201
Depauw University, 402
Dewey, Charles S., 380
Dickstein, Samuel, 411
Dieckhoff, Hans Heinrich, 410
Dillon, Clarence, 299
Dodd, William E., 184, 409-410, 434
Doherty, Henry, 172
Dominick and Dominick, 297
Donham, Wallace B., 185
Dorney, Joseph, 87-88, 95
Dos Passos, John, 418
Drew, Daniel, 86
Drummond, Sir Eric, 403

Dudley, Pendleton, 62, 82, 161, 219, 438, 448
Duffus, R. L., 189
Dulles, Foster Rhea, 217, 441, 448
Dulles, John Foster, 217, 339, 378

E

Easley, Ralph E., 387
Edgerton, John E., 295
Editor & Publisher, 82-83, 225, 419, 438
Eighteenth Amendment, 200
Electric Railway Association, 114, 131-133
Electric Railway Journal, 131
Elevated Express, 113, 237
Elkins Act, 88
Emory College, 38, 44, 49, 52, 56
English Speaking Union, 325, 367-368
Expedition Act, 88

F

Fairbanks, Douglas Sr., 285
Fall, Albert B., 201
Famous Players Film Company, 280
Famous Players-Lasky, 279-283, 285
Feature Player Company, 279
Federal Trade Commission, 132, 224, 346
Federalist Papers, 26-27
Finley, John H., 196, 341
Firestone, Harvey, 175
Fish, Hamilton Jr., 396
Fisk, Jim, 184, 187
Flynn, John T., 182-183, 205-206, 417
Foch, Marshal Ferdinand, 335, 345
Forbes, B. C., 295
Forbes Magazine, 295
Ford, Henry, 209
Fosdick, Harry Emerson, 326, 448

Fosdick, Raymond, 56, 160, 178, 184, 203, 206, 326, 448
"Four Minutemen," 352
Freeman, Edwin W., 436
Fuad, King, 195–96
Fundraising, 40, 218, 324–325, 348, 351
"Fundamentalist Controversy," 326
Fusion ticket, 67–68, 313

G

Gaeddert, G. R., 348, 349
Garland, Hamlin, 189
Garner, John, 316, 318
Garretson, Austin B., 152–153
Garrett, Charles, 321–322
Gary, Judge Elbert H., 223, 228
General Mills, 24, 257–258
Georgia Railway & Power Company, 132
Getz, Carl H., 210
Gibb, George, 246
Gibbons, Herbert Adams, 428
Glass-Steagall Bill, 302
Goebbels, Joseph, 406, 410
Gold Medal flour, 257
Goldwyn, Samuel, 280, 285
Gompers, Samuel, 192, 355
Goodwin, William A. R., 196–197
"Gospel of wealth," 45
Gould, Jay, 86
Grace, Eugene, 228–229
Grady, Henry W., 42–43, 401
Grange, 28, 87
Gras, N. S. B., 72
"Great Octopus," 159
Green, Jerome, 149
Green, William, 142
Greene, Evarts B., 184
Grenfell, Mrs. Helen, 145
Griffith, David W., 285
Grimm, Peter, 320, 322, 448
Guedalla, Philip, 185, 187–188
Guggenheim, Daniel, 24, 241, 249, 272, 273

Guggenheim, Harry F., 24, 217, 272–273, 332, 436, 437, 448
Guggenheim Foundation, 24, 241, 273–276

H

Hahn, Paul, 332, 448
Hall, Walter Phelps, 366
Harding, Warren, 284
Harriman, Edward H., 86
Harriman, W. Averill, 393
Harris, Joel Chandler, 42–45, 454
Harris, W. W., 109, 212, 216
Harris, Winthrop & Company, 94, 362
Harrison, Walter M., 427
Harvard Law School, 59
Hays, Will H., 284
Hearst, William Randolph, 318
Henderson, Rev. Howard, 50–51
Hendrick, Burton J., 189
Hepburn Act, 88, 92, 97
Hereford, W. R., 270–271
Hibben, John, 366
Hill, George Washington, 24, 213, 264–266, 332, 338, 436
Hill, James J., 66, 86
Hines, Walker D., 260
Hitler, Adolf, 25, 34, 404, 406–408, 410, 411–413, 433, 437
Hocking, W. E., 325
Hollingsworth, Sydney, 215, 438
Holloway, Emory, 189
Hoover, Herbert, 33, 218, 295–296, 299, 313, 315, 318, 339, 348, 402–403
Hopkins, Ernest M., 186
Household Finance Corporation, 297
Howard, Roy, 341
Howe, Mark Anthony DeWolfe, 189
Howells family, 42
Hubbard, Elbert, 143, 151
Hughes, Charles Evans, 203
Human Nature and Railroads, 131
Hurley, Edward N., 346
Hutchinson, William T., 184

I

I. G. Farben (Interessen Germenin-schaft Farben Industrie), 217, 404, 407–408, 410, 412–413, 434, 437
Illgner, Max, 406
Industrial associations, 209
Inglis, William O., 178–184
Institute of Pacific Relations, 368
Interborough Rapid Transit, 24, 108, 122, 132, 338, 347, 416
International Harvester Company, 79, 81, 82
International Red Cross Commission, 357
International Sugar Council, 261, 263, 332, 436
International United Mine Workers Union, 142
Interstate Commerce Commission, 88, 104, 127, 153, 415
Irving Trust Company, 281
Ivy Lee & Associates, 211, 212, 446
Ivy Lee & T. J. Ross, 216, 309, 432, 446

J

James, Henry, 184, 188
James, Marquis, 189
Javits, Benjamin, 24, 340–341, 448
Jefferson, Thomas, 26, 29
Jeffries, Jim, 61
Johns Hopkins University, 162
Jones, Jesse, 296, 298
Jones, Mother, 146, 149

K

Kahn, Otto, 24, 198, 281, 297, 305, 332
Keller, Helen, 318
Kellogg, Frank B., 393
Kellogg-Briand Pact, 403
Kempner, A. M., 397–398
Kendall, Amos, 27
Kern, Jerome, 286, 344
Kerr, J. B., 80

Keynes, John Maynard, 295
Khrushchev, Nikita, 373, 390, 399
King, Mackenzie, 145, 154, 160, 193, 276, 336
"Kitchen Cabinet," 27
Klein, Gertrude Wilde, 149
Knauth, Victor, 217, 277, 303–304, 338, 427, 437, 448
Knowlton, Evelyn, 246
Kuhn, Loeb & Company, 281, 297, 305

L

LaFollette, Robert M., 88, 92, 104, 105, 313, 314, 415, 447
Lamont, T. W., 295, 299
Landis, Judge K. M., 159
Langsam, Walter C., 184
Lasker, Albert, 265–266
Lasky, Jesse, 279–280, 282, 285
Law and Order League, 145–146
Lawrence, David, 341
Lawrence, T. E., 342
Lawson, Thomas W., 158
Ledbetter, Cornelia, 66–67, 233, 243, 367
Ledbetter, L. L., 38
Lee, Alfred McClung, 442
Lee, Alice (daughter), 67, 94, 243, 343
Lee, Alice (sister), 38, 233
Lee, Cornelia Bartlett Bigelow (wife), 66–67, 233, 243, 343, 432
Lee, Emma Eufaula (mother), 38
Lee, Harris, and Lee, 109, 208, 210, 223
Lee, Ivy
  ancestry, 37
  birth, 38
  courtship and marriage, 66
  death and funeral, 435–436
  description, 36
  education, 49–56
  journalistic career, 59–64
  philosophy, 22–23, 28–29, 32, 46, 57, 73–74, 75, 80–81, 98–99, 110–111, 131–133, 143–144, 211–212, 214–215, 224, 293–294, 313, 322, 368–370, 440–441, 443

Lee, Ivy Jr. (son), 94, 164, 215, 233, 243, 439, 447
Lee, James II (son), 94, 215, 243, 439, 447
Lee, James Melvin, 427
Lee, James Wideman (father), 37, 38, 40, 44, 50, 51
Lee, James Wideman Jr. (brother), 38, 90, 109, 149, 212, 215, 354
Lee, Kate (sister), 38, 233, 447
Lee, Laura (sister), 38, 233
Lee, Lewis (brother), 38, 215
Lee, Zachary (grandfather), 37–38
Lee-Higgenson, 297, 436
Leighton, Jack, 270, 271
Liberty National Bank, 296
Lincoln, Abraham, 26, 188
Lindbergh, Charles, 24, 213, 217, 274–277, 332, 350
Lippmann, Walter, 184, 290, 425
Litvinov, Maxim, 399
London School of Economics, 93, 95, 98
Long, Ray, 183
Long Island Lighting Company, 132
Low, Seth, 67, 68, 313
Luce, Henry, 340
Ludlow Massacre, 21, 57, 140, 142, 145, 147, 192, 234, 246, 337, 416–417, 431, 433
Ludwig, Emil, 185

M

McAdoo, William G., 118, 119, 313, 316
McCallum, James, 186
McClellan, George B., 67, 68
McClure, S. S., 66, 158
McCormack, John W., 411
McCosh, James, 44, 45
McKinley, William, 62, 72, 77
MacNeil, Neil, 420, 422
Mack, Frank N., 53
Malott, Deane, 36, 218, 448

Mann-Elkins Act, 88
Martineau, Harriet, 304–305
Masaryk, Jan, 383
Masaryk, Thomas, 383
Mass production, 29, 63, 208, 209, 257, 266, 291
Merritt, Wesley, 60
Methodist Episcopal Church South, 38, 326
Metro-Goldwyn-Mayer, 280
Milton, David, 171, 172
Mitchell, Charles, 299
Mitchell, John, 71
Mitchell, Nina, 51
Monnet, Jean Jacques, 378–379
Montana Power Company, 132
Mooney, J. D., 295
Morgan, J. P. & Co., 295, 297, 314, 346, 364, 365, 376, 377
Morgan, John Pierpont, 36, 70, 86, 301, 349
Morris and Company, 258
Morrow, Dwight, 24, 276, 297, 332, 343
Motion Picture Producers & Distribution Assoc., 284
Movietone News, 174
Muckrakers, 9, 30, 65, 98, 111, 112, 158, 290,
Mumford, John K., 60–61, 66, 215, 337–338, 348, 351, 354, 415, 423, 424
Murnane, George, 213, 446, 448
Murphy, Grayson M-P., 346
Murphy, Starr J., 156
Museum of Cairo, Egypt, 195–96
Mussolini, Benito, 25, 334, 372

N

National Automobile Chamber of Commerce, 308
National City Bank of New York, 346
National Civic Federation, 387
National Electric Light Association, 133, 135
National Petroleum War Service Committee, 356

Nevins, Allan, 27, 160, 164, 187, 190, 205
New Deal, 136, 303, 311, 313, 315, 319
New Orleans Railway and Light Company, 132
"New South," 42, 43
New York Central Railroad, 87, 91, 99, 104, 118, 120, 436
New York Herald, 159, 176, 217, 421
New York Journal, 53, 59, 60, 189, 238
New York Press, 53, 77
New York State Transit Commission, 115, 338, 447
New York Transit Authority, 415
New York Times, 12, 49, 61, 78, 187, 189, 195, 198, 318, 325, 341, 346, 359, 365, 386, 420, 436
New York Trust Co., 219, 296–297
New York World, 53, 62, 67, 75, 178, 179, 325, 419, 427
Newsom, Earl, 95
Niebuhr, Reinhold, 326
Nixon, Raymond B., 418
North American Review, 45
Norton, Bela W., 198, 218, 316
Norton, Charles D., 346

O

O'Brien, John P., 320
O'Brien, Terence, 25, 331
Ochs, Adolph, 61
Oregon Railroad, 94
Oregon Shortline, 94
Osgood, John C., 145

P

Page, Walter Hines, 42
Paine, Thomas, 8, 26
Panama Canal, 79, 89
Panic of 1907, 94, 97
Paramount, 280
Park Avenue Baptist Church, 325, 329
Park Street Church, 39

Parker, Alton B., 24, 76, 313, 315
Parker, George, 75, 76, 313, 344
Parker, Graham, 218, 448
Parker & Lee, 76, 77, 78, 82, 89, 90, 94
Parrish, Harcourt, 216, 316, 317, 318, 344, 380, 381, 382, 446
Parsons, Dudley, 219, 297, 448
Pecora, Ferdinand, 299
Pecora Committee, 300, 301
Pemberton, Brock, 171
Pennsylvania Railroad, 22, 24, 79, 88–108, 115, 119, 123–137, 144, 146, 206, 211, 266, 337, 339, 355, 358, 366, 386, 431, 435, 436
Pennsylvania Standard, 123
Penny press, 27, 64
Pershing, John J., 295, 348, 350, 355
"Personal Relation in Industry, The" 23, 192, 193
Phelps, Dodge & Co., 249
Philadelphia North American, 89
Pickford, Mary, 285
Pierce, Daniel T., 79, 97, 211, 253, 254, 255, 337
Pierson, Lewis, 387, 393
Pittenger, Dudley, 413
Pocantico Hills, 21, 165, 168
"Poison Ivy," 34, 153, 415, 417
Pound, Arthur, 189
Powell, Francis E., 262, 331, 332
"Power Trust," 136
Present-Day Russia, 388, 389
Press agentry, 23, 27, 78, 129, 159, 346, 442
Princeton, 36, 43, 44, 45, 46, 52, 53, 55, 59, 324, 328, 343
Pringle, Henry F., 57, 190, 419, 420, 422, 424
Profit sharing, 266
Progressive movement, 87
Prohibition, 251
Prosser, Seward, 347
Public Opinion, 79

469

Public Relations
  counsel, 131
  development of, 25, 27
  practice of, 211, 253–254
  two-way street, 369, 394
  use of term, 130–131
Public Utilities
  investigation of, 132–138
  Lee's advice to, 132
Public Utilities Executive
  Committee, 136, 339
Publicity
  definition, 31
  methods, 99–100
  philosophy of, 97, 99, 131
*Publicity For Public Service
Corporations*, 131
Pulitzer, Joseph, 62, 64
Pure Food and Drug Act, 65

Q
Quackenbush, James L., 338

R
Radek, Karl B., 390
Radio City, 199
"Railroad Valuation," 92
Railroad Valuation Act, 88
Railroads
  decline of, 96–97
  government control of, 117
  investigation of, 84
  labor unions, 120
  Lee's influence on, 93–94, 96, 104–105, 118–126
  material in Congressional Record, 103
  menu, 125
  problems of, 135
  publications for, 120, 121
  rate debate campaign, 98–105
  regulation of, 87
Rea, Samuel, 92, 113, 142

Reconstruction, The, 41
Reconstruction Finance Corporation, 196, 290–291
Reed, David A., 391
Reichenbach, Harry, 276
Reid, Wallace, 278
Republican Party, 20, 23, 75, 77, 307–309
Rickenbacker, Eddie, 311
Ripley, Joseph, 211–12
"Robber Barons," 85, 423, 425
Rockefeller, Abby, 169, 170, 171
Rockefeller, John D. Jr., 21, 22, 23, 48, 49, 133–207, 242, 45, 267, 292, 319, 350, 411, 426, 427, 428
Rockefeller, John D. Sr., 21, 32, 85, 133–207, 233, 380, 426, 427, 428
Rockefeller, John D. 3rd, 183, 184, 399
Rockefeller, Mrs. John D. Jr., 170
Rockefeller, Nelson, 20, 23, 179, 200, 428
Rockefeller Center, 194, 195, 196, 200, 213, 326, 399, 413, 414
Rockefeller Foundation, 24, 178, 200, 342, 343, 348, 351, 352
Rockefeller Institute, 160
Rockefellers, 138–202, 204, 206, 210, 225, 276, 291, 292, 325, 338, 359, 364, 399, 412, 413, 425
Rogers, James Harvey, 303
Roosevelt, Franklin D., 24, 132, 284, 292, 295, 297, 298, 301, 302, 303, 304, 305, 307, 309, 310, 312, 316, 366, 400, 402
Roosevelt, Theodore, 37, 40, 41, 44, 45, 133, 134, 216, 231, 260
Root, Elihu, 378, 379, 380
Rosenwald, William, 327
Ross, Pierce & Harris, 212
Ross, Thomas, 162, 184, 185, 186, 187, 202, 207, 211, 212, 333, 423, 428, 429, 430, 437
Russell, Charles Edward, 60, 186
Ryan, John, 245
Ryan, Thomas Fortune, 23, 78
Ryan Airlines, 274

S

Saar Basin, 408
Sandburg, Carl, 41
Sarnoff, David, 286, 341
"Savings Banks," 73, 74
Schacht, Hjalmar, 295, 336, 344
Schmitt, Karl, 406, 410
Schuster, M. Lincoln, 184, 187
Schwab, Charles, 24, 37, 214, 226–230, 281, 339, 344, 420
Sedgwick, Ellery, 184, 186
Seldes, Gilbert, 219, 441, 448
Seligmann, Herbert J., 417
Senate Banking and Currency Committee, 298
Seven Pillars of Wisdom, 342
Sewall, Ivy, 38
Sharkey, Tom, 61
Sherman Antitrust Act, 88, 314
Sinclair, Upton, 65, 143, 206, 417, 427
Slaten, William M., 51
Sloan, Alfred Jr., 308
Smith, Alfred E., 190, 313
Smith, Alfred H., 118
Socony-Vacuum, 249, 387
Sokolsky, George E., 341, 448
Southern Pacific Railroad, 94
Spectator, The, 367
"Spirit of St. Louis," 274, 275, 276
Standard Oil, 21, 24, 86, 149, 158, 159, 169, 174, 178, 182, 187, 190, 201, 203, 235, 240, 246, 247, 248, 249, 250, 347, 356, 386, 387, 393, 396, 404, 418, 423
Steffens, Lincoln, 65, 290
Stewart, Col. Robert W., 201, 202, 203
Stewart Case, 201, 202
Stinnes, Hugo, 335
Stock market crash, 277, 291–293, 378, 432
Stover, John, 138

Stresemann, Gustav, 410, 403
Struggle in Colorado for Industrial Freedom, 145, 152
Subways
    fare increase campaign, 115–116
    Lee's advice to, 111, 113
    publications for, 109, 111
Subway Sun, 113, 114, 115, 126, 237, 238
Success, 59, 181
Swope, Herbert Bayard, 427

T

T. J. Ross & Associates, 216
Taft, William Howard, 190, 347–348
Tammany Hall, 67, 68, 78, 320, 321
Tarbell, Ida, 65, 158, 160, 178, 180, 181, 182
Taylor, William Desmond, 283
Teapot Dome, 166, 168, 201, 202, 339, 431
Tennessee Valley Authority, 136
Tewson, Orton, 219
Thomas, E. B., 80
Thomas, Lowell, 341
Thomas, Norman, 294
Thomas notes (paper money), 311
Thornton, Sir Henry, 337
Tinkham, George Holden, 396
Todd, John R., 199
Trans-Atlantic Passenger Conference, 209, 268, 270, 271
Traylor, Melvin Alvah, 217, 304, 315–319
Trinity Church, 39
Truesdale, W. H., 80
Tweed, Sen. William M. (Boss), 86

U

Un-American Activities, Special House Committee on, 411, 415, 432–434, 441
Union Pacific Railroad, 79, 94

USSR: A World Enigma, 388
United Artists, 243, 280, 285, 286
United Mine Workers, 70, 71, 121, 141, 142, 145, 146
United Shareowners of America, Inc., 340
U.S. Chamber of Commerce, 33, 247, 307
U.S.-France Financial News Corporation, 377
U.S. Information Agency, 25, 373
U.S. Railroad Labor Board, 121
U.S. Rubber, 24
U.S. Steel, 223, 349, 392
United War Work Campaign, 356
Untermyer, Samuel, 115–116, 338

V

Vail, Theodore, 130
Van Anda, Carr, 61
Van Loon, Hendrick, 184
Vanderbilt, Cornelius, 86, 87
Vanderbilt, William, 86, 87
Viault, Van, 218, 448
Villard, Oswald Garrison, 106
Vincent, George, 160, 181
Von Neurath, Konstantin, 406
Von Papen, Franz, 406, 408
Von Ribbentrop, Joachim, 407, 408

W

Wadsworth, Eliot, 347
Waldorf-Astoria, 213
Walker, Jimmy, 319
Walker, Stanley, 421, 425
Wall Street, 36, 60, 61, 68, 72, 73, 217, 291, 296, 316, 379, 395, 434
Wall Street Journal, 395
Walsh, Frank P., 134, 135, 149, 150, 160–61
Walsh, Senator Thomas J., 201
Walsh Commission. 134, 135, 149, 160, 211

Ward, Charles S., 347
Washburn-Crosby, 257
Watson-Parker Bill, 193–194
"Wealth," 45
Welborn, J. F., 142, 144, 145, 147, 148, 152
West, George P., 141
Westinghouse, George, 24, 78
Wheeler-Rayburn bill (Utilities Holding Company Act), 136–137
White, Chester M., 417
White, F. Edson, 214
White, William Allen, 62, 181, 356
Whitney, George, 299
Whitney, Richard, 299
Who's Who on the Pennsylvania Railroad, 123
Wideman, Emma H., 37
Wiggin, A. H., 299–300
Willard, Daniel, 130
Willcox, David, 80
William & Mary Quarterly, 198
Williams, Morris, 80
Williamsburg, 50, 196–198, 218
Williamson, Frederick W., 436
Wilson, Woodrow, 42, 46, 55, 98, 106, 118, 142, 226, 314, 333, 346, 359
Winkler, John K., 182, 183
Women's Aid of the Pennsylvania Railroad, 123–124
Women's Peace Association, 146
Wood, R. E., 333
Woodbury, George E., 65
Woods, Col. Arthur, 203
World's Work, 160, 314
Wrench, Sir Evelyn, 367–368, 448

Y

Young, Owen D., 333, 344

Z

Zilberman, Bella, 149
Zukor, Adolph, 280, 281, 282, 284, 285

www.ingramcontent.com/pod-product-compliance
Lightning Source LLC
Chambersburg PA
CBHW050524300426
44113CB00012B/1946